MEDITERRANEAN INSTANT POT COOKBOOK

~ 555 ~

Quick & Easy Mediterranean Diet Instant Pot Recipes For Beginners: Healthy and Delicious Meals with 30 Day Meal Plan For Whole Family

JANET RANDOLPH

TABLE OF CONTENTS

DESCRIPTION 1
INTRODUCTION 1
BREAKFAST 2
    01. Traditional Pumpkin Pie Oatmeal 2
    02. Savory Breakfast Grits 2
    03. Spinach Bacon Frittata 2
    04. Fluffy Pancake 3
    05. Cheese Mushroom Frittata 3
    06. Banana Nut Oatmeal 3
    07. Delicious Berry Oatmeal 4
    08. Cinnamon Mash Banana Oats 4
    09. Flavored Avocado Kale Oats 4
    10. Brussels sprouts with Bacon 5
    11. Healthy Apple Dates Oatmeal 5
    12. Delicious Blueberry Oatmeal 5
    13. Blueberry French toast Casserole 6
    14. Healthy Green Beans 6
    15. Chocó Cherry Oatmeal 6
    16. Strawberry Oatmeal 6
    17. Delicious Egg Bake 7
    18. Apple Cinnamon Oatmeal 7
    19. Healthy Banana Oatmeal 7
    20. Crust-less Breakfast Quiche 8
    21. Creamy Lamb Stew 8
    22. Mediterranean Vichyssoise 9
    23. Lamb Stew with Bacon 9
    24. Spicy Mediterranean Chicken Curry 10
    25. Mediterranean Chili Verde 10
    26. Smoked Beef Chili 11
    27. Cauliflower Souffle 11
    28. Turkey Chili 11
    29. Beef Chili with Peppers 12
    30. Tomato Pollock Stew 12
    31. Spinach Soup 13
    32. Spring Vegetable Stew 13
    33. Poblano Cheese Frittata 14
    34. Fish Stew 14
    35. Cabbage Goulash 14
    36. Pork Stew with Basil 15
    37. Chinese-Style Spareribs 15
    38. Beef Neck Stew 16
    39. Beef Ragout 16
    40. Taco Soup 17
    41. Savory Cabbage Stew 17
    42. Sri Lankan Coconut Cabbage 17
    43. Chipotle Short Ribs Stew 18
    44. Buffalo Chicken Soup 18
MAINS 20
    45. Stuffed Eggplants 20
    46. Salmon Bowls 20
    47. Spicy Potato Salad 20
    48. Chicken and Rice Soup 21
    49. Chicken and Carrots Soup 21
    50. Roasted Peppers Soup 21
    51. Lentils Soup 22
    52. White Bean Soup 22
    53. Veggie Soup 22
    54. Seafood Gumbo 23
    55. Chicken and Orzo Soup 23
    56. Lentils Soup 24
    57. Zucchini Soup 24
    58. Tuscan Soup 24
    59. Cauliflower Cream 25
    60. White Beans and Orange Soup 25
    61. Basil Zucchini Soup 25
    62. Chicken and Leeks Soup 26
    63. Lemony Lamb Soup 26
    64. Sausage and Beans Soup 26
    65. Fish Soup 27
    66. Chickpeas Soup 27
    67. Tomato Soup 27
    68. Oyster Stew 28
    69. Potatoes and Lentils Stew 28
    70. Lamb and Potatoes Stew 28
    71. Ground Pork and Tomatoes Soup 29
SIDES 30
    72. Rich Beets Side Dish 30
    73. Green Beans Side Dish 30
    74. Sweet Potatoes Side Dish 30
    75. Wonderful And Special Side Dish 31
    76. Mashed Sweet Potatoes 31
    77. Tasty Side Dish 31
    78. Spinach Cauliflower Rice 32
    79. Squash Puree 32
    80. Healthy Mushrooms and Green Beans 32
    81. Delicious Cauliflower Rice 33
    82. Lovely Mash 33
    83. Carrot Puree 33
    84. Apple Mash 33
    85. Simple Fennel Side Dish 34
    86. Simple And Fast Side Dish 34
    87. Cauliflower Soup 34
    88. Cauliflower Mash 35
    89. Stuffed Peppers With Cheese 35
    90. Tomato Soup 36
    91. Yummy Bok Choy with Tofu 36
    92. Braised Garlic Treat 36
    93. Italian Soup with Pancetta and Cabbage 37
    94. Garlicky and Buttery Fennel 37
    95. Cheesy Artichokes On The Go 37
    96. Asian Bok Choy 38
    97. Cabbage with Bacon 38
    98. Superpower Broccoli Salad Bowl 38
    99. Spinach with Cheese 39
    100. Sausage with Turnip Greens 39
    101. Easy Cheesy Asparagus 39
    102. Zucchini with Tomato and Rosemary 40
    103. Chanterelles with Cheese 40
    104. Mediterranean Mexican Delight 40
    105. Swiss Chard with Ham Hock 41
    106. Mediterranean Beans with Canadian Bacon 41
    107. French Cauliflower Soup 42
    108. Family Autumn Pottage 42
    109. Easy Medley with Sausage 42
    110. Sausage Gumbo 43
    111. Fried Sauerkraut with Bacon 43
    112. Delicious Okra with Bacon 44
SEAFOOD 45

113. Thai Cauliflower Rice 45
114. Steamed Salmon Recipe 45
115. Mediterranean Seafood Stew 45
116. Mediterranean Green Pesto Tuna Steak 46
117. Spicy and Sweet Trout 46
118. King Prawn Stew 47
119. Squid Rings with Spinach and Potato 47
120. Tilapia Curry Recipe 48
121. Adobo Shrimps Recipe 48
122. Tilapia Fillets 49
123. Mussels with Asparagus 49
124. Cod Chowder with Bacon 50
125. Trout Casserole 50
126. Lobster Tomato Stew 51
127. Creamy Shrimp Stew 51
128. Spicy Shrimp Pasta 52
129. Creamy Mussel Soup 52
130. Jamaican Jerk Fish 52
131. Onion Prawn Stew 53
132. Catfish Stew 53
133. Quick Shrimp Soup 54
134. Lobster Tails in Butter Sauce 54
135. Mediterranean Chili Lime Salmon 55
136. Salmon with Vegetables 55

POULTRY **57**
137. Mouthwatering Maple Mustard Turkey Thighs .. 57
138. Chicken Cashew Butter 57
139. Classic Turkey Cheese Gnocchi 58
140. Delicious Orange Spice Chicken 58
141. Chicken with Smoked Paprika 59
142. Chicken with chilies 59
143. Green Chili Adobo Chicken 60
144. Instant Steamed Garlic Chicken 60
145. Spicy Chicken 60
146. Tso's Chicken 61
147. Chicken Salsa Recipe 62
148. Turkey and Cranberry Sauce 62
149. Chicken and Grape Tomatoes 63
150. Delightful Chicken with Lettuce Wrap 63
151. Turkey Noodle Soup Recipe 63
152. Delightful Chicken Garlic 64
153. Chicken and Black Beans 64
.154. Ranch Bacon Chicken 65
155. Shredded Chicken with Mayo Sauce 65
156. Greek Style Turkey Recipe 66
157. Spicy Herbs Wrapped Chicken 66
158. Steamed Chicken Wings 67
159. Instant Honey Chicken 67
160. Sweet Brown Chicken 68
161. California Style Chicken 68
162. Tangy and Spicy Honey Chicken 69
163. Chicken Curry with Zucchinis 69
164. Chicken Thighs with Rice 70
165. Chipotle Salsa Chicken 70
166. Garlic Chicken Thighs 71
167. BBQ Chicken 71
168. Lemongrass Coconut Chicken 72
169. Turkey Stacks 72
170. Quick Dumplings 73
171. Garlic Chicken 73
172. Butter Chicken 73
173. Instant Chicken Wings 74
174. Apple Turkey Curry Recipe 75
175. Chicken in Mushroom Sauce 75
176. Tasty Cajun Chicken with Rice 76
177. Cheesy Chicken Bowl 77
178. Sweet & Savory Adobo Chicken 77
179. Simple Shredded Chicken 78
180. Perfect Mississippi Chicken 78
181. Orange Chicken 78
182. Tasty Tamarind Chicken 78
183. Flavors Chicken Thighs 79
184. Italian Creamy Chicken 79
186. Chicken Pasta 80
186. Potato Mustard Chicken 80
187. Chicken & Rice 80
188. Herb Chicken Piccata 81
189. Sweet Mango Pineapple Chicken 81

MEAT **82**
190. Cheesy Pork Bombs 82
191. Cheesy Pork Macaroni 82
192. Spicy and Sour Pork Ribs 82
193. Pork Baby Back Ribs 83
194. Taco Pork Bowl Recipe 83
195. Loin Pork with Herbed Butter and Veggies 84
196. Pork Stew in Sweet Ginger Soy 84
197. Mustard Pork Chops 85
198. Lime Ginger Pork 85
199. Pork Roast Rosemary 86
200. Garlic Pork Rinds 86
201. Spicy Pork Ribs 86
202. Pork Ribs Barbecue 87
203. Pulled Pork 88
204. Pork Chops with Cinnamon 88
205. Mushroom Tomato Pork Meatloaf 88
206. Pork Sausages and Mushrooms Recipe 89
207. Tropical Pork Stew 89
208. Pork and Beef Gumbo Recipe 90
209. BBQ Pork Ribs Recipe 90
210. Beef, Bacon and Spinach Chili 90
211. Beef Steak with Rainbow Noodles 91
212. Zettuccini with Pepperoni and Cheese Sauce 91
213. Sinfully Delicious Cheeseburger Soup 91
214. Hamburgers with Kale and Cheese 92
215. Beef Stroganoff with a Twist 92
216. Spicy Broccoli, Leek and Beef Soup 93
217. Red Wine Stew with Smoked Cheddar Cheese ... 93
218. Bottom Eye Roast in Hoisin Sauce 94
219. Festive Bayrischer Gulasch 94
220. Garbure Gersoise Soup 95
221. Spezzatino di Manzo 95
222. German Leberkäse with Sauerkraut 96
223. Christmas Bacon Meatloaf 96
224. Perfect Filet Mignon in Beer Sauce 97
225. Restaurant-Style Oxtail Soup 97
226. Extraordinary Steak Sandwiches 97
227. Top Blade Roast with Horseradish Sauce 98
228. Chipolatas with Spinach and Cheese 99
229. Herbed Mustard Beef Shanks 99
230. Beef and Yogurt Curry 99
231. Beef Short Ribs with Cilantro Cream 100
232. Beef Black Pepper 100

233. French Style Beef Chuck Roast 101
234. Steamed Ground Beef Vegetables 101

BROTH, STOCKS AND SAUCES 102

235. Pineapple Sauce 102
236. Onion Sauce 102
237. Green Tomato Sauce 102
238. Plum Sauce 103
239. Clementine Sauce 103
240. Orange Sauce 103
241. Sriracha Sauce 104
242. Grape Sauce 104
243, Bread Sauce 104
244. Chili Jam 105
245. Pomegranate Sauce 105
246. Apricot Sauce 105
247. Broccoli Sauce 106
248. Carrot Sauce 106
249. Mustard Sauce 106
250. Eggplant Sauce 107
251. Cherry Sauce 107
252. Date Sauce 107
253. Pear Sauce 108
254. Guava Sauce 108
255. Sour Onion Sauce Recipe 108
256. Spicy Pepper Beef Stock 109
257. Celery and Tomato Fish Stock 109
258. Lamb Ribs Stock 109
259. Chicken Stock 110
260. Instant Sour Beef Stock 110
261. Pizza Sauce Recipe 111
262. Green Peppers Butter Sauce Recipe 111
263. Garlic Cauliflower Sauce Recipe 111
264. Sweet BBQ Sauce Recipe 112
265. Tuna Lemon Sauce Recipe 112
266. Creamy Spinach Sauce Recipe 113
267. Bolognese Recipe 113
268. Simple Fish Stock 113
269. Cabbage Beef Stock 114
270. Asparagus Sauce Recipe 114
271. Mushroom Sauce Recipe 115
272. Peanut Butter Sauce Recipe 115
273. Soy Sauce Recipe 116
274. Short Ribs Tomato Stock 116
275. Lamb Stock 116
276. Creamy Parsley Sauce Recipe 117
277. Dijon Sauce Recipe 117
278. Basil Tomato Sauce Recipe 117
279. Chicken Broth 118
280. Mixed Seafood Broth 118

RICE & PASTA RECIPES 119

281. Pretty Colorful Risotto 119
282. Lovely Rice Pilaf with Chicken 119
283. Sweet Apple and Apricot Wild Rice 119
284. Exquisite Spinach Vermouth Risotto 119
285. Superior Shrimp Risotto 120
286. Spring Pearl Barley Salad 120
287. Fresh Tagliatelle Pasta Bolognese 120
288. Elegant Fennel Jasmine Rice 121
289. Simple Mushroom Risotto 121
290. Creamy Coconut Rice Pudding 121
291. Satisfying Saucy Jasmine Rice 122

292. Ziti Pork Meatballs 122
293. Adorable Pizza Pasta 122
294. Delicious Quinoa Pilaf with Almonds 123
295. Cheese Tortellini with Broccoli and Turkey 123
296. Chili and Cheesy Beef Pasta 123
297. Rice Custard with Hazelnuts 124
298. Darling Spaghetti with Meatballs 124
299. Mellow Bulgur and Potato Soup 124
300. Lemony Rice with Veggies 125
301. Lush Sausage Penne 125
302. Pineapple and Honey Risotto 125
303. Buckwheat Breakfast Porridge with Figs 126
304. Heavenly Chicken Enchilada Pasta 126
305. Toothsome Noodles with Tuna 127

BEANS & GRAINS 128

306. Shrimp Rice Paella 128
307. Pea & Corn Rice 128
308. Chorizo Red Beans 128
309. Mix Fried Beans 129
310. Easy Cilantro Rice 129
311. Special Chorizo Pinto Beans 130
312. White Beans Curry 130
313. Easy Black Bean Gravy 130
314. Yummy Coconut Rice 131
315. Easy Bean Mustard Curry 131
316. Mexican Rice 131
317. Lentil Risotto 132
318. Instant Fennel Risotto 132
319. Healthy Almond Risotto 133
320. Mushrooms Risotto 133
321. Black Bean Burrito 133
322. Lentils Spinach Stew 134
323. Mexican Black Beans 134
324. Chickpea Spinach Curry 135
325. Lentil Chipotle Curry 135
326. Tasty Chickpea Tacos 136

VEGETABLES 137

327. Walnut Beets Bowl 137
328. Zuppa Toscana Recipe 137
329. Classic Lentil Gumbo 138
330. Green Beans Stew 138
331. Cheesy Asparagus Garlic 139
332. Green Beans Stir Fry 139
333. Quinoa Burrito Bowls Recipe 139
334. Quick Peas Risotto 140
335. Mushroom Soup Recipe 140
336. butternut Squash and Mushroom Meal 141
337. Garbanzo Beans and Potato 141
338. Glazed Cinnamon Honey Carrots 142
339. Spinach and Fusilli Pasta 142
340. Mushroom Risotto 143
341. Buttery Green Beans Recipe 143
342. Carrots with Dill 143
343. Cauliflower Florets 144
344. Brussels sprouts Tender 144
345. Mushroom and Navy Bean 144
346. Tuscan Pasta Recipe 145
347. Spicy Cabbage Wedges 145
348. Tomato Eggplant and Cheese Lasagna 146
349. Savoy Cabbage and Cream 146
350. Sweet and Spicy Cabbage 146

- 351. Sweet Carrots 147
- 352. Cabbage with Bacon 147
- 353. Cabbage and Sausages 147
- 354. Maple-glazed Carrots 148
- 355. Carrots with Molasses 148
- 356. Savory Collard Greens 148
- 357. Classic Collard Greens 149
- 358. Cauliflower with Pasta 149
- 359. Collard Greens and Bacon 150
- 360. Braised Endive 150
- 361. Endive with Ham 150
- 362. Eggplant Ratatouille 151
- 363. Eggplant Marinara 151
- 364. Sautéed Endive 151
- 365. Endive Risotto 152
- 366. Babaganoush 152
- 367. Eggplant Surprise 152
- 368. Kale with Garlic and Lemon 153
- 369. Braised Kale 153
- 370. Braised Fennel 153
- 371. Easy Cheesy Artichokes 154
- 372. Chinese Bok Choy 154
- 373. Green Cabbage with Bacon 155
- 374. Warm Broccoli Salad Bowl 155
- 375. Creamed Spinach with Cheese 155
- 376. Turnip Greens with Sausage 156
- 377. Asparagus with Colby Cheese 156
- 378. Mediterranean Aromatic Zucchini 156
- 379. Chanterelles with Cheddar Cheese 157
- 380. Family Cauliflower Soup 157
- 381. Cauliflower and Kohlrabi Mash 157
- 382. Old-Fashioned Stuffed Peppers 158
- 383. Aromatic Tomato Soup 158
- 384. Bok Choy with Tofu 159
- 385. Braised Garlicky Endive 159
- 386. Italian Pancetta and Cabbage Soup 159
- 387. Buttery and Garlicky Fennel 160
- 388. Vegetables à la Grecque 160
- 389. Caramelized Endive with Goat Cheese 160
- 390. Loaded Tuscan Rapini Soup 161
- 391. Nopales with Sour Cream 161

SOUPS AND STEWS **162**
- 392. Chicken Soup 162
- 393. Potato and Cheese Soup 162
- 394. Split Pea Soup 163
- 395. Corn Soup 163
- 396. Butternut Squash Soup 163
- 397. Beef and Rice Soup 164
- 398. Chicken Noodle Soup 164
- 399. Zuppa Toscana 165
- 400. Minestrone Soup 165
- 401. Chicken and Wild Rice Soup 166
- 402. Creamy Tomato Soup 166
- 403. Tomato Soup 167
- 404. Carrot Soup 167
- 405. Cabbage Soup 168
- 406. Cream of Asparagus 168
- 407. Ham and White Bean Soup 169
- 408. Lentil Soup 169
- 409. Artichoke Soup 169
- 410. Carrot Peanut Butter Soup 170
- 411. Healthy Chicken Vegetable Soup 170
- 412. Chicken Rice Noodle Soup 171
- 413. Creamy Squash Soup 171
- 414. Spicy Mushroom Soup 171
- 415. Kale Beef Soup 172
- 416. Creamy Cauliflower Soup 172
- 417. Kale Cottage Cheese Soup 172
- 418. Simple Kale Chicken Soup 173
- 419. Mushroom Chicken Soup 173
- 420. Coconut Chicken Soup 173
- 421. Taco Cheese Soup 174
- 422. Asparagus Garlic Ham Soup 174
- 423. Asian Pork Soup 174
- 424. Creamy Potato Soup 175
- 425. Mexican Chicken Fajita Soup 175
- 426. Butternut Squash Garlic Soup 176
- 427. Tomato Almond Milk Soup 176
- 428. Squash Nutmeg Soup 176
- 429. Tomato Basil Soup 177

SALADS **178**
- 430. Lentil Salmon Salad 178
- 431. Peppy Pepper Tomato Salad 178
- 432. Bulgur Salad 178
- 433. Tasty Tuna Salad 178
- 434. Sweet and Sour Spinach Salad 179
- 435. Easy Eggplant Salad 179
- 436. Sweetest Sweet Potato Salad 179
- 437. Delicious Chickpea Salad 180
- 438. Couscous Arugula Salad 180
- 439. Spinach and Grilled Feta Salad 180
- 440. Creamy Cool Salad 180
- 441. Grilled Salmon Summer Salad 180
- 442. Broccoli Salad with Caramelized Onions 181
- 443. Baked Cauliflower Mixed Salad 181
- 444. Quick Arugula Salad 181
- 445. Bell Pepper and Tomato Salad 182
- 446. One Bowl Spinach Salad 182
- 447. Olive and Red Bean Salad 182
- 448. Fresh and Light Cabbage Salad 182
- 449. Vegetable Patch Salad 183
- 450. Cucumber Greek yoghurt Salad 183
- 451. Chickpea Salad Recipe 183
- 452. Orange salad 183
- 453. Yogurt lettuce salad recipe 184
- 454. Fruit de salad recipe 184
- 455. Chickpea with mint salad recipe 184
- 456. Grapy Fennel salad 184
- 457. Greenie salad recipe 185

SNACKS **186**
- 458. Carrot Snack 186
- 459. Mushroom Appetizer 186
- 460. Zucchini Appetizer 186
- 461. Crazy And Unique Appetizer 187
- 462. Almonds Surprise 187
- 463. Sweet Potato Spread 187
- 464. Mint Dip 188
- 465. Popular Shrimp Appetizer 188
- 466. Incredible Scallops 188
- 467. Broiled Lobster Tails 188
- 468. Delightful Herring Appetizer 189
- 469. Salmon Patties 189

470. Clams And Mussels Appetizer 189
471. Special Shrimp Appetizer 190
472. Stuffed Squid 190
473. Asian-Style Appetizer Ribs 190
474. Two-Cheese Artichoke Dip 190
475. Easy Party Mushrooms 191
476. Herbed Party Shrimp 191
477. Crispy and Yummy Beef Bites 192
478. Asparagus with Greek Aioli 192
479. Carrot Sticks with Blue-Cheese Sauce 192
480. Zingy Zucchini Bites 193
481. Kohlrabi Sticks with Hungarian Mayo 193
482. Bok Choy Boats with Shrimp Salad 193
483. Game Day Sausage Dip 194
484. Stuffed Baby Bell Peppers 194
485. Party Garlic Prawns 194
486. Barbecue Lil Smokies 195
487. Two-Cheese and Caramelized Onion Dip 195
488. Hot Lager Chicken Wings 195
489. Braised Spring Kale Appetizer 196
490. Wax Beans with Pancetta 196
491. Middle-Eastern Eggplant Dip 196
492. Cheesy Cauliflower Bites 197
493. Goat Cheese and Chives Spread 197
494. Chickpeas Salsa 197
495. Ginger and Cream Cheese Dip 197
496. Walnuts Yogurt Dip 198
497. Herbed Goat Cheese Dip 198
498. Scallions Dip 198
499. Tomato Cream Cheese Spread 198
500. Pesto Dip 199
501. Vinegar Beet Bites 199
502. Zucchini and Olives Salsa 199
503. Strawberry and Carrots Salad 199
504. Hot Squash Wedges 200
505. Shrimp and Cucumber Bites 200
506. Salmon Rolls 200
507. Eggplant Bombs 200
508. Eggplant Bites 201
509. Sage Eggplant Chips 201
510. Tomato Dip 201
511. Oregano Avocado Salad 201
512. Lentils Spread 202
513. Chickpeas and Eggplant Bowls 202
514. Cheese and Egg Salad 202
515. Stuffed Zucchinis 203
516. Eggplant And Capers Dip 203
517. Pomegranate Dip 203
518. Lentils and Tomato Dip 203
519. Lentils Stuffed Potato Skins 204

DESSERTS 205
520. Bread Pudding 205
521. Ruby Pears 205
522. Pumpkin Rice Pudding 205
523. Lemon Marmalade 206
524. Rice Pudding 206
525. Ricotta Cake 207
526. Orange Marmalade 207
527. Berry Jam 207
528. Peach Jam 208
529. Raspberry Curd 208
530. Tomato Jam 208
531. Pear Jam 209
532. Berry Compote 209
533. Key Lime Pie 209
534. Fruit Cobbler 210
535. Simple Carrot Cake 210
536. Stuffed Peaches 211
537. Peach Compote 211
538. Zucchini Nut Bread 211
539. Samoa Cheesecake 212
540. Chocolate Pudding 212
541. Refreshing Curd 213
542. The Best Jam Ever 213
543. Divine Pears 213
544. Berry Marmalade 214
545. Orange Delight 214
546. Simple Squash Pie 214
547. Winter Pudding 214
548. Banana Dessert 215
549. Apple Cake 215
550. Special Vanilla Dessert 216
551. Tasty And Amazing Pear Dessert 216
552. Cranberries Jam 216
553. Lemon Jam 216
554. Special Dessert 217
555. Superb Banana Dessert 217
556. Rhubarb Dessert 217
557. Plum Delight 217
558. Refreshing Fruits Dish 218
559. Dessert Stew 218

30-DAY MEAL PLAN 219
CONCLUSION 219

DESCRIPTION

So many diets fail because people focus on what they cannot eat. With the Mediterranean diet, there is a wider variety of food that you are allowed to eat! Though you should try and limit your dairy, red meat, and poultry intake, there are still many delicious meals you can prepare. You can still eat a red meat or a chicken dish once a week, but try and use leaner cuts of meat and be conscious of your portion size. Incorporate more fish into your diet and have fresh fruits and vegetables on hand to create a quick salad. Also, remember that you should use extra virgin olive oil in your cooking and in your salad dressing. It's heart healthy and packed with antioxidants that keep your cells healthy and prevent inflammation in the body.

Here are some of the meals you will find in this book:

- Breakfast
- Mains
- Sides
- Seafood
- Poultry
- Meat
- Broth, Stocks And Sauces
- Beans and Grains
- Vegetables
- Soups and Stews
- Snacks
- Desserts

No other lifestyle allows you to drink wine, eat pasta, and enjoy your time with friends. If you're ready to find out what's next in your Mediterranean diet journey, there's no better place to begin than with the delicious cuisines you will be eating while you change your life for the better.

INTRODUCTION

Mediterranean diet is not just a dietary adjustment, but a complete lifestyle change. Ancel Keys was the first to notice the link between the people of the Mediterranean's heart healthy diet and longer lifespan. In order to correctly emulate that, we must improve not only our diet, but our physical activity as well. The people of the Mediterranean incorporated exercise into their routine regularly, and it's important that we try and do the same. It doesn't have to be a set workout time at the gym, but rather taking a walk around the neighborhood or taking a long bike ride can help you burn calories and spur weight loss. Weight loss can only occur if you are following a calorie deficit diet. Even if the Mediterranean diet is easy to follow in the sense that it doesn't require counting carbs or calories, it's still important you're aware of your portion size, snacking, and caloric intake if you want lose weight. That can only happen if you're burning off more calories than what you're taking in!

BREAKFAST

01. Traditional Pumpkin Pie Oatmeal

Servings: 4
Cooking Time: 13 minutes

Ingredients:

- 2 cups rolled old fashioned oats
- ½ cup maple syrup
- ½ tsp vanilla
- 1 tsp pumpkin pie spice
- ½ cup pumpkin puree
- 1 ¾ cup milk
- 2 cups water

Directions:

1. Pour 1 cup water in the instant pot. Set pot on sauté mode to boil the water.
2. Meanwhile, in a pyrex dish, mix together add oats, maple syrup, vanilla, pumpkin pie spice, pumpkin puree, milk, and 1 cup water. Cover dish with aluminum foil piece.
3. Press the cancel button of the instant pot.
4. Place trivet into the pot. Place Pyrex dish on top of the trivet.
5. Seal pot with lid and select manual high pressure for 8 minutes.
6. Allow to release pressure naturally for 5 minutes then release using quick release method.
7. Open the lid carefully. Remove dish from the instant pot and set aside to cool completely.
8. Stir well and serve.

Nutrition Value:

Calories: 360; Carbohydrates: 66.5g; Protein: 10.9g; Fat: 5.9g; Sugar: 30.4g; Sodium: 59mg

02. Savory Breakfast Grits

Servings: 6
Cooking Time: 15 minutes

Ingredients:

- 1 cup milk
- 2 ½ cups water
- 1 cup cheddar cheese, shredded
- 4 tbsp butter, melted
- 1 cup grits

Directions:

1. Pour 2 cups of water into the instant pot then place a trivet in the pot.
2. In a baking dish, mix together 2 tablespoons of butter, water, and grits. Cover dish with aluminum foil.
3. Place dish on top of the trivet.
4. Seal pot with lid and cook on manual high pressure for 15 minutes.
5. Release pressure using quick release method than open the lid.
6. Remove dish from the instant pot. Transfer grit mixture to the large mixing bowl.
7. Add milk and cheese to the grit mixture and stir until cheese melted.
8. Serve and enjoy.

Nutrition Value:

Calories: 184; Carbohydrates: 6.2g; Protein: 6.5g; Fat: 15g; Sugar: 2.4g; Sodium: 251mg

03. Spinach Bacon Frittata

Servings: 4
Cooking Time: 15 minutes

Ingredients:

- 6 eggs
- ¼ cup bacon, cooked and chopped
- ½ cup tomato, chopped
- 1 cup fresh spinach
- ½ tsp Italian seasoning
- 2 ½ tsp heavy cream
- ¼ tsp pepper
- ¼ tsp salt

Directions:

1. In a bowl, whisk eggs with spices and

heavy cream.
2. Spray 7" baking pan with cooking spray.
3. Add bacon, tomato, and spinach to the pan. Pour egg mixture over the bacon mixture.
4. Cover pan with aluminum foil piece.
5. Pour 1 ½ cups of water into the instant pot then place trivet to the pot.
6. Place baking pan on top of the trivet. Seal instant pot with lid and cook on manual high pressure for 15 minutes.
7. Release pressure using quick release method than open the lid.
8. Serve and enjoy.

Nutrition Value:

Calories: 120; Carbohydrates: 1.9g; Protein: 9.2g; Fat: 8.5g; Sugar: 1.2g; Sodium: 276mg

04. Fluffy Pancake

Servings: 2
Cooking Time: 17 minutes

Ingredients:

- 1 egg
- 1 ½ tbsp olive oil
- 1 ¼ cups buttermilk
- ¾ tsp baking soda
- ¾ tsp baking powder
- 3 tbsp sugar
- 1 cup all-purpose flour

Directions:

1. In a large mixing bowl, mix together flour, baking soda, baking powder, and sugar.
2. Add buttermilk, oil, and eggs and whisk until well combined.
3. Spray 7" spring-form pan with cooking spray. Pour batter into the prepared pan.
4. Pour 1 cup water into the instant pot then place a trivet in the pot.
5. Place pan on top of the trivet.
6. Seal pot with lid and cook on low pressure for 17 minutes.
7. Release pressure using quick release method than open the lid carefully.
8. Remove pan from the pot and set aside to cool completely.
9. Slice and serve.

Nutrition Value:

Calories: 480; Carbohydrates: 74.1g; Protein: 14.3g; Fat: 14.7g; Sugar: 25.7g; Sodium: 668mg

05. Cheese Mushroom Frittata

Servings: 2
Cooking Time: 15 minutes

Ingredients:

- 4 eggs
- 1 ½ cups water
- 2 Swiss cheese slices, cut each slice into 4 pieces
- 4 oz mushrooms, sliced
- 1/8 tsp white pepper
- 1/8 tsp onion powder
- 2 tsp heavy cream
- ¼ tsp salt

Directions:

1. In a bowl, whisk eggs with spices and heavy cream.
2. Spray 7" baking pan with cooking spray.
3. Add sliced mushrooms to the pan then pour egg mixture over the mushrooms.
4. Arrange cheese slices on top of mushroom and egg mixture.
5. Cover pan with aluminum foil piece.
6. Pour 1 ½ cups of water to the instant pot then place a trivet in the pot.
7. Place pan on top of the trivet.
8. Seal pot with lid and cook on manual high pressure for 15 minutes.
9. Release pressure using quick release method.
10. Serve and enjoy.

Nutrition Value:

Calories: 262; Carbohydrates: 18.5g; Protein: 20.5g; Fat: 18.5g; Sugar: 2.1g; Sodium: 478mg

06. Banana Nut Oatmeal

Servings: 4
Cooking Time: 3 minutes

Ingredients:

- 1 banana, chopped
- ¼ cup walnuts, chopped
- 1 tsp honey
- 2 cups milk
- 2 cups water
- 1 cup steel cut oats

Directions:

1. Add milk, water, and oats to the instant pot and stir well.
2. Seal pot with lid and select manual high pressure for 3 minutes.
3. Allow to release pressure naturally then open the lid.
4. Add walnuts, banana, and honey to the oats and stir well.
5. Serve and enjoy.

Nutrition Value:

Calories: 218; Carbohydrates: 28.8g; Protein: 8.9g; Fat: 85g; Sugar: 10.8g; Sodium: 63mg

07. Delicious Berry Oatmeal

Servings: 2

Cooking Time: 4 minutes

Ingredients:

- 4 oz fresh berries
- ¼ tsp cinnamon
- ½ tsp vanilla
- 2 tbsp honey
- 1 cup almond milk
- 15 oz coconut milk
- 1 cup steel cut oats

Directions:

1. Spray instant pot from inside with cooking spray.
2. Add all ingredients to the instant pot and stir well.
3. Seal pot with lid and select manual high pressure for 4 minutes.
4. Allow to release pressure naturally then open the lid.
5. Stir well and serve.

Nutrition Value:

Calories: 594; Carbohydrates: 60.3g; Protein: 9.3g; Fat: 37.5g; Sugar: 25.9g; Sodium: 36mg

08. Cinnamon Mash Banana Oats

Servings: 2

Cooking Time: 4 minutes

Ingredients:

- 2 bananas, sliced
- ½ tsp cinnamon
- 1 cup milk
- 1 cup water
- 2/3 cup rolled oats

Directions:

1. Spray instant pot from inside with cooking spray.
2. Add all ingredients to the instant pot and stir well.
3. Cover pot with lid and cook on manual high pressure for 4 minutes.
4. Release pressure using quick release method than open the lid.
5. Mash banana chunks with a fork and stir well.
6. Serve and enjoy.

Nutrition Value:

Calories: 271; Carbohydrates: 51.9g; Protein: 8.9g; Fat: 4.7g; Sugar: 20.2g; Sodium: 64mg

09. Flavored Avocado Kale Oats

Servings: 2

Cooking Time: 10 minutes

Ingredients:

- ½ cup steel cut oats
- 2 green onions, sliced
- ½ avocado, diced
- 1 tbsp tahini
- 1 tsp tamari
- 4 tbsp nutritional yeast
- 1 tbsp miso paste
- 1 cup frozen kale, chopped
- 1 cup water
- 1 cup unsweetened almond milk

Directions:
1. Add oats, almond milk, and water into the instant pot and stir well.
2. Cover pot with lid and select manual high pressure for 8 minutes.
3. Allow to release pressure naturally for 6 minutes then release using quick release method.
4. Set pot on sauté mode. Stir in nutritional yeast, tamari, tahini, miso paste, and kale and cook for 2-3 minutes on sauté mode.
5. Top with green onions and avocado.
6. Serve immediately and enjoy.

Nutrition Value:

Calories: 354; Carbohydrates: 36g; Protein: 17.7g; Fat: 18.6g; Sugar: 1.9g; Sodium: 616mg

10. Brussels sprouts with Bacon

Servings: 4
Cooking Time: 6 minutes

Ingredients:
- 1 lb Brussels sprouts, trimmed and halved
- 2 tsp orange zest
- ½ cup water
- ½ cup orange juice
- 2 bacon slices, diced
- 1 tbsp olive oil

Directions:
1. Add olive oil to the instant pot and set the pot on sauté mode.
2. Add bacon and sauté for 3-5 minutes or until crisp.
3. Add water and orange juice and deglaze the instant pot.
4. Add Brussels sprouts and stir well.
5. Seal pot with lid and cook on manual high pressure for 3 minutes.
6. Release pressure using quick release method.
7. Open the lid carefully.
8. Garnish with orange zest and serve.

Nutrition Value:

Calories: 145; Carbohydrates: 13.9g; Protein: 7.6g; Fat: 7.9g; Sugar: 5.1g; Sodium: 249mg

11. Healthy Apple Dates Oatmeal

Servings: 2
Cooking Time: 4 minutes

Ingredients:
- ¼ tsp vanilla
- ¼ tsp cinnamon
- 2 dates, chopped
- 1 apple, chopped
- ½ cup water
- ¼ cup instant oatmeal

Directions:
1. Add all ingredients to the instant pot and stir well.
2. Cover pot with lid and cook on manual high pressure for 4 minutes.
3. Allow to release pressure naturally for 5 minutes then release using quick release method.
4. Open the lid carefully.
5. Stir well and serve.

Nutrition Value:

Calories: 122; Carbohydrates: 28.9g; Protein: 1.9g; Fat: 0.9g; Sugar: 17g; Sodium: 4mg

12. Delicious Blueberry Oatmeal

Servings: 4
Cooking Time: 3 minutes

Ingredients:
- 1 cup steel cut oats
- 1 tbsp brown sugar
- 3 cups milk
- 1 cup blueberries
- 1/8 tsp cinnamon
- Pinch of salt

Directions:
1. Add all ingredients into the instant pot and stir well to combine.
2. Seal pot with lid and cook on manual

high pressure for 3 minutes.
3. Allow to release pressure naturally then open the lid.
4. Stir well and serve.

Nutrition Value:

Calories: 198; Carbohydrates: 30.4g; Protein: 9g; Fat: 5.2g; Sugar: 14.2g; Sodium: 127mg

13. Blueberry French toast Casserole

Servings: 4
Cooking Time: 25 minutes

Ingredients:

- 4 French bread slices, cut into pieces
- 1 cup blueberries
- ½ tsp cinnamon
- ½ tsp vanilla
- ¼ cup brown sugar
- 2 eggs
- 1 cup milk

Directions:

1. In a large mixing bowl, whisk eggs with cinnamon, vanilla, brown sugar, and milk.
2. Add bread pieces and blueberries and mix until well coated.
3. Spray baking dish with cooking spray.
4. Pour prepared mixture into the baking dish.
5. Pour ¾ cup water into the instant pot. Place trivet in the pot.
6. Place baking dish on top of the trivet.
7. Seal pot with lid and select pressure cook mode and set timer for 25 minutes.
8. Serve and enjoy.

Nutrition Value:

Calories: 212; Carbohydrates: 35.7g; Protein: 8.8g; Fat: 4.2g; Sugar: 16.2g; Sodium: 270mg

14. Healthy Green Beans

Servings: 10
Cooking Time: 8 minutes

Ingredients:

- 14 oz can green beans, undrained
- ½ cup butter
- 4 bacon slices, chopped
- Pepper
- Salt

Directions:

1. Add all ingredients into the instant pot and stir well.
2. Seal pot with lid and select manual high pressure for 8 minutes.
3. Allow to release pressure naturally then open the lid.
4. Stir well and serve.

Nutrition Value:

Calories: 151; Carbohydrates: 5.7g; Protein: 4.3g; Fat: 12.4g; Sugar: 2.8g; Sodium: 788mg

15. Chocó Cherry Oatmeal

Servings: 4
Cooking Time: 15 minutes

Ingredients:

- 2 cups steel cuts oats
- ¼ cup chocolate chips
- 2 cups cherries
- ½ tsp cinnamon
- 4 tbsp honey
- 2 cups water
- 2 cups milk
- Pinch of salt

Directions:

1. Spray instant pot from inside with cooking spray.
2. Add all ingredients to the instant pot and stir well.
3. Seal pot with lid and cook on manual high pressure for 15 minutes.
4. Allow to release pressure naturally then open the lid.
5. Stir well and serve.

Nutrition Value:

Calories: 307; Carbohydrates: 54.7g; Protein: 8.2g; Fat: 7.5g; Sugar: 38.4g; Sodium: 116mg

16. Strawberry Oatmeal

Servings: 4
Cooking Time: 5 minutes

Ingredients:

- ¼ cup sugar
- 1 cup strawberries, chopped
- 3 cups water
- 2 tsp vanilla
- 2 tbsp butter
- 1 cup steel cut oats
- ¼ tsp salt

Directions:

1. Add all ingredients except strawberries to the instant pot and stir well.
2. Seal pot with lid and cook on manual high pressure for 5 minutes.
3. Allow to release pressure naturally then open the lid.
4. Stir in strawberries and serve.

Nutrition Value:

Calories: 193; Carbohydrates: 29.4g; Protein: 3g; Fat: 7.2g; Sugar: 14.7g; Sodium: 195mg

17. Delicious Egg Bake

Servings: 2
Cooking Time: 9 minutes

Ingredients:

- 8 eggs
- 2 cups hash brown potatoes, thawed
- 5 bacon pieces, diced
- 1 cup cheddar cheese, shredded
- ½ cup milk
- ¼ tsp salt

Directions:

1. Set instant pot on sauté mode.
2. Add bacon to the instant pot and sauté for 1-2 minutes or until lightly brown.
3. Now add hash brown potatoes over the top of bacon. Sprinkle ½ cup cheese on top of potatoes.
4. In a bowl, whisk together eggs, milk, and salt and pour over the bacon and potatoes layers.
5. Sprinkle with remaining cheese.
6. Seal instant pot with lid and close the valve.
7. Select manual high for 7 minutes.
8. Once the timer goes off then remove the lid, there is no pressure to release.
9. Season with pepper and salt and serve.

Nutrition Value:

Calories: 484; Carbohydrates: 29.9g; Protein: 22.4g; Fat: 30.5g; Sugar: 3.4g; Sodium: 785mg

18. Apple Cinnamon Oatmeal

Servings: 4
Cooking Time: 5 minutes

Ingredients:

- 1 cup steel cut oats
- 3 tbsp butter
- 2 tbsp brown sugar
- 1 cup apple, peeled and diced
- 2 ½ cups water
- 1/8 tsp cinnamon
- 2 tbsp raisins

Directions:

1. Add butter into the instant pot and set the pot on sauté mode.
2. Once butter is melted then add turn off the sauté mode.
3. Add water, raisins, cinnamon, apples, brown sugar, and oats. Stir well.
4. Seal instant pot with lid and close steam valve and set the instant pot on manual high pressure for 5 minutes.
5. Release pressure using quick release method than open the lid.
6. Stir well and serve.

Nutrition Value:

Calories: 214; Carbohydrates: 29.6g; Protein: 3.1g; Fat: 5.7g; Sugar: 13.1g; Sodium: 69mg

19. Healthy Banana Oatmeal

Servings: 3
Cooking Time: 5 minutes

Ingredients:

- 1 cup old-fashioned oatmeal

- 1 tbsp brown sugar
- 2 tsp cinnamon
- 2 bananas
- 1 cup water
- 1 cup milk

Directions:

1. Spray instant pot bottom using cooking spray.
2. Add oatmeal, water, and milk. Stir well.
3. Slice one banana and add it into the instant pot.
4. Add brown sugar and cinnamon and stir well to combine.
5. Seal instant pot with lid and select manual high pressure for 5 minutes.
6. Allow to release pressure naturally for 10 minutes then release using quick release method.
7. Stir oatmeal and scoop into the serving bowls.
8. Slice remaining banana. Top with sliced banana and serve.

Nutrition Value:

Calorie: 256; Carbohydrates: 49.2g; Protein: 8.6 g; Fat: 1.6g; Sugar: 17.2g; Sodium: 42mg

20. Crust-less Breakfast Quiche

Servings: 6
Cooking Time: 30 minutes

Ingredients:

- 8 eggs
- 1 ½ cup mozzarella cheese, shredded
- 2 green onions, chopped
- 1 cup tomatoes, chopped
- 1 red pepper, chopped
- ½ cup flour
- ½ cup milk
- ¼ tsp pepper
- ¼ tsp salt

Directions:

1. Place trivet into the bottom of the instant pot.
2. Pour 1 cup water into the instant pot.
3. In a large bowl, whisk eggs, flour, milk, pepper, and salt.
4. Add vegetables and cheese and stir until combined.
5. Pour egg mixture into the dish that will fit inside your instant pot.
6. Cover dish with foil and place on the trivet.
7. Seal instant pot with lid and select manual high pressure for 30 minutes.
8. Allow to release pressure naturally for 10 minutes then release using quick release method.
9. Carefully remove the dish from the instant pot.
10. Serve and enjoy.

Nutrition Value:

Calorie: 166; Carbohydrates: 12.8g; Protein: 11.7g; Fat: 7.7g; Sugar: 3.3g; Sodium: 234mg

21. Creamy Lamb Stew

Preparation Time: 60 Minutes
Servings: 6

Ingredients:

- For stew:
- 1-pound lamb neck; chopped
- 1/2 cup cream cheese
- 4 tablespoon butter
- 1 cup cauliflower; chopped.
- 3 celery stalks; chopped
- 2 tablespoon oil
- 1 small red bell pepper; chopped.
- 1 garlic head; whole
- 1/4 cup fresh parsley; finely chopped
- 1 cup heavy cream
- 1/2 teaspoon black pepper
- 1/2 teaspoon dried thyme
- 1/2 salt

Directions:

1. Plug the instant pot and grease the inner pot with oil. Press the *Sauté* button and heat up. Add the meat and cook for 4-5 minutes, stirring constantly. Press the

Cancel' button to turn off the heat.
2. Add cauliflower, celery stalks, red pepper, and garlic head. Sprinkle with salt, pepper, and thyme and give it a good stir
3. Seal the lid and set the steam release handle to the *Sealing* position. Press the *Manual* button and set the timer for 25 minutes
4. When done; press the *Cancel'* button and release the pressure naturally. Carefully open the lid and stir in butter.
5. Chill for a while and then stir in cream cheese and heavy cream. Sprinkle with fresh parsley. Serve hot and enjoy.

Nutrition Value: Calories: 411; Total Fats: 32g; Net Carbs: 5.8g; Protein: 24.4g; Fiber: 1.1g

22. Mediterranean Vichyssoise

Preparation Time: 50 Minutes
Servings: 4

Ingredients:

- For soup:
- 2 cups cauliflower; chopped
- 5 cups vegetable stock
- 3 tablespoon butter
- 1 large leek; chopped.
- 1 small onion; finely chopped
- 1 teaspoon lemon juice; freshly squeezed
- 1 cup cream cheese
- 1/8 teaspoon nutmeg
- 1/4 teaspoon dried parsley
- 1/4 teaspoon white pepper; freshly ground.
- Freshly snipped chives; optional
- 1 bay leaf
- 1/2 teaspoon salt

Directions:
1. Plug in your instant pot and press the *Sauté* button. Melt the butter in the stainless steel insert and add the leeks and onions. Stir-fry for about 4-5 minutes without browning.
2. Add the cauliflower, vegetable stock, lemon juice, nutmeg, parsley, and bay leaf. Sprinkle with salt and pepper and securely lock the lid. Press the *Manual* button and set the timer for 10 minutes. Cook on high pressure
3. When done; press the *Cancel'* button and move the pressure valve to the *Venting* position to release the pressure. Remove and discard the bay leaf and pour the soup through a large sieve. Alternatively, transfer to a food processor and process until smooth.
4. Pour the soup back to the pot and press the *Sauté* button. Stir in the cream cheese and optionally sprinkle with some more salt or pepper to taste. Cook for another 5 minutes, stirring constantly
5. Press the *Cancel'* button to turn off the pot. Transfer the soup to serving bowls and sprinkle with chives. Serve hot and enjoy.

Nutrition Value: Calories: 320; Total Fats: 29.1g; Net Carbs: 7.4g; Protein: 6.5g; Fiber: 2.7g

23. Lamb Stew with Bacon

Preparation Time: 50 Minutes
Servings: 6

Ingredients:

For stew:

- 2 -pounds lamb leg; chopped.
- 2 tablespoon butter
- 8 garlic cloves
- 6 bacon slices
- 3 cups beef broth
- 1 large onion; finely chopped
- 1/4 teaspoon black pepper; freshly ground.
- 1 teaspoon dried rosemary
- 1/2 teaspoon salt

Directions:
1. Plug in the instant pot and grease the bottom with butter. Press the *Sauté* button and heat up
2. Add onions and bacon. Stir well and cook for 3 minutes. Press the *Cancel'* button and set aside.
3. Meanwhile, place the meat on a clean work surface. Using a sharp knife, make 8

incisions into the meat and place garlic clove in each. Rub with spices and transfer to the pot
4. Pour in the broth and seal the lid. Set the steam release handle to the *Sealing* position. Press the *Manual* button and set the timer for 25 minutes on high pressure.
5. When done; release the pressure naturally and carefully open the lid. Serve hot and enjoy.

Nutrition Value: Calories: 453; Total Fats: 23.6g; Net Carbs: 3.8g; Protein: 52.5g; Fiber: 0.6g

24. Spicy Mediterranean Chicken Curry

Preparation Time: 45 Minutes
Servings: 4

Ingredients:

For curry:

- 1-pound chicken fillets; chopped into bite-sized pieces
- 2 medium-sized tomatoes; finely chopped
- 6 garlic cloves; finely chopped
- 1 medium-sized onion; finely chopped.
- 1 small green chili pepper; chopped
- 1 tablespoon lemon juice
- 5 tablespoon olive oil
- 1 teaspoon fresh ginger; freshly grated
- 1 teaspoon coriander; ground
- 1/2 teaspoon garam masala
- 1/4 teaspoon turmeric powder
- 1/2 teaspoon cayenne pepper; ground.
- 1 teaspoon salt

Directions:

1. Rinse the fillets under cold running water and pat dry with a kitchen paper. Cut into bite-sized pieces and set aside.
2. Plug in the instant pot and grease the inner pot with olive oil. Press the *Sauté* button and add onions, green chili, garlic, coriander, cayenne pepper, garam masala, turmeric, and salt
3. Stir-fry for 3-4 minutes and add chicken. Give it a good stir and continue to cook for another 5 minutes
4. Add tomatoes and ginger. Pour in 2 cups of water and securely lock the lid. Set the steam release handle and press the *Manual* button. Set the timer for 8 minutes on high pressure
5. When you hear the cooker's end signal, perform a quick pressure release and open the lid
6. Transfer the curry to serving bowls and drizzle with lemon juice. Garnish with fresh parsley.

Nutrition Value: Calories: 396; Total Fats: 26.1g; Net Carbs: 5.1g; Protein: 34g; Fiber: 1.5g

25. Mediterranean Chili Verde

Preparation Time: 40 Minutes
Servings: 6

Ingredients:

For chili:

- 2-pounds beef stew meat
- 1 cup tomatillos; chopped
- 1 cup cherry tomatoes; chopped
- 1 onion; finely chopped.
- 3 garlic cloves; crushed
- 2 Serrano peppers; chopped.
- 3 cups beef broth
- 3 tablespoon oil
- 1/2 teaspoon chili powder
- 1/4 teaspoon freshly ground black pepper
- 1 teaspoon salt

Directions:

1. Plug in the instant pot and press the *Sauté* button. Grease the stainless steel insert with oil and add onions and garlic. Briefly cook for 3-4 minutes and add the remaining ingredients.
2. Give it a good stir and seal the lid. Set the steam release handle to the *Sealing* position and press the *Manual* button. Set the timer for 20 minutes on high pressure.
3. When done; release the pressure by moving the pressure valve to the

Venting position
4. Carefully open the lid and stir well again making sure to break down the tomatillos
5. Optionally, sprinkle with some freshly chopped parsley or Parmesan cheese and serve immediately

Nutrition Value: Calories: 383; Total Fats: 17.2g; Net Carbs: 4g; Protein: 49.1g; Fiber: 1.3g

26. Smoked Beef Chili

Preparation Time: 30 Minutes
Servings: 4

Ingredients:

For chili:

- 1-pound ground beef
- 2 cups cherry tomatoes; chopped
- 2 small chili peppers; chopped.
- 2 onions; chopped.
- 3 tablespoon butter
- 4 cups beef broth
- 1 cup button mushrooms; sliced
- 1 teaspoon smoked paprika
- 1/4 teaspoon dried basil
- 1/4 teaspoon chili powder
- 1 teaspoon salt

Directions:

1. Grease the bottom of the inner pot with oil and press the *Sauté* button. Add onions and cook for 2 minutes.
2. Now add chili peppers and continue to cook for another 2 minutes.
3. Add ground beef and sprinkle with salt, chili powder, smoked paprika, and dried basil. Stir in the butter and cook for 3-4 minutes or until lightly browned
4. Pour in the beef broth and add cherry tomatoes and mushrooms. Optionally, season with some more salt or pepper
5. Seal the lid and set the steam release handle to the *Sealing* position. Press the *Manual* button and set the timer for 12 minutes on high pressure
6. When you hear the end signal, perform a quick release and open the lid. Serve hot and enjoy.

Nutrition Value: Calories: 368; Total Fats: 17.4g; Net Carbs: 7.8g; Protein: 41.3g; Fiber: 2.5g

27. Cauliflower Souffle

Preparation Time: 32 Minutes
Servings: 6

Ingredients:

- 2 eggs
- 2 -ounce cream cheese
- 1 head cauliflower; chopped
- 1/4 cup chives
- 2 tablespoon butter; softened
- 1/2 cup sour cream or yogurt
- 1/2 cup Asiago cheese
- 1 cup cheddar cheese
- 1 cup of water
- 6 slices bacon; cooked, crumbled

Directions:

1. Add first five ingredients to a food processor and blend until smooth and frothy.
2. Add chopped cauliflower and pulse for 2 seconds at a time, until chunky. Fold in chives and butter.
3. Grease round 1 ¼ quart (1.4L) casserole dish, and fill it with the mixture.
4. Add 1 cup of water to Instant Pot. Put trivet in, and put casserole dish onto the trivet.
5. Put on and lock the lid. Cook at high pressure for 12 minutes. Release pressure after 10 minutes. Top with crumbled bacon, Serve.

Nutrition Value: Calories: 342 ; Total Carbs: 7 g; Net Carbs: 3.7 g; Fat: 28 g; Protein: 17 g

28. Turkey Chili

Preparation Time: 35 Minutes
Servings: 3

Ingredients:

- For chili:
- 1-pound ground turkey
- 1 onion; finely chopped.
- 3 cups chicken stock

- 2 garlic cloves
- 1/2 cup fire-roasted tomatoes
- 1 cup green chilies; diced
- 1/2 teaspoon pepper
- 1 teaspoon cumin powder
- 2 teaspoon chili powder
- 1 teaspoon salt

Directions:

1. Plug in the instant pot and press the *Sauté* button. Grease the inner pot with some oil and add onions and garlic. Sprinkle with some salt and pepper. Stir well and cook until translucent.
2. Now add the meat and fire-roasted tomatoes. Stir well and continue to cook for another 5-6 minutes, stirring constantly
3. Add the remaining ingredients and stir well. Seal the lid and set the steam release handle to the *Sealing* position.
4. Press the *Manual* button and set the timer for 13 minutes.
5. When done; release the pressure naturally for 10 minutes and then move the pressure handle to the *Venting* position to release any remaining pressure
6. Open the lid and transfer chili to serving bowls. Serve hot and enjoy.

Nutrition Value: Calories: 378; Total Fats: 19g; Net Carbs: 3.9g; Protein: 44.1g; Fiber: 2g

29. Beef Chili with Peppers

Preparation Time: 35 Minutes
Servings: 4

Ingredients:

For chili:

- 1-pound ground beef
- 1 cup tomatoes; finely chopped
- 2 medium-sized red bell peppers; chopped
- 1/2 teaspoon smoked paprika
- 3 cups beef broth
- 3 tablespoon olive oil
- 1/2 small onion; finely chopped.

- 1/4 teaspoon garlic powder
- 1 teaspoon salt
- 1/2 teaspoon black pepper; freshly ground.
- 1 teaspoon cumin powder

Directions:

1. Plug in the instant pot and press the *Sauté* button. Grease the inner pot with oil and heat up
2. Rinse the meat under cold running water and generously sprinkle with some salt. Add to the pot and cook for 4-5 minutes, stirring constantly
3. Now add onions and bell peppers. Continue to cook for another 1-2 minutes. Finally, add the remaining ingredients and give it a good stir.
4. Seal the lid and set the steam release handle to the *Sealing* position. Press the *Manual* button and cook for 20 minutes on high pressure
5. When done; release the pressure naturally and open the lid. Serve hot and enjoy.

Nutrition Value: Calories: 360; Total Fats: 18.9g; Net Carbs: 6.3g; Protein: 39.1g; Fiber: 1.5g

30. Tomato Pollock Stew

Preparation Time: 35 Minutes
Servings: 4

Ingredients:

For stew:

- 1-pound Pollock fillets
- 1 large onion; finely chopped
- 2 cups fish stock
- 1/2 cup olive oil
- 1 teaspoon white pepper; freshly ground
- 4 garlic cloves; crushed
- 1 cup tomatoes; finely chopped.
- 2 bay leaves
- 1 teaspoon sea salt

Directions:

1. Plug in the instant pot and press the *Sauté* button. Add about two tablespoons of olive oil in the pot and

heat up
2. Add onions and garlic. Sauté until translucent, stirring constantly
3. Add chopped tomatoes and cook until they soften, adding some fish stock from time to time
4. When tomatoes have completely soften and the liquid has evaporated, add the remaining ingredients and press the *Cancel'* button. Close the cooker's lid and set the steam release handle to the *Sealing* position.
5. Press the *Stew* button and cook for 15 minutes on high pressure
6. When done; press the *Cancel'* button again and open the lid
7. Serve warm and optionally sprinkle with some more olive oil or dried thyme

Nutrition Value: Calories: 479; Total Fats: 35.9g; Net Carbs: 4.8g; Protein: 33.8g; Fiber: 1.4g

31. Spinach Soup

Preparation Time: 30 Minutes
Servings: 2

Ingredients:

For soup:

- 3 cups spinach; chopped
- 2 tablespoon butter
- 3 cups beef broth
- 1 cup cauliflower; chopped.
- 1/2 cup heavy cream
- 1 teaspoon garlic powder
- 1/4 teaspoon sea salt
- 1/2 teaspoon black pepper; freshly ground.

Directions:

1. Plug in your instant pot and set the stainless steel insert
2. Place spinach in a large sieve and rinse well under running water. Transfer to the pot along with chopped cauliflower. Season with salt, pepper, and garlic
3. Stir well and pour in the broth. Seal the lid and set the steam release handle to the *Sealing* position. Press the *Manual* button and set the timer for 10 minutes on high pressure.
4. When done; press the *Cancel* button and release the pressure naturally for 10-15 minutes. Then move the pressure valve to the *Venting* position to release any remaining pressure
5. Carefully, open the lid and stir in two tablespoons of butter. Chill for a while
6. Transfer to a blender or a food processor and process until smooth. Stir in the heavy cream and optionally season with more salt or pepper. Serve hot and enjoy.

Nutrition Value: Calories: 286; Total Fats: 24.9g; Net Carbs: 4.3g; Protein: 10.3g; Fiber: 2.2g

32. Spring Vegetable Stew

Preparation Time: 40 Minutes
Servings: 6

Ingredients:

For stew:

- 2 -pounds beef stew meat
- 1 spring onion; chopped
- 2 large tomatoes; chopped.
- 4 tablespoon butter
- 1 cup broccoli; chopped
- 1 cup spinach; chopped.
- 1/4 cup fresh parsley leaves
- 2 celery stalks; chopped
- 4 tablespoon olive oil
- 1 red bell pepper; finely chopped
- 1 cup zucchini; chopped.
- 5 cups beef broth
- 1/4 teaspoon stevia powder
- 1 teaspoon smoked paprika
- 1/2 teaspoon dried rosemary
- 1 tablespoon cayenne pepper
- 1/2 teaspoon onion powder
- 1 teaspoon sea salt

Directions:

1. Plug in the instant pot and grease the inner pot with olive oil. Press the *Sauté* button and heat up. Add spring onions and tomatoes. Season with some salt and

cook for 4-5 minutes stirring constantly.
2. Press the *Cancel'* button to turn off the heat. Now add bell broccoli, zucchini, celery stalks, bell peppers, spinach, and parsley, creating layers as you go. Pour in the broth and sprinkle with the remaining spices. Top with beef stew meat.
3. Seal the lid and set the steam release handle to the *Sealing* position. Press the *Meat* button
4. When done; release the pressure naturally and open the lid. Mix all well and stir in the butter. Serve hot and enjoy.

Nutrition Value: Calories: 490; Total Fats: 27.9g; Net Carbs: 5g; Protein: 51.7g; Fiber: 2g

33. Poblano Cheese Frittata

Preparation Time: 40 Minutes
Servings: 4

Ingredients:

- 4 eggs
- 1 ½ cup Mexican cheese; any kind, blend shredded. divided
- 1/4 cup cilantro; chopped
- 1 cup half and half
- 10 -ounce canned green chiles; diced.
- 1/2 teaspoon ground cumin
- 1 teaspoon salt
- 2 cups water

Directions:

1. Whisk eggs. Mix in 1 cup cheese and remaining ingredients.
2. Grease a 6-inch metal or silicone pan thoroughly to prevent eggs sticking. Pour the prepared mixture into the pan
3. Add 2 cups water to the Instant Pot, and place a trivet in the pot. Place the greased pan on the trivet.
4. Cook at high pressure for 20 minutes. Let the pressure to release naturally for 10 minutes and then release any remaining pressure.
5. Top the quiche with remaining 1/2 cup cheese, and place under hot broiler for 5 minutes to brown until cheese is bubbling. Serve hot

Nutrition Value: Calories: 257 ; Total Carbs: 6 g; Net Carbs: 3.7 g; Fat: 19 g; Protein: 14g

34. Fish Stew

Preparation Time: 35 Minutes
Servings: 6

Ingredients:

For stew:

- 2 -pounds trout fillets
- 1-pound shrimps; peeled
- 4 cups fish stock
- 1/4 cup extra virgin olive oil
- 2 large onions; finely chopped
- 1/4 cup fresh parsley; finely chopped.
- 3 garlic cloves; crushed
- 1 cup cauliflower; chopped
- 1/2 teaspoon dried thyme
- 1 teaspoon sea salt

Directions:

1. Plug in the instant pot and add three tablespoons of olive oil in the inner pot. Press the *Sauté* button and heat up
2. Add onions and garlic. Stir-fry for 3-4 minutes, or until translucent
3. Now add shrimps and continue to cook for another 5 minutes. If necessary, add some more olive oil
4. Finally, add the remaining ingredients and seal the lid. Set the steam release handle to the *Sealing* position and press the *Manual* button
5. Set the timer for 10 minutes. When done; release the pressure naturally and open the lid.
6. Sprinkle with a few drops of freshly squeezed lemon juice before serving. This, however, is optional

Nutrition Value: Calories: 503; Total Fats: 23.9g; Net Carbs: 5.8g; Protein: 62g; Fiber: 1.6g

35. Cabbage Goulash

Preparation Time: 55 Minutes
Servings: 4

Ingredients:

For goulash:
- 1-pound beef stew meat
- 4 cups beef broth
- 3 tablespoon butter
- 1 cup cabbage; shredded
- 1/2 small zucchini; chopped
- 1 cup sun-dried tomatoes
- 1 large onion; finely chopped.
- 1/2 teaspoon Tabasco
- 1/2 teaspoon white pepper; freshly ground.
- 1 teaspoon salt

Directions:
1. Grease the bottom of your pot with oil and add onions. Press the *Sauté* button and cook until translucent, for 3-4 minutes. Now add tomatoes and continue to cook for another 5-6 minutes.
2. Press the *Cancel'* button and add the remaining ingredients. Stir well and securely lock the lid.
3. Set the steam release handle to the *Sealing* position and press the *Manual* button. Set the timer for 20 minutes on high pressure.
4. When done; perform a quick release and open the lid. Press the *Sauté* button and simmer for another 15-20 minutes or until the excess liquid evaporates

Nutrition Value: Calories: 356; Total Fats: 17.3g; Net Carbs: 5.9g; Protein: 40.6g; Fiber: 2.1g

36. Pork Stew with Basil
Preparation Time: 45 Minutes
Servings: 4

Ingredients:
For stew:
- 2-pounds pork tenderloin; chopped
- 1 tablespoon balsamic vinegar
- 5 cups beef broth
- 1 large onion; finely chopped.
- 2 tablespoon vegetable oil
- 1 cup cherry tomatoes; chopped

- 1/2 teaspoon pepper; freshly ground.
- A handful of fresh basil
- 1 teaspoon salt

Directions:
1. Plug in the instant pot and press the *Sauté* button. Grease the stainless steel insert with oil and add onions. Cook until translucent – about 3-4 minutes
2. Now add the meat and season with salt and pepper. Add balsamic vinegar and continue to cook for another 10 minutes.
3. Finally, add the remaining ingredients and stir well. Securely lock the lid and set the steam release handle to the *Sealing* position
4. Press the *Manual* button and set the timer for 25 minute
5. When done; release the pressure naturally and carefully open the lid. Serve hot and enjoy.

Nutrition Value: Calories: 456; Total Fats: 16.6g; Net Carbs: 5.1g; Protein: 66.2g; Fiber: 1.3g

37. Chinese-Style Spareribs
Preparation Time: 50 Minutes
Servings: 4

Ingredients:
- 1 tablespoon sesame oil
- 1 tablespoon Shaoxing wine
- 1 tablespoon dark soy sauce
- 1 teaspoon garlic; minced
- 1 teaspoon ginger; minced
- 1 tablespoon fermented black bean paste
- 1 tablespoon honey
- 1.5-pound spare ribs; cut into small pieces

Directions:
1. In a large mixing bowl, mix all ingredients except ribs for the marinade.
2. Add the spare ribs and stir. Marinate ribs for at least 30 minutes or up to 24 hours
3. Remove ribs from the marinade and place in the air fryer basket.
4. Set the air fryer at 375°F for 8 minutes.

5. Check to ensure the ribs have an internal temperature of 165°F before serving

Nutrition Value: Calories: 386 ; Total Carbs: 4 g; Net Carbs: 0.9 g; Fat: 31 g; Protein: 18 g

38. Beef Neck Stew

Preparation Time: 60 Minutes
Servings: 6.

Ingredients:

For stew:

- 2 -pounds beef neck; chopped into bite-sized pieces
- 1/2 eggplant; sliced
- 3 cups beef broth
- 1 tablespoon cayenne pepper
- 4 tablespoon olive oil
- 4 tablespoon Parmesan cheese
- 1 cup fire-roasted tomatoes
- 1 cup cauliflower; chopped into florets
- 2 bay leaves
- 1/2 teaspoon salt
- 1/2 teaspoon chili powder

Directions:

1. Rinse the meat and pat dry with a kitchen paper. Place on a large cutting board and cut into bite-sized pieces and place in a large bowl. Season with salt, cayenne pepper, and chili pepper, Set aside
2. Plug in the instant pot and press the *Sauté* button. Grease the bottom of the inner pot with olive oil and add the meat. Cook for 5-7 minutes, stirring constantly.
3. Now add the remaining ingredients and seal the lid. Adjust the steam release handle to the *Sealing* position and press the *Meat* button. Cook for 35 minutes on high pressure
4. When done; press the *Cancel* button to turn off the heat and release the pressure naturally. Make sure the pot stays covered for another 10 minutes before removing the lid.
5. Carefully, remove the lid and chill for a while. Divide the stew between serving bowls and sprinkle each with Parmesan Cheese to enjoy Serve it immediately.

Nutrition Value: Calories: 414; Total Fats: 20.6g; Net Carbs: 2.8g; Protein: 50.8g; Fiber: 2.1g

39. Beef Ragout

Preparation Time: 25 Minutes
Servings: 6

Ingredients:

For ragout:

- 2 -pounds beef stew meat
- 1 cup cauliflower; finely chopped.
- 2 tablespoon butter
- 3 small onions; finely chopped.
- 1 cup cherry tomatoes; chopped
- 1 celery rib; thinly sliced
- 3 tablespoon olive oil
- 2 tablespoon balsamic vinegar
- 1/2 teaspoon black pepper
- 1 tablespoon smoked paprika
- 1 teaspoon salt

Directions:

1. Rinse the meat under cold running water and pat dry with a kitchen paper. Cut into 1-inch thick pieces and set aside.
2. Plug in the instant pot and grease the bottom of the inner pot with olive oil. Rub the meat with salt and make the bottom layer
3. Add cherry tomatoes and cauliflower and season with salt, smoked paprika, and black pepper. Sprinkle with onions and pour in the vinegar and beef broth. Top with celery rib and seal the lid.
4. Set the steam release handle to the *Sealing* position and press the *Meat* button. Cook for 20 minutes on high pressure.
5. When done; press the *Cancel'* button to turn off the heat and release the pressure naturally. Open the lid and stir in the butter.
6. Let it chill for a while before serving

Nutrition Value: Calories: 400; Total Fats: 20.4g; Net Carbs: 4g; Protein: 46.9g; Fiber: 1.6g

Breakfast

40. Taco Soup

Preparation Time: 20 Minutes
Servings: 8

Ingredients:

- 2 pounds ground beef
- 20 -ounce tomatoes with chilis; diced.
- 32 -ounce beef broth
- 1 tablespoon onion flakes
- 4 cloves garlic; minced
- 2 tablespoon chili powder
- 2 teaspoon cumin
- Salt; pepper, to taste
- 8 -ounce cream cheese
- 1/2 cup heavy cream

Directions:

1. Press the *Sauté* button, brown ground beef in the Instant Pot. Drain excess grease if needed.
2. Stir in the next seven ingredients. Cover Instant Pot and cook on *Soup* setting for 5 minutes
3. When time is up, allow the pot to sit with the valve closed to depressurize for 1 minute before opening vent valve and removing the lid. Add cream cheese and heavy cream. Serve hot.

Nutrition Value: Calories: 368 ; Total Carbs: 8 g; Net Carbs: 3.7 g; Fat: 28 g; Protein: 27 g

41. Savory Cabbage Stew

Preparation Time: 40 Minutes
Servings: 6

Ingredients:

For stew:

- 2 -pounds beef chuck roast
- 2 small onions; finely chopped
- 3 cups beef broth
- 2 chipotle chilies; chopped.
- 1/4 teaspoon ground cloves
- 2 garlic cloves; crushed
- 2 tablespoon apple cider vinegar
- 1 tablespoon lime juice
- 3 tablespoon butter

- 1 cup cabbage; shredded
- 3 bay leaves
- 1 teaspoon dried oregano
- 1 teaspoon white pepper
- 1/2 teaspoon cumin powder
- 1 teaspoon salt

Directions:

1. Rinse the meat under cold running water and place on a clean work surface. Using a sharp knife cut into 4-6 large chunks, Set aside
2. Plug in the instant pot and press the *Sauté* button. Add the meat chunks and briefly brown on all sides, for 3-4 minutes. Remove from the pot and transfer to plate, Set aside.
3. Now add onions and cook until translucent, 3-4 minutes. Add garlic, oregano, and cumin. Stir well and continue to cook for another minute.
4. Add the remaining ingredients and stir well. Top with the meat and seal the lid. Set the steam release handle to the *Sealing* position and press the *Manual* mode. Set the timer for 20 minutes on high pressure
5. When done; release the pressure naturally and open the lid. Serve hot and enjoy.

Nutrition Value: Calories: 640; Total Fats: 48.6g; Net Carbs: 4.1g; Protein: 42.8g; Fiber: 1g

42. Sri Lankan Coconut Cabbage

Preparation Time: 30 Minutes
Servings: 4

Ingredients:

- 1 tablespoon coconut oil
- 1 medium brown onion; halved, sliced.
- 2 garlic cloves; diced.
- 1/2 long red chili; sliced.
- 1 tablespoon yellow mustard seeds
- 1 ½ teaspoon salt
- 1 tablespoon mild curry powder
- 1 tablespoon turmeric powder

- 1 medium cabbage; quartered, shredded.
- 1 medium carrot; peeled, sliced.
- 2 tablespoon lime or lemon juice
- 1/2 cup desiccated unsweetened coconut
- 1 tablespoon olive oil
- 1/3 cup water

Directions:
1. Turn the Instant Pot on and press the *Sauté* function key. Add the coconut oil, onion, and ½ teaspoon salt and cook for 3-4 minutes, until soft
2. Add the garlic, chili, and spices and stir, cooking for 1 minute.
3. Add the cabbage, carrots, lime juice, coconut, and olive oil. Add the water and stir thoroughly
4. Press *Keep Warm/Cancel. * Put on and lock the lid, the steam releasing handle pointing to *Sealing. *
5. Press *Manual* (High Pressure) and set to 5 minutes. After 3 beeps the pressure cooker will start the cooking process
6. Let the pressure release naturally for 5 minutes, then use the quick release to let off the rest of the steam.
7. Serve hot as a side dish.

Nutrition Value: Calories: 214; Total Carbs: 7.3 g; Net Carbs: 3.5 g; Fat: 16 g; Protein: 20 g

43. Chipotle Short Ribs Stew

Preparation Time: 60 Minutes
Servings: 6

Ingredients:

For stew:
- 2 -pounds beef short ribs
- 2 cups tomatoes; chopped.
- 3 cups beef broth
- 3 Poblano peppers; cut into strips
- 1 cup white onions; chopped
- 3 tablespoon olive oil
- 2 chipotle peppers; finely chopped.
- 1/2 teaspoon white pepper; freshly ground.
- 1 teaspoon salt

Directions:
1. Rub the meat with salt and pepper, Set aside.
2. Plug in the instant pot and grease the inner pot with olive oil. Press the *Sauté* button and add peppers, tomatoes, and onions. Cook for 15 minutes, stirring occasionally.
3. Now; pour in the broth and add the meat. Securely lock the lid and set the steam release handle to the *Sealing* position. Press the *Manual* button and set the timer for 35 minutes on high pressure
4. When you hear the end signal, perform a quick pressure release and open the lid. Serve warm

Nutrition Value: Calories: 423; Total Fats: 21.5g; Net Carbs: 6.4g; Protein: 47.6g; Fiber: 1.7g

44. Buffalo Chicken Soup

Preparation Time: 30 Minutes
Servings: 6

Ingredients:
- 1-pound chicken; cooked, shredded.
- 1 tablespoon extra-virgin olive oil
- 1/2 large onion; diced.
- 1/2 cup celery; diced.
- 4 cloves garlic; minced
- 4 cup chicken bone broth
- 3 tablespoon Buffalo sauce
- 6 -ounce cream cheese; cubed, at room temperature
- 1/2 cup heavy cream

Directions:
1. Press *Saute* button on the Instant Pot. Add the oil, chopped onion, and celery. Cook for 5-10 minutes, until onions are translucent and start to brown.
2. Add garlic. Saute for a minute, until fragrant. Press the *Off * button
3. Add the shredded chicken, broth, and buffalo sauce
4. Cover and seal the Instant Pot. Press the *Soup* button and adjust the time to 5

minutes.
5. After the time is up, allow the natural pressure release for 5 minutes, then switch to quick release and open the lid.
6. Ladle about a cup of liquid from the edge of the Instant Pot and put in blender. Add cream cheese and puree until smooth.
7. Add the mixture back into the Instant Pot with the heavy cream. Stir until smooth.

Nutrition Value: Calories: 270 ; Total Carbs: 4 g; Net Carbs: 2.6 g; Fat: 16 g; Protein: 27 g

MAINS

45. Stuffed Eggplants

Preparation time: 10 minutes
Cooking time: 35 minutes
Servings: 4

Ingredients:

- 2 eggplants, halved lengthwise and 2/3 of the flesh scooped out
- 3 tablespoons olive oil
- 1 red onion, chopped
- 2 garlic cloves, minced
- 1 pint white mushrooms, sliced
- 2 cups kale, torn
- 2 cups quinoa, cooked
- 1 tablespoon thyme, chopped
- Zest and juice of 1 lemon
- Salt and black pepper to the taste
- ½ cup Greek yogurt
- 3 tablespoons parsley, chopped

Directions:

1. Rub the inside of each eggplant half with half of the oil and arrange them on a baking sheet lined with parchment paper.
2. Heat up a pan with the rest of the oil over medium heat, add the onion and the garlic and sauté for 5 minutes.
3. Add the mushrooms and cook for 5 minutes more.
4. Add the kale, salt, pepper, thyme, lemon zest and juice, stir, cook for 5 minutes more and take off the heat.
5. Stuff the eggplant halves with the mushroom mix, introduce them in the oven and bake 400 degrees F for 20 minutes.
6. Divide the eggplants between plates, sprinkle the parsley and the yogurt on top and serve for lunch.

Nutrition Value: calories 512, fat 16.4, fiber 17.5, carbs 78, protein 17.2

46. Salmon Bowls

Preparation time: 10 minutes
Cooking time: 40 minutes
Servings: 4

Ingredients:

- 2 cups farro
- Juice of 2 lemons
- 1/3 cup olive oil+ 2 tablespoons
- Salt and black pepper
- 1 cucumber, chopped
- ¼ cup balsamic vinegar
- 1 garlic cloves, minced
- ¼ cup parsley, chopped
- ¼ cup mint, chopped
- 2 tablespoons mustard
- 4 salmon fillets, boneless

Directions:

1. Put water in a large pot, bring to a boil over medium-high heat, add salt and the farro, stir, simmer for 30 minutes, drain, transfer to a bowl, add the lemon juice, mustard, garlic, salt, pepper and 1/3 cup oil, toss and leave aside for now.
2. In another bowl, mash the cucumber with a fork, add the vinegar, salt, pepper, the parsley, dill and mint and whisk well.
3. Heat up a pan with the rest of the oil over medium heat, add the salmon fillets skin side down, cook for 5 minutes on each side, cool them down and break into pieces.
4. Add over the farro, add the cucumber dressing, toss and serve for lunch.

Nutrition Value: calories 281, fat 12.7, fiber 1.7, carbs 5.8, protein 36.5

47. Spicy Potato Salad

Preparation time: 10 minutes
Cooking time: 15 minutes
Servings: 4

Ingredients:

- 1 and ½ pounds baby potatoes, peeled

and halved
- A pinch of salt and black pepper
- 2 tablespoons harissa paste
- 6 ounces Greek yogurt
- Juice of 1 lemon
- ¼ cup red onion, chopped
- ¼ cup parsley, chopped

Directions:
1. Put the potatoes in a pot, add water to cover, add salt, bring to a boil over medium-high heat, cook for 12 minutes, drain and transfer them to a bowl.
2. Add the harissa and the rest of the ingredients, toss and serve for lunch.

Nutrition Value: calories 354, fat 19.2, fiber 4.5, carbs 24.7, protein 11.2

48. Chicken and Rice Soup

Preparation time: 10 minutes
Cooking time: 35 minutes
Servings: 4

Ingredients:
- 6 cups chicken stock
- 1 and ½ cups chicken meat, cooked and shredded
- 1 bay leaf
- 1 yellow onion, chopped
- 2 tablespoons olive oil
- 1/3 cup white rice
- 1 egg, whisked
- Juice of ½ lemon
- 1 cup asparagus, trimmed and halved
- 1 cup carrots, chopped
- ½ cup dill, chopped
- Salt and black pepper to the taste

1. **Directions:**
2. Heat up a pot with the oil over medium heat, add the onions and sauté for 5 minutes.
3. Add the stock, dill, the rice and the bay leaf, stir, bring to a boil over medium heat and cook for 10 minutes.
4. Add the rest of the ingredients except the egg and the lemon juice, stir and cook for 15 minutes more.
5. Add the egg whisked with the lemon juice gradually, whisk the soup, cook for 2 minutes more, divide into bowls an serve.

Nutrition Value: calories 263, fat 18.5, fiber 4.5, carbs 19.8, protein 14.5

49. Chicken and Carrots Soup

Preparation time: 10 minutes
Cooking time: 1 hour and 20 minutes
Servings: 6

Ingredients:
- 1 whole chicken, cut into medium pieces
- 3 carrots, sliced
- 4 eggs, whisked
- Juice of 2 lemons
- ¼ cup dill, chopped
- Salt and black pepper to the taste
- 8 cups water

Directions:
1. Put the chicken pieces in a pot, add the water, bring to a boil over medium heat, cover the pot and simmer for 1 hour.
2. Transfer the chicken to a plate, cool it down, discard bones, return the meat to the pot and heat it up again over medium heat.
3. Add the rest of the ingredients except the eggs, stir and simmer the soup for 10 minutes more.
4. Add the eggs mixed with 2 cups of stock, stir the soup, cook for 2-3 minutes more, divide into bowls and serve.

Nutrition Value: calories 264, fat 17.5, fiber 4.8, carbs 28.7, protein 16.3

50. Roasted Peppers Soup

Preparation time: 10 minutes
Cooking time: 55 minutes
Servings: 4

Ingredients:
- 2 tomatoes, halved

- 3 red bell peppers, halved and deseeded
- 1 yellow onion, quartered
- 2 garlic cloves, peeled and halved
- 2 tablespoons olive oil
- 2 cups veggie stock
- A pinch of salt and black pepper
- 2 tablespoons tomato paste
- ¼ cup parsley, chopped
- ¼ teaspoon Italian seasoning
- ¼ teaspoon sweet paprika

Directions:
1. Spread the bell peppers, tomatoes, onion and garlic on a baking sheet lined with parchment paper, add oil, salt and pepper and bake at 375 degrees F for 45 minutes.
2. Heat up a pot with the stock over medium heat, add the roasted vegetables and the rest of the ingredients, stir, bring to a simmer and cook for 10 minutes.
3. Blend the mix using an immersion blender, divide the soup into bowls and serve.

Nutrition Value: calories 273, fat 11.2, fiber 3.4, carbs 15.7, protein 5.6

51. Lentils Soup

Preparation time: 10 minutes
Cooking time: 45 minutes
Servings: 6

Ingredients:
- 1 yellow onion, chopped
- 2 tablespoons olive oil
- 2 celery stalks, chopped
- 1 carrot, sliced
- 1/3 cup parsley, chopped
- ½ cup cilantro, chopped
- 2 and ½ tablespoons garlic, minced
- 2 tablespoons ginger, grated
- 1 teaspoon turmeric powder
- 2 teaspoons sweet paprika
- 1 teaspoon cinnamon powder
- 1 and ¼ cups red lentils
- 15 ounces canned chickpeas, drained and rinsed
- 28 ounces canned tomatoes and juice, crushed
- 8 cups chicken stock
- A pinch of salt and black pepper

Directions:
1. Heat up a pot with the oil over medium heat, add the onion, ginger, garlic, celery and carrots and sauté for 5 minutes.
2. Add the rest of the ingredients, stir, bring to a simmer over medium heat and cook for 35 minutes.
3. Ladle the soup into bowls and serve right away.

Nutrition Value: calories 238, fat 7.3, fiber 6.3, carbs 32, protein 14

52. White Bean Soup

Preparation time: 10 minutes
Cooking time: 8 hours
Servings: 6

Ingredients:
- 1 cup celery, chopped
- 1 cup carrots, chopped
- 1 yellow onion, chopped
- 6 cups veggie stock
- 4 garlic cloves, minced
- 2 cup navy beans, dried
- ½ teaspoon basil, dried
- ½ teaspoon sage, dried
- 1 teaspoon thyme, dried
- A pinch of salt and black pepper

Directions:
1. In your slow cooker, combine the beans with the stock and the rest of the ingredients, put the lid on and cook on Low for 8 hours.
2. Divide the soup into bowls and serve right away.

Nutrition Value: calories 264, fat 17.5, fiber 4.5, carbs 23.7, protein 11.5

53. Veggie Soup

Preparation time: 10 minutes
Cooking time: 45 minutes
Servings: 8

Ingredients:

- 1 yellow onion, chopped
- 4 garlic cloves, minced
- ½ cup carrots, chopped
- 1 zucchini, chopped
- 1 yellow squash, peeled and cubed
- 2 tablespoons parsley, chopped
- 3 tablespoons olive oil
- ¼ cup celery, chopped
- 30 ounces canned cannellini beans, drained and rinsed
- 30 ounces canned red kidney beans, drained and rinsed
- 4 cups veggie stock
- 2 cups water
- ¼ teaspoon thyme, dried
- ½ teaspoon basil, dried
- A pinch of salt and black pepper
- 4 cups baby spinach
- ¼ cup parmesan, grated

Directions:

1. Heat up a pot with the oil over medium heat, add the onion, garlic, carrots, squash, zucchini, parsley and the celery, stir and sauté for 5 minutes.
2. Add the rest of the ingredients except the spinach and the parmesan, stir, bring to a simmer over medium heat and cook for 30 minutes.
3. Add the spinach, cook the soup for 10 minutes more, divide into bowls, sprinkle the cheese on top and serve.

Nutrition Value: calories 300, fat 11.3, fiber 3.4, carbs 17.5, protein 10

54. Seafood Gumbo

Preparation time: 10 minutes
Cooking time: 30 minutes
Servings: 4

Ingredients:

- ¼ cup tapioca flour
- ¼ cup olive oil
- 1 cup celery, chopped
- 1 white onion, chopped
- 1 red bell pepper, chopped
- 1 green bell pepper, chopped
- 1 red chili, chopped
- 2 cups okra, chopped
- 2 garlic cloves, minced
- 1 cup canned tomatoes, crushed
- 1 teaspoon thyme, dried
- 2 cups fish stock
- 1 bay leaf
- 16 ounces canned crab meat, drained
- 1 pound shrimp, peeled and deveined
- ¼ cup parsley, chopped
- Salt and black pepper to the taste

Directions:

1. Heat up a pot with the oil over medium heat, add the flour, whisk to obtain a paste and cook for about 5 minutes.
2. Add the bell peppers, the onions, celery and the okra and sauté for 5 minutes.
3. Add the rest of the ingredients except the crab, shrimp, and parsley, stir, bring to a simmer and cook for 15 minutes.
4. Add the remaining ingredients, simmer the soup for 10 minutes more, divide into bowls and serve.

Nutrition Value: calories 363, fat 2, fiber 5, carbs 18, protein 40

55. Chicken and Orzo Soup

Preparation time: 10 minutes
Cooking time: 11 minutes
Servings: 4

Ingredients:

- ½ cup carrot, chopped
- 1 yellow onion, chopped
- 12 cups chicken stock
- 2 cups kale, chopped
- 3 cups chicken meat, cooked and shredded

- 1 cup orzo
- ¼ cup lemon juice
- 1 tablespoon olive oil

Directions:
1. Heat up a pot with the oil over medium heat, add the onion and sauté for 3 minutes.
2. Add the carrots and the rest of the ingredients, stir, bring to a simmer and cook for 8 minutes more.
3. Ladle into bowls and serve hot.

Nutrition Value: calories 300, fat 12.2, fiber 5.4, carbs 16.5, protein 12.2

56. Lentils Soup

Preparation time: 10 minutes
Cooking time: 8 hours
Servings: 6

Ingredients:
- 2 cups red lentils, dried
- 1 yellow onion, chopped
- 2 celery stalks, chopped
- 2 carrots, sliced
- 3 garlic cloves, minced
- 15 ounces canned tomatoes, chopped
- 2 chipotle chili peppers, chopped
- 7 cups veggie stock
- 1 and ½ teaspoons cumin, ground
- Salt and black pepper to the taste
- 2 teaspoons adobo sauce
- ¼ cup cilantro, chopped
- 2 tablespoons lime juice

Directions:
1. In your slow cooker, combine the lentils with the tomatoes, chili peppers and the rest of the ingredients except the cilantro and the lime juice, put the lid on and cook on Low for 8 hours.
2. Add the cilantro and the lime juice, stir, ladle the soup into bowls and serve.

Nutrition Value: calories 276, fat 1, fiber 21, carbs 48, protein 17

57. Zucchini Soup

Preparation time: 10 minutes
Cooking time: 20 minutes
Servings: 8

Ingredients:
- 2 and ½ pounds zucchinis, roughly chopped
- 2 tablespoons olive oil
- 1 yellow onion, chopped
- 4 garlic cloves, minced
- 4 cups chicken stock
- ½ cup basil, chopped
- Salt and black pepper to the taste

Directions:
1. Heat up a pot with the oil over medium heat, add the zucchinis and the onion and sauté for 5 minutes.
2. Add the garlic and the rest of the ingredients except the basil, stir, bring to a simmer and cook for 15 minutes over medium heat.
3. Add the basil, blend the soup using an immersion blender, ladle into bowls and serve.

Nutrition Value: calories 182, fat 7.6, fiber 1.5, carbs 12.6, protein 2.3

58. Tuscan Soup

Preparation time: 10 minutes
Cooking time: 15 minutes
Servings: 6

Ingredients:
- 1 yellow onion, chopped
- 4 garlic cloves, minced
- 2 tablespoons olive oil
- ½ cup celery, chopped
- ½ cup carrots, chopped
- 15 ounces canned tomatoes, chopped
- 1 zucchini, chopped
- 6 cups veggie stock
- 2 tablespoons tomato paste
- 15 ounces canned white beans, drained and rinsed

- 2 handfuls baby spinach
- 1 tablespoon basil, chopped
- Salt and black pepper to the taste

Directions:

1. Heat up a pot with the oil over medium heat, add the garlic and the onion and sauté for 5 minutes.
2. Add the rest of the ingredients, stir, bring the soup to a simmer and cook for 10 minutes.
3. Ladle the soup into bowls and serve right away.

Nutrition Value: calories 471, fat 8.2, fiber 19.4, carbs 76.5, protein 27.6

59. Cauliflower Cream

Preparation time: 10 minutes
Cooking time: 1 hour and 10 minutes
Servings: 8

Ingredients:

- 1 cauliflower head, florets separated
- 1 teaspoon garlic powder
- 2 tablespoons olive oil
- 1 yellow onion, chopped
- Salt and black pepper to the taste
- 5 cups chicken stock
- 2 tablespoons garlic, minced
- 2 and ½ cups cheddar cheese, shredded

Directions:

1. Spread the cauliflower on a baking sheet lined with parchment paper, add garlic powder, half of the oil, salt and pepper and roast at 425 degrees F for 30 minutes.
2. Heat up a pot with the rest of the oil over medium heat, add the onion and sauté for 5 minutes.
3. Add the roasted cauliflower and the rest of the ingredients except the cheddar, stir and simmer the soup for 30 minutes.
4. Blend the soup using an immersion blender, add the cheese, stir, divide the soup into bowls and serve.

Nutrition Value: calories 243, fat 17, fiber 2.3, carbs 41.1, protein 13.7

60. White Beans and Orange Soup

Preparation time: 10 minutes
Cooking time: 37 minutes
Servings: 4

Ingredients:

- 1 yellow onion, chopped
- 5 celery sticks, chopped
- 4 carrots, chopped
- 1 cup olive oil
- ½ teaspoon oregano, dried
- 1 bay leaf
- 3 orange slices, peeled
- 30 ounces canned white beans, drained
- 2 tablespoons tomato paste
- 2 cups water
- 6 cups chicken stock

Directions:

1. Heat up a pot with the oil over medium heat, add the onion, celery, carrots, the bay leaf and the oregano, stir and sauté for 5 minutes.
2. Add the orange slices and cook for 2 minutes more.
3. Add the rest of the ingredients, stir, bring to a simmer and cook over medium heat for 30 minutes.
4. Ladle the soup into bowls and serve.

Nutrition Value: calories 273, fat 16.3, fiber 8.4, carbs 15.6, protein 7.4

61. Basil Zucchini Soup

Preparation time: 10 minutes
Cooking time: 20 minutes
Servings: 4

Ingredients:

- 2 tablespoons olive oil
- 3 garlic cloves, minced
- 1 yellow onion, chopped
- 4 zucchinis, cubed
- 4 cups chicken stock

- Zest of 1 lemon, grated
- ½ cup basil, chopped
- Salt and black pepper to the taste

Directions:
1. Heat up a pot with the oil over medium heat, add the onion and the garlic and sauté for 5 minutes.
2. Add the zucchinis and the rest of the ingredients except the basil, bring to a simmer and cook over medium heat for 15 minutes.
3. Add the basil, stir, divide the soup into bowls and serve.

Nutrition Value: calories 274, fat 11.1, fiber 4.5, carbs 16.5, protein 4.5

62. Chicken and Leeks Soup

Preparation time: 10 minutes
Cooking time: 50 minutes
Servings: 6

Ingredients:
- 2 pounds chicken breast, skinless, boneless and cubed
- ½ cup olive oil
- 2 leeks, sliced
- 4 spring onions, chopped
- 1 small green cabbage head, shredded
- 4 celery sticks, chopped
- 4 cups veggie stock
- ½ teaspoon sweet paprika
- A pinch of nutmeg, ground
- Salt and black pepper to the taste

Directions:
1. Heat up a pot with the oil over medium-high heat, add the chicken and brown for 2 minutes on each side.
2. Add the leeks, onions and celery and sauté for 1 minute more.
3. Add the rest of the ingredients, bring to a simmer and cook over medium heat for 45 minutes.
4. Ladle the soup into bowls and serve.

Nutrition Value: calories 310, fat 15.3, fiber 8.7, carbs 24.6, protein 18.4

63. Lemony Lamb Soup

Preparation time: 10 minutes
Cooking time: 1 hour and 5 minutes
Servings: 4

Ingredients:
- ½ cup olive oil
- 2 pounds lamb meat, cubed
- 5 cups water
- 5 spring onions, chopped
- 2 tablespoons dill, chopped
- Juice of 2 lemons
- Salt and black pepper to the taste
- 3 eggs, whisked
- 1 cup baby spinach

Directions:
1. Heat up a pot with the oil over medium heat, add the lamb and brown for 10 minutes stirring from time to time.
2. Add the onions and sauté for 3 minutes more.
3. Add the water, salt and pepper, stir and simmer over medium heat for 30 minutes.
4. Add the spinach, eggs whisked with the lemon juice and some of the soup, whisk the soup well and cook for 20 minutes more.
5. Add the dill, stir, ladle the soup into bowls and serve.

Nutrition Value: calories 275, fat 28.5, fiber 1, carbs 2.8, protein 5

64. Sausage and Beans Soup

Preparation time: 10 minutes
Cooking time: 20 minutes
Servings: 4

Ingredients:
- 1 pound Italian pork sausage, sliced
- ¼ cup olive oil
- 1 carrot, chopped
- 1 yellow onion, chopped
- 1 celery stalk, chopped
- 2 garlic cloves, minced

- ½ pound kale, chopped
- 4 cups chicken stock
- 28 ounces canned cannellini beans, drained and rinsed
- 1 bay leaf
- 1 teaspoon rosemary, dried
- Salt and black pepper to the taste
- ½ cup parmesan, grated

Directions:
1. Heat up a pot with the oil over medium heat, add the sausage and brown for 5 minutes.
2. Add the onion, carrots, garlic and celery and sauté for 3 minutes more.
3. Add the rest of the ingredients except the parmesan, bring to a simmer and cook over medium heat for 30 minutes.
4. Discard the bay leaf, ladle the soup into bowls, sprinkle the parmesan on top and serve.

Nutrition Value: calories 564, fat 26.5, fiber 15.4, carbs 37.4, protein 26.6

65. Fish Soup

Preparation time: 10 minutes
Cooking time: 20 minutes
Servings: 4

Ingredients:
- 2 tablespoons olive oil
- 1 tablespoon garlic, minced
- ½ cup tomatoes, crushed
- 1 yellow onion, chopped
- 1 quart veggie stock
- 1 pound cod, skinless, boneless and cubed
- ¼ teaspoon rosemary, dried
- A pinch of salt and black pepper

Directions:
1. Heat up a pot with the oil over medium heat, add the onion and the garlic and sauté for 5 minutes.
2. Add the rest of the ingredients, toss, simmer over medium heat for 15 minutes more, divide into bowls and serve for lunch.

Nutrition Value: calories 198, fat 8.1, fiber 1, carbs 4.2, protein 26.4

66. Chickpeas Soup

Preparation time: 10 minutes
Cooking time: 1 hour
Servings: 4

Ingredients:
- 3 tomatoes, cubed
- 2 yellow onions, chopped
- 2 tablespoons olive oil
- 4 celery stalks, chopped
- ½ cup parsley, chopped
- 2 garlic cloves, minced
- 16 ounces canned chickpeas, drained and rinsed
- 6 cups water
- 1 teaspoon cumin, ground
- Juice of ½ lemon
- 1 teaspoon turmeric powder
- ½ teaspoon cinnamon powder
- ½ teaspoon ginger, grated
- Salt and black pepper to the taste

Directions:
1. Heat up a pot with the oil over medium heat, add the onion and the garlic and sauté for 5 minutes.
2. Add the tomatoes, celery, cumin, turmeric, cinnamon and the ginger, stir and sauté for 5 minutes more.
3. Add the remaining ingredients, bring the soup to a boil over medium heat and simmer for 50 minutes.
4. Ladle the soup into bowls and serve.

Nutrition Value: calories 300, fat 15.4, fiber 4.5, carbs 29.5, protein 15.4

67. Tomato Soup

Preparation time: 10 minutes
Cooking time: 55 minutes
Servings: 8

Ingredients:

- 4 pounds tomatoes, halved
- 2 tablespoons olive oil
- 6 garlic cloves, minced
- 1 yellow onion, chopped
- Salt and black pepper to the taste
- 4 cups chicken stock
- ½ teaspoon red pepper flakes
- ½ cup basil, chopped
- ½ cup parmesan, grated

Directions:
1. Arrange the tomatoes in a roasting pan, add half of the oil, salt and pepper, toss, and bake at 400 degrees F for 20 minutes.
2. Heat up a pot with the rest of the oil over medium heat, add the onion and sauté for 5 minutes.
3. Add the tomatoes and the rest of the ingredients except the basil and the parmesan, bring to a simmer and cook for 30 minutes.
4. Blend the soup using an immersion blender, add the basil and the parmesan, stir, divide into bowls and serve.

Nutrition Value: calories 237, fat 10, fiber 3.4, carbs 15.3, protein 7.4

68. Oyster Stew

Preparation time: 10 minutes
Cooking time: 1 hour and 10 minutes
Servings: 6

Ingredients:
- 2 garlic cloves, minced
- ¼ cup jarred roasted red peppers
- 2 teaspoons oregano, chopped
- 1 pound lamb meat, ground
- 1 tablespoon red wine vinegar
- Salt and black pepper to the taste
- 1 teaspoon red pepper flakes
- 2 tablespoons olive oil
- 1 and ½ cups chicken stock
- 36 oysters, shucked
- 1 and ½ cups canned black eyed peas, drained

Directions:
1. Heat up a pot with the oil over medium heat, add the meat and the garlic and brown for 5 minutes.
2. Add the peppers and the rest of the ingredients, bring to a simmer and cook for 15 minutes.
3. Divide the stew into bowls and serve.

Nutrition Value: calories 264, fat 9.3, fiber 1.2, carbs 2.3, protein 1.2

69. Potatoes and Lentils Stew

Preparation time: 10 minutes
Cooking time: 35 minutes
Servings: 4

Ingredients:
- 4 cups water
- 1 cup carrots, sliced
- 1 yellow onion, chopped
- 1 tablespoon olive oil
- 1 cup celery, chopped
- 2 garlic cloves, minced
- 2 pounds gold potatoes, cubed
- 1 and ½ cup lentils, dried
- ½ teaspoon smoked paprika
- ½ teaspoon oregano, dried
- Salt and black pepper to the taste
- 14 ounces canned tomatoes, chopped
- ½ cup cilantro, chopped

Directions:
1. Heat up a pot with the oil over medium-high heat, add the onion, garlic, celery and carrots, stir and cook for 5 minutes.
2. Add the rest of the ingredients except the cilantro, stir, bring to a simmer and cook over medium heat for 25 minutes.
3. Add the cilantro, divide the stew into bowls and serve.

Nutrition Value: calories 325, fat 17.3, fiber 6.8, carbs 26.4, protein 16.4

70. Lamb and Potatoes Stew

Preparation time: 10 minutes
Cooking time: 1 hour and 20 minutes

Servings: 4

Ingredients:

- 2 pounds lamb shoulder, boneless and cubed
- Salt and black pepper to the taste
- 1 yellow onion, chopped
- 3 tablespoons olive oil
- 3 tomatoes, grated
- 2 cups chicken stock
- 2 and ½ pounds gold potatoes, cubed
- ¾ cup green olives, pitted and sliced
- 1 tablespoon cilantro, chopped

Directions:

1. Heat up a pot with the oil over medium-high heat, add the lamb, and brown for 5 minutes on each side.
2. Add the onion and sauté for 5 minutes more.
3. Add the rest of the ingredients, bring to a simmer and cook over medium heat and cook for 1 hour and 10 minutes.
4. Divide the stew into bowls and serve.

Nutrition Value: calories 411, fat 17.4, fiber 8.4, carbs 25.5, protein 34.3

71. Ground Pork and Tomatoes

Soup

Preparation time: 10 minutes
Cooking time: 40 minutes
Servings: 4

Ingredients:

- 1 pound pork meat, ground
- Salt and black pepper to the taste
- 2 garlic cloves, minced
- 2 teaspoons thyme, dried
- 2 tablespoons olive oil
- 4 cups beef stock
- A pinch of saffron powder
- 15 ounces canned tomatoes, crushed
- 1 tablespoons parsley, chopped

Directions:

1. Heat up a pot with the oil over medium heat, add the meat and the garlic and brown for 5 minutes.
2. Add the rest of the ingredients except the parsley, bring to a simmer and cook for 25 minutes.
3. Divide the soup into bowls, sprinkle the parsley on top and serve.

Nutrition Value: calories 372, fat 17.3, fiber 5.5, carbs 28.4, protein 17.4

SIDES

72. Rich Beets Side Dish

Preparation time: 10 minutes
Cooking time: 12 minutes
Servings: 6

Ingredients:

- 6 beets, peeled and cut into wedges
- A pinch of sea salt
- Black pepper to the taste
- 2 tablespoons lemon juice
- 2 tablespoons olive oil
- 2 tablespoons agave nectar
- 1 tablespoon cider vinegar
- ½ teaspoon lemon rind, grated
- 2 rosemary sprigs

Directions:

1. Put the beets in your slow cooker.
2. Add a pinch of salt, black pepper, lemon juice, oil, agave nectar, rosemary and vinegar.
3. Stir everything, cover and cook on Low for 8 hours.
4. Add lemon rind, stir, divide among plates and serve.
5. Enjoy!

Nutrition Value: calories 120, fat 1, fiber 2, carbs 6, protein 6

73. Green Beans Side Dish

Preparation time: 10 minutes
Cooking time: 14 minutes
Servings: 6

Ingredients:

- 5 cups water
- 1 tablespoon olive oil
- 2 tablespoons thyme, chopped
- 1 cup yellow onion, chopped
- 5 garlic cloves, minced
- 3 tablespoons balsamic vinegar
- ½ cup tomato paste
- ½ cup maple syrup
- 2 tablespoons coconut aminos
- 2 tablespoons red chili paste
- 2 tablespoons mustard
- 1 and ½ cups green beans
- A pinch of sea salt and black pepper

Directions:

1. Set your instant pot on sauté mode, add the oil, heat it up, add onion, stir and sauté for 3 minutes.
2. Add garlic, thyme, vinegar and tomato paste, stir and cook for 1 minute more.
3. Add green beans, water, maple syrup, mustard, chili paste, salt, pepper and aminos, stir, cover and cook on High for 10 minutes
4. Divide among plates and serve as a side dish.
5. Enjoy!

Nutrition Value: calories 160, fat 2, fiber 4, carbs 7, protein 8

74. Sweet Potatoes Side Dish

Preparation time: 10 minutes
Cooking time: 20 minutes
Servings: 6

Ingredients:

- 4 pounds sweet potatoes, peeled and sliced
- 2 tablespoons olive oil
- 1 cup water
- ½ cup orange juice
- 2 tablespoons maple syrup
- ½ teaspoon thyme, dried
- A pinch of sea salt and black pepper
- ½ teaspoon sage, dried

Directions:

1. Set your instant pot on sauté mode, add the oil, heat it up, add sweet potato slices and cook for 4 minutes.
2. In a bowl, mix orange juice with honey,

thyme, sage, a pinch of salt and black pepper and whisk well.
3. Add this over potatoes, toss to coat, cover and cook on High for 16 minutes.
4. Divide among plates and serve as a side dish.
5. Enjoy!

Nutrition Value: calories 130, fat 3, fiber 2, carbs 5, protein 6

75. Wonderful And Special Side Dish

Preparation time: 10 minutes
Cooking time: 20 minutes
Servings: 12

Ingredients:
- 42 ounces veggie stock
- 1 cup carrot, shredded
- 2 and ½ cups cauliflower rice
- 2 tablespoons olive oil
- 2 teaspoons marjoram, dried
- 4 ounces mushrooms, sliced
- A pinch of sea salt and black pepper
- 2/3 cup cherries, dried
- ½ cup pecans, chopped
- 2/3 cup green onions, chopped

Directions:
1. Put the stock in your instant pot, add cauliflower rice, carrots, mushrooms, oil, salt, pepper and marjoram, stir, cover and cook on High for 12 minutes.
2. Add cherries and green onions, stir, cover and cook for 5 minutes more.
3. Divide among plates and serve as a side dish with chopped pecans on top.
4. Enjoy!

Nutrition Value: calories 130, fat 2, fiber 3, carbs 4, protein 6

76. Mashed Sweet Potatoes

Preparation time: 10 minutes
Cooking time: 16 minutes
Servings: 12

Ingredients:
- 3 pounds sweet potatoes, peeled and cubed
- 1 cup coconut milk, hot
- 6 garlic cloves, minced
- 28 ounces veggie stock
- 1 bay leaf
- ¼ cup ghee, melted
- A pinch of sea salt and black pepper

Directions:
1. Put potatoes in your instant pot, add stock, garlic and bay leaf, stir, cover and cook on High for 16 minutes
2. Drain potatoes, discard bay leaf, transfer them to a bowl, mash using a potato masher, mix with coconut milk and ghee and whisk really well.
3. Season with a pinch of salt and pepper, stir well, divide among plates and serve as a side dish.
4. Enjoy!

Nutrition Value: calories 135, fat 4, fiber 2, carbs 6, protein 4

77. Tasty Side Dish

Preparation time: 10 minutes
Cooking time: 10 minutes
Servings: 7

Ingredients:
- 2 tablespoons extra virgin olive oil
- ½ cup yellow onion, chopped
- ½ teaspoon saffron threads, crushed
- 2 tablespoons coconut milk, heated up
- 1 and ½ cups cauliflower rice
- 3 and ½ cups veggie stock
- A pinch of salt
- 1 tablespoon honey
- 1 cinnamon stick
- 1/3 cup almonds, chopped
- 1/3 cup currants, dried

Directions:
1. In a bowl, mix coconut milk with saffron and stir.
2. Set your instant pot on Sauté mode, add

oil, heat it up, add onions, stir and sauté them for 5 minutes.
3. Add cauliflower rice, stock, saffron and milk, honey, salt, almonds, cinnamon stick and currants, stir, cover and cook on High for 5 minutes.
4. Discard cinnamon stick, divide it between plates and serve as a side dish.
5. Enjoy!

Nutrition Value: calories 243, fat 3, fiber 1, carbs 5, protein 5

78. Spinach Cauliflower Rice

Preparation time: 10 minutes
Cooking time: 10 minutes
Servings: 6

Ingredients:

- 2 garlic cloves, minced
- ¾ cup yellow onion, chopped
- 2 tablespoons extra virgin olive oil
- 1 and ½ cups cauliflower rice
- ½ cup water
- 12 ounces spinach, chopped
- 3 and ½ cups hot veggie stock
- A pinch of sea salt and black pepper
- 2 tablespoons lemon juice
- 1/3 cup pecans, toasted and chopped

Directions:

1. Set your instant pot on sauté mode, add the oil, heat it up, add garlic and onions, stir and sauté for 5 minutes.
2. Add cauliflower rice and water, stir and cook for 1 minute more.
3. Add 3 cups stock, cover the pot and cook on High for 4 minutes.
4. Add spinach, stir, and set instant pot on Simmer mode, cook for 3 minutes and mix with the rest of the stock, salt, pepper and lemon juice.
5. Stir; divide among plates, sprinkle pecans on top and serve as a side dish.
6. Enjoy!

Nutrition Value: calories 243, fat 2, fiber 2, carbs 6, protein 12

79. Squash Puree

Preparation time: 10 minutes
Cooking time: 20 minutes
Servings: 4

Ingredients:

- ½ cup water
- 2 tablespoons ghee
- 2 acorn squash, halved
- A pinch of salt and black pepper
- ¼ teaspoon baking soda
- ½ teaspoon nutmeg, grated
- 2 tablespoons maple syrup

Directions:

1. Put the water in your instant pot, add the steamer basket, add squash halves inside, season with a pinch of salt, pepper and baking soda, rub a bit, cover and cook them on High for 20 minutes.
2. Transfer squash to a plate, cool it down, scrape flesh, transfer to a bowl and mix with ghee, maple syrup and nutmeg.
3. Mash using a potato masher, whisk well, divide among plates and serve as a side dish.
4. Enjoy!

Nutrition Value: calories 143, fat 2, fiber 2, carbs 7, protein 2

80. Healthy Mushrooms and Green Beans

Preparation time: 10 minutes
Cooking time: 6 minutes
Servings: 4

Ingredients:

- 1 pound fresh green beans, trimmed
- 2 cups water
- 6 ounces bacon, chopped
- 1 small yellow onion, chopped
- 1 garlic clove, minced
- 8 ounces mushrooms, sliced
- A pinch of sea salt and black pepper
- A splash of balsamic vinegar

Directions:

1. Put the beans in your instant pot, add water to cover them, cover the pot, cook at High for 3 minutes, drain and leave them aside.
2. Set your instant pot on Sauté mode, add bacon, brown it for 1 minute and mix with onion and garlic.
3. Stir, cook 2 more minutes, add mushrooms, stir and cook until they are done.
4. Return green beans to instant pot, add salt, pepper and a splash of vinegar, toss, divide among plates and serve as a side dish.
5. Enjoy!

Nutrition Value: calories 123, fat 2, fiber 3, carbs 4, protein 3

81. Delicious Cauliflower Rice

Preparation time: 10 minutes
Cooking time: 20 minutes
Servings: 6

Ingredients:

- 2 cups cauliflower rice
- 2 cups water
- 1 small pineapple, peeled and chopped
- A pinch of sea salt and black pepper
- 2 teaspoons olive oil

Directions:

1. In your instant pot, mix cauliflower rice with pineapple, water, oil, salt and pepper, stir, cover and cook on Low for 20 minutes.
2. Divide among plates and serve as a side dish.
3. Enjoy!

Nutrition Value: calories 100, fat 2, fiber 2, carbs 6, protein 5

82. Lovely Mash

Preparation time: 10 minutes
Cooking time: 5 minutes
Servings: 4

Ingredients:

- 4 turnips, peeled and chopped
- 1 yellow onion, chopped
- ½ cup chicken stock
- A pinch of sea salt and black pepper
- ¼ cup coconut cream

Directions:

1. Put turnips, stock and onion in your instant pot, stir, cover and cook on High for 5 minutes
2. Drain turnips, transfer them to a bowl, blend using an immersion blender, mix with a pinch of salt, pepper and coconut cream.
3. Blend again, divide among plates and serve as a side dish.
4. Enjoy!

Nutrition Value: calories 100, fat 2, fiber 2, carbs 6, protein 3

83. Carrot Puree

Preparation time: 5 minutes
Cooking time: 5 minutes
Servings: 4

Ingredients:

- 1 and ½ pounds carrots, chopped
- A pinch of salt and white pepper
- 1 tablespoon ghee, melted
- 1 teaspoon stevia
- 1 cup water
- 1 tablespoon honey

Directions:

1. Put carrots in your instant pot, add the water, cover, cook on High for 4 minutes, drain, transfer to a bowl and mash using an immersion blender.
2. Add ghee, honey, a pinch of salt, pepper and stevia, blend again, divide among plates and serve.
3. Enjoy!

Nutrition Value: calories 73, fat 2, fiber 2, carbs 4, protein 6

84. Apple Mash

Preparation time: 10 minutes
Cooking time: 15 minutes

Servings: 4

Ingredients:

- 1 cup water
- 2 apples, peeled, cored and sliced
- A pinch of sea salt
- 1 butternut squash, peeled and cut into medium chunks
- 2 tablespoons maple syrup
- 1 yellow onion, chopped
- ½ teaspoon apple pie spice

Directions:

1. Put the water in your instant pot, add the steamer basket inside, add squash pieces, onion and apple slices inside, cover and cook on High for 8 minutes/
2. Transfer squash, onion and apple to a bowl, mash using a potato masher, add a pinch of salt, maple syrup and pie spices, stir well, divide among plates and serve as a side dish.
3. Enjoy!

Nutrition Value: calories 142, fat 2, fiber 3, carbs 5, protein 6

85. Simple Fennel Side Dish

Preparation time: 5 minutes
Cooking time: 6 minutes
Servings: 3

Ingredients:

- 2 fennel bulbs, sliced
- 1 tablespoon coconut flour
- 2 tablespoons olive oil
- A pinch of sea salt
- 2 cups coconut milk
- A pinch of nutmeg, ground

Directions:

1. Set your instant pot on Sauté mode, add ghee, heat it up, add fennel, brown for a couple of minutes and mix with salt, pepper, nutmeg, coconut milk and flour.
2. Stir gently, cover and cook on Low for 6 minutes.
3. Divide among plates and serve.
4. Enjoy!

Nutrition Value: calories 152, fat 2, fiber 3, carbs 5, protein 6

86. Simple And Fast Side Dish

Preparation time: 10 minutes
Cooking time: 10 minutes
Servings: 4

Ingredients:

- 5 bok choy bunches
- 1 tablespoon olive oil
- 2 garlic cloves, minced
- 5 cups water
- 1 teaspoon ginger, grated
- A pinch of sea salt

Directions:

1. Put bok choy in your instant pot, add the water, cover, cook on High for 7 minutes, drain and transfer to a bowl.
2. Clean the pot, set it on Sauté mode, add the oil and heat it up.
3. Return bok choy to the pot, add a pinch of salt, garlic and ginger, stir and sauté for 3 minutes.
4. Divide among plates and serve as a side dish.
5. Enjoy!

Nutrition Value: calories 75, fat 1, fiber 1, carbs 3, protein 5

87. Cauliflower Soup

Preparation Time: 10 minutes
Servings 4)

Nutrition Value: 167 Calories; 13.7g Fat; 5.7g Total Carbs; 3.8g Protein; 3.1g Sugars

Ingredients

- 4 tablespoons butter, softened
- 1/2 cup leeks, thinly sliced
- 2 cloves garlic, minced
- 3/4 pound cauliflower, broken into florets
- 1 cup water
- 2 cups chicken stock

- 1 cup full-fat milk
- Kosher salt, to taste
- 1/3 teaspoon ground black pepper

Directions

1. Press the "Sauté" button to heat up your Instant Pot. Then, melt the butter; sauté the leeks until softened.
2. Then, sauté the garlic until fragrant, about 30 seconds. Add the remaining ingredients and gently stir to combine.
3. Secure the lid. Choose "Manual" mode and Low pressure; cook for 5 minutes. Once cooking is complete, use a quick pressure release; carefully remove the lid.
4. Ladle into individual bowls and serve warm. Bon appétit!

88. Cauliflower Mash

Preparation Time: 15 minutes
Servings 4)

Nutrition Value: 89 Calories; 4.7g Fat; 6.5g Total Carbs; 3.6g Protein; 2.6g Sugars

Ingredients

- 1/2 pound cauliflower, cut into florets
- 1/2 pound kohlrabi, peeled and diced
- 1 cup water
- 3/4 cup sour cream
- 1 garlic clove, minced
- Sea salt, to taste
- 1/3 teaspoon ground black pepper
- 1/2 teaspoon cayenne pepper

Directions

1. Add 1 cup of water and a steamer basket to the bottom of your Instant Pot.
2. Then, arrange cauliflower and kohlrabi in the steamer basket.
3. Secure the lid. Choose "Manual" mode and Low pressure; cook for 3 minutes. Once cooking is complete, use a quick pressure release; carefully remove the lid.
4. Now, puree the cauliflower and kohlrabi with a potato masher. Add the remaining ingredients and stir well. Bon appétit!

89. Stuffed Peppers With Cheese

Preparation Time: 20 minutes
Servings 3)

Nutrition Value: 488 Calories; 38.2g Fat; 5.1g Total Carbs; 29.1g Protein; 2.9g Sugars

Ingredients

- 2 tablespoons olive oil
- 1 yellow onion, chopped
- 2 garlic cloves, smashed
- 2 tablespoons coriander, chopped
- 1/3 pound ground beef
- 1/2 pound ground pork
- Sea salt, to taste
- 1/4 teaspoon black peppercorns, freshly crushed
- 3 bell peppers, deveined, tops removed
- 2 ripe tomatoes, puréed
- 1 teaspoon dried basil
- 1/2 teaspoon dried oregano
- 1/2 teaspoon dried rosemary
- 1/2 cup Romano cheese, freshly grated

Directions

1. Press the "Sauté" button to heat up the Instant Pot; heat the oil.
2. Once hot, sweat the onions for 2 minutes. Add garlic and coriander cook an additional 30 seconds. Then, stir in ground meat and cook until no longer pink. Season with salt and black peppercorns.
3. Stuff the peppers with this meat mixture; do not pack the peppers too tightly.
4. In a mixing bowl, thoroughly combine pureed tomatoes, basil, oregano, and rosemary. Pour this mixture over the peppers.
5. Wipe down the Instant Pot with a damp cloth; add 1 ½ cups of water and a metal trivet to the Instant Pot.
6. Place the peppers on the trivet and secure the lid. Choose "Poultry" mode and High pressure; cook for 15 minutes. Once cooking is complete, use a quick pressure

release; carefully remove the lid.
7. Top with grated Romano cheese, cover, and let it sit in the residual heat. Serve warm and enjoy!

90. Tomato Soup

Preparation Time: 10 minutes
Servings 2)

Nutrition Value: 339 Calories; 29.5g Fat; 6.1g Total Carbs; 10.8g Protein; 4.2g Sugars

Ingredients

- 1 tablespoon avocado oil
- 2 cloves garlic, minced
- 2 ripe tomatoes, puréed
- 1/2 cup double cream
- 1/3 cup water
- 1/2 teaspoon basil
- 1 teaspoon dried sage
- Salt, to taste
- 1/4 teaspoon ground black pepper
- 1/2 teaspoon cayenne pepper
- 1/2 cup Colby cheese, shredded

Directions

1. Press the "Sauté" button to heat up the Instant Pot; heat the oil. Once hot, cook the garlic until aromatic.
2. Add the remaining ingredients and stir to combine.
3. Secure the lid. Choose "Manual" mode and Low pressure; cook for 3 minutes. Once cooking is complete, use a quick pressure release; carefully remove the lid.
4. Ladle into individual bowls and serve immediately. Bon appétit!

91. Yummy Bok Choy with Tofu

Preparation Time: 8 minutes
Servings 4)

Nutrition Value: 133 Calories; 8.6g Fat; 5.1g Total Carbs; 11.1g Protein; 2g Sugars

Ingredients

- 1 tablespoon olive oil
- 12 ounces extra-firm tofu, pressed and cubed
- 1 ½ teaspoons ginger-garlic paste
- 1 ½ pounds Bok choy
- 1 cup water
- 2 tablespoons coconut aminos
- 1/4 cup rice wine vinegar
- 1 teaspoon smoked paprika
- Himalayan pink salt, to taste
- 1/4 teaspoon ground black pepper

Directions

1. Press the "Sauté" button to heat up the Instant Pot; heat the oil. Once hot, cook the tofu until delicately browned.
2. Add the ginger-garlic paste and Bok choy; sauté 1 minute more. Add the remaining ingredients.
3. Secure the lid. Choose "Manual" mode and Low pressure; cook for 4 minutes. Once cooking is complete, use a quick pressure release; carefully remove the lid.
4. Serve immediately. Bon appétit!

92. Braised Garlic Treat

Preparation Time: 6 minutes
Servings 3)

Nutrition Value: 91 Calories; 5.3g Fat; 6.4g Total Carbs; 3.6g Protein; 1.8g Sugars

Ingredients

- 1 tablespoon extra-virgin olive oil
- 2 garlic cloves, minced
- 2 large-sized Belgian endive, halved lengthwise
- 1/2 cup apple cider vinegar
- 1/2 cup broth, preferably homemade
- Sea salt and freshly ground black pepper, to taste
- 1 teaspoon cayenne pepper

Directions

1. Press the "Sauté" button to heat up the Instant Pot; heat the oil. Once hot, cook the garlic for 30 seconds or until aromatic and browned.
2. Add Belgian endive, vinegar, broth, salt, black pepper, and cayenne pepper.

3. Secure the lid. Choose "Manual" mode and Low pressure; cook for 2 minutes or until tender when pierced with the tip of a knife.
   4. Once cooking is complete, use a quick pressure release; carefully remove the lid. Bon appétit!

93. Italian Soup with Pancetta and Cabbage

Preparation Time: 10 minutes
Servings 4)

Nutrition Value: 196 Calories; 17.8g Fat; 6.3g Total Carbs; 2.2g Protein; 2.5g Sugars

Ingredients

- 1 tablespoon olive oil
- 2 ounces pancetta, finely diced
- 1/2 cup shallots, chopped
- 1 red bell pepper, deveined and sliced
- 1 green bell pepper, deveined and sliced
- 1 carrot, sliced
- 2 celery stalks with leaves, diced
- 2 cloves garlic
- 2 ripe Roma tomatoes, puréed
- 3/4 pound green cabbage, cut into wedges
- 4 cups water
- 2 bouillon cubes
- 1 tablespoon Italian seasoning blend
- 1 cup baby spinach

Directions
1. Press the "Sauté" button to heat up your Instant Pot; heat the olive oil. Once hot, cook pancetta until crisp, about 3 minutes; reserve.
2. Now, cook the shallots, peppers, carrot, celery, and garlic until tender.
3. Add tomatoes, cabbage, water, bouillon cubes, Italian seasoning blend; stir to combine.
4. Secure the lid. Choose "Manual" mode and Low pressure; cook for 3 minutes. Once cooking is complete, use a quick pressure release; carefully remove the lid.
5. Lastly, add baby spinach, cover, and let it sit in the residual heat until it wilts. Ladle into four soup bowls and top with the reserved pancetta. Enjoy!

94. Garlicky and Buttery Fennel

Preparation Time: 6 minutes
Servings 6)

Nutrition Value: 111 Calories; 7.8g Fat; 5.7g Total Carbs; 2.1g Protein; 2.7g Sugars

Ingredients

- 1/2 stick butter
- 2 garlic cloves, sliced
- 1/2 teaspoon sea salt
- 1 ½ pounds fennel bulbs, cut into wedges
- 1/4 teaspoon ground black pepper, or more to taste
- 1/2 teaspoon cayenne pepper
- 1/4 teaspoon dried dill weed
- 1/3 cup dry white wine
- 2/3 cup chicken stock

Directions
1. Press the "Sauté" button to heat up your Instant Pot; now, melt the butter. Cook garlic for 30 seconds, stirring periodically.
2. Add the remaining ingredients.
3. Secure the lid. Choose "Manual" mode and Low pressure; cook for 3 minutes. Once cooking is complete, use a quick pressure release; carefully remove the lid. Bon appétit!

95. Cheesy Artichokes On The Go

Preparation Time: 10 minutes
Servings 3)

Nutrition Value: 173 Calories; 12.5g Fat; 6g Total Carbs; 8.1g Protein; 0.9g Sugars

Ingredients

- 3 medium-sized artichokes, cleaned and trimmed
- 3 cloves garlic, smashed

- 3 tablespoons butter, melted
- Sea salt, to taste
- 1/2 teaspoon cayenne pepper
- 1/4 teaspoon ground black pepper, or more to taste
- 1 lemon, freshly squeezed
- 1 cup Monterey-Jack cheese, shredded
- 1 tablespoon fresh parsley, roughly chopped

Directions

1. Start by adding 1 cup of water and a steamer basket to the Instant Pot. Place the artichokes in the steamer basket; add garlic and butter.
2. Secure the lid. Choose "Manual" mode and High pressure; cook for 8 minutes. Once cooking is complete, use a quick pressure release; carefully remove the lid.
3. Season your artichokes with salt, cayenne pepper, and black pepper. Now, drizzle them with lemon juice.
4. Top with cheese and parsley and serve immediately. Bon appétit!

96. Asian Bok Choy

Preparation Time: 10 minutes
Servings 4)

Nutrition Value: 83 Calories; 6.1g Fat; 5.7g Total Carbs; 3.2g Protein; 2.4g Sugars

Ingredients

- 2 tablespoons butter, melted
- 2 cloves garlic, minced
- 1 (1/2-inch) slice fresh ginger root, grated
- 1 ½ pounds Bok choy, trimmed
- 1 cup vegetable stock
- Celery salt and ground black pepper to taste
- 1 teaspoon Five-spice powder
- 2 tablespoons soy sauce

Directions

1. Press the "Sauté" button to heat up the Instant Pot. Now, warm the butter and sauté the garlic until tender and fragrant.
2. Now, add grated ginger and cook for a further 40 seconds.
3. Add Bok choy, stock, salt, black pepper, and Five-spice powder.
4. Secure the lid. Choose "Manual" mode and High pressure; cook for 6 minutes. Once cooking is complete, use a quick pressure release; carefully remove the lid.
5. Drizzle soy sauce over your Bok choy and serve immediately. Bon appétit!

97. Cabbage with Bacon

Preparation Time: 10 minutes
Servings 4)

Nutrition Value: 166 Calories; 13g Fat; 5.8g Total Carbs; 6.8g Protein; 2.7g Sugars

Ingredients

- 2 teaspoons olive oil
- 4 slices bacon, chopped
- 1 head green cabbage, cored and cut into wedges
- 1 cups vegetable stock
- Sea salt, to taste
- 1/2 teaspoon whole black peppercorns
- 1 teaspoon cayenne pepper
- 1 bay leaf

Directions

1. Press the "Sauté" button to heat up the Instant Pot. Then, heat olive oil and cook the bacon until it is nice and delicately browned.
2. Then, add the remaining ingredients; gently stir to combine.
3. Secure the lid. Choose "Manual" mode and High pressure; cook for 3 minutes. Once cooking is complete, use a quick pressure release; carefully remove the lid.
4. Serve warm and enjoy!

98. Superpower Broccoli Salad Bowl

Preparation Time: 10 minutes
Servings 4)

Nutrition Value: 95 Calories; 3.1g Fat; 5.6g Total Carbs; 9.9g Protein; 2.8g Sugars

Sides

Ingredients

- 1 pound broccoli, broken into florets
- 2 tablespoons balsamic vinegar
- 2 garlic cloves, minced
- 1 teaspoon mustard seeds
- 1 teaspoon cumin seeds
- Salt and pepper, to taste
- 1 cup Cottage cheese, crumbled

Directions

1. Place 1 cup of water and a steamer basket in your Instant Pot.
2. Place the broccoli in the steamer basket.
3. Secure the lid. Choose "Manual" mode and High pressure; cook for 5 minutes. Once cooking is complete, use a quick pressure release; carefully remove the lid.
4. Then, toss your broccoli with the other ingredients. Serve and enjoy!

99. Spinach with Cheese

Preparation Time: 10 minutes
Servings 4)

Nutrition Value: 283 Calories; 23.9g Fat; 6.4g Total Carbs; 10.7g Protein; 2.2g Sugars

Ingredients

- 2 tablespoons butter, melted
- 1/2 cup scallions, chopped
- 2 cloves garlic, smashed
- 1 ½ pounds fresh spinach
- 1 cup vegetable broth, preferably homemade
- 1 cup cream cheese, cubed
- Seasoned salt and ground black pepper, to taste
- 1/2 teaspoon dried dill weed

Directions

1. Press the "Sauté" button to heat up the Instant Pot. Then, melt the butter; cook the scallions and garlic until tender and aromatic.
2. Add the remaining ingredients and stir to combine well.
3. Secure the lid. Choose "Manual" mode and High pressure; cook for 2 minutes. Once cooking is complete, use a quick pressure release; carefully remove the lid.
4. Ladle into individual bowls and serve warm. Bon appétit!

100. Sausage with Turnip Greens

Preparation Time: 10 minutes
Servings 4)

Nutrition Value: 149 Calories; 7.2g Fat; 6.1g Total Carbs; 14.2g Protein; 2.2g Sugars

Ingredients

- 2 teaspoons sesame oil
- 2 pork sausages, casing removed sliced
- 2 garlic cloves, minced
- 1 medium-sized leek, chopped
- 1 pound turnip greens
- 1 cup turkey bone stock
- Sea salt, to taste
- 1/4 teaspoon ground black pepper, or more to taste
- 1 bay leaf
- 1 tablespoon black sesame seeds

Directions

1. Press the "Sauté" button to heat up the Instant Pot. Then, heat the sesame oil; cook the sausage until nice and delicately browned; set aside.
2. Add the garlic and leeks; continue to cook in pan drippings for a minute or two.
3. Add the greens, stock, salt, black pepper, and bay leaf.
4. Secure the lid. Choose "Manual" mode and Low pressure; cook for 3 minutes. Once cooking is complete, use a quick pressure release; carefully remove the lid.
5. Serve garnished with black sesame seeds and enjoy!

101. Easy Cheesy Asparagus

Preparation Time: 10 minutes
Servings 4)

Nutrition Value: 164 Calories; 12.2g Fat; 5.9g

Total Carbs; 7.8g Protein; 3.2g Sugars

Ingredients

- 1 ½ pounds fresh asparagus
- 2 tablespoons olive oil
- 4 garlic cloves, minced
- Sea salt, to taste
- 1/4 teaspoon ground black pepper
- 1/2 cup Colby cheese, shredded

Directions

1. Add 1 cup of water and a steamer basket to your Instant Pot.
2. Now, place the asparagus on the steamer basket; drizzle your asparagus with olive oil. Scatter garlic over the top of the asparagus.
3. Season with salt and black pepper.
4. Secure the lid. Choose "Manual" mode and High pressure; cook for 1 minute. Once cooking is complete, use a quick pressure release; carefully remove the lid.
5. Transfer the prepared asparagus to a nice serving platter and scatter shredded cheese over the top. Enjoy!

102. Zucchini with Tomato and Rosemary

Preparation Time: 10 minutes
Servings 4)

Nutrition Value: 85 Calories; 7.1g Fat; 4.7g Total Carbs; 1.6g Protein; 3.3g Sugars

Ingredients

- 2 tablespoons olive oil
- 2 garlic cloves, chopped
- 1 pound zucchini, sliced
- 1/2 cup tomato purée
- 1/2 cup water
- 1 teaspoon dried thyme
- 1/2 teaspoon dried oregano
- 1/2 teaspoon dried rosemary

Directions

1. Press the "Sauté" button to heat up the Instant Pot. Then, heat the olive oil; sauté the garlic until aromatic.
2. Add the remaining ingredients.
3. Secure the lid. Choose "Manual" mode and Low pressure; cook for 3 minutes. Once cooking is complete, use a quick pressure release; carefully remove the lid. Bon appétit!

103. Chanterelles with Cheese

Preparation Time: 10 minutes
Servings 4)

Nutrition Value: 218 Calories; 15.1g Fat; 5.5g Total Carbs; 9.9g Protein; 2.3g Sugars

Ingredients

- 1 tablespoon olive oil
- 2 cloves garlic, minced
- 1 (1-inch) ginger root, grated
- 1/2 teaspoon dried dill weed
- 1 teaspoon dried basil
- 1/2 teaspoon dried thyme
- 16 ounces Chanterelle mushrooms, brushed clean and sliced
- 1/2 cup water
- 1/2 cup tomato purée
- 2 tablespoons dry white wine
- 1/3 teaspoon freshly ground black pepper
- Kosher salt, to taste
- 1 cup Cheddar cheese

Directions

1. Press the "Sauté" button to heat up the Instant Pot. Then, heat the olive oil; sauté the garlic and grated ginger for 1 minute or until aromatic.
2. Add dried dill, basil, thyme, Chanterelles, water, tomato purée, dry white wine, black pepper, and salt.
3. Secure the lid. Choose "Manual" mode and Low pressure; cook for 5 minutes. Once cooking is complete, use a quick pressure release; carefully remove the lid.
4. Top with shredded cheese and serve immediately. Bon appétit!

104. Mediterranean Mexican Delight

Preparation Time: 8 minutes
Servings 4)

Nutrition Value: 109 Calories; 7.3g Fat; 6.8g Total Carbs; 3.5g Protein; 3.7g Sugars

Ingredients

- 1 pound nopales, cleaned and diced
- 1 white onion, chopped
- 2 garlic cloves, smashed
- 2 tablespoons fresh parsley, chopped
- 2 dried chiles negros
- 1 cup ripe tomatoes, chopped
- 1/2 teaspoon mustard seeds
- 1/2 teaspoon Mexican oregano
- 2 tablespoons olive oil
- Sea salt and ground black pepper, to taste
- 1 cup chicken broth
- 1/2 cup sour cream

Directions

1. Place all ingredients, except for sour cream, in your Instant Pot.
2. Secure the lid. Choose "Manual" mode and High pressure; cook for 5 minutes. Once cooking is complete, use a quick pressure release; carefully remove the lid.
3. Spoon into serving bowls and serve dolloped with sour cream. Bon appétit!

105. Swiss Chard with Ham Hock

Preparation Time: 45 minutes
Servings 4)

Nutrition Value: 268 Calories; 12.3g Fat; 6.1g Total Carbs; 30.9g Protein; 2.2g Sugars

Ingredients

- 2 tablespoons olive oil
- 1 cup leeks, chopped
- 2 garlic cloves, minced
- Sea salt and ground black pepper, to taste
- 1/2 teaspoon cayenne pepper
- 3 cups beef bone broth
- 1 (1-pound) ham hock
- 1 pound Swiss chard, torn into pieces

Directions

1. Press the "Sauté" button to heat up your Instant Pot; now, heat the olive oil. Cook the leeks for about 2 minutes or until softened.
2. Stir in the garlic and cook an additional 40 seconds or until aromatic.
3. Add the salt, black pepper, cayenne pepper, broth, and ham hock.
4. Secure the lid. Choose "Meat/Stew" mode and High pressure; cook for 35 minutes. Once cooking is complete, use a natural pressure release; carefully remove the lid.
5. Then, add Swiss chard and choose "Manual" mode; cook for 5 minutes. Once cooking is complete, use a quick pressure release; carefully remove the lid. Bon appétit!

106. Mediterranean Beans with Canadian Bacon

Preparation Time: 10 minutes
Servings 6)

Nutrition Value: 133 Calories; 2.9g Fat; 6.6g Total Carbs; 19.1g Protein; 2.6g Sugars

Ingredients

- 2 (6-ounce) packages Canadian bacon, chopped
- 1/2 cup scallions, chopped
- 2 cloves garlic, minced
- 1 pound green beans, trimmed
- Kosher salt and ground black pepper, to taste
- 1/2 teaspoon paprika
- 1/2 teaspoon dried dill weed
- 1/2 teaspoon red pepper flakes
- 2 tablespoons apple cider vinegar
- 1 cup water

Directions

1. Press the "Sauté" button to heat up your Instant Pot. Once hot, cook Canadian bacon until crisp, about 4 minutes; reserve.
2. Add the scallions and garlic. Cook an

additional 1 minute or until aromatic.
3. Add the other ingredients; stir to combine
4. Secure the lid. Choose "Manual" mode and Low pressure; cook for 3 minutes. Once cooking is complete, use a quick pressure release; carefully remove the lid.
5. Serve warm, garnished with the reserved bacon. Bon appétit!

107. French Cauliflower Soup

Preparation Time: 10 minutes
Servings 4)

Nutrition Value: 221 Calories; 15.7g Fat; 5.9g Total Carbs; 11.4g Protein; 2.9g Sugars

Ingredients

- 2 tablespoons ghee, melted
- 1 medium-sized shallot, chopped
- 2 garlic cloves, minced
- 1 cup cauliflower, chopped into small florets
- 1 celery stalk, chopped
- 1 cup half-and-half
- 2 ½ cups vegetable broth
- A pinch of grated nutmeg
- 1 dried chile negro
- 1/4 teaspoon ground black pepper
- 1/3 teaspoon sea salt
- 4 ounces blue cheese, crumbled

Directions

1. Press the "Sauté" button to heat up your Instant Pot. Once hot, melt the ghee. Sauté the shallot and garlic until aromatic or approximately 2 minutes.
2. Now, add the cauliflower, celery stalk, half-and-half, vegetable broth, nutmeg, chile, pepper, and salt.
3. Secure the lid. Choose "Manual" mode and Low pressure; cook for 3 minutes. Once cooking is complete, use a quick pressure release; carefully remove the lid.
4. Ladle into soup bowls, top with blue cheese, and serve warm. Bon appétit!

108. Family Autumn Pottage

Preparation Time: 15 minutes
Servings 4)

Nutrition Value: 151 Calories; 11.5g Fat; 5.8g Total Carbs; 4.2g Protein; 2.1g Sugars

Ingredients

- 2 tablespoons olive oil
- 1 white onion, chopped
- 2 cloves garlic
- 1 red bell pepper, seeded and sliced
- 1 green bell pepper, seeded and sliced
- 2 ripe tomatoes, puréed
- 1/2 teaspoon turmeric
- 1 teaspoon paprika
- 1/2 teaspoon dried oregano
- Kosher salt and ground black pepper, to taste
- 1 cup water
- 4 large eggs, lightly whisked

Directions

1. Press the "Sauté" button to heat up your Instant Pot. Heat the oil and sauté the onion and garlic until aromatic, about 2 minutes.
2. Add the peppers, tomatoes, turmeric, paprika, oregano, salt, black pepper, and water.
3. Secure the lid. Choose "Manual" mode and High pressure; cook for 3 minutes. Once cooking is complete, use a quick pressure release; carefully remove the lid.
4. Fold in the eggs and stir to combine. Cover with the lid and let it sit in the residual heat for 5 minutes. Serve warm.

109. Easy Medley with Sausage

Preparation Time: 15 minutes
Servings 4)

Nutrition Value: 248 Calories; 20.5g Fat;5.6g Total Carbs; 9.1g Protein; 2.9g Sugars

Ingredients

- 2 tablespoons olive oil
- 2 garlic cloves, minced
- 1/2 cup scallions

- 2 pork sausages, casing removed, sliced
- 2 cups cauliflower, chopped into small florets
- 1/2 pound button mushrooms, sliced
- 2 bell peppers, chopped
- 1 red chili pepper, chopped
- 2 cups turnip greens
- Sea salt and freshly ground black pepper, to taste
- 1 teaspoon cayenne pepper
- 2 bay leaves
- 1 cup water

Directions
1. Press the "Sauté" button to heat up your Instant Pot. Heat the oil and sauté the garlic and scallions until aromatic, about 2 minutes.
2. Add sausage and cook an additional 3 minutes or until it is no longer pink. Now, stir in the remaining ingredients.
3. Secure the lid. Choose "Manual" mode and High pressure; cook for 5 minutes. Once cooking is complete, use a quick pressure release; carefully remove the lid. Bon appétit!

110. Sausage Gumbo

Preparation Time: 10 minutes
Servings 6)

Nutrition Value: 303 Calories; 17.8g Fat; 6.2g Total Carbs; 27g Protein; 2.4g Sugars

Ingredients
- 2 tablespoons olive oil
- 2 pounds Gyulai sausage links, sliced
- 1/2 cup leeks, chopped
- 3 cloves garlic, minced
- 1 celery, diced
- 1/2 cup tomato purée
- 1 ½ cups water
- 1 ½ cups beef bone broth
- 1 tablespoon coconut aminos
- Kosher salt, to taste
- 1/2 teaspoon black peppercorns, crushed

- 1/2 teaspoon caraway seeds
- 1 bay leaf
- 2 cups frozen okra, chopped

Directions
1. Press the "Sauté" button to heat up your Instant Pot. Heat the oil and cook the sausage until no longer pink; reserve.
2. Then, sauté the leeks until translucent, about 2 minutes. Now, add the garlic and cook an additional 30 seconds.
3. Add the celery, tomato, water, broth, coconut aminos, salt, pepper, caraway seeds, bay leaf, and okra. Stir to combine.
4. Secure the lid. Choose "Manual" mode and Low pressure; cook for 3 minutes. Once cooking is complete, use a quick pressure release; carefully remove the lid.
5. Ladle into individual bowls and serve warm. Bon appétit!

111. Fried Sauerkraut with Bacon

Preparation Time: 15 minutes
Servings 6)

Nutrition Value: 184 Calories; 13.5g Fat; 6.1g Total Carbs; 7.1g Protein; 3g Sugars

Ingredients
- 6 ounces meaty bacon, roughly chopped
- 1 yellow onion, chopped
- 2 garlic cloves, minced
- 1/4 cup dry white wine
- 1 carrot, grated
- 1 bell pepper, chopped
- 2 anchos, minced
- 3 cups sauerkraut, rinsed and drained
- 1 teaspoon cayenne pepper
- 1 bay leaf
- 1 teaspoon mixed peppercorns
- 4 cups beef bone broth

Directions
1. Press the "Sauté" button to heat up your Instant Pot. Once hot, cook the bacon until crisp; reserve.
2. Now, cook the onion and garlic in pan

drippings. Add a splash of wine to deglaze the bottom of the Instant Pot.
3. Then, stir in the remaining ingredients.
4. Secure the lid. Choose "Manual" mode and High pressure; cook for 10 minutes. Once cooking is complete, use a natural pressure release; carefully remove the lid.
5. Divide your sauerkraut among serving bowls and top with the reserved bacon. Bon appétit!

112. Delicious Okra with Bacon

Preparation Time: 10 minutes
Servings 4)

Nutrition Value: 202 Calories; 17.1g Fat; 6.4g Total Carbs; 4.9g Protein; 3.2g Sugars

Ingredients

- 2 tablespoons olive oil
- 1 red onion, chopped
- 1/2 pound okra
- 1 teaspoon ginger-garlic paste
- 4 slices pancetta, chopped
- 1 teaspoon celery seeds
- 1/2 teaspoon caraway seeds
- 1/2 teaspoon cayenne pepper
- 1/2 teaspoon turmeric powder
- 1 cup water
- 1 cup tomato purée

Directions

1. Press the "Sauté" button to heat up your Instant Pot. Once hot, heat the olive oil; sauté the onion until softened.
2. Add okra, ginger-garlic paste, and pancetta; sauté for 1 minute more or until fragrant. Add the remaining ingredients and stir to combine.
3. Secure the lid. Choose "Manual" mode and High pressure; cook for 3 minutes. Once cooking is complete, use a natural pressure release; carefully remove the lid. Bon appétit!

SEAFOOD

113. Thai Cauliflower Rice

Preparation Time: 25 Minutes
Servings: 4

Ingredients:

- 2 cups cauliflower florets; finely chopped
- 1 medium-sized onion; finely chopped.
- 1 cup Thai basil; finely chopped
- 1 cup bean sprouts
- 4 tablespoon fish sauce
- 2 cups seafood mix; frozen
- 3 tablespoon coconut oil
- 1 jalapeno pepper; finely chopped.
- 3 garlic cloves; crushed
- 1/2 cup chicken stock
- 2 teaspoon fresh ginger; grated
- 2 teaspoon stevia powder
- 1 teaspoon sea salt

Directions:

1. Plug in the instant pot and grease the inner pot with coconut oil. Press the *Sauté* button and add jalapeno pepper and garlic. Briefly cook for 2-3 minutes, stirring constantly.
2. Now add seafood and continue to cook for 5 minutes. Sprinkle with salt, ginger, and stevia. Add bean sprouts, cauliflower, and onions. Pour in the stock and seal the lid.
3. Set the steam release handle to the *Sealing* position and press the *Manual* button. Set the timer for 5 minutes on high pressure
4. When done, release the pressure naturally and open the lid. Stir in chopped Thai basil and drizzle with fish sauce. Stir well and serve immediately.

Nutrition Value: Calories: 188; Total Fats: 11.2g; Net Carbs: 8.1g; Protein: 12.6g; Fiber: 2.1g

114. Steamed Salmon Recipe

Preparation Time: 15 Minutes
Servings: 4

Ingredients:

- 1-pound salmon fillets; sliced into 4 pieces
- 2 lemons; juiced
- 2 cups fish stock
- 1/4 cup Parmesan cheese; freshly grated
- 4 tablespoon butter
- 1 teaspoon white pepper; freshly ground.
- 1 teaspoon smoked salt

Directions:

1. Plug in the instant pot and pour in the stock. Drizzle with lemon juice and set the steam basket.
2. Rinse the salmon fillets and sprinkle with salt and pepper. Place in the basket and seal the lid.
3. Set the steam release handle to the *Sealing* position and press the *Manual* button
4. Set the timer for 5 minutes.
5. When done, perform a quick release and open the lid. Remove the salmon fillets and set asideRemove the stock from the pot.
6. Press the *Sauté* button and melt the butter. Add salmon steaks and cook for 2-3 minutes on each side
7. Sprinkle with grated parmesan and serve immediately

Nutrition Value: Calories: 257; Total Fats: 18.9g; Net Carbs: 0.1g; Protein: 22.7g; Fiber: 0g

115. Mediterranean Seafood Stew

Preparation Time: 20 Minutes
Servings: 5

Ingredients:

- 2 -pounds sea bass fillets; cut into chunks
- 7-ounce shrimps; peeled and deveined

- 2 small tomatoes; roughly chopped.
- 3 tablespoon soy sauce
- 1 large onion; finely chopped
- 5 cups fish stock
- 4 tablespoon olive oil; extra-virgin
- 3 celery stalks; finely chopped
- 2 bay leaves
- 1 teaspoon black pepper; freshly ground.
- 1 tablespoon Creole seasoning
- 2 teaspoon sea salt

Directions:
1. Clean and rinse fish fillets. Pat dry with some kitchen paper and set aside.
2. In a small bowl, combine Creole seasoning with salt and pepper. Rub the fish with this mixture making sure to coat on all sides.
3. Plug in the instant pot and press the *Sauté* button. Grease the inner pot with olive oil and heat up. Add the prepared fish and cook for 4-5 minutes, stirring occasionally.
4. When the fish has nicely browned, gently remove from the pot and set aside
5. Grease the inner pot with some more oil and add onions and celery stalk. Season with some salt and stir well. Continue to cook for 2-3 minutes
6. Now press the *Cancel'* button and add the fish, shrimps, and tomatoes. Drizzle with soy sauce and pour in the stock.
7. Seal the lid and set the steam release handle to the *Sealing* position. Press the *Manual* button and set the timer for 5 minutes on high pressure
8. When done; release the pressure naturally and open the lid. Optionally, stir in some fresh parsley and serve.

Nutrition Value: Calories: 433; Total Fats: 18.5g; Net Carbs: 4.6g; Protein: 58.5g; Fiber: 1.3g

116. Mediterranean Green Pesto Tuna Steak

Preparation Time: 40 Minutes
Servings: 4

Ingredients:
- 2 tuna steaks; about 1-inch thick
- 3 tablespoon mozzarella; shredded
- 1 cup basil leaves; finely chopped.
- 1 cup cauliflower; finely chopped
- 1/4 cup olive oil
- 2 garlic cloves
- 3 tablespoon butter
- 1 teaspoon sea salt

Directions:
1. Plug in the instant pot and set the steam basket. Pour in one cup of water and add tuna steaks in the basket
2. Season with salt and seal the lid. Set the steam release handle to the *Sealing* position and press the *Manual* button. Cook for 7 minutes on high pressure
3. When done, perform a quick release and open the lid. Using oven mitts, gently remove the steam basket and set aside
4. Remove the water from the pot and add butter. Press the *Sauté* button and heat up
5. Briefly cook each tuna steak for 3-4 minutes on each side
6. Remove from the pot and set aside
7. Now; prepare the pesto. Combine the remaining ingredients in a food processor and process until completely smooth. Coat each tuna steak with pesto and place on a small baking sheet lined with some parchment paper
8. Bake for 15 minutes at 400 degrees or until lightly brown and crispy. Serve and enjoy.

Nutrition Value: Calories: 484; Total Fats: 32.9g; Net Carbs: 2g; Protein: 44.3g; Fiber: 0.8g

117. Spicy and Sweet Trout

Preparation Time: 15 Minutes
Servings: 2

Ingredients:
- 1-pound trout fillet; chopped
- 2 chili peppers; finely chopped.
- 3 tablespoon butter

- 2 tablespoon swerve
- 1/4 cup fish stock
- 1 tablespoon fish sauce
- 3 garlic cloves; crushed
- 1 tablespoon ginger; freshly grated
- 1/2 teaspoon cumin powder
- 1 teaspoon salt
- 1 teaspoon black pepper; freshly ground.

Directions:

1. Generously rub fillets with salt and pepper. Place on a large plate and cover with aluminum foil, Set aside
2. In a small bowl, whisk together fish stock, swerve, and fish sauce. Add grated ginger and cumin powder and stir well again
3. Plug in the instant pot and set the steam basket. Place the fish fillets in the basket and generously brush with the previously prepared mixture on all sides
4. Pour in one cup of water and seal the lid. Set the steam release handle to the *Sealing* position and press the *Manual* button. Set the timer for 5 minutes on high heat.
5. When done; perform a quick release and carefully open the lid. Remove the fish and set aside
6. Melt the butter over medium heat and drizzle over fish. Serve and enjoy

Nutrition Value: Calories: 600; Total Fats: 36.8g; Net Carbs: 2g; Protein: 62g; Fiber: 0.2g

118. King Prawn Stew

Preparation Time: 45 Minutes
Servings: 6

Ingredients:

- 2 -pounds king prawns; whole
- 2 large celery stalks; chopped.
- 1 cup olive oil
- 4 tablespoon balsamic vinegar
- 7-ounce cauliflower; chopped into florets
- 5 cups fish stock
- 1 avocado; chopped into bite-sized pieces
- 2 small tomatoes; roughly chopped
- 1 small onion; finely chopped.
- 1/2 teaspoon dried thyme
- 1 teaspoon chili flakes
- 1 teaspoon sea salt
- 1 teaspoon dried marjoram

Directions:

1. Place prawns in a large colander and rinse well, Set aside.
2. In a medium-sized bowl, combine together oil, balsamic vinegar, salt, marjoram, thyme, and chili flakes. Stir well and add prawns. If necessary, add some fish stock to the bowl and submerge prawns in this mixture. Refrigerate for 20 minutes
3. Meanwhile, prepare the vegetables and plug in the Instant pot. Press the *Sauté* button and add onions and celery stalks. Drizzle with some oil and cook for 4-5 minutes. Now add avocado, cauliflower, and tomatoes. Stir well and continue to cook for another 5 minutes.
4. Remove the prawns from the refrigerator and transfer to the pot. Press the *Cancel'* button and pour in the remaining stock. Stir well and seal the lid.
5. Set the steam release handle and press the *Manual* button. Set the timer for 15 minutes
6. When you hear the end signal, perform a quick pressure release and carefully open the lid.
7. Transfer the stew to serving bowls and optionally sprinkle with some pepper. Serve and enjoy.

Nutrition Value: Calories: 593; Total Fats: 44.4g; Net Carbs: 5.9g; Protein: 40.7g; Fiber: 4g

119. Squid Rings with Spinach and Potato

Preparation Time: 35 Minutes
Servings: 3

Ingredients:

- 1-pound squid rings; frozen
- 2 cups cauliflower; roughly chopped

- 1-pound fresh spinach; torn
- 2 tablespoon lemon juice
- 4 tablespoon extra virgin olive oil
- 1 teaspoon dried rosemary; crushed
- 2 thyme sprigs; fresh
- 1 teaspoon garlic paste
- 1 teaspoon sea salt

Directions:
1. Place squid rings in a deep bowl and pour in enough warm water to cover. Let it sit for a while. Transfer to a large colander and drain, Set aside.
2. Plug in the instant pot and grease the inner pot with two tablespoons of olive oil. Press the *Sauté* button and add garlic paste and rosemary. Stir-fry for one minute and then add the spinach. Season with salt and cook for 3-4 minutes or until wilted. Remove the spinach from the pot and set aside.
3. Add the remaining oil to the pot and heat up on the *Sauté* mode. Add chopped cauliflower making an even layer. Top with squid rings and drizzle with lemon juice and optionally some more olive oil to taste Sprinkle with salt, add thyme sprigs, and pour in one cup of water (or fish stock)
4. Seal the lid and set the steam release handle to the *Sealing* position. Press the '*Fish* button and set the timer for 9 minutes
5. When you hear the cooker's end signal, carefully move the pressure valve to the *Venting* position to release the pressure
6. Open the pot and stir in the spinach. Optionally, season with some more garlic powder or dried thyme. Serve and enjoy.

Nutrition Value: Calories: 353; Total Fats: 21.5g; Net Carbs: 8.9g; Protein: 29.3g; Fiber: 5g

120. Tilapia Curry Recipe

Preparation Time: 15 Minutes
Servings: 4

Ingredients:
- 10-ounce tilapia fillets; chopped.
- 3 tablespoon olive oil
- 1 teaspoon lemon juice
- 3 garlic cloves; crushed
- 2 cups coconut milk; full-fat
- 1 small onion; finely chopped
- 1/2 cup Thai basil; chopped.
- 1/2 cup cherry tomatoes; chopped
- 1 small chili pepper; chopped.
- 2 teaspoon chili powder
- 1 teaspoon cumin powder
- 1/2 teaspoon turmeric powder
- 2 teaspoon fresh ginger; grated
- 1 teaspoon coriander powder
- 1 teaspoon sea salt

Directions:
1. Plug in the instant pot and grease the inner pot with oil. Press the *Sauté* button and add onions, garlic, ginger, coriander, chili, cumin powder, turmeric, and salt. Give it a good stir and cook for 3-4 minutes or until translucent
2. Now; pour in the coconut milk and give it a good stir. Add cherry tomatoes, tilapia fillets, and chopped chili pepper.
3. Seal the lid and set the steam release handle to the *Sealing* position. Press the *Manual* button and set the timer for 4 minutes on high pressure.
4. When you hear the end signal, perform a quick pressure release and open the pot. Sprinkle with Thai basil and serve immediately

Nutrition Value: Calories: 440; Total Fats: 39.9g; Net Carbs: 6.7g; Protein: 16.6g; Fiber: 3.4g

121. Adobo Shrimps Recipe

Preparation Time: 50 Minutes
Servings: 4

Ingredients:
- 1-pound shrimps; peeled and deveined
- 2 tablespoon green onions; finely chopped
- 2 cups fish stock
- 1/4 cup soy sauce

- 1/4 cup olive oil
- 1/4 cup rice vinegar
- 1 small onion; finely chopped
- 1 red chili pepper; finely chopped.
- 5 garlic cloves; crushed
- 2 tablespoon fish sauce
- 1 tablespoon peppercorn
- 1 teaspoon stevia powder
- 2 teaspoon salt

Directions:
1. In a large bowl, whisk together olive oil, rice vinegar, soy sauce, green onions, garlic, fish sauce, chopped onion, chili pepper, salt, peppercorn, and stevia
2. Add shrimps and give it a good stir making sure to coat shrimps well in the marinade. Transfer to a large Ziploc bag and refrigerate for at least 30 minutes (up to 2 hours)
3. Plug in the instant pot and pour in the stock. Remove the shrimps from the Ziploc and place in the pot along with 1/4 cup of the marinade
4. Stir well and seal the lid. Set the steam release handle to the *Sealing* position and press the *Manual* button
5. Set the timer for 10 minutes. When done, perform a quick release and serve immediately.

Nutrition Value: Calories: 298; Total Fats: 15.5g; Net Carbs: 5.7g; Protein: 30.4g; Fiber: 0.7g

122. Tilapia Fillets

Preparation Time: 40 Minutes
Servings: 2

Ingredients:
- 1-pound tilapia fillets; chopped.
- 1 cup fish stock
- 2 tablespoon peanut oil
- 1 spring onion; finely chopped
- 1/4 cup celery leaves; finely chopped.
- 3 tablespoon soy sauce
- 1 tablespoon rice vinegar
- 1 teaspoon garlic powder
- 1 tablespoon fresh ginger; grated
- 1 teaspoon sea salt

Directions:
1. In a small bowl, whisk together peanut oil, soy sauce, rice vinegar, ginger, garlic powder, and sea salt. Rub the fish with this mixture and place in a large Ziploc bag. Seal the bag and refrigerate for at least 30 minutes
2. Plug in the instant pot and pour in the stock. Remove the fish from the refrigerator and place in the pot along with the marinade. Sprinkle with celery and seal the lid
3. Set the steam release handle to the *Sealing* position and press the *Manual* button. Set the timer for 6 minutes on high pressure

Nutrition Value: Calories: 348; Total Fats: 16.5g; Net Carbs: 2.2g; Protein: 46.6g; Fiber: 0.6g

123. Mussels with Asparagus

Preparation Time: 15 Minutes
Servings: 4

Ingredients:
- 1-pound mussels; cleaned
- 1 large green bell pepper; finely chopped.
- 2 teaspoon lemon juice; freshly squeezed
- 7-ounce asparagus; chopped into bite-sized pieces
- 1 cup sun-dried tomatoes
- 3 tablespoon avocado oil
- 4 cups fish stock
- 1/2 teaspoon garlic powder
- 1 ½ teaspoon smoked paprika
- 1/2 teaspoon pepper
- 1 teaspoon sea salt

Directions:
1. Plug in the instant pot and press the *Sauté* button. Grease the stainless steel insert with avocado oil and heat up. Optionally, use olive oil
2. Add asparagus and stir-fry for 2-3 minutes. Now add sun dried tomatoes

and mussels. Sprinkle with salt, pepper, garlic powder, and smoked paprika.
3. Continue to cook for 4-5 minutes
4. Finally add bell peppers and pour in the stock. Stir well and seal the lid. Set the steam release handle to the *Sealing* position and press the *Manual* button
5. Set the timer for 5 minutes on high pressure.
6. When done, perform a quick release and open the lid. Serve and enjoy.

Nutrition Value: Calories: 179; Total Fats: 6g; Net Carbs: 8.2g; Protein: 20.7g; Fiber: 2.5g

124. Cod Chowder with Bacon

Preparation Time: 25 Minutes
Servings: 5

Ingredients:

- 1-pound cod fillets
- 3 tablespoon butter
- 1/4 cup heavy cream
- 5 bacon slices; chopped
- 2 cups cauliflower; cut into florets
- 3 cups fish stock
- 1 cup button mushrooms; sliced
- 1/4 cup fish sauce
- 1/2 cup onions; finely chopped.
- 1 cup full-fat milk
- 1 teaspoon dried basil
- 1/2 teaspoon black pepper; freshly ground.
- 1 teaspoon salt

Directions:

1. Plug in the instant pot and press the *Sauté* button. Grease the inner pot with butter and heat up. Add onions and mushrooms and stir well. Cook for 5 minutes, stirring occasionally
2. Now add the fish stock and cauliflower. Add cod fillets and season with salt, pepper, and basil.
3. Add bacon and stir well again.
4. Seal the lid and set the steam release handle to the *Sealing* position. Press the *Manual* button and set the timer for 8 minutes on high pressure
5. When done, perform a quick pressure release and carefully open the lid
6. Stir in the milk and heavy cream. Drizzle with the fish sauce and chill for a while. Serve with some freshly chopped parsley.

Nutrition Value: Calories: 333; Total Fats: 20.7g; Net Carbs: 5.6g; Protein: 30.1g; Fiber: 1.4g

125. Trout Casserole

Preparation Time: 40 Minutes
Servings: 4

Ingredients:

- 1-pound trout fillets; without skin
- 1 cup cherry tomatoes; halved
- 1 cup cauliflower; chopped into florets
- 1 small onion; sliced
- 1/2 zucchini; sliced
- 4 tablespoon olive oil
- 1 teaspoon dried thyme
- 1/2 teaspoon garlic powder
- 2 teaspoon sea salt
- 1 teaspoon dried rosemary

Directions:

1. Line a small square pan with some parchment paper and sprinkle with two tablespoons of olive oil
2. Arrange onions at the bottom of the pan and make a layer with sliced zucchini. Top with cherry tomatoes and onions. Sprinkle with some salt and drizzle with the remaining olive oil
3. Top with trout fillets and season with some more salt, rosemary, thyme, and garlic powder
4. Tightly wrap with aluminum foil and set aside
5. Plug in the instant pot and pour in 2 cups of water. Set the trivet at the bottom of the inner pot and place the pan on top.
6. Seal the lid and set the steam release handle to the *Sealing* position. Press the *Manual* button and set the timer for 20 minutes on high pressure
7. When done, perform a quick release and

open the lid. Carefully remove the pan and chill for a while

8. Remove the aluminum foil and optionally, bake for 15 minutes at 450 degrees F. Serve and enjoy

Nutrition Value: Calories: 361; Total Fats: 23.8g; Net Carbs: 3.7g; Protein: 31.6g; Fiber: 1.8g

126. Lobster Tomato Stew

Preparation Time: 15 Minutes
Servings: 4

Ingredients:

- 4 lobster tails; defrosted
- 2 cups cherry tomatoes; chopped.
- 2 cups heavy cream
- 2 cups fish stock
- 3 tablespoon olive oil
- 2 tablespoon butter
- 1 cup celery; finely chopped
- 2 shallots; diced
- 1 teaspoon black pepper; freshly ground.
- 1/2 teaspoon smoked paprika
- 1 tablespoon Old Bay seasoning
- 1 teaspoon dill

Directions:

- In a large bowl, combine tomatoes, celery, shallots, olive oil, and dill. Mix until well incorporated and set aside
- Plug in the instant pot and press the *Sauté* button. Grease the inner pot with butter and add lobster tails. Season with salt, pepper, and Old Bay seasoning. Cook for 3-4 minutes on each side
- Pour in the tomato mixture, fish stock, and sprinkle with smoked paprika
- Give it a good stir and seal the lid. Set the steam release handle and press the *Manual* button. Set the timer for 5 minutes on high pressure
- When done, press the *Cancel'* button and release the pressure naturally. Carefully open the lid and stir in the heavy cream. Chill for a while and serve

Nutrition Value: Calories: 468; Total Fats: 40.3g; Net Carbs: 5.3g; Protein: 21.2g; Fiber: 1.5g

127. Creamy Shrimp Stew

Preparation Time: 35 Minutes
Servings: 4

Ingredients:

- 1-pound shrimps; peeled and deveined
- 3 bacon slices; chopped
- 1/4 cup bell peppers; diced
- 1 cup cherry tomatoes; sliced in half
- 1/2 cup heavy cream
- 1/4 cup scallions; chopped
- 2 cups fish stock
- 4 tablespoon olive oil
- 1 cup onion; finely chopped.
- 1/4 teaspoon white pepper; freshly ground.
- 2 teaspoon apple cider vinegar
- 1 teaspoon Old Bay seasoning
- 1/2 teaspoon garlic powder
- 1/2 teaspoon salt

Directions:

1. Plug in the instant pot and press the *Sauté* button. Grease the inner pot with olive oil and add bacon. Cook for 3-4 minutes or until lightly golden brown and crisp. Remove the bacon from the pot and set aside.
2. Now add onions and bell peppers. Cook until translucent and add cherry tomatoes and scallions. Continue to cook for 10 minutes, stirring occasionally. If necessary, pour in some of the stock
3. Now add shrimps and give it a good stir. Pour in the remaining stock and season with Old Bay seasoning, garlic powder, salt, and pepper. Sprinkle with some apple cider and seal the lid.
4. Set the steam release handle to the *Sealing* position and press the *Manual* button. Cook for 8 minutes on high pressure
5. When done, release the pressure naturally and open the lid. Serve and enjoy.

Nutrition Value: Calories: 427; Total Fats: 28.5g;

Net Carbs: 6.4g; Protein: 35g; Fiber: 1.4g

128. Spicy Shrimp Pasta

Preparation Time: 15 Minutes
Servings: 4

Ingredients:

- 7-ounce shrimps; cleaned
- 3 cups chicken stock
- 2 garlic cloves; crushed
- 2 tablespoon olive oil
- 1 teaspoon apple cider vinegar
- 2 cups cauliflower; chopped into florets
- 1 cup cream cheese
- 1/4 cup mayonnaise
- 1/2 teaspoon red pepper flakes
- 1/2 teaspoon onion powder
- 1 teaspoon smoked salt

Directions:

1. Place shrimps and cauliflower in the pot. Add garlic and pour in the stock. Sprinkle with olive oil and apple cider and stir well.
2. Seal the lid and set the steam release handle to the *Sealing* position. Press the *Manual* button and cook for 9 minutes on high pressure
3. When done, perform a quick release and open the lid. Remove the shrimp mixture and drain the remaining liquid in the pot. Transfer to a deep bowl and set aside
4. Now press the *Sauté* button and heat up the inner pot. add cream cheese and mayonnaise. Season with smoked salt, onion powder, and red pepper flakes.
5. Briefly cook, for about a minute and stir in the shrimp mixture. Mix well and press the *Cancel* button
6. Serve immediately and optionally sprinkle with some shredded mozzarella or grated parmesan

Nutrition Value: Calories: 401; Total Fats: 33.5g; Net Carbs: 8.2g; Protein: 17.4g; Fiber: 1.3g

129. Creamy Mussel Soup

Preparation Time: 15 Minutes
Servings: 4

Ingredients:

- 2 cups mussels; defrosted
- 2 tablespoon butter; unsalted
- 1 tablespoon soy sauce
- 1/4 cup Parmesan cheese
- 1-pound cauliflower; chopped into florets
- 1 cup broccoli; chopped.
- 2 cups fish stock
- 1 cup heavy cream
- 1/2 teaspoon fresh pepper; ground.
- 2 bay leaves

Directions:

1. Place mussels in a large sieve and rinse thoroughly under cold running water. Drain and place in a deep bowl. Season with pepper and set aside
2. Plug in the instant pot and press the *Sauté* button. Add cauliflower and broccoli. Stir well and cook for 5 minutes.
3. Now add mussels and pour in the fish stock. Drizzle with soy sauce and add bay leaves
4. Seal the lid and set the steam release handle to the *Sealing* position. Press the *Manual* button and set the timer for 5 minutes on high pressure.
5. When done, perform a quick release and open the lid. Remove the bay leaves and stir in the heavy cream and Parmesan. Chill for a while before serving

Nutrition Value: Calories: 283; Total Fats: 20g; Net Carbs: 8g; Protein: 15.9g; Fiber: 3.5g

130. Jamaican Jerk Fish

Preparation Time: 35 Minutes
Servings: 4

Ingredients:

- 2-pounds cod fillets; cut into 1-inch slices
- 2 cups cherry tomatoes; chopped.
- 2 tablespoon butter
- 1/4 cup fish stock

- 2 tablespoon swerve
- 3 tablespoon soy sauce
- 1 tablespoon Jamaican Jerk seasoning
- 2 teaspoon chili powder

Directions:

1. Rinse the fillets under cold running water and pat dry with a kitchen paper, Set aside
2. Plug in the instant pot and grease the inner pot with butter. Add fish fillets and cook for 4-5 minutes on each side. You will probably have to do this in several batches.
3. Remove from the pot and transfer to a plate, Set aside
4. Now add cherry tomatoes and pour in the stock. Bring it to a boil and drizzle with soy sauce. Season with Jamaican Jerk seasoning and chili powder. Add swerve and cook until tomatoes soften
5. Add fish fillets and coat well with the sauce
6. Press the *Cancel* button and remove from the pot. Serve and enjoy

Nutrition Value: Calories: 507; Total Fats: 25.3g; Net Carbs: 3.2g; Protein: 62.3g; Fiber: 1.2g

131. Onion Prawn Stew

Preparation Time: 45 Minutes
Servings: 6

Ingredients:

- 7oz chicken breast; chopped into bite-sized pieces
- 20 king prawn tails; peeled
- 1 cup cherry tomatoes; chopped
- 1 spring onion; chopped
- 3 tablespoon fresh parsley; chopped.
- 1/2 cup olive oil
- 5 cups fish stock
- 1 cup onions; chopped
- 1 small green bell pepper; finely chopped
- 2 celery stalks; chopped.
- 3 garlic cloves; crushed
- 1 teaspoon stevia powder
- 1 teaspoon chili powder
- 1/2 teaspoon black pepper; freshly ground.
- 2 teaspoon cayenne pepper; ground.
- 1 tablespoon dried celery
- 1 teaspoon white pepper; freshly ground.
- 1 teaspoon sea salt

Directions:

1. Rinse well and clean prawns. Place in a deep bowl and season with salt and pepper, Set aside
2. Rinse the meat and pat-dry with some kitchen paper. Place on a large cutting board and cut into bite-sized pieces. Season with the remaining salt and pepper and set aside
3. Plug in the instant pot and grease the inner pot with some oil. Add onions, spring onions, celery stalk, and green pepper. Stir well and cook for 5-6 minutes, stirring constantly
4. Now add the meat and prawns. Give it a good stir and season with the remaining spices
5. Continue to cook for another 5-6 minutes. Pour in the fish stock and the remaining olive oil. Press the *Cancel* button
6. Seal the lid and set the steam release handle to the *Sealing* position. Press the *Manual* button and set the timer for 20 minutes on high pressure
7. When done, perform a quick pressure release and open the lid. Stir in garlic and parsley. Let it sit for 5 minutes and serve

Nutrition Value: Calories: 418; Total Fats: 21.9g; Net Carbs: 6.4g; Protein: 46.8g; Fiber: 1.3g

132. Catfish Stew

Preparation Time: 10 Minutes
Servings: 2

Ingredients:

- 10-ounce catfish fillets; cut into bite-sized pieces
- 2 cups collard greens; finely chopped (can be replaced with spinach or kale)

- 2 cups cherry tomatoes; chopped
- 3 tablespoon olive oil
- 2 cups fish stock
- 1 teaspoon garlic powder
- 1/2 teaspoon sea salt
- 1 teaspoon dried dill
- 1 teaspoon Italian seasoning
- 1/4 teaspoon chili flakes

Directions:
1. Combine the ingredients in the instant pot and stir well. Seal the lid and set the steam release handle to the *Sealing* position.
2. Press the *Manual* button and set the timer for 7 minutes on high pressure.
3. When done, release the pressure for about 10 minutes and then move the pressure valve to the *Venting* position
4. Carefully open the lid and optionally sprinkle with some fresh parsley or grated Parmesan before serving.

Nutrition Value: Calories: 456; Total Fats: 34.3g; Net Carbs: 5.8g; Protein: 29.9g; Fiber: 3.7g

133. Quick Shrimp Soup

Preparation Time: 40 Minutes
Servings: 5

Ingredients:
- 2 -pounds shrimps; tail-on
- 3 tablespoon olive oil
- 3 tablespoon butter
- 4 garlic cloves; minced
- 1 cup broccoli; cut into florets
- 4 cups fish stock
- 1 large tomato; roughly chopped
- 1/2 cup fresh parsley; finely chopped.
- 1 teaspoon dried rosemary
- 2 teaspoon sea salt

Directions:
1. Plug in the instant pot. Heat up the olive oil on the *Sauté* mode and add broccoli. Stir well and cook until golden brown. Sprinkle with garlic and cook for one more minute
2. Now add tomatoes and pour in some fish stock – about three tablespoons will be enough. Cook for 7-8 minutes, or until most of the liquid evaporates
3. Now add shrimps and briefly brown. Stir well and season with salt and rosemary.
4. Add the remaining ingredients and give it a good stir. Seal the lid and set the steam release handle and press the *Manual* button
5. Set the timer for 15 minutes
6. When done, perform a quick pressure release and open the lid. Optionally, sprinkle with some more herbs or spices and serve immediately

Nutrition Value: Calories: 399; Total Fats: 20.1g; Net Carbs: 5.4g; Protein: 46.8g; Fiber: 1.2g

134. Lobster Tails in Butter Sauce

Preparation Time: 15 Minutes
Servings: 4

Ingredients:
- 1-pound fresh lobster tails; cleaned
- 5 tablespoon butter; unsalted
- 1/4 teaspoon dried rosemary
- 1/4 teaspoon garlic powder
- 1/4 cup fish stock
- 1 cup water
- 1 tablespoon apple cider vinegar
- 1/2 cup mayonnaise
- 1/2 teaspoon black pepper; freshly ground.
- 1/4 teaspoon dried thyme
- 1 teaspoon salt

Directions:
1. Place lobster tails in the steam basket and transfer to the pot. Pour in one cup of water and seal the lid. Set the steam release handle to the *Sealing* position and press the *Steam* button. Cook for 5 minutes on high pressure.
2. When done, preform a quick pressure release and open the lid. Remove the

lobster tails from the pot and press the *Sauté* button.
3. Pour in the stock and bring it to a boil. Stir in butter and mayonnaise and sprinkle with apple cider
4. Season with salt, pepper, thyme, rosemary, and garlic powder. Cook for 2-3 minutes
5. Press the *Cancel'* button and remove the sauce from the pot. Drizzle over steamed lobster tails and serve immediately. Optionally, sprinkle with fresh dill

Nutrition Value: Calories: 347; Total Fats: 25.3g; Net Carbs: 7.1g; Protein: 22.3g; Fiber: 0g

135. Mediterranean Chili Lime Salmon

Preparation Time: 15 Minutes
Servings: 1

Ingredients:

- 7-ounce salmon fillets
- 1 cup fish stock
- 1 tablespoon freshly squeezed lime juice
- 1 tablespoon swerve
- 1 jalapeno pepper; chopped
- 1 tablespoon olive oil
- 2 garlic cloves; crushed
- 1/4 teaspoon cumin powder
- 1/2 teaspoon smoked paprika
- 1 tablespoon fresh parsley; finely chopped
- 1 teaspoon sea salt
- 1/2 teaspoon black pepper

Directions:

1. Rinse the fillets under cold running water and rub with salt and pepper. Place in the steam basket and pour in one cup of water
2. Seal the lid and set the steam release handle to the *Sealing* position. Press the *Steam* button and set the timer for 4 minutes on high pressure.
3. When done, perform a quick release and open the lid

4. Meanwhile, in a small bowl, combine olive oil, swerve, garlic, lime juice, cumin powder, paprika, and parsley
5. Press the *Sauté* button and pour the mixture in the pot. Heat up and add chopped pepper. Stir in the salmon and cook for 2 minutes.
6. Press the *Cancel'* button to turn off the pot. Serve and enjoy

Nutrition Value: Calories: 399; Total Fats: 26.5g; Net Carbs: 2.5g; Protein: 39.2g; Fiber: 0.6g

136. Salmon with Vegetables

Preparation Time: 45 Minutes
Servings: 4

Ingredients:

- 4 medium-sized salmon steaks
- 7-ounce kale; chopped.
- 2 tablespoon rice vinegar
- 7-ounce broccoli; chopped
- 1 garlic clove; crushed
- 1 cup chicken stock
- 2 tablespoon soy sauce
- 2 tablespoon sesame oil
- 2 teaspoon ginger; freshly grated
- 1/4 teaspoon chili powder
- 1/2 teaspoon black pepper; freshly ground.
- 1 teaspoon sea salt

Directions:

1. Rub steaks with garlic, ginger, and chili powder. Sprinkle with some salt and pepper place in a small baking dish. Loosely cover with the aluminum foil and set aside
2. Plug in the instant pot and add vegetables. Pour in the chicken stock and season with salt and some pepper. Seal the lid and set the steam release handle
3. Press the *Manual* button and set the timer for 10 minute
4. When done, perform a quick release and open the lid. Remove the vegetables and drain. Place in a deep bowl and drizzle with some sesame oil, soy sauce, and rice

vinegar, Set aside.

5. Position a trivet in the inner pot and place the baking dish on top. Pour in 2 cups of water and seal the lid
6. Set the steam release handle again and press the *Manual* button. Set the timer for 8 minutes on high pressure
7. When done, perform a quick release and open the lid. Remove the steaks from the pot and set aside
8. Now press the *Sauté* button and add the vegetable mixture. Briefly cook – for 3-4 minutes, stirring constantly. Press the *Cancel'* button
9. Remove the vegetables from the pot and place on a large serving platter. Top with salmon steaks and optionally season with some more salt or pepper to taste. Serve and enjoy.

Nutrition Value: Calories: 313; Total Fats: 16.4g; Net Carbs: 7.4g; Protein: 32.7g; Fiber: 2.1g

POULTRY

137. Mouthwatering Maple Mustard Turkey Thighs

Preparation Time: 60 minutes
Servings: 4

Nutrition Values:

Calories: 633
Carbohydrate: 41g
Protein: 44g
Fat: 34g
Sugar: 30g
Sodium: 1.81g

Ingredients

- 2 (3 lb) turkey thighs bone-in skin-on; washed and dried (3 lb)
- 1/2 cup butter; unsalted
- 1 tsp. fresh rosemary; chopped.
- 1 tsp. fresh thyme; chopped
- 1 tbsp. smoked paprika
- 2 tbsp. Dijon mustard
- 1/2 cup maple syrup
- 1 large onion; chopped.
- 5 stalks celery; chopped
- 5 carrots; chopped.
- 4 sprigs rosemary
- 2 sprigs thyme
- 1 tsp. salt
- 1/2 tsp. pepper
- 1 cup water

Directions:
1. Add the melted butter, thyme, rosemary, maple syrup, smoked paprika and Dijon mustard to the instant pot.
2. Boil the mixture on *Sauté* function, stirring occasionally.
3. Add the salt, pepper and half the maple syrup mixture to the turkey thighs, Toss it well.
4. Add the water, celery, onion, rosemary, thyme and carrots to the instant pot.
5. Place the trivet in the pot then place turkey thighs over the trivet.
6. Pour the remaining maple syrup mixture over the thighs,
7. Select *Manual* and set to high pressure for 30 minutes and let it cook.
8. When it beeps; vent the steam, using *Natural Release* for 10 minutes then use *Quick Release*.
9. Remove the lid and take out the turkey thighs, Leave for 10 minutes then cut them into slices, Pour the maple mustard mixture over the sliced thighs and serve.

138. Chicken Cashew Butter

Preparation Time: 13 minutes
Servings: 6

Nutrition Values:

Calories: 640
Carbohydrate: 26.3g
Protein: 69.9g
Fat: 27.6g
Sugar: 13.7g
Sodium: 0.85g

Ingredients

- 2 lbs. chicken breasts
- 3 cloves garlic minced
- 3 tbsp. cilantro (chopped)
- 3 tbsp. cashews (chopped)
- 1/4 cup rice vinegar
- 1/2 cup smooth cashew butter
- 1/4 cup Soy Sauce
- 1 tbsp. chili sauce
- 1/2 cup chicken broth
- 1/4 cup honey

Directions:
1. Cut the chicken breasts into small, 2-inch chunks, Put the pieces in the cooker pot.
2. Put the cashew butter, honey, rice, soy sauce, chilli sauce, vinegar, chicken broth and garlic in a separate bowl and mix all the Ingredients well.

3. Pour the butter mixture over the chicken pieces, Then cover with the lid.
4. After securing the lid select *Manual* function, set high pressure and 7 minutes on the timer.
5. Let it cook till it beeps, Then use the *Quick Release* method to vent the steam. Serve the chicken on a platter with chopped cashews on top.

139. Classic Turkey Cheese Gnocchi

Preparation Time: 30 minutes
Servings: 6

Nutrition Values:
Calories: 1033
Carbohydrate: 32.6g
Protein: 99.2g
Fat: 19.9g
Sugar: 2.3g
Sodium: 0.89g

Ingredients

- 1 pound turkey boneless pieces,
- 2 cups fresh spinach chopped
- 2 cups mozzarella cheese shredded
- 1/2 cup parmesan cheese shredded
- 2 tbsp. olive oil
- 1/2 tsp. black pepper
- 1/4 cup shallots chopped.
- 2 cloves garlic minced
- 1/4 cup sun-dried tomatoes,
- 1 cup cream
- 2 cups chicken broth
- 2 lbs. gnocchi
- 1/2 tsp. salt

Directions:
1. Select the *Sauté* option on your instant pot. Pour in the oil and heat.
2. Add the turkey, with salt and pepper. Let it cook for 3 minutes on each side,
3. Now add the garlic tomatoes and the shallots to the pot. Cook for 2 minutes while stirring.
4. Add the cream and chicken broth to the pot. Secure the cooker lid.
5. Select *Manual* settings at high pressure for 10 minutes,
6. When it beeps; release the steam naturally then remove the lid.
7. Add the gnocchi to the mixture,
8. Select the *Sauté* function and let it all cook for 5 minutes until gnocchi is tender.
9. Switch off the appliance then add the cheese to the pot. Serve immediately.

140. Delicious Orange Spice Chicken

Preparation Time: 30 minutes
Servings: 6

Nutrition Values:
Calories: 818
Carbohydrate: 23.7g
Protein: 128.2g
Fat: 19.6g
Sugar: 19.6g
Sodium: 1.12g

Ingredients

- 2 lb. chicken breast cut into two-inch pieces
- 2 tbsp. vegetable oil
- Two garlic heads; minced
- 1/4 cup granulated sugar
- 1/4 cup brown sugar
- 1/4 cup soy sauce
- 1 cup tomato sauce
- 1 cup orange juice
- 4 tbsp. corn starch
- 4 green onions and orange zest
- Salt and pepper to taste

Directions:
1. Dry the chicken pieces with a paper towel.
2. Add oil and chicken to the pot of the cooker.
3. Press the *Sauté* key and cook the chicken on a medium-high heat for 2-3 minutes, stirring constantly.

4. When the chicken turns golden brown; add the rest of the Ingredients to the pot.
5. Mix all the Ingredients well. Cover and lock the cooker lid.
6. Select the *poultry* option and set the timer for 7 minutes,
7. After it beeps sound; use *Natural Release* to vent the steam for 10 minutes, Then open the lid.
8. Mix the corn-starch with the orange juice in a separate bowl and add it to the pot.
9. Select the *Sauté* function and cook the chicken in the sauce for 5 minutes, Stir constantly until it thickens, Garnish with chopped green onions and orange zest on top.

141. Chicken with Smoked Paprika

Preparation Time: 20 minutes
Servings: 6

Nutrition Values:

Calories: 524
Carbohydrate: 29.3g
Protein: 68.5g
Fat: 10.3g
Sugar: 1.2g
Sodium: 0.31g

Ingredients

- 1 1/2-pound chicken breasts cut into small pieces
- 2 tsp. smoked paprika
- 1 tsp. olive oil
- 3 strips bacon; chopped
- 1 small onion; chopped
- 2 garlic cloves; minced.
- 1 small red bell pepper; chopped.
- 1 tsp. salt
- 1 (12 oz.) can of beer.
- 1 cup white rice
- 2 strips bacon; cooked (topping)

Directions:

1. Put the oil and bacon in the pot. Sauté it, without covering the lid, for 3 minutes,
2. Add the bell pepper to the oil and bacon and sauté for 3 more minutes,
3. Add chopped onion and sauté for 2 minutes,
4. Add garlic and cook for 1 minute,
5. Add all the seasoning to the pot and turn off the *Sauté* function.
6. Add the beer to the mixture, Mix all the Ingredients well.
7. Add the chicken and rice to the pot and select *manual* settings.
8. Set to high pressure for 10 minutes and leave it to cook.
9. Use *Quick Release* to vent all the steam then remove the lid. Serve the dish with the bacon strips on top.

142. Chicken with chilies

Preparation Time: 15 minutes
Servings: 6

Nutrition Values:

Calories: 697
Carbohydrate: 2.9g
Protein: 127.3g
Fat: 15.1g
Sugar: 0.7
Sodium: 0.40g

Ingredients

- 2 lb. chicken breasts
- 1/4 cup white wine,
- 1 large lemon juiced.
- 4 tsp. arrowroot flour
- 1 onion; diced
- 1 tbsp. olive oil.
- 5 garlic cloves; minced
- 1/2 cup organic chicken broth
- 1 tsp. dried parsley
- 1/4 tsp. paprika
- 1 tsp. sea salt

Directions:

1. Put the cooking oil and chopped onion in the instant pot. Select the *Sauté* function to cook the onion for 5-10 minutes; until it turns light brown.

2. Add all the remaining Ingredients to the pot and select the *poultry* function without changing the settings,
3. Allow it cook. Release the steam after the beep.
4. Remove the lid. Check the sauce is thick enough.
5. If not, add dissolved arrowroot flour into the sauce to increase thickness, Transfer the cooked chicken onto a platter and serve immediately.

143. Green Chili Adobo Chicken

Preparation Time: 31 minutes
Servings: 6

Nutrition Values:

Calories: 204
Carbohydrate: 7.6g
Protein: 32.9g
Fat: 4.2g
Sugar: 2.2g
Sodium: 0.73g

Ingredients

6 boneless; skinless chicken breasts
1 tbsp. GOYA Adobo all-purpose seasoning with pepper
two cups diced tomatoes
1/2 cup water
1 tbsp. turmeric
1 cup diced green chilies

Directions:

1. Place the chicken breasts in the inner pot.
2. Add Adobo seasoning pepper to the chicken. Sprinkle on both sides,
3. Add the sliced tomatoes to the chicken.
4. Pour half-cup of water over the chicken.
5. Cover and lock the lid. Use manual settings and set the time to 25 minutes,
6. When cooking is complete at the beep, use *Natural Release* to vent the steam for 15 minutes,
7. Use quick the release option to vent all remaining steam.
8. Remove the pot and shred the chicken inside using two forks, Serve with rice, or fill the tacos with the shredded chicken.

144. Instant Steamed Garlic Chicken

Preparation Time: 14 minutes
Servings: 3

Nutrition Values:

Calories: 155
Carbohydrate: 0.3g
Protein: 21.3g
Fat: 7.2g
Sugar: 4.3g
Sodium: 55mg

Ingredients

- 3 boneless chicken breasts
- 1/4 tsp. garlic powder
- 1 tsp. black pepper
- 1/8 tsp. dried oregano
- 1/8 tsp. dried basil
- 1 tbsp. olive oil
- 1 cup water
- Salt to taste

Directions:

1. Add the oil to the pot and select the *Sauté* function. Let it up heat without the lid on.
2. Sprinkle seasonings on both sides of the chicken.
3. Put the seasoned chicken into the pot with the oil and cook each side for 3-4 minutes until they turn golden brown.
4. Add the water to the pot then set the trivet in the pot.
5. Place the chicken pieces on the trivet.
6. Select *Manual* settings; high pressure and 5 minutes on the timer. Let it cook.
7. Use the *Natural Release*; after the beep; to release the steam. Use *Quick Release* afterwards to make sure all the steam has been vented.
8. Remove the lid. Transfer the chicken to a platter. Wait 5 minutes and serve with lime wedges, sprinkled oregano and basil on top.

145. Spicy Chicken

Preparation Time: 18 minutes
Servings: 4

Nutrition Values:

Calories: 270
Carbohydrate: 6.6g
Protein: 17.9g
Fat: 20.1g
Sugar: 2.8g
Sodium: 51mg

Ingredients

- 3 large boneless; skinless chicken breasts
- 1/2 an onion; chopped..
- 1 can full-fat coconut milk
- 3 cloves garlic; minced
- 1 ½ tsp. black pepper
- 1 tsp. turmeric
- 1/2 cup of water
- 1 tbsp. olive oil
- 2 tsp. smoked paprika
- 1 ½ tsp. ground cumin
- Sea salt to taste

Directions:

1. Place the chicken and water in the instant pot. Cover with the lid and lock.
2. Use manual settings for high pressure and set timer to 15minutes,
3. When the timer beeps; use natural release pressure to release the steam.
4. Remove the chicken from the pot and shred it using two forks,
5. Add the oil onion and garlic to the instant pot; keeping the *Sauté* mode on.
6. Let the Ingredients cook for 3 minutes; stirring constantly.
7. Turn the *Sauté* function off then add the shredded chicken, cumin, turmeric, coconut milk, smoked paprika, black pepper and salt to the pot.
8. Mix all the Ingredients well with the chicken. Serve with steaming boiled rice,

146. Tso's Chicken

Preparation Time: 13 minutes

Servings: 6

Nutrition Values:

Calories: 617
Carbohydrate: 15g
Protein: 96.6g
Fat: 16.1g
Sugar: 9.4g
Sodium: 1.43g

Ingredients

- 1 ½ lb. chicken breast (cut into 2-inch pieces)
- ⅓ cup white wine vinegar
- 2 tbsp. tomato paste
- 3 tbsp. arrowroot powder
- 2 tbsp. minced ginger
- 3 tbsp. red hot chili pepper
- 1/2 cup water
- 2 tbsp. sesame seeds
- 1/4 cup chopped green onion
- 1 tbsp. honey
- 1/2 cup soy sauce
- 2 tbsp. olive oil
- 1 tbsp. almond butter
- 1/4 cup coconut sugar
- 2 cloves garlic crushed

Directions:

1. Roll the chicken pieces in the arrowroot powder until each one is covered with a uniform layer.
2. Select the *Sauté* option on your instant cooker. Add the oil, garlic and chicken to the pot.
3. Let it cook, stirring occasionally; until the chicken turns golden brown. Don't forget to cancel the sauté function.
4. Mix all the remaining Ingredients together in a separate bowl and whisk them to make a smooth paste,
5. Add this mixture to the pot then secure the cooker lid.
6. Use *Manual* settings, with high pressure and 8 minutes cooking time,
7. When it beeps; carefully release the steam and open the lid. Sprinkle sesame seeds

and green onion over the dish then serve.

147. Chicken Salsa Recipe

Preparation Time: 20 minutes
Servings: 2

Nutrition Values:
Calories: 387
Carbohydrate:4.5g
Protein: 21.7g
Fat: 3.4g
Sugar: 1.4g
Sodium: 0.56g

Ingredients

- 1 pound frozen; skinless, boneless chicken breast halves
- 1/2 cup salsa
- 1(1 oz.) packet taco seasoning mix
- 1/2 cup chicken broth.

Directions:

1. Place the chicken breasts in the instant pot.
2. Sprinkle taco seasoning uniformly over both sides of the chicken breasts,
3. Add the salsa and chicken broth to the pot.
4. Secure the lid.
5. Set the *poultry* function on your pressure cooker to cook for 15 minutes,
6. When it beeps; release the steam naturally for 20 minutes, Use *Quick Release* to vent any remaining steam.
7. Remove the chicken and shred it. Serve the shredded chicken with the steaming hot sauce.

148. Turkey and Cranberry Sauce

Preparation Time: 50 minutes
Servings: 6

Nutrition Values:
Calories: 600
Carbohydrate:51.8g
Protein:70.8g
Fat: 9.6g
Sugar: 32.2g
Sodium: 0.19g

Ingredients

- 4-pound turkey breast with skin
- 3 cups cranberries; fresh or frozen
- 1 cup orange juice
- 1 cup apple jelly
- 1/2 tsp. five-spice
- 3 tbsp. corn-starch
- 4 tbsp. unsalted butter
- 2 medium onions; chopped
- 1 tbsp. fresh rosemary; chopped.
- 1/2 tsp. dried thyme
- 1/2 cup chicken broth
- Salt and pepper to taste

Directions:

1. Put the 2 cups of cranberries, apple jelly, Five Spice, orange juice and corn-starch into a blender. Blend well to form a smooth paste,
2. Add the melted butter and the prepared mixture to the instant pot. Select the *Sauté* function to boil then keep it aside,
3. Sprinkle salt, pepper, thyme and rosemary generously over the turkey breasts,
4. Add butter to the instant pot. Select *Sauté* function then add the turkey to the pot.
5. Let it cook until it turns brown on both sides, Then keep it aside,
6. Add butter, onion, salt and pepper to the pot and *Sauté* for 5 minutes,
7. Add the cranberry mixture to the pot and bring it to the boil while stirring constantly.
8. Add the remaining cup of cranberries to the sauce and mix well.
9. Add the chicken broth and place the turkey breasts in the pot. Secure the cooker lid.
10. Select *Manual* function to high pressure for 25 minutes,
11. When it beeps; release the steam

completely then remove the lid. Serve the steaming hot turkey breasts with cranberry sauce,

149. Chicken and Grape Tomatoes

Preparation Time: 35 minutes
Servings: 2

Nutrition Values:
Calories: 407
Carbohydrate: 11g
Protein: 32g
Fat: 25g
Sugar: 9g
Sodium: 0.26g

Ingredients

- ⅔ pound boneless; skinless chicken breast
- 3 cups of cold water
- 1/2 tsp salt
- 1 tbsp. Dijon mustard
- 1 tbsp. honey
- 1 tbsp. balsamic vinegar
- 3 cloves garlic; finely minced
- 3 tbsp. olive oil
- Grape tomatoes; cut in half
- Field greens,

Directions:

1. Take a large bowl and put two cups of water and the chicken pieces into it. Let it refrigerate for 45 minutes,
2. Pour 1 cup of water into the instant pot and place a trivet over it.
3. Place the chicken pieces on the trivet and select *Manual* function to set high pressure for 5 minutes,
4. After it beeps sound; release the steam naturally then let the chicken stay for 5 minutes,
5. Meanwhile; put the Dijon mustard, olive oil, garlic, balsamic vinegar and honey into a bowl and mix them all together.
6. Slice the chicken and add the field greens and tomatoes, Pour the honey mixture over the chicken and serve.

150. Delightful Chicken with Lettuce Wrap

Preparation Time: 25 minutes
Servings: 4

Nutrition Values:
Calories: 564
Carbohydrate: 6.2g
Protein: 99.2g
Fat: 11.9g
Sugar: 4.3g
Sodium: 0.88g

Ingredients

- 1 large boneless; skinless chicken breast
- 1 celery stalk
- 1 clove garlic
- 1/2 cup buffalo wing sauce
- 1/2 cup shredded carrots
- 1 medium onion; chopped.
- 2 cups chicken broth
- large lettuce leaves

Directions:

1. Put chopped onions, minced garlic, chicken broth, buffalo wing sauce and chicken into the inner pot of the pressure cooker.
2. Cover with the cooker lid and lock it.
3. Select the *poultry* function. Do not change the pressure and time settings,
4. Wait for the completion beep. Then use the *Natural Release* method to vent the steam.
5. Then use the *Quick Release* function to release the remaining pressure,
6. Shred the chicken while still in the pot using two forks,
7. Mix the chicken well with all the other ingredients,
8. Pour the chicken and sauce over the lettuce leaves, Garnish the dish with the shredded carrots and chopped celery then serve.

151. Turkey Noodle Soup Recipe

Preparation Time: 30 minutes
Servings: 8

Nutrition Values:

Calories: 458
Carbohydrate: 9.4g
Protein: 76.7g
Fat: 11.6g
Sugar: 2.7g
Sodium: 0.67g

Ingredients

Broth:
- 1 cup shredded turkey
- 1 turkey carcass left over from a carved turkey
- 14 cups water
- 1 large onion; peeled
- 3 carrots; peeled and cleaned
- 2 stalks celery; washed
- Salt and pepper to taste

Soup:
- 3 cups turkey meat; chopped, white or dark
- 8 oz. egg noodles (cooked)
- Scallions; chopped
- Salt and pepper to taste

Directions:

1. Put the, water, onion, celery sticks, carrots, salt, pepper and turkey pieces into the instant pot. Secure the lid and select the *Soup* function.
2. Let the mixture cook until the cooker beeps, Release the steam using *Natural Release*.
3. Strain the turkey broth to separate the liquid from the solid.
4. Pour the broth back into the pot.
5. Add the shredded turkey carrots and the celery. Select the *Sauté* function. Allow the soup to boil.
6. Add the precooked noodles, Cook for 1 more minute then serve with scallions garnishing.

152. Delightful Chicken Garlic

Preparation Time: 25 minutes
Servings: 6

Nutrition Values:

Calories: 925
Carbohydrate: 16.2g
Protein: 53.7g
Fat: 9.1g
Sugar: 0.9g
Sodium: 0.77g

Ingredients

- 6 bone-in chicken thighs
- 1 tbsp. olive oil
- 1 tbsp. butter
- 40 peeled garlic cloves
- 2 thyme sprigs
- 1/4 cup dry white wine
- 1/4 cup chicken broth
- Chopped parsley leaves (garnish)
- 1 ½ tsp. kosher salt
- 1/2 tsp. ground black pepper

Directions:

1. Select the *Sauté* function on your instant pot. After 5 minutes, pour in the oil.
2. Season the chicken thighs with salt and pepper then put them into the oil.
3. Let the chicken cook on each side for 3 minutes until it turns golden brown.
4. Remove the chicken from the pot then add garlic and thyme to it.
5. Let it cook for one minute with occasional stirring. Then add the broth and the wine to the pot.
6. Put the chicken back in the pot and secure the lid.
7. Use *Manual* settings at high pressure and 15 minutes cooking time,
8. When it's done; let it stay for 5 minutes then use the *Natural Release* to vent the steam. Serve it with parsley sprinkled on top.

153. Chicken and Black Beans

Preparation Time: 16 minutes

Servings: 6

Nutrition Values:

Calories: 447
Carbohydrate: 15.2g
Protein: 66.2g
Fat: 11.7g
Sugar: 3.9g
Sodium: 0.18g

Ingredients

- 1 pound boneless; skinless chicken breasts
- 1 can organic black beans drained and rinsed
- 1 cup jasmine rice (uncooked)
- 2 tsp. sea salt.
- 1/2 tsp. ground black pepper
- 2 tbsp. butter.
- 1/2 cup water
- 1/2 lime; juiced
- 1 small onion chopped.
- 4 cups diced tomatoes with juice
- 1 tbsp. chipotle peppers

Directions:

1. Put the chicken, tomatoes, peppers, water, rice, salt, lemon juice, butter and onion in your electric cooker pot.
2. Use *Manual* settings and adjust pressure to high for 6 minutes,
3. Let it cook until the cooker beeps,
4. Use the *Quick release* pressure to vent the steam.
5. Add black beans to the chicken then stir well.
6. Add salt and pepper to taste, Serve with shredded cheese and sour cream on top.

.154. Ranch Bacon Chicken

Servings: 4
Cooking Time: 15 minutes

Ingredients:

- 1 cup cheddar cheese, shredded
- ½ cup water
- 8 oz cream cheese
- 1 packet ranch seasoning
- 2 lbs chicken breast, boneless
- 6 bacon slices, cooked and chopped

Directions:

1. Add cream cheese and chicken into the instant pot.
2. Sprinkle ranch seasoning on top of chicken. Add water.
3. Seal pot with lid and cook on high pressure for 15 minutes.
4. Release pressure using quick release method than open the lid.
5. Remove chicken from pot and shred using a fork.
6. Return shredded chicken to the pot. Add bacon and cheese and stir well.
7. Serve and enjoy.

Nutrition Value:

Calories: 724; Carbohydrates: 2.3g; Protein: 70g; Fat: 46.7g; Sugar: 0.3g; Sodium: 1118mg

155. Shredded Chicken with Mayo Sauce

Preparation Time: 17 minutes
Servings: 2

Ingredients:

- 1/2 lb. boneless chicken breast
- 1/2 teaspoon cumin
- 1/4 teaspoon garlic powder
- 1/2 teaspoon grated orange zest
- 1/4 cup orange juice
- 2 tablespoons chicken broth
- 3 teaspoons minced' garlic
- 2 tablespoons chopped' onion
- 1 bay leaf
- 2 tablespoons mayonnaise
- 1 tablespoon tomato chili sauce
- 1/4 teaspoon chili powder
- 1/4 teaspoon oregano
- 1/4 teaspoon salt
- 1/4 teaspoon pepper
- 1/4 teaspoon salt

Directions:

1. Place boneless chicken breast in the inner pot of an Instant Pot then add cumin, chili powder, oregano, salt, pepper, grated orange zest, minced' garlic, chopped' onion and bay leaf
2. Pour chicken broth and orange juice over the chicken then close the Instant Pot with the lid. Seal the Instant Pot properly and close the steam valve
3. Select *Chicken* setting on the Instant Pot and cook the chicken on high. Set the time to 12 minutes.
4. Meanwhile, combine mayonnaise with tomato chili sauce, salt and garlic powder. Stir until incorporated then set aside
5. Once the chicken is done, naturally release the Instant Pot and open the lid
6. Take the chicken out of the Instant Pot then place on a flat surface. Leave the liquid in the Instant Pot
7. Using a fork shred the chicken then place in the Instant Pot. Stir the shredded chicken until completely coated with the liquid
8. Transfer the shredded chicken together with the liquid to a serving dish then drizzle mayonnaise mixture on top

Nutrition Value:

Calories: 352; Net Carbs: 7g; Total Fat: 24.7g; Protein: 26.1g; Carbs: 7.8g;

156. Greek Style Turkey Recipe

Preparation Time: 10 minutes
Servings: 3

Ingredients:

- 1 sliced turkey breast
- 1/2 minced Poblano pepper
- 1/2 teaspoon chili flakes
- 3 tablespoon sliced olives
- 1/2 cup diced tomatoes
- 1/2 cup crumbled feta cheese
- 2 tablespoon lemon juice
- 1 cup water
- 2 tablespoon olive oil
- 3 minced garlic cloves
- Rosemary
- Basil
- Chopped parsley
- Salt and pepper to taste

Directions:

1. Take a large bowl and put the olive oil, Poblano pepper, garlic, lemon juice, salt, chili flakes, rosemary, basil and pepper in it.
2. Mix all the Ingredients well then immerse the turkey in the mixture to marinate, Let it simmer in the marinade,
3. Cover the bowl with a plastic wrap and put it in a refrigerator for 3 hours,
4. Add water to the instant pot and place a trivet in it, Now place the turkey pieces on the trivet. Pour the marinade generously over the turkey.
5. Secure the cooker lid. Select the *Manual* function and set *HIGH* pressure for 50 minutes,
6. Release all the steam after the beep and remove the lid.
7. Top each piece with a tomato slice, sliced olives and cheese then grill them for 10 minutes in an oven. Garnish with fresh parsley and serve.

Nutrition Value:

Calories: 932, Fat: 32.2g, Carbs: 15.7g, Protein: 84.7g

157. Spicy Herbs Wrapped Chicken

Preparation Time: 22 minutes
Servings: 2

Ingredients:

- 1/2 lb. bone-in chicken
- 1/2 teaspoon turmeric
- 1 lemon grass
- 1 bay leaf
- 1/4 cup diced' red tomatoes
- 1/2 cup water
- 2 cloves garlic
- 2 shallots

- 2 red chilies
- 1/2 teaspoon cayenne pepper
- 1/4 teaspoon salt

Directions:
1. Place the garlic, shallots, red chilies, cayenne pepper, salt and turmeric in a food processor. Process until smooth
2. Transfer the smooth spice mixture to a bowl then add diced' red tomatoes to the bowl. Mix until just combined
3. Cut the chicken into medium pieces then rub with the spice mixture. Place the seasoned chicken on a sheet of aluminum foil then place lemon grass and bay leaf on top
4. Wrap the chicken with the aluminum foil then set aside
5. Pour water into the Instant Pot and place a trivet in it.
6. Place the wrapped chicken on the trivet then cover the Instant Pot properly. Close the steam valve
7. Select *Manual* setting on the Instant Pot and cook the chicken on high for 12 minutes.
8. Once it is done; naturally release the Instant Pot then open the lid.
9. Take the wrapped chicken out of the Instant Pot and let it sit for a few minutes or until warm
10. Unwrap the steamed chicken then transfer to a serving dish. Serve and enjoy with a bowl of warm white rice

Nutrition Value:
Calories: 276; Net Carbs: 6.8 g; Total Fat: 17.4g; Protein: 21.4g; Carbs: 8g

158. Steamed Chicken Wings

Preparation Time: 16 minutes
Servings: 2

Ingredients:
- 1/2 lb. chicken wings
- 1/2 teaspoon brown sugar
- 1/2 teaspoon honey
- 1/2 teaspoon maple syrup
- 1/2 teaspoon Tabasco
- 1/4 teaspoon ketchup
- 1/4 teaspoon BBQ sauce
- 3/4 cup chicken broth
- 1/4 cup hot sauce
- 2 tablespoons butter
- 1/2 teaspoon molasses
- 1/4 teaspoon salt
- 1/4 teaspoon pepper

Directions:
1. Rub the chicken wings with salt and pepper then set aside. Place a trivet in an Instant Pot then pour chicken broth into the Instant Pot
2. Arrange the seasoned chicken wings on the trivet then cover the Instant Pot with the lid. Seal it properly.
3. Select *Manual* setting on the Instant Pot and cook the chicken on high for 8 minutes
4. Once it is done; quick release the Instant Pot then take the cooked chicken out of the Instant Pot. Remove the trivet.
5. Place the chicken wings on a plate then set aside. Add hot sauce, butter, molasses, brown sugar, honey, maple syrup, Tabasco, ketchup and BBQ sauce to the Instant Pot then stir well
6. Select *Sauté* menu on the Instant Pot then cook the sauce for approximately 2-3 minutes
7. Return the chicken wings back to the Instant Pot then stir until the chicken wings are coated with the sauce.
8. Transfer the chicken wings together with the sauce to a serving dish then serve

Nutrition Value:
Calories: 338; Net Carbs: 5.8g; Total Fat: 24.4g; Protein: 23.1g; Carbs: 6g;

159. Instant Honey Chicken

Preparation Time: 35 minutes
Servings: 3

Ingredients:
- 2-pounds boneless chicken thighs; fresh

or frozen
- 1/4 cup ghee
- 1/4 cup honey
- 3 tablespoons tamari
- 3 tablespoons ketchup
- 2 teaspoons garlic powder
- 1 ½ teaspoons sea salt
- 1/2 teaspoon black pepper

Directions:
1. Place your instant pot on a flat kitchen surface', plug it and turn it on. Open the lid and one by one add the mentioned ingredients in the pot. Carefully close its lid and firmly lock it. Then after, seal the valve too.
2. To start making the recipe, press *Manual* button. Now you have to set cooking time', set the timer for 18 minutes for fresh chicken and 40 minutes if you are using frozen chicken. Allow the pot to cook the mixture until the timer goes off.
3. Turn off the pot and press *Cancel.* Allow the built up pressure to vent out naturally', it will take 8-10 minutes to completely release inside pressure.
4. Open its lid and transfer the cooked mixture into serving container/containers. Serve warm with vegetables and rice.

Nutrition Value:
Calories 544; Fat: 22g; Carbohydrates: 48.2g; Fiber: –4g; Protein 36.2g

160. Sweet Brown Chicken

Preparation Time: 5 hours
Servings: 2

Ingredients:
- 1/2 lb. chicken wings
- 1¼ teaspoons brown sugar
- 1/2 cup water
- 1 teaspoon minced' garlic
- 1/4 teaspoon salt
- 1/4 teaspoon pepper

Directions:
1. Rub the chicken wings with minced' garlic, salt and pepper then place in the inner pot of an Instant Pot.
2. Pour water into the Instant Pot and sprinkle brown sugar over the chicken
3. Cover the Instant Pot with the lid and seal it properly. Select *Slow Cooker* setting on the Instant Pot and set the time to 5 hours. Adjust the temperature on low and ensure that the pressure valve is in the *Venting* position
4. Once the chicken is done, naturally release the Instant Pot then open the lid. Transfer the cooked chicken to a serving dish then serve. Enjoy!

Nutrition Value:
Calories: 276; Net Carbs: 6.5g; Total Fat: 18g; Protein: 21.1g; Carbs: 6.5g;

161. California Style Chicken

Preparation Time: 25 minutes
Servings: 3

Ingredients:
- 3 chicken breast halves; boneless and skinless
- 1/2 lemon; thinly sliced
- 1/2 cup white wine
- 1/4 cup parsley; chopped
- 2 tablespoons olive oil
- 1 cup chicken broth
- 1 teaspoon rosemary
- 2 garlic cloves; peeled and sliced
- Salt and Pepper to taste

Directions:
1. Add oil to Instant Pot and press "Sauté" button (*Normal* preset), wait till you see Hot on the display.
2. Add chicken breasts, cook for 6-7 minutes both sides with the lid open until all sides are browned.
3. Season the chicken with rosemary and add garlic. Press *Cancel* button.
4. Mix wine, broth and parsley in a bowl. Add the mixture to the pot.

5. Close the lid and turn the vent to *Sealed*. Press *Pressure Cook* (Manual) button, use *+* or *-* button to set the timer for 8 minutes. Use *Pressure level* button to set Pressure to *HIGH*.
6. Once the timer is up; press *Cancel* button and turn the steam release handle to "Venting" position for quick release, until the float valve drops down. Open the lid; Put lemon slices on top before serving.

Nutrition Value:
Calories: 192 g; Total Fat: 27.7 g; Total Carbohydrate: 1.9 g; Protein: 14.4

162. Tangy and Spicy Honey Chicken

Preparation Time: 20 minutes
Servings: 4

Ingredients:

- 4 chicken breasts
- 3 tablespoon honey
- 1/4 cup soy sauce
- 1 teaspoon Worcestershire sauce
- 1/2 sliced onion
- 1 tablespoon sriracha sauce
- 2 green onions
- 1 tablespoon sesame seeds
- 2 tablespoon cornstarch
- 1 tablespoon brown sugar
- 1 tablespoon minced garlic
- 1 ½ tablespoon minced ginger

Directions:

1. Before you start cooking, you should cut the chicken breasts into bite–size chunks.
2. The onions should be diced into chunks as well.
3. The chicken and onions should be put inside the Mini Instant Pot pressure cooker.
4. Now take a bowl and mix all the other ingredients except the cornstarch. Pour the mixture on the chicken and cover it with the marinade.
5. Close the lid of the steam valve and set it to Manual cooking in High Pressure for 4 minutes.
6. Once the cooking time is over; you need to do a quick release of the steam by carefully lifting the lid.
7. Take another bowl and add the hot sauce along with the cornstarch and whisk it quickly before putting it inside the pot.
8. Now turn on the Sauté function of the Instant Pot, switch on the normal mode; and allow everything to bubble for a few minutes.
9. Allow the chicken to sit for a few minutes; the sauce will thicken by now.
10. The spicy honey chicken is ready to be served with plain rice.
11. This is a good quick fix if you are really hungry and do not want to go for an elaborate cooking process.

Nutrition Value:
Calories: 155, Fat: 2g, Carbs: 15g, Protein: 17g

163. Chicken Curry with Zucchinis

Preparation Time: 18 minutes
Servings: 2

Ingredients:

- 1/2 lb. boneless chicken breast
- 1/4 cup chopped' zucchinis
- 2 tablespoons chopped' onion
- 2 teaspoons minced' garlic
- 1 teaspoon curry powder
- 1/4 teaspoon brown sugar
- 1/2 cup water
- 1/4 cup pineapple chunks
- 1/4 teaspoon turmeric
- 1/4 teaspoon ginger
- 1/4 teaspoon salt
- 1/4 teaspoon pepper

Directions:

1. Cut the boneless chicken breast into cubes then place in a bowl. Rub the chicken with minced' garlic, curry

powder, turmeric, ginger, salt, pepper and brown sugar then place in the inner pot of an Instant Pot
2. Sprinkle chopped' onion and pineapple chunks over the chicken then pour water into the Instant Pot
3. Cover the Instant Pot with the lid then seal it properly. Close the steam valve
4. Select *Manual* setting on the Instant Pot then cook the chicken on high. Set the time to 10 minutes.
5. Once it is done; naturally release the Instant Pot then open the lid
6. Add chopped' zucchinis to the Instant Pot and stir until just wilted. Transfer the chicken curry to a serving dish then serve with a bowl of brown rice

Nutrition Value:

Calories: 243; Net Carbs: 5.3g; Total Fat: 8.7g; Protein: 33.6g; Carbs: 6.5g;

164. Chicken Thighs with Rice

Preparation Time: 18 minutes
Servings: 2

Ingredients:

- 2 skinless chicken thighs
- 3/4 cup long–grain white rice
- 1/2 diced small onion
- 1 tablespoon Jamaican jerk seasoning
- 2 teaspoons olive oil
- 1 minced garlic clove
- 1 cup chicken broth

Directions:

1. Begin with rinsing the rice; you will know that the rice is rinsed properly when the water runs clear. Drain the rice and keep it aside.
2. Turn the Sauté function in the Mini Instant Pot. Once the display reads Hot, you can add the olive oil.
3. Start by stirring the onions, cook it for a few minutes and stir them from time to time. You know that the onions are done once they turn translucent.
4. Keep on adding the other ingredients such as garlic; keep stirring for about 20 seconds, Pour the jerk seasoning as well; continue to stir.
5. Now add the chicken broth. Bring the concoction to simmer and then add the rice. Ensure that all the ingredients are fully submerged in the chicken broth.
6. Place the chicken thighs on the broth mixture; they will shrink when they are cooked. Let the thighs sink in the broth as well.
7. Secure the lid on the pot and lock it. Switch the Steam Release knob to Sealing position.
8. Press Pressure or the Manual mode and then choose 7 minutes.
9. Once the cooking is done, you should allow the pot to sit for about 5 minutes.
10. You can now turn the Steam Release knob to Venting position. The remaining steam will be released.
11. Once the pin in the lid drops, you can safely open the lid and simply remove the chicken thighs.
12. You can either serve the thighs with some rice in a bowl or shred the chicken and mix it with the rice. Give one last stir and the rice is ready to be served.
13. This is one of the guilt–free fuss–free meals which you can enjoy at both lunch and dinner.

Nutrition Value:

Calories: 283, Fat: 2.5g, Carbs: 47g, Protein: 22g

165. Chipotle Salsa Chicken

Preparation Time: 4 hours
Servings: 2

Ingredients:

- 1/2 lb. chicken thighs
- 1 teaspoon avocado oil
- 1/4 cup chipotle salsa
- 1/4 teaspoon salt
- 1/4 teaspoon pepper

Directions:

1. Brush the inner pot of an Instant Pot with avocado oil. Rub the chicken thighs

with salt and pepper then place in the Instant Pot
2. Top the chicken thighs with chipotle salsa then cover the Instant Pot properly
3. Select *Slow Cooker* setting on the Instant Pot and set the time to 4 hours. Adjust the temperature on high and ensure that the pressure valve is in the *Venting* position
4. Once the Instant Pot beeps naturally release the Instant Pot and open the lid. Transfer the cooked chicken to a serving dish

Nutrition Value:
Calories: 239; Net Carbs: 4.1g; Total Fat: 8.7g; Protein: 32.9g; Carbs: 4.3g;

166. Garlic Chicken Thighs

Preparation Time: 35 minutes
Servings: 2

Ingredients:
- 4 chicken thighs
- 3/4 cup ketchup
- 3/4 cup soy sauce
- 1/2 cup water or chicken stock
- 1 teaspoon fresh basil; chopped
- 1/2 teaspoon garlic cloves; minced
- 1 teaspoon chili garlic sauce
- 1 tablespoon arrowroot starch; dissolved in 2 tablespoons of water

Directions:
1. Add oil to Instant Pot and press *Sauté* button (*Normal* preset), wait till you see Hot on the display.
2. Add chicken thighs, cook for 6-7 minutes both sides with the lid open until all sides are browned. Press *Cancel* button.
3. Add soy sauce, chili sauce, garlic, water or stock and organic ketchup to the pot. Stir the ingredients and close the lid, turn the vent to *Sealed*.
4. Press *Pressure Cook* (Manual) button, use *+* or *-* button to set the timer for 10 minutes. Use *Pressure level* button to set Pressure to *HIGH*.

5. Once the timer is up; press *Cancel* button and turn the steam release handle to "Venting" position for quick release, until the float valve drops down.
6. Open the lid; Transfer the meat to a plate. Add arrowroot starch mixture to the pot. Press "Sauté" button, adjust to *Less* preset and stir until the sauce thickens. Pour the sauce over the meat before serving.

Nutrition Value:
Calories: 532 g; Total Fat: 55.4 g; Total Carbohydrate: 15.2 g; Protein: 30.2

167. BBQ Chicken

Preparation Time: 20 minutes
Servings: 2

Ingredients:
- 2-pounds. chicken wings
- 1/2 cup barbecue sauce
- 1-cup water
- 1/2 cup chopped onion
- 2 ½ tablespoons raw honey
- 1/2 teaspoon pepper
- 1/4 teaspoon salt

Directions:
1. In a bowl, mix the barbecue sauce with water, raw honey, salt and pepper. Switch on the pot after placing it on a clean and dry platform.
2. Open the pot lid and place the chicken and sauce in the cooking pot area. Give the ingredients a little stir. Close the pot by closing the top lid. Also, ensure to seal the valve.
3. Press *Manual* cooking function and set cooking time to 10 minutes. It will start cooking after a few minutes. Let the pot mix cook under pressure until the timer reads zero.
4. Press *Cancel* cooking function and press *Quick release* setting.
5. Open the pot, preheat a pan over medium heat; add the chicken mix to the pan. Bring to simmer and stir until the barbecue sauce is thickened. Serve warm!

Nutrition Value:

Calories 334; Fat: 10g; Carbohydrates: 45g; Fiber: 1.5g; Protein 10.5g

168. Lemongrass Coconut Chicken

Preparation Time: 20 minutes
Servings: 2

Ingredients:

- 4 chicken drumsticks
- 1 teaspoon ginger
- 1/2 teaspoon coconut oil
- 3/4 cup coconut milk
- 2 teaspoons minced garlic
- 3 teaspoons fish sauce
- 1/4 teaspoon pepper
- 1 tablespoon lemon juice
- 1/4 cup chopped onion
- 1 lemongrass

Directions:

1. Chop the lemongrass and add in a blender. Add the garlic, ginger, fish sauce, pepper and lemon juice; combine well.
2. Add the coconut milk. Blend until smooth and incorporated. Switch on the pot after placing it on a clean and dry platform. Press *Sauté* cooking function.
3. Open the lid; add the oil and onions in the pot; cook for 2 minutes to cook well and soften.
4. Add the drumsticks to the pot; top with the coconut mixture over the chicken. Close the pot by closing the top lid. Also, ensure to seal the valve.
5. Press *Manual* cooking function and set cooking time to 10 minutes. It will start cooking after a few minutes. Let the pot mix cook under pressure until the timer reads zero.
6. Press *Cancel* cooking function and press *Natural release* setting.
7. It will take 8-10 minutes for natural pressure release. Open the pot and serve warm.

Nutrition Value:

Calories: 342; Fat: 28.5g; Carbohydrates: 9.5g; Fiber: 2.5g; Protein 13g

169. Turkey Stacks

Preparation Time: 35 minutes
Servings: 4

Ingredients:

- 1–pound ground turkey
- 1 sliced tomato
- 4 slices turkey bacon
- 4 lettuce leaves
- 1/4 teaspoon cayenne pepper
- 1 teaspoon Herbs de Provence
- 1 tablespoon olive oil
- 4 slices Swiss cheese
- 4 eggs
- Salt and pepper to taste

Directions:

1. Put the ground turkey, cayenne pepper, salt, herbs de Provence and pepper into a bowl and mix all the Ingredients well.
2. Make 4 burger patties using this mixture. To the instant pot, add olive oil and select the *Sauté* function. Carefully place the turkey patties in the pot.
3. Cook them from both sides until they turn golden brown, Remove the patties from the pot and put them aside,
4. Add 1 cup of water to the pot and place the trivet in it.
5. Place the fried patties on the trivet and cover each one with a cheese slice, Place the turkey bacon strips on the trivet too.
6. Secure the lid and select *Manual* function, setting at *HIGH* pressure for 5 minutes,
7. When it beeps; release the steam completely and remove the lid. To serve; take the lettuce leaves and stack them up with a tomato slice, a turkey patty, bacon and fried egg on top.

Nutrition Value:

Calories: 720, Fat: 18.9g, Carbs: 1.7g, Protein: 122.3g

170. Quick Dumplings

Preparation Time: 20 minutes
Servings: 4

Ingredients:

- 1 ½–pound cubed chicken breast
- 16–ounce refrigerated biscuits
- 1 teaspoon olive oil
- 1 cup frozen peas
- 2 teaspoon oregano
- 1 teaspoon onion powder
- 1 teaspoon basil
- 1 cup water
- 2 cup chicken broth
- 2 minced garlic cloves
- 1 cup chopped carrots
- 1/2 teaspoon salt
- 1/2 teaspoon pepper

Directions:

1. Press the biscuits to flatten them then cut them into 2–inch strips with a sharp knife,
2. Put the olive oil, onion powder, oregano, chicken, garlic, salt, pepper and basil into the pot and mix them well.
3. Select the *Sauté* function on your pressure cooker and allow it to cook until the chicken turns brown.
4. Cancel the *Sauté* function when the cooking is finished.
5. Add the water, peas, carrots and chicken broth to the pot. Add the biscuits then stir well.
6. Cover with the lid and lock it, Select the *Manual* function and set the timer for 5 minutes,
7. When it beeps; use the *Natural Release* for 10 minutes to vent all steam.
8. Press *Cancel* to turn the cooker off then remove the lid. Serve the cooked chicken in a bowl.

Nutrition Value:
Calories: 610, Fat: 12.1g, Carbs: 13.6g, Protein: 100.5g

171. Garlic Chicken

Preparation Time: 18 minutes
Servings: 2

Ingredients:

- 3/4-pound chopped boneless chicken
- 1-cup low sodium chicken broth
- 2 tablespoons minced garlic
- 1 ½ teaspoons olive oil
- 1 bay leaf
- 1 tablespoon chopped rosemary
- 2 tablespoons chopped celery
- 1/2 cup chopped onion
- 1/4 teaspoon thyme
- 1/2 teaspoon salt
- 1/2 teaspoon pepper

Directions:

- Switch on the pot after placing it on a clean and dry platform. Press *Sauté* cooking function.
- Open the lid; add the oil, garlic and onions in the pot; cook for 2 minutes to cook well and turn lightly golden.
- Add chicken cubes to the pot. Mix the salt, pepper, bay leaf, chopped rosemary and thyme. Close the pot by closing the top lid. Also, ensure to seal the valve.
- Press *Manual* cooking function and set cooking time to 10 minutes. It will start cooking after a few minutes. Let the pot mix cook under pressure until the timer reads zero.
- Press *Cancel* cooking function and press *Natural release* setting.
- It will take 8-10 minutes for natural pressure release. Open the instant pot; topped with some celery and serve warm.

Nutrition Value:
Calories: 176; Fat: 8g; Carbohydrates: 7.5g; Fiber: 2g; Protein 17g

172. Butter Chicken

Preparation Time: 35 minutes
Servings: 6

Ingredients:

- 2–pound skinless chicken breasts
- 1 teaspoon ground turmeric
- 1 teaspoon ground coriander
- 1 can diced tomatoes
- 1 chopped onion
- 1/2 cup coconut milk
- 1 tablespoon Garam masala
- 4 tablespoon Unsalted butter
- 3 chopped garlic cloves
- 1 chopped fresh ginger
- 1 teaspoon kosher salt

Directions:

1. Turn on the Sauté function in the Pressure Cooker in the Mini Instant Pot and melt the butter first. Use 2 tablespoons of butter.
2. Start adding the garlic, onion; and gingers along with the spices and sauté them by stirring them occasionally.
3. The onions will start to brown in about 4 minutes. Now you can add the spices like the garam masala, salt; and turmeric and cook them until they become fragrant.
4. Now add the tomatoes; their juices will start to come out. Combine the tomatoes with the other ingredients. It is time to add the chicken breasts; cover the breasts with the sauce.
5. Seal the pressure cooker but please ensure that the vent is closed properly.
6. The cooker should be set to Manual mode in high temperature. The cooking time should be set for 10 minutes.
7. The pressure cooker will take about 10-12 minutes to come to the pressure mode.
8. The cooking time should not be more than 10 minutes. The cooker will release all the pressure in another 10 minutes.
9. Transfer the chicken breasts to a cutting board and let them cool down.
10. In the sauce, add the rest of the butter along with either coconut milk or heavy cream and transfer the sauce to make a fine puree. If required, you can reserve some of the additional sauce for later use.
11. The chicken should be cut into 1–inch pieces, returned to the sauce; and a gentle stir is required for the final touch.
12. You can serve this delicious dish with basmati rice; a healthier option can be brown rice, cauliflower rice, or quinoa.
13. Whatever is your preference, this finger–licking dish will definitely win the hearts of your guests.

Nutrition Value:

Calories: 537, Fat: 29.3g, Carbs: 14.5g, Protein: 54.2g

173. Instant Chicken Wings

Preparation Time: 30 minutes
Servings: 2

Ingredients:

- 1-pound. chicken wings
- 2 teaspoons minced garlic
- 2 tablespoons chopped onion
- 1 ½ tablespoons low sodium soy sauce
- 1/2 tablespoon rice wine
- 1/2 tablespoon sesame oil
- 1/2 teaspoon ginger
- 1 cup your choice of cola

Directions:

1. Switch on the pot after placing it on a clean and dry platform. Press *Sauté* cooking function.
2. Open the lid; add the oil, garlic and onions in the pot; cook for 2 minutes to cook well and soften.
3. Add the chicken wings and sauté until brown. Mix in the cola, soy sauce and rice wine then stir well. Close the pot by closing the top lid. Also, ensure to seal the valve.
4. Press *Manual* cooking function and set cooking time to 20 minutes. It will start cooking after a few minutes. Let the pot mix cook under pressure until the timer reads zero.
5. Press *Cancel* cooking function and press *Natural release* setting.

6. It will take 8-10 minutes for natural pressure release. Open the pot and serve warm.

Nutrition Value:
Calories: 228; Fat: 8.5g; Carbohydrates: 32g; Fiber: 0.5g; Protein 5.5g

174. Apple Turkey Curry Recipe

Preparation Time: 30 minutes
Servings: 3

Ingredients:

- 1 pound. cooked turkey breasts; chopped
- 1 apple; cored and finely sliced
- 1/2 cup full fat yogurt
- 1 teaspoon Curry powder
- 2 garlic cloves; minced
- 2 tablespoons lemon juice
- 1 cup water
- 2 tablespoons olive oil
- 1 cup onion; sliced
- Salt and Pepper to taste

Directions:

1. Add oil to Instant Pot and press "Sauté" button (*Normal* preset), wait till you see Hot on the display.
2. Add onion, sauté until golden brown. Add garlic, sauté for 20 more seconds. Add Curry powder.
3. Add apple, turkey, water, salt and pepper. Mix well. Close the lid and turn the vent to "Sealed". Press *Pressure Cook* (Manual) button, use *+* or *-* button to set the timer for 12 minutes. Use *Pressure level* button to set Pressure to *HIGH*.
4. Once the timer is up; press *Cancel* button and turn the steam release handle to "Venting" position for quick release, until the float valve drops down. Open the lid; Add yogurt, sprinkle with lemon juice and mix well.
5. Press "Sauté" button and adjust to *Less* preset, cook for 5 minutes stirring well.

Nutrition Value:
Calories: 320 g; Total Fat: 28 g; Total Carbohydrate: 5 g; Protein: 18

175. Chicken in Mushroom Sauce

Preparation Time: 25 minutes
Servings: 4

Ingredients:

- 8–ounce sliced cremini mushrooms
- 1 whole chicken
- 1/2 teaspoon black pepper
- 1 cup low–sodium chicken broth
- 2 tablespoon all–purpose flour
- 2 teaspoon kosher salt
- 1 sliced yellow onion
- 1 teaspoon paprika
- 2 tablespoon avocado oil
- 1 chopped garlic clove
- 1/2 teaspoon dried oregano
- 1/2 teaspoon dried thyme
- 1 tablespoon tomato paste

Directions:

1. Take a dry chicken towel and pat the chicken dry. You need to tuck the wings of the chicken under so that they remain flat.
2. As for the drumsticks, you can tie them with kitchen string. Spread the seasoning of salt, pepper; and paprika on the chicken.
3. Turn on the Sauté function of the Mini Instant Pot. Let the oil heat for about 2 minutes.
4. The center of the Pot should be coated well with oil. Use tongs to place the chicken inside the pot with the breast–side up.
5. The chicken should be seared without any interruptions; the chicken will turn brown in 5 minutes. Do not worry if some of the chicken skin sticks to the bottom of the pan.
6. You can now flip the chicken to the breast side and sear it for 5 minutes or

until it turns brown. Take the chicken out on the plate and keep it aside.

7. In the Mini Pot, add the mushrooms, onions; and garlic and sauté them until the onion is soft and the mushrooms have wilted completely.
8. Pour the tomato paste along with oregano and thyme and sauté for another 2 minutes until you have a flavorful concoction.
9. You can now add the broth and stir it with a wooden spoon. If there are brown bits at the bottom of the pot, you can easily scrape it with the wooden spoon.
10. Put the trivet in the Instant Pot just on the top of mushrooms and onions. Use the tongs to place the chicken breast–side up on the trivet.
11. Safely place the lid and set the Pressure Release to Sealing position.
12. Select the Poultry button and set the cooking time for 20 minutes at *HIGH* pressure.
13. You need to do a quick release by moving the Pressure Release to Venting position. Use heat–resistant mittens to take out the chicken with the trivet.
14. Put the chicken on the carving board. Strain the liquid through a fine–mesh strainer in a fat–separator bowl. Keep the onions and mushrooms by the side.
15. The liquid minus the fat should be poured back into the Instant Pot; discard the remaining fat. Scoop the fat with a ladle and discard.
16. Select the Sauté function in the Mini Instant Pot and let the sauce boil until it thickens. It will be done within a minute.
17. Taste the sauce and adjust the salt as required, Carve the chicken and arrange it on a platter.
18. Pour the sauce generously on the top and you are ready for a nice cozy meal with your entire family.

Nutrition Value:

Calories: 370, Fat: 21g, Carbs: 1.4g, Protein: 50.3g

176. Tasty Cajun Chicken with Rice

Preparation Time: 30 minutes
Servings: 5

Ingredients:

- 1–pound chicken breast
- 1.5 cup white rice
- 1.75 cup chicken broth
- 1 tablespoon olive oil
- 1 tablespoon Cajun seasoning
- 1 diced bell pepper
- 1 tablespoon tomato paste
- 1 minced garlic clove
- 1 diced onion

Directions:

1. You should start by rinsing the rice; you will know that the rice is ready when the water runs clear. It will help you to remove the starch from the rice which might get stuck at the bottom of the Mini Instant Pot.
2. To make the chicken breasts thinner, you should cut them in half lengthwise. Take the Cajun seasoning and spread it lavishly on both sides.
3. Turn on the Sauté function of the Mini Instant Pot and soften both the onion and garlic.
4. If there are brown bits stuck at the bottom, deglaze with a few spoons of water. Remember if anything remains stuck at the bottom, it will prevent the Mini Pot from pressurizing properly.
5. Add the rice, bell peppers; and tomato paste along with 1 teaspoon of Cajun seasoning.
6. The Cajun seasoning is optional and should be only added if you want more heat and more paste. Stir everything until the ingredients are mixed well.
7. Now you can pour the chicken broth over the rice and arrange the chicken breasts on the top.
8. Close the lid of the Mini Instant Pot and turn the valve to Sealing position. Cook

everything in *HIGH* pressure on Manual mode for 7-8 minutes.
9. Naturally release pressure for 5 minutes; the remaining pressure can be released by turning the *Venting* mode.
10. Carefully open the lid once the pin drops. Shred the chicken and combine it with rice. Put more salt or pepper if required.
11. Serve it in a bowl with a generous topping of freshly chopped cilantro and just a hint of lime.

Nutrition Value:
Calories: 473, Fat: 7.4g, Carbs: 64.9g, Protein: 33.4g

177. Cheesy Chicken Bowl

Preparation Time: 19 minutes
Servings: 2

Ingredients:

- 1½ teaspoons olive oil
- 1/2 teaspoon cumin
- 1/2 cup chicken broth
- 1/2 lb. boneless chicken breast
- 3 tablespoons chopped' onion
- 1 teaspoon minced' garlic
- 1½ teaspoons chili powder
- 1/2 cup salsa
- 1/4 cup grated cheddar cheese
- 1/4 teaspoon pepper
- 1/4 teaspoon salt

Directions:

1. Pour olive oil into the inner pot of an Instant Pot then select *Sauté* menu. Stir in chopped' onion and minced' garlic then sauté until wilted and aromatic. Press the *Cancel* button
2. Cut the boneless chicken breast into small cubes then add to the Instant Pot
3. Season with chili powder, cumin, salt and pepper then pour chicken broth and salsa over the chicken. Stir well.
4. Close the Instant Pot with the lid then seal it properly. Close the steam valve.
5. Select *Manual* setting and cook the chicken on high. Set the time to 12 minutes
6. Once it is done; quick release the Instant Pot then open the lid
7. Sprinkle grated cheddar cheese over the chicken then stir quickly. Serve the cheesy chicken over two bowls of brown rice then enjoy immediately

Nutrition Value:
Calories: 241; Net Carbs: 5.6g; Total Fat: 10.6g; Protein: 31.4g; Carbs: 7.8g;

178. Sweet & Savory Adobo Chicken

Servings: 2
Cooking Time: 25 minutes

Ingredients:

- 3 chicken thighs, boneless
- 1 tbsp scallion, chopped
- 1 tbsp cilantro, chopped
- ½ cup water
- ½ cup chicken stock
- ½ tsp red chili flakes
- 2 tbsp sugar
- 2 tbsp white vinegar
- 5 tbsp soy sauce
- 2 garlic cloves, minced
- ½ onion, sliced
- Pepper
- Salt

Directions:

1. Season chicken with pepper and salt. Place chicken into the instant pot.
2. Add sliced onion on top of chicken.
3. In a small bowl, mix together soy sauce, stock, chili flakes, sugar, water, and vinegar. Pour to the instant pot.
4. Seal pot with lid and select poultry mode and set timer for 10 minutes.
5. Release pressure using quick release method than open the lid.
6. Remove chicken from pot and set the pot on sauté mode. Cook sauce on sauté mode until sauce thickens, about 15 minutes.

7. Return chicken to the pot and stir well.
8. Serve and enjoy.

Nutrition Value:

Calories: 505; Carbohydrates: 19.2g; Protein: 66.6g; Fat: 16.5g; Sugar: 14.2g; Sodium: 3296mg

179. Simple Shredded Chicken

Servings: 6
Cooking Time: 30 minutes

Ingredients:

- 2 chicken breasts, boneless and skinless
- 14.5 oz chicken broth
- ¼ tsp pepper
- ½ tsp salt

Directions:

1. Add all ingredients into the instant pot.
2. Seal pot with lid and cook on high pressure for 30 minutes.
3. Allow to release pressure naturally then open the lid.
4. Remove chicken from pot and shred using a fork.
5. Serve and enjoy.

Nutrition Value:

Calories: 104; Carbohydrates: 0.3g; Protein: 15.5g; Fat: 4g; Sugar: 0.2g; Sodium: 454mg

180. Perfect Mississippi Chicken

Servings: 6
Cooking Time: 8 minutes

Ingredients:

- 6 pepperoncini
- 2 tbsp brown gravy mix
- 2 tbsp ranch mix
- 1 cup pepperoncini juice
- 1 cup chicken stock
- 3 lbs chicken thighs, boneless

Directions:

1. Add all ingredients into the instant pot and stir well.
2. Seal pot with lid and cook on high pressure for 8 minutes.
3. Allow to release pressure naturally for 10 minutes then release using quick release method.
4. Remove chicken from pot and shred using a fork.
5. Return shredded chicken to the pot and stir well.
6. Serve and enjoy.

Nutrition Value:

Calories: 440; Carbohydrates: 17.1g; Protein: 65.9g; Fat: 17.1g; Sugar: 0.1g; Sodium: 1009mg

181. Orange Chicken

Servings: 6
Cooking Time: 15 minutes

Ingredients:

- 4 chicken breasts, boneless and cut into chunks
- 2 tsp cornstarch
- ¾ cup orange marmalade
- 2 tbsp soy sauce
- ¾ cup BBQ sauce

Directions:

1. Add chicken, soy sauce, and BBQ sauce into the instant pot and stir well.
2. Seal pot with lid and cook on high for 4 minutes.
3. Release pressure using quick release method than open the lid.
4. Remove ¼ cup sauce mixture from instant pot and mix with cornstarch in a bowl.
5. Pour cornstarch mixture into the instant pot and stir well.
6. Add marmalade and stir well to mix.
7. Set pot on sauté mode and sauté chicken until sauce thickens, about 5-6 minutes.
8. Stir well and serve.

Nutrition Value:

Calories: 336; Carbohydrates: 39.1g; Protein: 28.6 g; Fat: 7.3g; Sugar: 32.2g; Sodium: 756mg

182. Tasty Tamarind Chicken

Servings: 4

Cooking Time: 15 minutes

Ingredients:

- 2 lbs chicken breasts, skinless, boneless, and cut into pieces
- 1 tbsp arrowroot powder
- ½ cup tamarind paste
- ½ tsp salt
- 2 tbsp brown sugar
- 1 tbsp ketchup
- 1 tbsp vinegar
- 2 tbsp ginger, grated
- 2 garlic cloves, minced
- 3 tbsp olive oil
- ½ tsp salt

Directions:

1. Add oil into the instant pot and set the pot on sauté mode.
2. Add ginger and garlic and sauté for 30 seconds.
3. Add chicken and sauté for 3-4 minutes or until chicken is lightly brown.
4. In a small bowl, combine together tamarind paste, brown sugar, ketchup, vinegar, and salt and pour into the instant pot. Stir well.
5. Seal pot with lid and cook on high for 8 minutes.
6. Release pressure using quick release method than open the lid.
7. Remove ¼ cup sauce mixture from instant pot and combine with arrowroot powder in a small bowl. Pour into the pot and stir everything well.
8. Serve and enjoy.

Nutrition Value:

Calories: 599; Carbohydrates: 27.6g; Protein: 66.5g; Fat: 27.6g; Sugar: 14g; Sodium: 825mg

183. Flavors Chicken Thighs

Servings: 6
Cooking Time: 15 minutes

Ingredients:

- 6 chicken thighs, remove skin
- 1 cup water
- 2 tbsp olive oil
- 1 tsp smoked paprika
- 1 tsp garlic powder
- Pepper
- Salt

Directions:

1. Season chicken with paprika, garlic powder, pepper, and salt.
2. Add oil into the instant pot and set the pot on sauté mode.
3. Add chicken into the pot and sauté until lightly brown.
4. Remove chicken from pot.
5. Add water to the pot and stir well.
6. Place trivet into the pot. Place chicken on top of the trivet.
7. Seal pot with lid and cook on high for 10 minutes.
8. Allow to release pressure naturally then open the lid.
9. Serve and enjoy.

Nutrition Value:

Calories: 320; Carbohydrates: 0.6g; Protein: 42.4g; Fat: 15.5g; Sugar: 0.2g; Sodium: 154mg

184. Italian Creamy Chicken

Servings: 8
Cooking Time: 10 minutes

Ingredients:

- 2 lbs chicken breasts, skinless and boneless
- 8 oz cream cheese
- ¼ cup butter
- 14 oz can cream of chicken soup
- 0.5 oz dry Italian dressing mix
- 1 cup chicken stock

Directions:

1. Add stock to the instant pot.
2. Add cream of chicken soup, Italian dressing mix, and butter into the pot and stir well.
3. Seal pot with lid and cook on high for 10 minutes.
4. Release pressure using quick release

method than open the lid.
5. Add cream cheese and stir until cheese is melted
6. Serve and enjoy.

Nutrition Value:

Calories: 416; Carbohydrates: 5.5g; Protein: 36.3g; Fat: 27g; Sugar: 0.4g; Sodium: 738mg

186. Chicken Pasta

Servings: 4
Cooking Time: 8 minutes

Ingredients:

- 8 oz penne pasta, dry
- 1 lb chicken breasts, boneless and skinless, cut into bite-size pieces
- 3 tbsp fajita seasoning, divided into half
- 7 oz can tomatoes
- 4 garlic cloves, minced
- 1 onion, diced
- 1 cup chicken stock
- 2 bell peppers, seeded and diced
- 2 tbsp olive oil

Directions:

1. Add olive oil in instant pot and set the pot on sauté mode.
2. Add chicken and half fajita seasoning. Stir well and sauté until chicken looks like white.
3. Add garlic, bell pepper, onions, and remaining fajitas seasoning. Stir well and sauté for 2 minutes.
4. Add tomatoes, stock, and pasta in the pot. Stir well.
5. Seal pot with lid and cook on high for 6 minutes.
6. Release pressure using quick release method than open the lid.
7. Serve and enjoy.

Nutrition Value:

Calories: 510; Carbohydrates: 46.5g; Protein: 40.9g; Fat: 17g; Sugar: 6.1g; Sodium: 806mg

186. Potato Mustard Chicken

Servings: 4
Cooking Time: 15 minutes

Ingredients:

- 2 lb chicken thighs, boneless and skinless
- 3/4 cup chicken stock
- 4 tbsp lemon juice
- 2 tbsp Italian seasoning
- 3 tbsp Dijon mustard
- 2 lb potatoes, quartered
- 2 tbsp olive oil
- Pepper
- Salt

Directions:

1. Add olive oil into the instant pot and set the pot on sauté mode.
2. Season chicken with pepper and salt and place into the instant pot.
3. In a small bowl, mix together lemon juice, stock, and Dijon mustard stir well and pour over the chicken.
4. Add potatoes and Italian seasoning in the pot.
5. Seal pot with lid and cook on high for 15 minutes.
6. Release pressure using quick release method the open lid carefully.
7. Serve and enjoy.

Nutrition Value:

Calories: 682; Carbohydrates: 37.5g; Protein: 70.2g; Fat: 26.8g; Sugar: 3.8g; Sodium: 529mg

187. Chicken & Rice

Servings: 2
Cooking Time: 7 minutes

Ingredients:

- 2 chicken thighs, skinless and boneless
- 1 garlic clove, minced
- 1/2 small onion, diced
- 3/4 cup long grain rice, rinsed
- 2 tsp olive oil
- 1 cup chicken broth
- 1 tbsp jerk seasoning

Directions:

1. Add oil into the instant pot and set the instant pot on sauté mode.
2. Add onion and sauté for few minutes or until onion softens.
3. Add garlic and sauté for 10 seconds. Stir well.
4. Add jerk seasoning and stir well to combine.
5. Add rice and chicken broth and stir well. Add chicken.
6. Seal instant pot with lid and select pressure cook mode and set the timer for 7 minutes.
7. Allow to release pressure naturally for 5 minutes then release using quick release method than open the lid.
8. Stir well and serve.

Nutrition Value:
Calories: 599; Carbohydrates: 58.1g; Protein: 49.9g; Fat: 16.7g; Sugar: 1.2g; Sodium: 512mg

188. Herb Chicken Piccata

Servings: 4
Cooking Time: 10 minutes

Ingredients:

- 1 1/2 lbs chicken breasts, skinless and boneless
- 4 oz capers, drained
- 3/4 cup chicken stock
- 1 garlic clove, minced
- 1 tbsp olive oil
- 1 tsp dried basil
- 1 tsp dried oregano
- 1/4 cup lemon juice
- Pepper
- Salt

Directions:

1. Add olive oil into the instant pot and select sauté.
2. Season chicken with pepper and salt. Place chicken into the pot and sauté until lightly brown on all sides.
3. Remove chicken from pot and place on a plate.
4. Add garlic and sauté for a minute.
5. Add broth, basil, oregano, and lemon juice and stir well.
6. Return chicken into the pot and top with capers.
7. Seal pot with lid and select manual high pressure for 10 minutes.
8. Release pressure using quick release method than open the lid.
9. Serve and enjoy.

Nutrition Value:
Calories: 368; Carbohydrates: 2.4g; Protein: 50.2g; Fat: 16.6g; Sugar: 0.6g; Sodium: 1172mg

189. Sweet Mango Pineapple Chicken

Servings: 4
Cooking Time: 10 minutes

Ingredients:

- 3 chicken breasts, skinless and boneless
- 14 oz pineapple mango salsa
- 1 tsp red pepper flakes
- 1 cup pineapple, cubed
- 1 mango, peel and cube
- Pepper
- Salt

Directions:

1. Set instant pot on sauté mode.
2. Season chicken with pepper and salt.
3. Place chicken into the instant pot and sauté until brown.
4. Add remaining ingredients into the pot and stir well.
5. Seal pot with lid and cook on high pressure for 10 minutes.
6. Release pressure using quick release method than open the lid.
7. Serve and enjoy.

Nutrition Value:
Calories: 332; Carbohydrates: 32g; Protein: 32.6g; Fat: 8.6g; Sugar: 25.8g; Sodium: 134mg

MEAT

190. Cheesy Pork Bombs

Preparation Time: 20 minutes
Servings: 2

Ingredients:

- 1/2 lb. ground pork
- 2 tablespoons diced' onion
- 2 tablespoons fresh milk
- 2 tablespoons chopped' red chilies
- 1/4 cup Mozzarella cheese cubes
- 1 tablespoon flour
- 3/4 teaspoon Worcestershire sauce
- 1 egg white
- 1/4 teaspoon salt
- 1/4 teaspoon pepper

Directions:

- Combine ground pork with egg white, diced' onion, fresh milk, flour, Worcestershire sauce, salt and pepper.
- Mix well using your hand, shape the pork mixture into medium balls. Fill each ball with red chili and Mozzarella cubes. Set aside
- Pour water into the Instant Pot and place a trivet in it. Arrange the pork balls on the trivet then cover and seal the Instant Pot properly. Close the steam valve
- Select *Steam* setting on the Instant Pot and cook the pork balls on high for 15 minutes.
- Once it is done; naturally release the Instant Pot and open the lid
- Remove the pork balls from the Instant Pot and place on a serving dish. Let them cool.
- Serve and enjoy with any kind of sauce, as you desired

Nutrition Value:

Calories: 146; Net Carbs: 6.2g; Total Fat: 7.9g; Protein: 11.2g; Carbs: 7.3g;

191. Cheesy Pork Macaroni

Preparation Time: 25 minutes
Servings: 2

Ingredients:

- 1/4 lb. ground pork
- 1/4 cup grated cheddar
- 1/4 cup cooked macaroni
- 1 tablespoon olive oil
- 2 tablespoons diced' mushroom
- 2 eggs
- 2 teaspoons garlic powder
- 1/2 teaspoon pepper

Directions:

1. Combine the entire ingredients except cheese in a bowl then mix well. Transfer the mixture in a disposable aluminum pan then spread evenly
2. Sprinkle grated cheddar cheese on top then set aside. Pour water into the Instant Pot and place a trivet in it.
3. Place the disposable aluminum pan on the trivet then cover and seal the Instant Pot properly
4. Select *Manual* setting on the Instant Pot and cook the pork on high for 20 minutes
5. Once it is done; naturally release the Instant Pot then open the lid. Take the disposable aluminum pan out of the Instant Pot and let it sit for a few minutes

Nutrition Value:

Calories: 368; Net Carbs: 3.4g; Total Fat: 30.7g; Protein: 19.2g; Carbs: 3.8g

192. Spicy and Sour Pork Ribs

Preparation Time: 30 minutes
Servings: 2

Ingredients:

- 3/4 lb. pork ribs
- 2 cloves garlic

- 1 lemon grass
- 1/2 teaspoon tamarind
- 3 tablespoons coconut milk
- 1 teaspoon cayenne
- 2 shallots
- 1/4 cup water
- 1 tablespoon red chili flakes
- 1/2 teaspoon turmeric
- 1/4 teaspoon ginger
- 1/4 teaspoon salt

Directions:
1. Place red chili flakes, cayenne, shallots, garlic, turmeric, ginger, tamarind water and salt in a food processor. Process until smooth
2. Chop the pork ribs then place in the inner pot of an Instant Pot. Add the spice mixture to the Instant Pot then pour coconut milk and water over the pork ribs. Stir well
3. Cover the Instant Pot with the lid then seal it properly. Close the steam valve
4. Select *Pressure cook* setting on the Instant Pot then cook the pork ribs on high. Set the time to 25 minutes.
5. Once it is done; naturally release the Instant Pot then open the lid. Transfer the cooked pork ribs and the gravy to a serving dish then serve warm

Nutrition Value:
Calories: 398; Net Carbs: 6.9g; Total Fat: 25.2g; Protein: 36.1g; Carbs: 8.2g

193. Pork Baby Back Ribs

Preparation Time: 45 minutes
Servings: 2

Ingredients:
- 2-pound. rack of baby back ribs
- 2 tablespoons BBQ rub
- 1 tablespoon liquid smoke
- 1 cup BBQ sauce
- 1/2 onion
- 2 cups water
- Salt and Pepper to taste

Directions:
1. Season baby back ribs with barbecue rub, salt and pepper, sprinkle both sides with liquid smoke.
2. Pour water into Instant Pot and insert a trivet. Put seasoned ribs bones and onion on the trivet.
3. Close the lid and turn the vent to *Sealed*. Press *Pressure Cook* (Manual) button, use *+* or *-* button to set the timer for 25 minutes. Use *Pressure level* button to set Pressure to *HIGH*.
4. Once the timer is up; press *Cancel* button and allow the pressure to be released naturally; until the float valve drops down.
5. Open the lid; Top cooked ribs with BBQ sauce and put on a baking sheet.
6. Preheat the oven to 375 F and cook the ribs for 5-10 minutes. Serve with more BBQ sauce.

Nutrition Value:
Calories: 559 g; Total Fat: 37.1 g; Total Carbohydrate: 23.9 g; Protein: 30.1

194. Taco Pork Bowl Recipe

Preparation Time: 1 hour 10 minutes
Servings: 8

Ingredients:
- 2–pound pork sirloin roast; thickly sliced
- 20–ounce green chili tomatillo salsa
- 2 teaspoon cumin powder
- 2 teaspoon garlic powder
- 2 teaspoons black pepper
- 2 tablespoons olive oil
- 2 teaspoon salt

Directions:
1. Put the garlic powder, salt, pepper and ground cumin in a bowl and mix together
2. Put the pork in the bowl and dredge it in the spice mixture. Pour the oil into the instant pot and select the *Sauté* function.
3. Place the pork in the oil then add the

tomatillo salsa.

4. Secure the lid and cook for 45 minutes at *HIGH* pressure using the *Manual* function.
5. Release the steam naturally for 15 minutes then remove the lid. Serve warm.

Nutrition Value:

Calories: 295, Fat: 14.3g, Carbs: 6.1g, Protein: 32.6g

195. Loin Pork with Herbed Butter and Veggies

Preparation Time: 1 hour 10 minutes
Servings: 3

Ingredients:

- 1 (3/4-pound) pork tenderloin
- 1 tablespoon fresh herbs (sage; thyme and chives), chopped
- 2 tablespoons lemon juice
- 1 celery stalk; sliced
- 1 red onion; diced
- 2 tablespoons olive oil
- 2 garlic cloves; minced
- 2 carrots; sliced or cubed
- 1 cup chicken stock
- 1/4 cup softened unsalted butter
- 2 teaspoons dried rosemary
- Salt and Pepper to taste

Directions:

1. Mix oil, lemon juice, minced garlic, rosemary, salt and pepper in a bowl. Pour stock into the Instant pot and add pork loin.
2. Pour lemon juice mixture over the pork. Close the lid and turn the vent to *Sealed*.
3. Press *Pressure Cook* (Manual) button, use *+* or *-* button to set the timer for 30 minutes. Use *Pressure level* button to set Pressure to *HIGH*.
4. Once the timer is up; press *Cancel* button and turn the steam release handle to *Venting* position for quick release, until the float valve drops down.
5. Open the lid; Add onion, celery and carrots and close the lid again. Press *Pressure Cook* (Manual) button, use *+* or *-* button to set the timer for 6 minutes. Use *Pressure level* button to set Pressure to *HIGH*.
6. Once the timer is up; press *Cancel* button and turn the steam release handle to *Venting* position for quick release, until the float valve drops down.
7. Open the lid; Now make the herbed butter by simply mixing softened butter with herbs. Slice pork and serve with butter and veggies on top.

Nutrition Value:

Calories: 450 g; Total Fat: 39 g; Total Carbohydrate: 7.5 g; Protein: 20.3

196. Pork Stew in Sweet Ginger Soy

Preparation Time: 25 minutes
Servings: 2

Ingredients:

- 1/2 lb. pork sirloin
- 3 tablespoons chopped' leek
- 1/4 cup water
- 2 tablespoons soy sauce
- 1/2 teaspoon ginger
- 1/2 teaspoon pepper
- 1 teaspoon cornstarch
- 1 teaspoon sesame seeds
- 1 teaspoon vegetable oil
- 1/4 cup chopped' onions
- 1 teaspoon sugar
- 1 tablespoon oyster sauce
- 1/4 teaspoon salt

Directions:

1. Cut the pork into very thin slices then set aside. Pour vegetable oil into the inner pot of an Instant Pot then select *Sauté* menu
2. Stir in chopped' onion and sauté until wilted aromatic. Add sliced pork to the Instant Pot then sauté until wilted and no

longer pink. Press the *Cancel* button
3. Pour water into the Instant Pot and season the pork with soy sauce, ginger, pepper, sugar, oyster sauce and salt.
4. Cover the Instant Pot with the lid properly and close the steam valve
5. Select *Manual* menu on the Instant Pot and cook the pork for 15 minutes
6. Once it is done; quick release the Instant Pot then open the lid
7. Take about 3 tablespoons of gravy and mix with cornstarch
8. Pour the cornstarch mixture over the pork and stir well. add chopped' leek to the Instant Pot
9. Select *Sauté* menu again and cook the pork for another 2 minutes or until the gravy is thickened. Transfer the pork together with the gravy to a serving dish then sprinkle sesame seeds on top

Nutrition Value:
Calories: 253; Net Carbs: 7g; Total Fat: 13.1g; Protein: 24.7g; Carbs: 7.9g;

197. Mustard Pork Chops

Preparation Time: 30 minutes
Servings: 2

Ingredients:
- 2 pork chops
- 1/2 teaspoon paprika
- 1/2 teaspoon thyme
- 1 teaspoon apple cider vinegar
- 1 tablespoon mustard
- 1 tablespoon olive oil
- 1/2 cup chicken stock
- 1/4 cup heavy cream
- 2 tablespoons lemon juice
- Salt and Pepper to taste

Directions:
1. Season pork chops with salt, pepper, paprika and thyme.
2. Add oil to Instant Pot and press "Sauté" button (*Normal* preset), wait till you see Hot on the display.
3. Add pork chops and cook for 2 to 3 minutes on both sides until slightly brown. Mix stock, vinegar, mustard, heavy cream and lemon juice in a bowl, add to the Instant pot.
4. Close the lid and turn the vent to *Sealed*. Press *Pressure Cook* (Manual) button, use *+* or *-* button to set the timer for 15 minutes. Use *Pressure level* button to set Pressure to *HIGH*.
5. Once the timer is up; press *Cancel* button and turn the steam release handle to *Venting* position for quick release, until the float valve drops down.
6. Open the lid; Serve chops with the sauce from the Instant pot.

Nutrition Value:
Calories: 331 g; Total Fat: 27.2 g; Total Carbohydrate: 2 g; Protein: 19.1

198. Lime Ginger Pork

Preparation Time: 40 minutes
Servings: 2

Ingredients:
- 3/4-pound. pork loin
- 2 garlic cloves; minced
- 1 teaspoon fresh ginger; grounded
- 2 tablespoons honey
- 1 tablespoon Worcestershire Sauce
- 1/2 lime; juiced
- 1 tablespoon cornstarch or agar agar
- 1 cup water
- 1 tablespoon olive oil
- Salt and Pepper to taste

Directions:
1. Add oil to Instant Pot and press "Sauté" button (*Normal* preset), wait till you see Hot on the display.
2. Season pork with salt and pepper, then put it into Instant pot. Cook for 2-5 minutes both sides. Press *Cancel* button.
3. Mix honey, Worcestershire sauce, lime juice, garlic cloves and ginger in a bowl. Pour the mixture over pork, add water.

4. Close the lid and turn the vent to *Sealed*. Press *Meat/Stew* button and adjust to *Less* preset.
5. Once the timer is up; press *Cancel* button and turn the steam release handle to *Venting* position for quick release, until the float valve drops down.
6. Open the lid; Transfer the pork to a plate and press "Sauté" button, adjust to *Less*.
7. Add cornstarch to the cooker. Stir until the sauce thickens. Pour over the pork and serve.

Nutrition Value:

Calories: 442 g; Total Fat: 23.4 g; Total Carbohydrate: 15.1 g; Protein: 41.5

199. Pork Roast Rosemary

Preparation Time: 25 minutes
Servings: 2

Ingredients:

- 1/2 lb. boneless pork roast
- 1½ tablespoons butter
- 1½ teaspoons brown sugar
- 1/4 cup chopped' onion
- 1/2 teaspoon mustard
- 1 tablespoon rosemary
- 2 teaspoons minced' garlic
- 1/2 cup chopped' carrots
- 2 tablespoons chopped' celeries
- 1/4 cup apple juice
- 2 teaspoons Worcestershire sauce
- 1/2 teaspoon salt
- 1/4 teaspoon pepper

Directions:

1. Cut the pork loin into small pieces then set aside. Place butter in the inner pot of an Instant Pot then select *Sauté* menu
2. Stir in pork loin pieces and sauté until wilted. Press the *Cancel* button
3. Sprinkle chopped' carrots and onion then season with salt, pepper, minced' garlic, brown sugar, mustard, Worcestershire sauce and rosemary

4. Pour apple juice over the pork then cover the Instant Pot properly. Close the steam valve.
5. Select *Pressure cook* menu and cook the pork on high. Set the time to 25 minutes
6. Once it is done; naturally release the Instant Pot and open the lid. Transfer the cooked pork to a serving dish then serve

Nutrition Value:

Calories: 137; Net Carbs: 5.6g; Total Fat: 5.2g; Protein: 17.8g; Carbs: 6.7g;

200. Garlic Pork Rinds

Preparation Time: 20 minutes
Servings: 2

Ingredients:

- 1/2 lb. pork rinds
- 1/4 teaspoon ginger
- 3 teaspoons minced' garlic
- 1/2 cup water
- 3 tablespoons soy sauce
- 1/4 teaspoon salt
- 1/2 teaspoon pepper

Directions:

1. Cut the pork rinds into medium cubes then rub with minced' garlic, soy sauce, salt, pepper and ginger. Let it sit for about 10 minutes. Pour water into the inner pot of an Instant Pot then place the seasoned pork rinds in it
2. Cover the Instant Pot with the lid and seal it properly. Close the steam valve
3. Select *Manual* setting on the Instant Pot and cook the pork rinds on high. Set the time to 15 minutes.
4. Once it is done; naturally release the Instant Pot and open the lid. Transfer the cooked pork rinds to a serving dish then serve

Nutrition Value:

Calories: 621; Net Carbs: 3.2g; Total Fat: 37.6g; Protein: 69.4g; Carbs: 3.7g

201. Spicy Pork Ribs

Preparation Time: 55 minutes
Servings: 3

Ingredients:

- 2–pound pork ribs
- 1/2 teaspoon garlic powder
- 1/4 teaspoon coriander powder
- 1/4 cup tomato ketchup
- 1/4 teaspoon black pepper
- 1/2 teaspoon onion powder
- 1/4 teaspoon liquid smoke
- 3/4 tablespoon red wine vinegar
- 1/2 teaspoon ground mustard
- 3/4 teaspoon erythritol
- 1/2 teaspoon allspice
- 1/2 teaspoon salt

Directions:

1. Add all the dry spices to the pork and marinate for 1 hour.
2. In a different bowl; mix the mustard, vinegar, ketchup and liquid smoke to prepare a sauce,
3. Place the marinated ribs in the instant pot and pour the sauce over it.
4. Secure the lid and select the *Manual* function. Cook for 35 minutes at *HIGH* pressure,
5. Natural release the steam for 5 minutes then remove the lid.
6. Transfer the ribs to a platter, Cook the remaining sauce in the pot on the *Sauté* setting for 5 minutes, to serve; drizzle the sauce over the ribs,

Nutrition Value:

Calories: 852, Fat: 53.8g, Carbs: 7.3g, Protein: 80.7g

202. Pork Ribs Barbecue

Preparation Time: 25 minutes
Servings: 2

Ingredients:

- 3/4 lb. pork ribs
- 1/4 cup red wine vinegar
- 1/2 teaspoon onion powder
- 1/2 teaspoon garlic powder
- 1/4 teaspoon paprika
- 1/4 teaspoon mustard
- 1/4 teaspoon cinnamon
- 1/2 teaspoon chili powder
- 1/2 cup water
- 2 tablespoons tomato sauce
- 2 tablespoons ketchup
- 2 tablespoons brown sugar
- 1/2 teaspoon salt
- 1/2 teaspoon pepper

Directions:

1. Pour water into the inner pot of an Instant Pot then place a trivet in it
2. Now, rub the pork ribs with salt, pepper and garlic powder then place on the trivet. Cover and seal the Instant Pot properly then close the steam valve
3. Select *Pressure cook* setting on the Instant Pot and cook the pork on high. Set the time to 10 minutes
4. In the meantime, combine tomato sauce with ketchup, brown sugar, red wine vinegar, paprika, mustard, cinnamon, chili powder and onion powder. Stir well
5. Once the pork is done, quick release the Instant Pot and open the lid.
6. Take the pork out of the Instant Pot and glaze with the sauce mixture
7. Wrap the glazed pork with aluminum foil then return it back to the Instant Pot. Place on the trivet.
8. Select *Manual* setting and cook the wrapped pork on high for another 10 minutes
9. Once it is done; naturally release the Instant Pot and open the lid
10. Remove the wrapped pork from the Instant Pot and let it cool for a few minutes. Unwrap the pork then place on a serving dish
11. Cut into thick slices then serve. Enjoy right away. The pork barbecue is best to be served with mashed potatoes

Nutrition Value:

Calories: 354; Net Carbs: 6.7g; Total Fat: 19.9g; Protein: 35.4g; Carbs: 7.8g;

203. Pulled Pork

Preparation Time: 50 minutes
Servings: 2

Ingredients:

- 1-pound pork belly; make cubes
- 1 ½ teaspoons black pepper
- 1 tablespoon cornstarch
- 1/2 cup beef broth
- 1/2 cup chopped onion
- 3 tablespoons water
- 1 teaspoon thyme
- 1/4 teaspoon salt

Directions:

1. Switch on the pot after placing it on a clean and dry platform.
2. Open the pot lid and place the above-mentioned ingredients in the cooking pot area. Give the ingredients a little stir. Do not add the water and cornstarch.
3. Close the pot by closing the top lid. Also, ensure to seal the valve. Press *Manual* cooking function and set cooking time to 35 minutes.
4. It will start cooking after a few minutes. Let the pot mix cook under pressure until the timer reads zero. Press *Cancel* cooking function and press *Quick release* setting.
5. Open the pot. Combine cornstarch with water then stir into the Instant Pot. Add the liquid over the pork then serve warm!

Nutrition Value:

Calories: 188; Fat: 15g; Carbohydrates: 8g; Fiber: 1.5g; Protein 4.5g

204. Pork Chops with Cinnamon

Preparation Time: 25 minutes
Servings: 2

Ingredients:

- 1/2 lb. pork chops
- 1/4 teaspoon cinnamon
- 1/2 apple
- 1 teaspoon brown sugar
- 1 tablespoon butter
- 1/4 teaspoon nutmeg
- 1/2 cup water
- 1/4 teaspoon salt
- 1/4 teaspoon pepper

Directions:

1. Rub the pork chops with salt and pepper then let it sit. Meanwhile, cut the apple into slices then place in a bowl
2. Sprinkle brown sugar, cinnamon and nutmeg over the sliced apple then toss to combine
3. Now, pour water into the inner pot of an Instant Pot then sprinkle the sliced apple in it
4. After that; place the seasoned pork chops on top then cover and seal the Instant Pot properly. Close the steam valve.
5. Select *Manual* setting on the Instant Pot and cook the pork chops on high for 20 minutes
6. Once it is done; naturally release the Instant Pot and open the lid. Transfer the cooked pork chops to a serving dish then garnish with the apples

Nutrition Value:

Calories: 267; Net Carbs: 7g; Total Fat: 16.6g; Protein: 21.1g; Carbs: 8.5g;

205. Mushroom Tomato Pork Meatloaf

Preparation Time: 25 minutes
Servings: 2

Ingredients:

- 3/4 lbs. ground pork
- 1/2 teaspoon ginger
- 1/4 teaspoon nutmeg
- 1/2 cup chopped' mushrooms
- 3/4 teaspoon Worcestershire sauce
- 1/4 teaspoon salt
- 1/4 cup diced' tomatoes

- 1 egg white
- 2 tablespoons diced' onion
- 1/2 tablespoon flour
- 1/4 teaspoon pepper

Directions:
1. Combine ground beef with egg white, diced' onion, flour, Worcestershire sauce, salt, pepper, mushrooms and carrots in a bowl then mix well
2. Transfer the pork mixture to loaf pan then spread evenly. Pour water into the Instant Pot then place a trivet in it
3. Put the beef loaf on the trivet then cover and seal the Instant Pot properly. Close the steam valve
4. Select *Steam* setting on the Instant Pot and cook the pork on high for 20 minutes
5. Once it is done; naturally release the Instant Pot and open the lid.
6. Remove the pork loaf from the Instant Pot and let it cool for a few minutes
7. Now, take the pork loaf out of the loaf pan then place on a flat surface. Cut the pork loaf into thick slices then arrange on a serving dish

Nutrition Value:
Calories: 378; Net Carbs: 4.5g; Total Fat: 24.3g; Protein: 33g; Carbs: 5g;

206. Pork Sausages and Mushrooms Recipe

Preparation Time: 55 minutes
Servings: 2

Ingredients:
- 6–ounce pork sausages
- 1/2 cup marinara sauce
- 2 large Portobello mushrooms
- 1/2 cup shredded mozzarella cheese
- 1/4 cup chopped parsley
- 1/2 cup whole milk ricotta cheese

Directions:
1. Stuff each mushroom with pork sausage,
2. Place the ricotta cheese over the sausages and carve a dent in the center.
3. Drizzle the marinara sauce over the ricotta cheese,
4. Cover with mozzarella cheese on top and place the mushrooms in the instant pot.
5. Secure the lid; select the *Manual* function and cook for 35 minutes at *HIGH* pressure. Natural release the steam then remove the lid. Serve immediately.

Nutrition Value:
Calories: 624, Fat: 41.7g, Carbs: 27.2g, Protein: 34.9g

207. Tropical Pork Stew

Preparation Time: 20 minutes
Servings: 2

Ingredients:
- 1/2 lb. pork sirloin
- 1/4 teaspoon oregano
- 1 tablespoon soy sauce
- 1/2 cup water
- 1/2 cup chopped' pineapple
- 1/4 tablespoon honey
- 1/2 teaspoon ginger
- 2 tablespoons chopped' onion
- 1 teaspoon red chili
- 1/4 teaspoon salt
- 1/4 teaspoon pepper

Directions:
1. Cut the pork sirloin into slices then place in the inner pot of an Instant Pot
2. Pour water over the pork then season it with soy sauce, ginger, chopped' onion, red chili, salt, pepper and oregano
3. Sprinkle chopped' pineapple on top then cover and seal the Instant Pot properly. Close the steam valve.
4. Select *Manual* setting on the Instant Pot and cook the pork on high. Set the time to 15 minutes.
5. Once it is done; naturally release the Instant Pot and open the lid. Transfer the cooked pork to a serving dish then drizzle honey on top

Nutrition Value:

Calories: 250; Net Carbs: 5.9g; Total Fat: 10.1g; Protein: 23.4g; Carbs: 6.7g

208. Pork and Beef Gumbo Recipe

Preparation Time: 25 minutes
Servings: 3

Ingredients:

- 1/4–pound ground pork
- 1/4–pound grass–fed ground beef
- 1/4 tablespoon olive oil
- 1/4 tablespoon chili powder
- 1/4 tablespoon ground cumin
- 1 chopped tomatillo.
- 1/8 chopped yellow onion.
- 1/2 chopped jalapeño pepper.
- 1/2 minced garlic clove
- 2 tablespoon shredded cheddar cheese
- 6-ounce sugar–free tomato sauce
- 1 tablespoon water
- Salt and black pepper

Directions:

1. Put the oil and all the Ingredients into the instant pot.
2. Stir well and secure the lid, Set the cooker to *Slow cook* at high heat for 4 hours,
3. Natural release the steam and remove the lid. Serve hot.

Nutrition Value:

Calories: 181, Fat: 8.5g, Carbs: 4.8g, Protein: 20.4g

209. BBQ Pork Ribs Recipe

Preparation Time: 1 hour 45 minutes
Servings: 4

Ingredients:

- 2–pound baby back pork ribs
- 1/2 teaspoon ground cumin
- 1/2 teaspoon brown sugar
- 1/2 teaspoon garlic powder
- 2 tablespoon apple cider vinegar
- 2 cup apple juice
- 1/4 cup BBQ sauce
- 1/4 cup tomato ketchup
- 1 tablespoon Worcestershire sauce
- 1 tablespoon liquid smoke
- 1/2 teaspoon black pepper
- 1 teaspoon salt

Directions:

1. Combine the salt, pepper, brown sugar, cumin and garlic powder in a bowl to prepare the seasoning.
2. Add pork and mix well.
3. Now put the seasoned pork, apple cider vinegar, liquid smoke and apple juice into the instant pot.
4. Cook for 20 minutes at *HIGH* pressure using the *meat stew* function.
5. Natural release the steam for 15 minutes then remove the lid, Stir in the Worcestershire sauce BBQ sauce and the tomato ketchup. Allow to cool before serving.

Nutrition Value:

Calories: 746, Fat: 54.5g, Carbs: 25.2g, Protein: 36.6g

210. Beef, Bacon and Spinach Chili

Preparation Time: 15 minutes
Servings 6)
Ready to cook a gourmet meal in less than 15 minutes? Serve with Dijon mustard on the side.

Nutrition Value: 392 Calories; 25.4g Fat; 5.8g Carbs; 33.6g Protein; 1.8g Sugars

Ingredients

- 1 ½ pounds ground beef
- 4 slices bacon, chopped
- 8 ounces tomato puréed
- 1 onion, chopped
- 2 garlic cloves, minced
- 2 cups chicken stock, preferably homemade
- 1/2 teaspoon ground cumin
- 1 teaspoon smoked paprika

- 1/2 teaspoon dried basil
- 1/2 teaspoon dried oregano
- Sea salt and ground black pepper, to taste
- 1 teaspoon red pepper flakes, crushed
- 2 bay leaves
- 1/4 teaspoon ground allspice
- 2 cups spinach, fresh or frozen

Directions

1. Press the "Sauté" button to heat up the Instant Pot. Once hot, cook ground beef and bacon for 2 to 3 minutes, crumbling them with a fork.
2. Add the remaining ingredients, except for spinach.
3. Secure the lid. Choose "Manual" mode and High pressure; cook for 6 minutes. Once cooking is complete, use a quick pressure release; carefully remove the lid.
4. Add spinach and cover with the lid. Let it sit until the spinach wilts. Ladle into individual bowls and serve warm. Bon appétit!

211. Beef Steak with Rainbow Noodles

Preparation Time: 45 minutes
Servings 6)
Beef steak is the most versatile ingredient ever! In this recipe, we will serve it with innovative, colorful and delicious low-carb veggie noodles.

Nutrition Value: 259 Calories; 12.2g Fat; 3g Carbs; 32.4g Protein; 1.2g Sugars

Ingredients

- 1 zucchini
- 1 carrot
- 1 yellow onion
- 2 tablespoons ghee
- Sea salt, to taste
- 2 pounds beef steak
- 2 large cloves garlic
- 1/3 teaspoon ground black pepper

Directions

1. Slice the zucchini, carrot, and yellow onion using a mandolin.
2. Preheat an oven to 390 degrees F. Grease a baking sheet with the ghee; toss the vegetables with salt and bake for 18 to 22 minutes, tossing once or twice.
3. Meanwhile, add the beef, garlic, and black pepper to your Instant Pot.
4. Secure the lid. Choose "Manual" mode and High pressure; cook for 20 minutes. Once cooking is complete, use a quick pressure release; carefully remove the lid. Salt the beef to taste.
5. Serve the prepared beef steak over roasted vegetable noodles and enjoy!

212. Zettuccini with Pepperoni and Cheese Sauce

Preparation Time: 10 minutes
Servings 4)
Try different veggie noodles every day. You can use sweet bell peppers, onions, carrots, and so on.

Nutrition Value: 437 Calories; 38.3g Fat; 2.6g Carbs; 19.5g Protein; 1.7g Sugars

Ingredients

- 2 zucchini
- 1/2 pound pepperoni, sliced
- 1/2 cup cream cheese
- Sea salt and ground black pepper, to taste
- 1/2 teaspoon red pepper flakes, crushed
- 1 teaspoon cayenne pepper
- 1/2 cup Romano cheese, grated

Directions

1. Slice the zucchini with a mandolin; add your zettuccini to the Instant Pot.
2. Now, stir in the pepperoni, cream cheese, salt, black pepper, red pepper, and cayenne pepper.
3. Secure the lid. Choose "Manual" mode and High pressure; cook for 5 minutes. Once cooking is complete, use a quick pressure release; carefully remove the lid.
4. Afterwards, stir in Romano cheese, cover and let it melt for a couple of minutes. Bon appétit!

213. Sinfully Delicious

Cheeseburger Soup

Preparation Time: 20 minutes

Servings 4)

Make this all-star cheeseburger soup using only one revolutionary kitchen gadget – Instant Pot electric pressure cooker! Serve with fresh Iceberg lettuce and mustard.

Nutrition Value: 571 Calories; 39g Fat; 3.6g Carbs; 48.4g Protein; 1.6g Sugars

Ingredients

- 2 slices bacon, chopped
- 1 pound ground chuck
- 1 teaspoon ghee, room temperature
- Salt and ground black pepper, to taste
- 4 cups vegetable stock, preferably homemade
- 2 garlic cloves, minced
- 1/2 cup scallions, chopped
- 1 teaspoon mustard seeds
- 1 teaspoon paprika
- 1 teaspoon chili powder
- 1/2 cup tomato puree
- 1 bay leaf
- 1 ½ cups Monterey-Jack cheese, shredded
- 2 ounces sour cream
- 1 small handful fresh parsley, roughly chopped

Directions

1. Press the "Sauté" button to heat up the Instant Pot. Once hot, cook the bacon and ground beef for 2 to 3 minutes, crumbling them with a fork.
2. Add the ghee, salt, black pepper, vegetable stock, garlic, scallions, mustard seeds, paprika, chili powder, tomato puree, and bay leaf.
3. Secure the lid. Choose "Manual" mode and High pressure; cook for 8 minutes. Once cooking is complete, use a natural pressure release; carefully remove the lid.
4. After that, add Monterey-Jack cheese and sour cream; seal the lid and let it stand for at least 5 minutes.
5. Serve warm in individual bowls garnished with fresh parsley. Bon appétit!

214. Hamburgers with Kale and Cheese

Preparation Time: 15 minutes

Servings 6)

Here's a great combo of ground meat, sausage, kale, and cheese. It's no shocker that burger is one of the most popular dishes in the world!

Nutrition Value: 323 Calories; 20.3g Fat; 5.8g Carbs; 29.9g Protein; 0.6g Sugars

Ingredients

- 1 pound ground beef
- 1/2 pound beef sausage, crumbled
- 1 ½ cups kale, chopped
- 1/4 cup scallions, chopped
- 2 garlic cloves, minced
- 1/2 Romano cheese, grated
- 1/3 cup blue cheese, crumbled
- Salt and ground black pepper, to taste
- 1 teaspoon crushed dried sage
- 1/2 teaspoon oregano
- 1/2 teaspoon dried basil
- 1 tablespoon olive oil

Directions

1. Place 1 ½ cups of water and a steamer basket in your Instant Pot.
2. Mix all ingredients until everything is well incorporated.
3. Shape the mixture into 6 equal sized patties. Place the burgers on the steamer basket.
4. Secure the lid. Choose "Manual" mode and High pressure; cook for 6 minutes. Once cooking is complete, use a quick pressure release; carefully remove the lid. Bon appétit!

215. Beef Stroganoff with a Twist

Preparation Time: 20 minutes

Servings 6)

An Instant Pot transforms the beef and regular

vegetables into a magical satisfying stew in record time. This appetizing stew showcases mushrooms at its finest.

Nutrition Value: 347 Calories; 20.7g Fat; 7.9g Carbs; 33.5g Protein; 2.2g Sugars

Ingredients

- 1 tablespoon lard
- 1 ½ pounds beef stew meat, cubed
- 1 yellow onion, chopped
- 2 garlic cloves, chopped
- 1 red bell pepper, chopped
- Kosher salt and freshly ground black pepper, to taste
- 1/2 teaspoon dried rosemary
- 1/2 teaspoon dried thyme
- 2 cups mushrooms, chopped
- 2 ½ cups broth, preferably homemade
- 1 (10-ounce) box frozen chopped spinach, thawed and squeezed dry
- 1 cup sour cream
- 4 slices Muenster cheese

Directions

1. Press the "Sauté" button to heat up the Instant Pot. Now, melt the lard; once hot, cook the beef for 3 to 4 minutes.
2. Add the onion, garlic, bell pepper, salt, black pepper, rosemary, thyme, mushrooms, and broth.
3. Secure the lid. Choose "Manual" mode and High pressure; cook for 10 minutes. Once cooking is complete, use a quick pressure release; carefully remove the lid.
4. Lastly, stir in the spinach, sour cream and cheese. Let it stand in the residual heat until everything is well incorporated. Ladle into soup bowls and serve warm. Bon appétit!

216. Spicy Broccoli, Leek and Beef Soup

Preparation Time: 20 minutes
Servings 6)
Dump all ingredients into your Instant Pot, turn on the cooker and enjoy a real feast!
Nutrition Value: 373 Calories; 29.2g Fat; 5.7g Carbs; 21.2g Protein; 2.4g Sugars

Ingredients

- 1 tablespoon olive oil
- 1 ½ pounds beef stew meat
- 1/2 cup leeks
- 1 cup broccoli, chopped into florets
- 1 carrot, chopped
- 1 celery with leaves, chopped
- 1 cup tomatoes, puréed
- 4 ½ cups roasted vegetable stock
- 1 teaspoon garlic powder
- 1 teaspoon dried basil
- 1 (1-inch) piece ginger root, grated
- 1 teaspoon Sriracha

Directions

1. Press the "Sauté" button to heat up the Instant Pot. Now, heat the oil; once hot, cook the beef for 3 to 4 minutes; reserve.
2. Now, sauté the leeks in pan drippings until tender and fragrant. Add the remaining ingredients, including the reserved beef.
3. Secure the lid. Choose "Manual" mode and High pressure; cook for 15 minutes. Once cooking is complete, use a quick pressure release; carefully remove the lid.
4. Ladle into individual bowls and garnish with some extra leek leaves if desired. Bon appétit!

217. Red Wine Stew with Smoked Cheddar Cheese

Preparation Time: 30 minutes
Servings 6)
Cooking with dry red wine brings a layer of depth and balance to your favorite beef recipes. You can enjoy a glass of red wine while you cook, too. Win-win!

Nutrition Value: 381 Calories; 16.7g Fat; 4.5g Carbs; 49.2g Protein; 1.8g Sugars

Ingredients

- 1 tablespoon tallow, at room temperature
- 2 pounds bottom round roast, trimmed and diced

- Coarse sea salt and ground black pepper, to taste
- 1 tablespoon Montreal steak seasoning
- 1 banana shallot, chopped
- 1 carrot, chopped
- 1 celery, chopped
- 1/2 cup dry red wine
- 2 cups beef stock
- 2 bay leaves
- 1 cup smoked cheddar cheese, grated

Directions

1. Press the "Sauté" button to heat up the Instant Pot. Now, melt the tallow; once hot, cook the bottom round roast for 3 to 4 minutes. Season with salt and black pepper.
2. Now, add Montreal steak seasoning, shallot, carrot, celery, wine, beef stock, and bay leaves to your Instant Pot.
3. Secure the lid. Choose "Meat/Stew" mode and High pressure; cook for 25 minutes. Once cooking is complete, use a quick pressure release; carefully remove the lid.
4. Divide the stew among 6 serving bowls; top each serving with grated cheese and serve warm. Bon appétit!

218. Bottom Eye Roast in Hoisin Sauce

Preparation Time: 45 minutes
Servings 8)
Here is a classic Chinese beef! Do not forget to add a hot sauce to make the recipe outstanding!

Nutrition Value: 313 Calories; 17.3g Fat; 3.8g Carbs; 35.8g Protein; 2.3g Sugars

Ingredients

- 1 tablespoon tallow
- 3 pounds bottom eye roast
- Sea salt and ground black pepper, to taste
- 3 garlic cloves, halved

Hoisin Sauce:

- 3 tablespoons soy sauce
- 2 tablespoons peanut butter
- 1 tablespoon black vinegar
- 2 cloves garlic, minced
- 2 ½ tablespoons toasted sesame oil
- 1 teaspoon Chinese chili sauce
- 1/2 teaspoon Chinese five spice powder
- 1 tablespoon Splenda

Directions

1. Press the "Sauté" button to heat up the Instant Pot. Now, melt the tallow; once hot, cook the bottom eye roast for 2 to 3 minutes on each side. Season with salt and black pepper.
2. Then, make small slits along the surface of the beef cut and place garlic in them.
3. Secure the lid. Choose "Meat/Stew" mode and High pressure; cook for 40 minutes. Once cooking is complete, use a natural pressure release; carefully remove the lid.
4. Meanwhile, process all sauce ingredients in your blender; blitz until everything is well mixed.
5. Add the hoisin sauce to the Instant Pot; stir for a couple of minutes more. Serve immediately and enjoy!

219. Festive Bayrischer Gulasch

Preparation Time: 30 minutes
Servings 8)
This German dish is rich, flavorful, and sophisticated. A rump roast pairs well with German red wines like Siegrist Dornfelder, Spätburgunder (Pinot Noir), etc.

Nutrition Value: 334 Calories; 15.3g Fat; 8g Carbs; 38.2g Protein; 3.3g Sugars

Ingredients

- 1 tablespoon olive oil
- 3 pounds rump roast, boneless and cubed
- Salt and ground black pepper, to taste
- 1 red onion, chopped
- 2 cloves garlic, minced
- 2 tomatoes, puréed
- 1 habanero pepper, seeded and sliced

- 1 green bell pepper, seeded and sliced
- 1 red bell peppers, seeded and sliced
- 2 cups chicken stock
- 1/2 cup dry red wine
- 1/2 teaspoon dried rosemary
- 1/2 teaspoon dried basil
- 1/2 teaspoon dried oregano
- 1/2 teaspoon caraway seed
- 1 tablespoon coconut aminos
- 1 cup sour cream, to serve

Directions

1. Press the "Sauté" button to heat up the Instant Pot. Now, heat the oil; once hot, cook the rump roast for 3 to 4 minutes.
2. Season with salt and black pepper to taste. Add a splash of wine to scrape up any browned bits from the bottom.
3. Add the onion, garlic, tomatoes, peppers, chicken stock, remaining wine, rosemary, basil, oregano, caraway seeds, and coconut aminos.
4. Secure the lid. Choose "Meat/Stew" mode and High pressure; cook for 25 minutes. Once cooking is complete, use a natural pressure release; carefully remove the lid.
5. Ladle into serving bowls; serve dolloped with sour cream. Bon appétit!

220. Garbure Gersoise Soup

Preparation Time: 30 minutes
Servings 6)
The key to the amazing and unique flavor of this French soup is the slab bacon. Be sure to find a meaty bacon and good quality veggies.

Nutrition Value: 324 Calories; 17.9g Fat; 6.8g Carbs; 34.6g Protein; 1.9g Sugars

Ingredients

- 1 tablespoon grapeseed oil
- 2 pounds top chuck, trimmed, boneless and cubed
- 3 slices slab bacon, chopped
- 1/2 cup yellow onion, chopped
- 1 celery ribs, sliced
- 1 parsnip, sliced
- 4 teaspoons beef base
- 6 cups water
- 1/4 cup dry white wine
- 7 ounces tomato purée
- 1 head savoy cabbage
- Sea salt, to your liking
- 1 teaspoon dried juniper berries
- 1/2 teaspoon dried sage, crushed
- 1/2 teaspoon dried rosemary, leaves picked
- 1 teaspoon whole mixed peppercorns
- 2 sprigs parsley, roughly chopped

Directions

1. Press the "Sauté" button to heat up the Instant Pot. Now, heat the oil; once hot, cook the chuck for 2 to 3 minutes on each side.
2. Add the remaining ingredients and stir to combine well.
3. Secure the lid. Choose "Meat/Stew" mode and High pressure; cook for 25 minutes. Once cooking is complete, use a quick pressure release; carefully remove the lid.
4. Serve in individual bowls garnished with some extra fresh parsley if desired. Bon appétit!

221. Spezzatino di Manzo

Preparation Time: 50 minutes
Servings 6)

- Italian dishes are one of the most popular dishes in the world thanks to their authenticity and abundance of flavors. Spezzatino di Manzo is an Italian beef stew that is enriched with tons of spices.

Nutrition Value: 324 Calories; 17.9g Fat; 6.8g Carbs; 34.6g Protein; 1.9g Sugars

Ingredients

- 1 tablespoon bacon grease
- 2 pounds chuck roast, trimmed and cubed
- 1 onion, diced

- 2 cloves garlic, sliced
- 4 ounces celery, diced
- 1 cup cabbage, diced
- 1 cup fennel, diced
- 1 carrot, sliced
- 1/2 cup tomato puree
- 4 cups broth, preferably homemade
- 2 tablespoons balsamic vinegar
- 2 bay leaves
- 1 teaspoon winter savory
- 1/2 teaspoon black peppercorns, crushed
- 1 teaspoon dried rosemary
- 1 teaspoon dried thyme
- Sea salt, to taste
- 2 tablespoons fresh basil, snipped

Directions

1. Press the "Sauté" button to heat up the Instant Pot. Now, melt the bacon grease; once hot, cook the chuck for 2 to 3 minutes on each side; reserve.
2. Add the onion and cook an additional 3 minutes or until it is translucent.
3. Add the vegetables to the Instant Pot. Then, stir in tomato puree, broth, balsamic vinegar, bay leaves, winter savory, black peppercorns, dried rosemary, thyme, and sea salt.
4. Secure the lid. Choose "Meat/Stew" mode and High pressure; cook for 40 minutes. Once cooking is complete, use a natural pressure release; carefully remove the lid.
5. Serve garnished with fresh basil. Bon appétit!

222. German Leberkäse with Sauerkraut

Preparation Time: 15 minutes
Servings 6

Nutrition Value: 382 Calories; 27.1g Fat; 9.1g Carbs; 24.5g Protein; 5.7g Sugars

Ingredients

- 2 pounds Leberkäse
- 18 ounces sauerkraut plus 1 cup sauerkraut juice
- 2 garlic cloves, minced
- 1 yellow onion, sliced
- 1 teaspoon dried thyme
- 1/2 cup water
- 1/2 cup chicken stock
- 1 bay leaf

Directions

1. Press the "Sauté" button to heat up the Instant Pot. Once hot, cook your Leberkäse for 2 to 3 minutes, turning periodically.
2. Place all ingredients in your Instant Pot.
3. Secure the lid. Choose "Manual" mode and High pressure; cook for 8 minutes. Once cooking is complete, use a quick pressure release; carefully remove the lid.
4. Discard bay leaf and serve warm. Bon appétit!

223. Christmas Bacon Meatloaf

Preparation Time: 40 minutes
Servings 6

Nutrition Value: 589 Calories; 44.9g Fat; 6.9g Carbs; 38.6g Protein; 3.9g Sugars

Ingredients

- 1 ½ pounds ground chuck
- 1/2 cup heavy whipping cream
- 1 cup cheddar cheese, shredded
- Sea salt and ground black pepper, to taste
- 1 tablespoon dried parsley
- 1 shallot, chopped
- 1 cup mushrooms, diced
- 2 eggs, whisked
- 1 teaspoon fresh thyme
- 1/2 teaspoon dried rosemary
- 1 teaspoon dried marjoram
- 1/2 teaspoon caraway seeds
- 1 teaspoon mustard powder
- 16 long slices bacon
- 1/2 cup tomato chili sauce

Directions

1. Prepare your Instant Pot by adding 1 ½

cups of water and a metal rack to the bottom of the inner pot.
2. In a mixing bowl, thoroughly combine all ingredients, except for bacon and tomato chili sauce.
3. Shape the mixture into a loaf. Place the bacon slices on the top. Weave the bacon (under, over…under, over)
4. Place the meatloaf in a lightly greased baking pan; lower the baking pan onto the rack.
5. Secure the lid. Choose "Manual" mode and High pressure; cook for 23 minutes. Once cooking is complete, use a quick pressure release; carefully remove the lid.
6. Spread the tomato chili sauce over the meatloaf. Place the meatloaf under the broiler for 6 to 7 minutes. Allow your meatloaf to sit for 10 minutes before slicing. Bon appétit!

224. Perfect Filet Mignon in Beer Sauce

Preparation Time: 20 minutes
Servings 4

Nutrition Value: 499 Calories; 38g Fat; 5.6g Carbs; 32.1g Protein; 1.9g Sugars

Ingredients

- 2 tablespoons sesame oil
- 4 (8-ounce) filet mignon steaks
- 1 onion, diced
- 2 garlic cloves, minced
- 1/2 teaspoon dried rosemary
- 1 teaspoon cayenne pepper
- Sea salt and ground black pepper, to taste
- 1/3 cup ale beer
- 1 cup stock, preferably homemade

Directions

1. Press the "Sauté" button to heat up the Instant Pot. Heat the sesame oil. Once hot, cook filet mignon steaks for 2 to 3 minutes per side.
2. Now, add the remaining ingredients and secure the lid.
3. Secure the lid. Choose "Manual" mode and High pressure; cook for 12 minutes. Once cooking is complete, use a natural pressure release; carefully remove the lid.
4. Serve with a fresh salad of choice. Bon appétit!

225. Restaurant-Style Oxtail Soup

Preparation Time: 55 minutes
Servings 6

Nutrition Value: 474 Calories; 25.9g Fat; 5.3g Carbs; 51.4g Protein; 2.3g Sugars

Ingredients

- 2 tablespoons canola oil
- 2 pounds meaty oxtails
- 5 cups broth, preferably homemade
- 1 cup tomato puree
- 1 onion, chopped
- 1 carrot, diced
- 1 celery, diced
- 1 teaspoon granulated garlic
- 1/2 teaspoon dried marjoram
- 1/2 teaspoon dried basil
- 1/2 teaspoon dried thyme
- 1/2 teaspoon ground bay leaf
- 2 cups Swiss chard

Directions

1. Press the "Sauté" button to heat up the Instant Pot. Heat the canola oil. Once hot, cook oxtails for 7 to 10 minutes.
2. Stir in the remaining ingredients, except for Swiss chard.
3. Secure the lid. Choose "Meat/Stew" mode and High pressure; cook for 45 minutes. Once cooking is complete, use a natural pressure release; carefully remove the lid.
4. Add Swiss chard and seal the lid; let it stand until the green wilts. Taste, adjust the seasonings, and ladle into individual bowls. Bon appétit!

226. Extraordinary Steak Sandwiches

Preparation Time: 40 minutes
Servings 4

Nutrition Value: 486 Calories; 30.2g Fat; 4.9g Carbs; 49.3g Protein; 2.9g Sugars

Ingredients

- 1 ½ pounds beef rump steak, boneless
- Sea salt and ground black pepper, to taste
- 1 teaspoon garlic powder
- 1 teaspoon dried oregano
- 1 teaspoon dried basil
- 1/2 teaspoon caraway seeds
- 1/2 teaspoon red pepper flakes, crushed
- 1 cucumber, sliced
- 2 plum tomatoes, sliced
- 1/2 red onion, sliced
- 8 leaves lettuce
- 1 tablespoon Dijon mustard

Low Carb Wraps:

- 4 ounces pork rinds, crushed
- 1/2 teaspoon baking soda
- 4 ounces cream cheese, softened
- 2 eggs, whisked
- 1/4 teaspoon turmeric powder
- 1/2 teaspoon shallot powder
- 1/4 cup water

Directions

1. Place beef rump steak along with the salt, black pepper, garlic powder, oregano, basil, caraway seeds, and red pepper flakes, in your Instant Pot.
2. Secure the lid. Choose "Manual" mode and High pressure; cook for 25 minutes. Once cooking is complete, use a natural pressure release; carefully remove the lid.
3. Slice the beef against the grain.
4. To make low-carb wraps, blitz the pork rinds in your food processor until they become a fine powder.
5. Add the other ingredients; process until everything is well mixed. Allow the batter to rest approximately 12 minutes.
6. Cook four wraps on the preheated pancake griddle over a moderate flame. To assemble your sandwiches, divide the prepared beef steak slices among low-carb wraps.
7. Add cucumber, tomatoes, onions, lettuce and mustard. Serve and enjoy!

227. Top Blade Roast with Horseradish Sauce

Preparation Time: 35 minutes
Servings 6

Nutrition Value: 406 Calories; 24.6g Fat; 4.8g Carbs; 41.9g Protein; 1.3g Sugars

Ingredients

- 1 tablespoon sesame oil
- 2 pounds top blade roast
- Sea salt and ground black pepper, to taste
- 1/2 teaspoon cayenne pepper
- 1/3 cup port wine
- 1 cup water
- 1 bouillon cube
- 2 tablespoons green onions
- 3 cloves garlic
- 1 teaspoon mustard seeds
- 1 teaspoon fennel seeds

Horseradish Sauce:

- 1 teaspoon stone-ground mustard
- 1/4 cup sour cream
- 2 tablespoons mayonnaise
- 3 tablespoons prepared horseradish

Directions

1. Press the "Sauté" button to heat up the Instant Pot. Heat the oil. Once hot, cook the top blade roast for 3 minutes on each side.
2. Season with salt, black pepper, and cayenne pepper. Now, add the wine, water, bouillon cube, green onions, garlic, mustard seeds, and fennel seeds.
3. Secure the lid. Choose "Manual" mode and High pressure; cook for 25 minutes. Once cooking is complete, use a natural pressure release; carefully remove the lid.
4. Meanwhile, mix all of the ingredients for the horseradish sauce. Serve your blade roast with horseradish sauce on the side.

Bon appétit!

228. Chipolatas with Spinach and Cheese

Preparation Time: 15 minutes
Servings 6

Nutrition Value: 403 Calories; 33g Fat; 5.5g Carbs; 16g Protein; 0.7g Sugars

Ingredients

- 1 tablespoon lard, at room temperature
- 2 pounds chipolata sausages
- 1 yellow onion, chopped
- 1/2 cup dry red wine
- 1 cup water
- Freshly ground black pepper, to taste

Directions

1. Press the "Sauté" button to heat up the Instant Pot. Heat the oil. Once hot, cook the sausage for a couple of minutes, moving them around.
2. Add the remaining ingredients.
3. Secure the lid. Choose "Manual" mode and High pressure; cook for 8 minutes. Once cooking is complete, use a quick pressure release; carefully remove the lid. Serve warm. Bon appétit!

229. Herbed Mustard Beef Shanks

Preparation Time: 35 minutes
Servings 8

Nutrition Value: 210 Calories; 6.6g Fat; 4.2g Carbs; 31.1g Protein; 0g Sugars

Ingredients

- 2 teaspoons lard, room temperature
- 2 ½ pounds beef shanks, 1 ½-inch wide
- 1 ½ cups beef broth
- 1 teaspoon Dijon mustard
- 1/2 teaspoon cayenne pepper
- 1/4 teaspoon freshly cracked black pepper
- 1 teaspoon salt
- 1 bay leaf
- 1/2 teaspoon dried marjoram, crushed
- 1/2 teaspoon caraway seeds
- 1 teaspoon dried sage, crushed
- 2 sprigs mint, roughly chopped

Directions

1. Press the "Sauté" button to heat up the Instant Pot. Melt the lard. Once hot, sear the beef shanks for 2 to 3 minutes per side.
2. Add the remaining ingredients, except for the mint.
3. Secure the lid. Choose "Meat/Stew" mode and High pressure; cook for 30 minutes. Once cooking is complete, use a quick pressure release; carefully remove the lid.
4. Serve garnished with fresh mint and enjoy!

230. Beef and Yogurt Curry

Preparation Time: 30 minutes
Servings 6

Nutrition Value: 375 Calories; 17.7g Fat; 7.4g Carbs; 43.9g Protein; 4.9g Sugars

Ingredients

- 2 tablespoons olive oil
- 2 ½ pounds beef steaks, cubed
- Sea salt and ground black pepper, to taste
- 1/2 teaspoon red pepper flakes, crushed
- 1 shallot, chopped
- 2 garlic cloves, minced
- 1 habanero pepper, minced
- 1 ½ teaspoons red curry paste
- 1/4 teaspoon ground cinnamon
- 1 ½ tablespoons rice vinegar
- 1 ½ cups chicken stock, preferably homemade
- 1 cup canned coconut milk, unsweetened
- 1/2 cup yogurt
- A small handful coriander, chopped

Directions

1. Press the "Sauté" button to heat up the Instant Pot. Now, heat the olive oil.

Once hot, sear the beef steaks for 3 to 4 minutes, stirring periodically; season with salt, black pepper, and red pepper; reserve.
2. Then, cook the shallot, garlic and habanero pepper in pan drippings until fragrant.
3. Add red curry paste, cinnamon, vinegar, and chicken stock.
4. Secure the lid. Choose "Manual" mode and High pressure; cook for 18 minutes. Once cooking is complete, use a quick pressure release; carefully remove the lid.
5. Then, add coconut milk and yogurt. Stir to combine well and press the "Sauté" button one more time; let it simmer until thoroughly heated.
6. Serve in individual bowls, garnished with fresh coriander. Bon appétit!

231. Beef Short Ribs with Cilantro Cream

Preparation Time: 25 minutes
Servings 8

Nutrition Value: 346 Calories; 24.1g Fat; 2.1g Carbs; 31g Protein; 1.1g Sugars

Ingredients

- 1 tablespoon sesame oil
- 2 ½ pounds beef short ribs
- 1/2 teaspoon red pepper flakes, crushed
- Sea salt and ground black pepper, to taste

Cilantro Cream:
- 1 cup cream cheese, softened
- 1/3 cup sour cream
- A pinch of celery salt
- A pinch of paprika
- 1 teaspoon garlic powder
- 1 bunch fresh cilantro, chopped
- 1 tablespoon fresh lime juice

Directions

- Press the "Sauté" button to heat up the Instant Pot. Now, heat the sesame oil. Sear the ribs until nicely browned on all sides.
- Season the ribs with red pepper, salt, and black pepper.
- Secure the lid. Choose "Manual" mode and High pressure; cook for 20 minutes. Once cooking is complete, use a quick pressure release; carefully remove the lid.
- Meanwhile, mix all ingredients for the cilantro cream. Place in the refrigerator until ready to serve. Serve warm ribs with the chilled cilantro cream on the side. Bon appétit!

232. Beef Black Pepper

Preparation Time: 26 minutes
Servings: 2

Ingredients:

- 1/2 lb. beef tenderloin
- 1/4 teaspoon sugar
- 1/4 cup chopped' onion
- 2 tablespoons tomato sauce
- 1 tablespoon soy sauce
- 2 tablespoons butter
- 1/2 cup water
- 1/4 teaspoon salt
- 1/2 teaspoon black pepper

Directions:

1. Cut the beef tenderloin into thick slices then rub with soy sauce, salt, black pepper, sugar, onion and tomato sauce. Place butter in the inner pot of an Instant Pot then select *Sauté* setting
2. Stir in the seasoned beef then sauté until wilted. Press the *Cancel* button
3. Pour water over the beef then cover and seal the Instant Pot properly. Closet the steam valve.
4. Select *Manual* setting and cook the beef on high. Set the time to 22 minutes
5. Once it is done; naturally release the Instant Pot and open the lid. Arrange the beef to a serving dish then serve with sautéed carrots and fried potatoes

Nutrition Value:

Calories: 299; Net Carbs: 2.9g; Total Fat: 19.6g; Protein: 26g; Carbs: 3.6g

233. French Style Beef Chuck Roast

Preparation Time: 55 minutes
Servings: 3

Ingredients:

- 2-pound. beef chuck roast
- 2 carrots; peeled and cut into 1-inch pieces
- 2 garlic cloves; minced
- 2 cups beef broth
- 2 tablespoons unsalted butter
- 1 yellow onion; cut in 4 pieces
- 1 tablespoon fresh lemon juice
- Salt and Pepper to taste

Directions:

1. Season beef with salt and pepper, add lemon juice and toss to coat.
2. Add butter to the Instant Pot and press *Sauté* button (*Normal* preset), wait till you see Hot on the display.
3. Add onion and cook for 2 to 3 minutes. Add garlic and cook for 1 more minute.
4. Press *Cancel* and add broth and beef. Close the lid and turn the vent to *Sealed*. Press *Pressure Cook* (Manual) button, use *+* or *-* button to set the timer for 40 minutes. Use *Pressure level* button to set Pressure to *HIGH*.
5. Once the timer is up; press *Cancel* button and turn the steam release handle to *Venting* position for quick release, until the float valve drops down.
6. Open the lid; Add carrots to the Instant pot and press *Sauté* button, adjust to *Less*.
7. Cook for 10 minutes with the lid open. Add more salt if needed and serve.

Nutrition Value:
Calories: 674 g; Total Fat: 50.6 g; Total Carbohydrate: 5 g; Protein: 36.4

;

234. Steamed Ground Beef Vegetables

Preparation Time: 20 minutes
Servings: 2

Ingredients:

- 1/2 lb. ground beef
- 1/4 teaspoon nutmeg
- 1/4 cup carrot sticks
- 1/4 teaspoon salt
- 1/2 cup broccoli florets
- 1/4 cup chopped' onion
- 2 teaspoons minced' garlic
- 1 teaspoon olive oil
- 1/4 teaspoon pepper

Directions:

1. Pour olive oil into the inner pot of an Instant Pot then select *Sauté* setting. Stir in chopped' onion, minced' garlic and ground beef then sauté until wilted and aromatic. Press the *Cancel* button
2. Transfer the half-cooked beef to a disposable aluminum pan then mix with broccoli florets and chopped' carrots.
3. Season with salt, pepper and nutmeg then stir until combined
4. Pour water into the Instant Pot then place a trivet in it. Put the disposable aluminum pan with beef and vegetables on the trivet then cover and seal the Instant Pot properly. Close the steam valve
5. Select *Steam* setting on the Instant Pot and cook the beef on high for 10 minutes
6. Once it is done; naturally release the Instant Pot and remove the aluminum pan out of the Instant Pot.
7. Transfer the beef and vegetables to a serving dish and serve right away

Nutrition Value:
Calories: 374; Net Carbs: 3.8g; Total Fat: 30.5g; Protein: 19.2g; Carbs: 5.1g

BROTH, STOCKS AND SAUCES

235. Pineapple Sauce

Preparation time: 10 minutes
Cooking time: 3 minutes
Servings: 4

Ingredients:

- 3 cups pineapple chunks
- 3 tablespoons rum
- 3 tablespoons butter
- 4 tablespoons brown sugar
- 1 teaspoon ground cinnamon
- 1 teaspoon allspice
- 1 teaspoon nutmeg
- 1 teaspoon ground ginger

Directions:

1. Set the Instant Pot on sauté mode, add the butter and melt it. Add the sugar, pineapple, rum, allspice, nutmeg, cinnamon, and ginger, stir, cover, and cook on the Manual setting for 3 minutes. Release the pressure, uncover the Instant Pot, stir sauce one more time, and serve.

Nutrition Value:
Calories: 160
Fat: 0
Fiber: 0
Carbs: 23
Protein: 0

236. Onion Sauce

Preparation time: 10 minutes
Cooking time: 30 minutes
Servings: 8

Ingredients:

- 6 tablespoons butter
- 3 pounds yellow onion, peeled and chopped
- Salt and ground black pepper, to taste
- ½ teaspoon baking soda

Directions:

1. Set the Instant Pot on Sauté mode, add the butter and heat it up. Add the onions and baking soda, stir, and cook for 3 minutes. Cover the Instant Pot and cook on the Manual setting for 20 minutes. Release the pressure, uncover the Instant Pot, set it on Sauté mode again, and cook for 5 minutes, stirring often. Serve when needed.

Nutrition Value:
Calories: 100
Fat: 0.4
Fiber: 0
Carbs: 9
Protein: 0

237. Green Tomato Sauce

Preparation time: 5 minutes
Cooking time: 10 minutes
Servings: 12

Ingredients:

- 2 pounds green tomatoes, cored and chopped
- 1 white onion, peeled and chopped
- ¼ cup currants
- 1 Anaheim chili pepper, chopped
- 4 red chili peppers, chopped
- 2 tablespoons ginger, grated
- ¾ cup brown sugar
- ¾ cup white vinegar

Directions:

1. In the Instant Pot, mix green tomatoes with onion, currants, Anaheim pepper, chili pepper, ginger, sugar, and vinegar, stir, cover and cook on the Manual setting for 10 minutes. Release the pressure for 5 minutes, uncover the Instant Pot, transfer sauce to jars, and serve.

Nutrition Value:

Calories: 50
Fat: 2
Fiber: 2.4
Carbs: 10
Protein: 1.5

238. Plum Sauce

Preparation time: 10 minutes
Cooking time: 15 minutes
Servings: 20

Ingredients:

- 3 pounds plums, pitted and chopped
- 2 onions, peeled and chopped
- 2 apples, cored and chopped
- 4 tablespoons ground ginger
- 4 tablespoons ground cinnamon
- 4 tablespoons allspice
- 1½ tablespoons salt
- 1 pint vinegar
- ¾ pound sugar

Directions:

2. Put the plums, apples, and onions into the Instant Pot. Add the ginger, cinnamon, allspice, salt, and almost all the vinegar, stir, cover, and cook on the Manual setting for 10 minutes. Release the pressure, uncover the Instant Pot, set it on Manual mode, add the rest of the vinegar and the sugar, stir, and cook until sugar dissolves. Keep sauce refrigerated until ready to use.

Nutrition Value:

Calories: 100
Fat: 10
Fiber: 3
Carbs: 23
Protein: 26

239. Clementine Sauce

Preparation time: 10 minutes
Cooking time: 6 minutes
Servings: 4

Ingredients:

- 12 ounces cranberries
- 1 cup water
- Juice and peel from 1 clementine
- 1 cup sugar

Directions:

1. In the Instant Pot, mix the cranberries with clementine juice and peel, water, and sugar, stir, cover and cook on the Manual setting for 6 minutes. Release the pressure, uncover the Instant Pot, and serve.

Nutrition Value:

Calories: 50
Fat: 0
Fiber: 0
Carbs: 0.3
Protein: 0

240. Orange Sauce

Preparation time: 10 minutes
Cooking time: 7 minutes
Servings: 6

Ingredients:

- ¼ cup white wine vinegar
- 1 teaspoon ginger paste
- 2 tablespoons tomato paste
- 3 tablespoons sugar
- 1 cup orange juice
- 1 teaspoon garlic, diced
- 2 tablespoons agave nectar
- 1 teaspoon sesame oil
- 1 teaspoon chili sauce
- 2 tablespoons soy sauce
- ¼ cup vegetable stock
- 2 tablespoons cornstarch

Directions:

1. Set the Instant Pot on Sauté mode, add the oil and heat it up. Add the garlic and ginger paste, stir, and cook for 2 minutes. Add the tomato paste, sugar, orange juice, vinegar, agave nectar, soy sauce, and chili sauce, stir, cover, and cook on the Manual setting for 3 minutes. Release the pressure, uncover the Instant Pot,

add the stock and cornstarch, stir, cover again, and cook on the Manual setting for 4 minutes. Release the pressure again, and serve your sauce.

Nutrition Value:

Calories: 80
Fat: 7
Fiber: 1.4
Carbs: 5
Protein: 13

241. Sriracha Sauce

Preparation time: 10 minutes
Cooking time: 17 minutes
Servings: 6

Ingredients:

- 4 ounces red chilies, seeded and chopped
- 3 tablespoons brown sugar
- 3 ounces arbol chilies, dried
- 12 garlic cloves, peeled and minced
- 5 ounces distilled vinegar
- 5 ounces water

Directions:

1. In the Instant Pot, mix the water with the brown sugar and stir. Add all the chilies and garlic, stir, cover and cook on the Manual setting for 7 minutes. Release the pressure, uncover the Instant Pot, blend sauce using an immersion blender, add the vinegar, stir, set the Instant Pot on Manual mode, and cook the sauce for 10 minutes. Serve when needed.

Nutrition Value:

Calories: 90
Fat: 0.4
Fiber: 0.3
Carbs: 19
Protein: 2.4

242. Grape Sauce

Preparation time: 10 minutes
Cooking time: 10 minutes
Servings: 6

Ingredients:

- 6 ounces black grapes
- ½ cup water
- 2½ tablespoons sugar
- 1 cup corn flour
- Lemon juice

Directions:

2. Put grapes into the Instant Pot, add enough water to cover, cook on the Manual setting for 7 minutes, release the pressure, set the mixture aside to cool down, blend using an immersion blender, strain the sauce, and set the dish aside. Heat up a pan over medium heat, add the grapes, sugar, water, and corn flour, stir, and boil until it thickens. Add the lemon juice, stir, take off heat, and serve.

Nutrition Value:

Calories: 60
Fiber: 0.3
Carbs: 0
Protein: 3

243, Bread Sauce

Preparation time: 10 minutes
Cooking time: 10 minutes
Servings: 12

Ingredients:

- 1 yellow onion, peeled and chopped
- 2 garlic cloves, peeled and crushed
- 6 cloves
- 26 ounces milk
- 6 bread slices, torn
- 2 bay leaves
- Salt, to taste
- 2 tablespoons butter
- Heavy cream

Directions:

3. Set the Instant Pot on Manual mode, add the milk and heat it up. Add the garlic, cloves, onion, bay leaves, and salt, stir well, and cook for 3 minutes. Add the bread, stir, cover, and cook on the Manual setting for 4 minutes. Release the pressure, uncover the Instant Pot,

transfer the sauce to a blender, add the butter and cream, discard the bay leaves, and blend well. Return the sauce to the Instant Pot set it on Manual mode and simmer sauce for 3 minutes.

Nutrition Value:

Calories: 113
Fat: 5
Fiber: 2.4
Carbs: 11
Protein: 3

244. Chili Jam

Preparation time: 10 minutes
Cooking time: 40 minutes
Servings: 12

Ingredients:

- 4 garlic cloves, peeled and minced
- 2 red onions, peeled and diced
- 4 red chili peppers, seeded and chopped
- 17 ounces cranberries
- 4 ounces sugar
- Olive oil
- Salt and ground black pepper, to taste
- 2 tablespoons red wine vinegar
- 3 tablespoons water

Directions:

1. Set the Instant Pot on Sauté mode, add the oil and heat it up. Add the onions, garlic, and chilies, stir, and cook for 8 minutes. Add the cranberries, vinegar, water, and sugar, stir, cover the Instant Pot, and cook on the Manual setting for 14 minutes. Release the pressure, uncover the Instant Pot, puree sauce using an immersion blender, set the Instant Pot on Manual mode, and cook the sauce for 15 minutes. Add the salt and pepper, transfer to jars, and serve when needed.

Nutrition Value:

Calories: 20
Fat: 0.2
Fiber: 0.4
Carbs: 4

Protein: 0.2

245. Pomegranate Sauce

Preparation time: 10 minutes
Cooking time: 25 minutes
Servings: 4

Ingredients:

- 5 cups pomegranate juice
- ½ cup lemon juice
- 1 cup white sugar

Directions:

1. In the Instant Pot, mix the pomegranate juice with sugar, and lemon juice, stir, cover, and cook on the Manual setting for 25 minutes. Release the pressure, uncover the Instant Pot, divide sauce into jars, and serve when needed.

Nutrition Value:

Calories: 136
Fat: 0.4
Fiber: 0.8
Carbs: 35
Protein: 1.2

246. Apricot Sauce

Preparation time: 10 minutes
Cooking time: 20 minutes
Servings: 6

Ingredients:

- 3 ounces apricots, dried and cut into halves
- 2 cups water
- ⅔ cup sugar
- 1 teaspoon vanilla extract

Directions:

1. In the Instant Pot, mix the apricots with water, sugar, and vanilla, stir, cover, and cook on Manual for 20 minutes. Release the pressure, uncover the Instant Pot, transfer the sauce to a blender, and pulse well. Divide into jars, and serve with a poultry dish.

Nutrition Value:

Calories: 100
Fat: 0.6
Fiber: 0
Carbs: 10
Protein: 1

247. Broccoli Sauce

Preparation time: 10 minutes
Cooking time: 6 minutes
Servings: 4

Ingredients:

- 6 cups water
- 3 cups broccoli florets
- 2 garlic cloves, minced
- Salt and ground black pepper, to taste
- ⅓ cup coconut milk
- 1 tablespoon white wine vinegar
- 1 tablespoons nutritional yeast
- 1 tablespoon olive oil

Directions:

1. Put the water into the Instant Pot. Add the broccoli, salt, pepper, and garlic, stir, cover, and cook on the Manual setting for 6 minutes. Release the pressure, uncover the Instant Pot, strain the broccoli and garlic, and transfer to a food processor. Add the coconut milk, vinegar, yeast, olive oil, salt, and pepper and blend well. Serve over pasta.

Nutrition Value:

Calories: 128
Fat: 10
Fiber: 1.4
Carbs: 6
Protein: 5.4

248. Carrot Sauce

Preparation time: 10 minutes
Cooking time: 15 minutes
Servings: 6

Ingredients:

- 4 tablespoons butter
- 2 cups carrot juice
- Ground cinnamon
- Salt and ground black pepper, to taste
- Cayenne pepper
- 1 teaspoon dried chervil
- 1 teaspoon dried chives
- 1 teaspoon dried tarragon

Directions:

2. Put the carrot juice into the Instant Pot, set the Instant Pot on Manual mode, and bring to a boil. Add the butter, salt, pepper, cayenne and cinnamon, stir, cover and cook on the Manual setting for 5 minutes. Release the pressure, uncover the Instant Pot, add the chervil, chives, and tarragon, stir, and serve.

Nutrition Value:

Calories: 149
Fat: 7
Fiber: 4
Carbs: 19
Protein: 2
Sugars 8

249. Mustard Sauce

Preparation time: 10 minutes
Cooking time: 7 minutes
Servings: 4

Ingredients:

- 6 ounces mushrooms, chopped
- 3 tablespoon olive oil
- ounces dry sherry
- 1 thyme sprig
- 1 garlic clove, peeled and minced
- ounces beef stock
- 1 tablespoon balsamic vinegar
- 1 tablespoon mustard
- 2 tablespoon crème fraiche
- 2 tablespoons fresh parsley, diced

Directions:

1. Set the Instant Pot on Sauté mode, add the oil and heat it up. Add the garlic, thyme, and mushrooms, stir, and cook for 5 minutes. Add the sherry, vinegar, and stock, stir, cover, and cook on the

Manual setting for 3 minutes. Release the pressure, uncover the Instant Pot, discard the thyme, add the crème fraiche, mustard, and parsley, stir, set the Instant Pot on Manual mode, and cook the sauce for 3 minutes, and serve.

Nutrition Value:

Calories: 67
Fat: 0.4
Fiber: 0.2
Carbs: 4
Protein: 1

250. Eggplant Sauce

Preparation time: 10 minutes
Cooking time: 20 minutes
Servings: 6

Ingredients:

- 1 pound ground beef
- 28 ounces canned diced tomatoes
- 5 garlic cloves, peeled and minced
- 5 ounces canned tomato paste
- 1 onion, peeled and chopped
- 1 eggplant, chopped
- ½ cup olive oil
- ½ teaspoon turmeric
- 1 cup vegetable stock
- 1 tablespoon apple cider vinegar
- ½ teaspoon dried dill
- Salt and ground black pepper, to taste
- ¼ cup fresh parsley, chopped

Directions:

1. Set the Instant Pot on Sauté mode, add the beef, brown for a few minutes, and transfer to a bowl. Heat up the oil into the Instant Pot, add the onion and some salt, and cook for 2 minutes. Add the eggplant and garlic, stir, and cook for 1 minute. Add the vinegar, stir, and cook for 2 minutes. Add the tomato paste, tomatoes, meat, salt, pepper, parsley, dill, turmeric, and stock, stir, cover, and cook on the Manual setting for 15 minutes. Release the pressure, uncover the Instant Pot, add more salt and pepper, and a splash of lemon juice, stir well, and serve.

Nutrition Value:

Calories: 142
Fat: 11
Fiber: 4.4
Carbs: 10
Protein: 2.1

251. Cherry Sauce

Preparation time: 10 minutes
Cooking time: 5 minutes
Servings: 4

Ingredients:

- 1 tablespoon lemon juice
- ¼ cup water
- 1 teaspoon kirsch
- Salt
- 1 tablespoon sugar
- 2 tablespoons cornstarch
- 2 cups cherries

Directions:

1. In the Instant Pot, mix the water with lemon juice, salt, sugar, kirsch, and cornstarch. Add the cherries, stir, cover, and cook on the Manual setting for 5 minutes. Release the pressure, uncover the Instant Pot, transfer the sauce to a bowl, and serve after chilling.

Nutrition Value:

Calories: 60
Fat: 0
Fiber: 0
Carbs: 13
Protein: 0

252. Date Sauce

Preparation time: 10 minutes
Cooking time: 9 minutes
Servings: 6

Ingredients:

- 2 cups apple juice
- 2 cups dates, dried

- 1 tablespoon lemon juice

Directions:

1. In the Instant Pot, mix the apple juice with the lemon juice and dates, stir, cover and cook on the Manual setting for 9 minutes. Release the pressure, uncover the Instant Pot, blend using an immersion blender, and transfer to a container. Serve when needed.

Nutrition Value:

Calories: 30
Fat: 0
Fiber: 1
Carbs: 5
Protein: 0
Sugar: 5

253. Pear Sauce

Preparation time: 10 minutes
Cooking time: 15 minutes
Servings: 5 pints

Ingredients:

- 10 cups pears, sliced
- 2 teaspoons ground cinnamon
- 1 cup pear juice
- ½ teaspoon nutmeg

Directions:

- Put pear pieces into the Instant Pot, add the cinnamon, nutmeg, and pear juice. Stir, cover the Instant Pot, and cook on the Manual setting for 10 minutes. Release the pressure, uncover the Instant Pot, blend using an immersion blender, and serve when needed.

Nutrition Value:

Calories: 80
Fat: 0.1
Fiber: 0
Carbs: 20
Protein: 0.1

254. Guava Sauce

Preparation time: 10 minutes
Cooking time: 20 minutes
Servings: 6

Ingredients:

- 1 can guava shells and syrup
- 2 onions, peeled and chopped
- ¼ cup vegetable oil
- Juice from 2 lemons
- 2 garlic cloves, peeled and chopped
- 1-inch ginger piece, peeled and minced
- ½ teaspoon nutmeg
- 2 Serrano chilies, chopped

Directions:

1. Put guava shells and syrup into the blender, pulse well and set aside. Set the Instant Pot on Sauté mode, add the oil and heat it up. Add the onion and garlic, stir and cook for 4 minutes. Add the guava mix, ginger, lemon juice, chilies, and nutmeg, stir, cover, and cook on High for 15 minutes. Release the pressure, uncover the Instant Pot, and serve sauce with fish.

Nutrition Value:

Calories: 85
Fat: 2.3
Fiber: 8
Carbs: 22
Protein: 3

255. Sour Onion Sauce Recipe

Preparation Time: 15 Minutes
Servings: 2

Ingredients:

- 1 large onion; sliced
- 1-2 tablespoon apple cider vinegar
- 1 cup water or chicken stock
- 1 tablespoon olive oil
- 2 teaspoon almond flour
- 1 teaspoon cayenne pepper
- 1 teaspoon stevia powder
- 1/4 teaspoon salt

Directions:

1. Plug in the instant pot and press the *Saute* button. Heat up the olive oil and

add onions. Sprinkle with salt and stevia and cook for 2-3 minutes, or until translucent
2. Now add almond flour and give it a good stir. Continue to cook for one more minute and then add cayenne pepper. Pour in water or chicken stock and sprinkle with apple cider vinegar
3. Bring it to a boil and press the *Cancel'* button. Chill for a while and store until use

Nutrition Value: Calories: 108; Total Fats: 8.4g; Net Carbs: 6g; Protein: 1.4g; Fiber: 2.1g

256. Spicy Pepper Beef Stock

Preparation Time: 40 Minutes
Servings: 6

Ingredients:

- 2 -pounds beef bones
- 3 chili peppers; whole
- 4 garlic cloves; whole
- 1/4 cup celery stalk; chopped.
- 1/4 cup celery leaves; chopped
- 1/4 cup onions; chopped.
- 3 tablespoon red wine vinegar
- 1/2 teaspoon red pepper flakes
- 2 teaspoon chili pepper
- 1 teaspoon salt

Directions:

1. Place the bones in the pot and pour in enough water to cover. Add vegetables and drizzle with red wine vinegar. Season with salt, chili pepper, and pepper flakes
2. Stir well and seal the lid. Set the steam release handle to the *Sealing* position and press the *Manual* button. Set the timer for 35 minutes on high pressure
3. When done; release the pressure naturally and open the lid. Stir well again and strain the liquid.
4. Chill for a while and refrigerate

Nutrition Value: Calories: 17; Total Fats: 0.4g; Net Carbs: 0.8g; Protein: 2g; Fiber: 0.3g

257. Celery and Tomato Fish Stock

Preparation Time: 25 Minutes
Servings: 6

Ingredients:

- 2 -pounds halibut bones; cleaned
- 2 small onions; sliced
- 1/4 cup apple cider vinegar
- 2 celery stalks; chopped
- 1 fresh rosemary sprig
- 2 fresh thyme sprigs
- 2 teaspoon sea salt

Directions:

1. Place the bones in the pot and pour in one cup of water and apple cider vinegar. Sprinkle with one teaspoon of salt and press the *Saute* button
2. Bring it to a boil and gently simmer for 10-15 minutes. Make sure to skim of the foam that might appear on top
3. Now press the *Cancel'* button and add the remaining ingredients. Pour in 7 cups of water and seal the lid. Set the steam release handle to the *Sealing* position and press the *Manual* button. Set the timer for 12 minutes on high pressure
4. When done, release the pressure naturally and open the lid. Chill for a while and strain the stock.
5. Optionally, sprinkle with some white pepper and refrigerate

Nutrition Value: Calories: 43; Total Fats: 1.9g; Net Carbs: 0.3g; Protein: 5.3g; Fiber: 0.1g

258. Lamb Ribs Stock

Preparation Time: 40 Minutes
Servings: 6

Ingredients:

- 2 -pounds lamb ribs; meat on
- 1 carrot; sliced
- 2 small onions; sliced
- 1 large tomato; whole
- 3 tablespoon olive oil
- 1 tablespoon smoked paprika
- 1 teaspoon black pepper; freshly ground.

- 1 teaspoon sea salt

Directions:
1. Rinse the lamb under cold running water and drain in a large colander. Chop in smaller pieces and place in the pot
2. Pour in enough water to cover and season with salt. Seal the lid and set the steam release handle. Press the *Manual* button and cook for 20 minutes on high pressure
3. When you hear the cooker's end signal, perform a quick release and open the lid. Add sliced carrot, onions, tomato, pepper, and smoked paprika.
4. Stir well and seal the lid again. Set the steam release handle to the sealing position and press the *Manual* button again. Continue to cook for 10 more minutes
5. When done; release the pressure naturally and open the lid. Strain the liquid and stir in the olive oil.
6. Chill for a while and transfer to glass jars. Refrigerate until use

Nutrition Value: Calories: 77; Total Fats: 7.5g; Net Carbs: 0.7g; Protein: 2.1g; Fiber: 0.6g

259. Chicken Stock

Preparation Time: 2 hours 5 Minutes
Servings: 4

Ingredients:
- 3 -pounds chicken necks and back
- 1 cup spring onions; finely chopped.
- 1 tablespoon apple cider vinegar
- 2 teaspoon dried celery
- 1 teaspoon white pepper
- 2 teaspoon salt

Directions:
1. Place the bones in your instant pot and pour in enough water to cover. Season with salt and add vinegar. Seal the lid and set the steam release handle to the *Sealing* position. Press the *Manual* button and set the timer for 5 minutes on high pressure
2. When you hear the cooker's end signal, perform a quick pressure release and open the lid. Stir in spring onions and sprinkle with pepper and celery
3. Seal the lid again and set the steam release handle. Press the *Slow Cook* button and set the timer for 2 hours on low pressure
4. When done; release the pressure naturally and optionally season with some more salt or pepper to taste. Strain the liquid and refrigerate until use

Nutrition Value: Calories: 13; Total Fats: 0.6g; Net Carbs: 1.1g; Protein: 0.8g; Fiber: 0.2g

260. Instant Sour Beef Stock

Preparation Time: 35 Minutes
Servings: 6

Ingredients:
- 2 -pounds beef bones
- 1 cup apple cider vinegar
- 1 large onion; wedged
- 2 celery stalks; chopped.
- 1 cup sauerkraut
- 1 cup tomatoes; chopped
- 1 teaspoon peppercorn
- 1 teaspoon black pepper
- 1 teaspoon salt

Directions:
1. Place the bones in a deep bowl and pour in apple cider vinegar and enough water to cover. Soak for 1 hour
2. Transfer to the instant pot and add celery stalks. Seal the lid and set the steam release handle
3. Press the *Manual* button and cook for 15 minutes on high pressure
4. When you hear the end signal, perform a quick pressure release and open the lid.
5. Now stir in the remaining vegetables and sauerkraut. Season with pepper and seal the lid again.
6. Set the steam release handle and press the *Manual* button. Set the timer for 12 minutes on high pressure

7. When done, release the pressure naturally and carefully open the lid. Strain the stock and transfer to jars with tight lids. Refrigerate until use

Nutrition Value: Calories: 28; Total Fats: 0.6g; Net Carbs: 0.9g; Protein: 2.9g; Fiber: 0.3g

261. Pizza Sauce Recipe

Preparation Time: 10 Minutes
Servings: 4

Ingredients:

- 1 cup cherry tomatoes; sliced
- 2 tablespoon apple cider vinegar
- 2 cups tomato sauce; sugar-free
- 1 small onion; finely chopped.
- 1 tablespoon tomato paste
- 2 tablespoon chopped parsley; finely chopped
- 1 garlic clove; crushed
- 2 tablespoon olive oil
- 2 tablespoon swerve
- 1 teaspoon dried oregano
- 1/4 teaspoon black pepper
- 2 teaspoon sea salt

Directions:

1. Place tomatoes, parsley, onions, garlic, and apple cider in a food processor. Process until smooth and set aside
2. Plug in the instant pot and press the *Saute* button. Heat up the oil and pour in the processed mixture. Add tomato paste and season with salt, oregano, pepper, and swerve
3. Cook for 4-5 minutes
4. Press the *Cancel'* button and remove from the pot. Serve immediately or store for later.

Nutrition Value: Calories: 111; Total Fats: 7.4g; Net Carbs: 8.2g; Protein: 2.5g; Fiber: 3g

262. Green Peppers Butter Sauce Recipe

Preparation Time: 20 Minutes
Servings: 3

Ingredients:

- 1/2 small onion; finely chopped.
- 2 tablespoon olive oil
- 2 green bell peppers; chopped
- 1/4 cup whole milk
- 1/4 cup butter
- 2 tablespoon almond flour
- 1/4 teaspoon freshly ground black pepper
- 1/2 teaspoon dried basil
- 1/4 teaspoon garlic powder
- 1/2 teaspoon salt

Directions:

1. Melt the butter on the *Saute* mode and add bell peppers and onions. Sprinkle with salt and cook until peppers have softened
2. Now add olive oil and season with black pepper, garlic powder, and basil. Stir in almond flour and continue to cook for another minute
3. Pour in the milk and give it a good stir. Bring it to a boil and press the *Cancel'* button.
4. Remove the sauce from the pot and use immediately

Nutrition Value: Calories: 287; Total Fats: 27.8g; Net Carbs: 7.4g; Protein: 2.8g; Fiber: 1.9g

263. Garlic Cauliflower Sauce Recipe

Preparation Time: 20 Minutes
Servings: 6

Ingr edients:

- 4 cups cauliflower; chopped into florets
- 2 tablespoon Parmesan cheese
- 3 tablespoon nutritional yeast
- 3 tablespoon butter
- 1 tablespoon lemon juice; freshly squeezed
- 2 garlic cloves; crushed
- 1/4 cup heavy cream
- 1/4 cup whole milk

- 1/2 teaspoon dried rosemary
- 1/2 teaspoon white pepper
- 1 teaspoon salt

Directions:

1. Plug in the instant pot and add cauliflower. Pour in enough water to cover and seal the lid. Set the steam release handle to the *Sealing* position and press the *Manual* button. Set the timer for 8 minutes
2. When done, release the pressure naturally and open the lid. Drain the cauliflower and chill for a while
3. Meanwhile, melt the butter on the *Saute* mode. Add garlic and briefly cook – for one minute
4. Now add cauliflower and cook for 3-4 minutes, stirring constantly. Pour in the heavy cream and milk. Season with salt, pepper, and rosemary. Bring it to a boil and then press the *Cancel'* button. Stir in the nutritional yeast and Parmesan cheese
5. Finally, sprinkle with lemon juice and serve. Optionally, transfer the mixture to a food processor and process until smooth.

Nutrition Value: Calories: 126; Total Fats: 9.3g; Net Carbs: 4g; Protein: 5.7g; Fiber: 3g

264. Sweet BBQ Sauce Recipe

Preparation Time: 35 Minutes
Servings: 4

Ingredients:

- 2 -pounds tomatoes; chopped
- 1 cup swerve
- 1/4 cup soy sauce
- 3 tablespoon apple cider vinegar
- 2 teaspoon agar powder
- 4 garlic cloves
- 1/2 teaspoon cinnamon powder
- 1/2 teaspoon curry powder
- 1/2 teaspoon black pepper; freshly ground.
- 2 cloves
- 2 teaspoon salt

Directions:

1. Place tomatoes in the pot and sprinkle with salt. Pour in 3 cups of water and seal the lid. Set the steam release handle to the *Sealing* position and press the *Manual* button
2. Set the timer for 5 minutes
3. When done, perform a quick pressure release and open the lid. Stir in apple cider, stevia, garlic, and cloves. Press the *Saute* button and bring it to a boil. Gently simmer for 15 minutes.
4. Finally, add soy sauce, agar powder, and the remaining spices. Continue to cook for 2-3 minutes, stirring constantly
5. Press the *Cancel'* button and chill for a while. Transfer the mixture to a food processor and process until smooth.

Nutrition Value: Calories: 59; Total Fats: 0.5g; Net Carbs: 8.9g; Protein: 3.3g; Fiber: 3.2g

265. Tuna Lemon Sauce Recipe

Preparation Time: 15 Minutes
Servings: 4

Ingredients:

- 2 cups canned tuna; drained
- 2 tablespoon apple cider vinegar
- 4 cups tomato sauce; sugar-free
- 2 tablespoon soy sauce
- 1 onion; finely chopped
- 1/4 cup mozzarella; shredded
- 2 tablespoon olive oil
- 3 garlic cloves; crushed
- 2 teaspoon basil; dried
- 1 tablespoon oregano; dried
- 1/2 teaspoon sea salt

Directions:

1. Heat up the olive oil in the *Saute* mode and add onions and garlic. Cook for 2-3 minutes and then add tomato sauce. Sprinkle with apple cider and soy sauce
2. Continue to cook for 2 more minute
3. Finally, add tna and mozzarella. Season

with basil, oregano, and salt. Give it a good stir and cook for 2-3 more minutes.
4. Press the *Cancel* button and serve

Nutrition Value: Calories: 313; Total Fats: 15.1g; Net Carbs: 13.9g; Protein: 28.4g; Fiber: 4.9g

266. Creamy Spinach Sauce Recipe

Preparation Time: 15 Minutes
Servings: 5

Ingredients:

- 2 cups heavy cream
- 2 tablespoon pine nuts; finely chopped.
- 3 tablespoon olive oil
- 1 small onion; finely chopped
- 2 cups spinach; shredded
- 2 garlic cloves; sliced
- 2 tablespoon Parmesan cheese
- 1/2 cup gorgonzola cheese
- 1 teaspoon dried celery
- 1/2 teaspoon black pepper; freshly ground
- 1/4 teaspoon nutmeg
- 1/4 teaspoon dried basil
- 1 teaspoon salt

Directions:

1. Plug in the instant pot and press the *Saute* button. Grease the inner pot with olive oil and add onions and garlic. Cook until translucent and then add spinach.
2. Continue to cook until wilted
3. Now add gorgonzola and parmesan cheese. Pour in the heavy cream and season with spices.
4. Give it a good stir and warm up
5. Press the *Cancel* button and transfer the mixture to a food processor along with pine nuts.
6. Process until smooth.

Nutrition Value: Calories: 366; Total Fats: 35.8g; Net Carbs: 4.1g; Protein: 9.4g; Fiber: 1.3g

267. Bolognese Recipe

Preparation Time: 2 hours 20 Minutes
Servings: 6

Ingredients:

- 1-pound ground pork
- 1 small chili pepper; sliced
- 10-ounce ground beef
- 1/4 cup celery stalks; chopped.
- 6 tablespoon tomato sauce; sugar-free
- 1 onion; sliced
- 1/4 cup balsamic vinegar
- 4 tablespoon olive oil
- 2 garlic cloves; crushed
- 2 tablespoon parsley leaves
- 1/2 teaspoon dried basil
- 1/2 teaspoon black pepper; freshly ground.
- 1/2 teaspoon dried oregano
- 1 ½ teaspoon salt

Directions:

1. Plug in the instant pot and press the *Saute* button. Grease the inner pot with olive oil and heat up. Add onions, garlic, chili pepper, and celery. Sprinkle with salt and cook for 5-6 minutes, stirring occasionally
2. Now add the meat, tomato sauce, and red wine vinegar. Sprinkle with pepper, basil, and oregano. Stir well again and continue to cook for 5 minutes
3. Finally, pour in 4 cups of water and sprinkle with parsley. Press the *Cancel* button and seal the lid.
4. Set the steam release handle to the *Sealing* position and press the *Slow Cook* button. Set the timer for 2 hours
5. When done; release the pressure naturally and open the lid. Serve immediately or store for later.

Nutrition Value: Calories: 293; Total Fats: 15g; Net Carbs: 2.5g; Protein: 34.7g; Fiber: 0.9g

268. Simple Fish Stock

Preparation Time: 2 hours 15 Minutes
Servings: 6

Ingredients:

- 1-pound fish bones and heads
- 1 large onion; sliced
- 1 small carrot; sliced
- 1 small celery stalk; chopped
- 3 tablespoon fresh parsley leaves
- 1/2 teaspoon red pepper flakes
- 1/2 teaspoon wite pepper
- 1 teaspoon sea salt

Directions:
1. Place the bones in the pot and add onions, celery, and carrot. Pour in one cup of water and press the *Saute* button
2. Bring it to a boil and simmer for 10-12 minutes. Using a large wooden spoon, remove the foam from the top and press the *Cancel'* button
3. Now add the remaining ingredients and pour in 6 cups of water. Seal the lid and set the steam release handle to the *Sealing* position. Press the *Slow Cook* button and set the timer for 2 hours on low pressure
4. When done, release the pressure naturally and open the lid. Chill for a while and strain the stock.
5. Optionally, sprinkle with some dried celery and refrigerate until use

Nutrition Value: Calories: 38; Total Fats: 1.3g; Net Carbs: 1.9g; Protein: 3.9g; Fiber: 0.7g

269. Cabbage Beef Stock

Preparation Time: 1 hour 15 Minutes
Servings: 6

Ingredients:
- 2 -pounds beef marrow bones
- 2 cups green cabbage; shredded
- 1 cup celery stalk; chopped.
- 1 medium-sized onion; sliced
- 1/2 cup fresh parsley; chopped
- 1/4 cup apple cider vinegar
- 2 tablespoon tomato paste; sugar-free
- 1 teaspoon fresh rosemary; finely chopped.
- 1 teaspoon cayenne pepper
- 1 teaspoon salt

Directions:
1. Place bones in a deep bowl and pour in apple cider vinegar and enough water to cover. Sprinkle with salt and soak for 30-40 minutes
2. Transfer to the pot and stir in tomato paste. Add celery stalks, onion, cayenne, and rosemary
3. Give it a good stir and seal the lid. Set the steam release handle to the *Sealing* position and press the *Manual* button. Set the timer for 25 minutes on high pressure
4. When done; perform a quick pressure release and open the lid. Add cabbage and seal the lid again.
5. Cook for 10 more minutes on the *Manual* mode
6. When done, release the pressure naturally and open the lid. Remove the bones and strain the liquid. Transfer the broth to glass jars with tight lids. Refrigerate until use

Nutrition Value: Calories: 28; Total Fats: 0.6g; Net Carbs: 1.8g; Protein: 2.9g; Fiber: 0.6g

270. Asparagus Sauce Recipe

Preparation Time: 15 Minutes
Servings: 4

Ingredients:
- 1 cup asparagus; chopped
- 1/2 cup whole milk
- 2 tablespoon butter
- 1/4 cup parsley; finely chopped
- 1 cup heavy cream
- 1 teaspoon Dijon mustard
- 1 teaspoon agar powder
- 1/2 teaspoon dried marjoram
- 1/2 teaspoon black pepper; freshly ground.
- 1/2 teaspoon dried rosemary
- 1 teaspoon salt

Directions:

1. Melt the butter on the *Sauté* mode and add asparagus. Sprinkle with salt and cook for 2-3 minutes.
2. Pour in the milk and heavy cream. Add parsley, Dijon and season with the remaining spices.
3. Give it a good stir and cook for 5 minutes
4. Finally, stir in agar powder and briefly cook – for about one minute
5. Press the *Cancel'* button and remove from the pot
6. Transfer the mixture to a food processor and process until smooth. Serve immediately or store for later.

Nutrition Value: Calories: 182; Total Fats: 18g; Net Carbs: 3g; Protein: 2.6g; Fiber: 0.9g

271. Mushroom Sauce Recipe

Preparation Time: 10 Minutes
Servings: 4

Ingredients:

- 2 cups button mushrooms; sliced
- 2 tablespoon Parmesan cheese; freshly grated
- 3 tablespoon sour cream
- 2 tablespoon soy sauce
- 1 teaspoon agar powder
- 1 cup heavy cream
- 2 tablespoon butter
- 3 tablespoon gorgonzola cheese
- 1 tablespoon sesame oil
- 1 teaspoon dried celery
- 1/3 teaspoon black pepper
- 1 teaspoon salt

Directions:

1. Melt the butter on the *Saute* mode and add mushrooms. Season with salt and pepper.
2. Give it a good stir and cook until the liquid from the mushrooms evaporates
3. Njow add sour cream, gorgonzola cheese, and heavy cream. Sprinkle with dried celery and cook until cheese melts
4. Finally, pour in the soy sauce and add sesame oil. Stir in agar powder and briefly cook – for another minute
5. Press the *Cancel'* button and remove the sauce from the pot. Serve hot and enjoy!

Nutrition Value: Calories: 265; Total Fats: 26g; Net Carbs: 3.1g; Protein: 6.6g; Fiber: 0.7g

272. Peanut Butter Sauce Recipe

Preparation Time: 15 Minutes
Servings: 6

Ingredients:

- 2 large tomatoes; chopped.
- 1 small onion; finely chopped.
- 2 tablespoon olive oil
- 1 small chili pepper; finely chopped
- 1 garlic clove; crushed
- 3 tablespoon peanut butter
- 1/4 cup chicken stock
- 2 tablespoon freshly chopped celery leaves
- 2 tablespoon fish sauce
- 2 tablespoon lemon juice; freshly squeezed
- 2 teaspoon stevia powder
- 1 teaspoon ginger powder

Directions:

1. Grease the bottom of the stainless steel insert with olive oil and press the *Saute* button. Add onions, garlic, and chili pepper. Give it a good stir and cook for 3-4 minutes
2. Now add tomatoes and sauté until the liquid evaporates. Stir in the peanut butter, celery leaves, fish sauce, and lemon juice. Sprinkle with ginger powder and stevia powder. Stir well and cook for 1 minute
3. Now pour in the chicken stock and bring it to a boil. Cook for 4-5 minutes
4. Press the *Cancel'* button and transfer to a bowl. Chill for a while and serve

Nutrition Value: Calories: 109; Total Fats: 8.9g; Net Carbs: 4.3g; Protein: 3.1g; Fiber: 1.6g

273. Soy Sauce Recipe

Preparation Time: 10 Minutes
Servings: 2

Ingredients:

- 1/2 cup soy sauce
- 2 garlic cloves; crushed
- 2 tablespoon oil
- 3 tablespoon rice vinegar
- 3 tablespoon swerve
- 2 tablespoon balsamic vinegar
- 1/4 teaspoon garlic powder
- 1/2 teaspoon ginger powder

Directions:

1. Pour the soy sauce in the instant pot and press the *Saute* button. Add swerve and gently bring it to a boil. Stir well and cook for 1-2 minutes
2. Now add balsamic vinegar, rice vinegar, oil, and garlic. Season with garlic powder and ginger powder.
3. Stir well and cook for 5 minutes
4. When done, press the *Cancel'* button and remove the sauce from the pot. Serve hot and enjoy!

Nutrition Value: Calories: 177; Total Fats: 13.7g; Net Carbs: 5.4g; Protein: 4.2g; Fiber: 0.6g

274. Short Ribs Tomato Stock

Preparation Time: 1 hour
Servings: 5

Ingredients:

- 2 -pounds short ribs
- 2 onions; sliced
- 4 garlic cloves; whole
- 1/4 cup fresh parsley; chopped
- 4 tablespoon olive oil
- 1 cup tomatoes; diced
- 3 teaspoon stevia powder
- 1 teaspoon black pepper; ground.
- 2 teaspoon pink Himalayan salt

Directions:

1. Preheat the oven to 350 degrees F. Line some parchment paper over a baking sheet and set aside
2. Rub the ribs with olive oil and place on a baking sheet along with diced tomatoes, sliced onion, and garlic. Sprinkle with some salt and roast for 25 minutes
3. Remove from the oven and chill for a while. Transfer to the pot and pour in enough water to cover. Sprinkle with salt, pepper, and stevia powder. Add freshly chopped parsley and seal the lid
4. Set the steam release handle to the *Sealing* position and press the *Manual* button. Set the timer for 30 minutes
5. When done, release the pressure naturally and open the lid. Strain the liquid and refrigerate until use

Nutrition Value: Calories: 115; Total Fats: 11.7g; Net Carbs: 1g; Protein: 2.5g; Fiber: 0.3g

275. Lamb Stock

Preparation Time: 6 hours
Servings: 5

Ingredients:

- 2 -pounds lamb bones
- 1/4 cup celery root; chopped
- 1/4 cup red wine vinegar
- 1 garlic head; whole
- 1 large onion; sliced
- 1/2 teaspoon white pepper
- 2 teaspoon chili powder
- 1 teaspoon red pepper flakes
- 1 teaspoon salt

Directions:

1. Place bones in the pot and pour in enough water to cover. Add red wine vinegar, chopped celery root, one garlic head, and one onion
2. Season with salt, chili powder, red pepper flakes, and white pepper. Optionally, add some dried herbs to taste
3. Seal the lid and set the steam release

handle. Press the *Slow Cook* button and set the timer for 6 hours on low pressure
4. When done, release the pressure naturally and open the lid. Strain the stock and cool to a room temperature before refrigerating.

Nutrition Value: Calories: 24; Total Fats: 0.7g; Net Carbs: 1.3g; Protein: 2.5g; Fiber: 0.6g

276. Creamy Parsley Sauce Recipe

Preparation Time: 15 Minutes
Servings: 5

Ingredients:

- 4 tablespoon heavy cream
- 4 tablespoon cream cheese
- 2 cups fresh parsley; finely chopped
- 1/2 teaspoon agar powder
- 3 tablespoon butter; unsalted
- 2 tablespoon gorgonzola cheese
- 1 ½ cup whole milk
- 1/2 teaspoon black pepper; freshly ground.
- 1/2 teaspoon salt

Directions:

1. Plug in the instant pot and press the *Saute* button. Melt the butter in the inner pot and add cream cheese and gorgonzola cheese
2. Stir well and cook until the cheese melts. Now pour in the heavy cream and milk. Sprinkle with parsley and season with salt and pepper
3. Stir well and season with salt and pepper. Cook for 2 minutes or until the sauce thickens.
4. Press the *Cancel'* button and serve immediately

Nutrition Value: Calories: 198; Total Fats: 17.9g; Net Carbs: 4.8g; Protein: 4.9g; Fiber: 1g

277. Dijon Sauce Recipe

Preparation Time: 20 Minutes
Servings: 4

Ingredients:

1 cup heavy cream

- 1/4 cup parmesan; freshly grated
- 2 tablespoon fresh parsley; finely chopped
- 2 tablespoon olive oil
- 2 teaspoon lemon juice; freshly squeezed
- 1 garlic clove; crushed
- 2 teaspoon Dijon mustard
- 1/4 cup feta cheese
- 1/2 teaspoon cayenne pepper
- 1/4 teaspoon black pepper; freshly ground.
- 1 teaspoon pink Himalayan salt

Directions:

1. Plug in the instant pot and press the *Saute* button. Grease the inner pot with olive oil and heat up. Add garlic and cook for one minute
2. Now add heavy cream, cheese, and Dijon. Sprinkle with lemon juice and fresh parsley. Season with salt, cayenne pepper,
3. Give it a good stir and cook for 2-3 minutes
4. Press the *Cancel'* button and optionally transfer to a food processor. Process until completely smooth. Serve

Nutrition Value: Calories: 215; Total Fats: 21.7g; Net Carbs: 1.8g; Protein: 4.4g; Fiber: 0.2g

278. Basil Tomato Sauce Recipe

Preparation Time: 30 Minutes
Servings: 5

Ingredients:

- 10-ounce ground beef
- 2 tomatoes; chopped
- 2 tablespoon olive oil
- 1/4 cup sun-dried tomatoes; diced
- 1 onion; chopped.
- 1 cup chicken stock
- 1/4 cup grated Parmesan cheese

- 1/2 teaspoon freshly chopped rosemary
- 1 teaspoon dried thyme
- 1/2 teaspoon oregano
- 1 teaspoon salt

Directions:
1. Grease the inner pot with oil and press the *Saute* button. Add onions and sauté for 3-4 minutes. Now add the meat and season with salt, thyme oregano, and rosemary. Continue to cook for another 5-6 minutes, stirring occasionally
2. Add chopped tomatoes and pour in about 1/4 cup of the stock. Bring it to a boil and gently simmer for 5 minutes
3. Finally, add sun-dried tomatoes and the remaining stock. Press the *Cancel'* button and seal the lid.
4. Cook for 5 minutes on the *Manual* mode
5. When done; release the pressure naturally and open the lid. Serve and enjoy!

Nutrition Value: Calories: 192; Total Fats: 10.6g; Net Carbs: 3.4g; Protein: 19.9g; Fiber: 1.2g

279. Chicken Broth

Preparation Time: 1 hour 35 minutes
Servings: 3 to 4 cups

Ingredients

- 2 tbsp Olive oil
- 2 lb Chicken Carcass
- 4 Carrots, halved
- 4 Celery Stalks, halved
- 2 medium Onions, halved
- 1 Tomato, halved
- 1 cup fresh Parsley
- 1 cup fresh Thyme
- Salt to taste
- Water as desired

Directions

1. Set on Sauté. Heat oil, and brown the chicken carcass for 10 minutes. Add carrots, onions, tomato, celery stalks, parsley, thyme, and salt. Pour the water over to cover the vegetables, about ⅔ of the pot. Stir.
2. Seal the lid, select Manual and cook on High Pressure mode for 1 hour. Once ready, quickly release the pressure. Strain the pot's content through a fine strainer and transfer the broth to a storage container. Let cool and use for your chicken soups or stews.
3. Tip: If refrigerated, after 6 hours, remove the solidified fat on top of the broth.

Nutrition Value: Calories 12, Protein 0.9g, Net Carbs 1.5g, Fat 0.9g

280. Mixed Seafood Broth

Preparation Time: 3 hours 20 minutes
Servings: 4 cups

Ingredients

- 8 cups Seafood Bones and Shells, washed
- 4 tsp Olive oil
- 2 tsp Black Peppercorns
- 2 large Onion, halved
- 4 Carrots, halved
- 6 stalks Celery
- 4 cloves Garlic
- 1 cup Parsley
- 2 Bay Leaves
- 5 cups Water

Directions

1. Set on Sauté. Heat oil, and add the onion, garlic, black peppercorns, celery, and carrots. Cook until fragrant. Add the seafood bones and shells; sauté them for 5 minutes. Stir occasionally.
2. Stir in the water, parsley and bay leaves. Seal the lid, select Manual and cook on High Pressure for 3 hours. Once ready, quickly release the pressure. Strain the content in the pot through a fine sieve, and discard the solids. Pour the stock into a storage bowl and leave to cool.

Nutrition Value: Calories 10, Protein 2g, Net Carbs 0g, Fat 0g

RICE & PASTA RECIPES

281. Pretty Colorful Risotto

Preparation Time: 40 minutes
Servings: 6

Nutrition Value: Calories 324; Carbs 58g; Fat 5g; Protein 11g

Ingredients

- 2 cups Brown Rice
- 4 cups Veggie Broth
- ½ cup Carrots, chopped
- 1 Yellow Bell Pepper, chopped
- 1 Green Bell Pepper, chopped
- 2 Tomatoes, chopped
- 1 Red Onion, chopped
- 3 tsp Oil
- 1 cups Green Peas
- Salt and Pepper, to taste

Directions

1. Heat oil on SAUTÉ mode at High, add the onions and cook for a few minutes, until soft. Add carrots and peppers and cook for 2 more minutes. Stir in the remaining ingredients.
2. Seal the lid and cook for 20 minutes PRESSURE COOK/MANUAL at High pressure. Do a quick pressure release.

282. Lovely Rice Pilaf with Chicken

Preparation Time: 40 minutes
Servings: 8

Nutrition Value: Calories 341; Carbs 41g; Fat 9g; Protein 21g

Ingredients

1. 2 cups Rice
2. 2 Chicken Breasts, diced
3. 1 tsp Garlic, minced
4. 1 Onion, chopped
5. 2 Bell Peppers, chopped
6. 1 tbsp Oil
7. 4 cups Chicken Broth
8. 1 tsp Rosemary
9. Salt and Pepper, to taste

Directions

1. Heat oil on SAUTÉ mode at High, and cook the onions for 2 minutes, until translucent. Stir in garlic and cook for 1 more minute, until fragrant. Add peppers and cook for 2 minutes, until soft
2. Stir in the remaining ingredients. Seal the lid and cook for 25 minutes on MEAT/STEW mode at High. When cooking is over, do a quick pressure release. Serve and enjoy!

283. Sweet Apple and Apricot Wild Rice

Preparation Time: 30 minutes
Servings: 8

Nutrition Value: Calories 246; Carbs 50g; Fat 3g; Protein 8g

Ingredients

- 2 cups Wild Rice
- ¼ cup Maple Syrup
- ½ cup dried Apricots, chopped
- 1 ½ cups Apple Juice
- ½ cup Milk
- 3 Egg Yolks
- ¼ tsp ground Ginger
- ½ tsp Cinnamon
- A pinch of Salt
- 4 cups Water

Directions

1. Combine all ingredients, except the apricots, in your pressure cooker. Seal the lid and cook on MEAT/STEW mode for 25 minutes at High. Do a quick pressure release. Stir in the apricots, serve and enjoy!

284. Exquisite Spinach Vermouth Risotto

Preparation Time: 20 minutes
Servings: 4

Nutrition Value: Calories 327; Carbs 44g; Fat 8g; Protein 10g

Ingredients

- 1 cup Mushrooms, sliced
- 2 cups Spinach, chopped
- ½ cup Vermouth
- 1 cup Rice
- 1 Zucchini, sliced
- ½ cup Parmesan Cheese, shredded
- 1 Shallot, chopped
- 1 tsp Garlic, minced
- 1 tbsp Oil
- 2 cups Chicken Stock

Directions

1. Heat oil on SAUTÉ mode at High. Cook the shallot and garlic for 2 minutes, until translucent and fragrant. Add mushrooms and cook for 3 more minutes, until soft.
2. Stir in the remaining ingredients, except the cheese. Seal the lid, and cook for 8 minutes on RICE mode, at High. When done, do a quick release. Stir in the cheese, and serve warm.

285. Superior Shrimp Risotto

Preparation Time: 20 minutes
Servings: 4

Nutrition Value: Calories 476; Carbs 59g; Fat 12g; Protein 32g

Ingredients

- 1 pound Shrimp, peeled and deveined
- 1 ½ cups White Rice
- 1 tbsp Oil
- 3 tbsp Butter
- 3 cups Fish Stock
- 2 tsp Garlic, minced
- 2 Shallots, chopped
- ¼ cup White Wine
- Salt and Pepper, to taste

Directions

1. Heat oil on SAUTÉ mode at High, and cook onion and garlic for 3 minutes, until soft. Add shrimp and cook for 3 minutes, until lightly browned. Stir in the remaining ingredients and seal the lid.
2. Cook for 8 minutes on RICE mode at High. When ready, do a quick pressure release.

286. Spring Pearl Barley Salad

Preparation Time: 25 minutes
Servings: 4

Nutrition Value: Calories 350; Fat 9g; Carbs 62g; Protein 9g

Ingredients

- ¼ cups Pearl Barley, rinsed and drained
- ½ cup Onion, thinly sliced
- ½ cup Kalamata Olives, pitted and sliced
- 1 tbsp Olive Oil
- 2 Bell Peppers, thinly sliced
- 1 cup grape Tomatoes, diced
- 2 tbsp Vinegar
- ½ cup Goat Cheese, crumbled to serve
- ½ tsp Sea Salt
- 1 tsp dried Basil
- ½ tsp dried Oregano
- ½ tsp ground Black Pepper
- 4 cups Water

Directions

1. Add the barley, water and salt. Seal the lid and cook for 15 minutes on PRESSURE COOK/MANUAL at High. When ready, do a quick pressure release and open the lid. Transfer the barley to a bowl to let cool.
2. Stir in slowly the remaining ingredients. Season to taste and enjoy.

287. Fresh Tagliatelle Pasta Bolognese

Preparation Time: 20 minutes
Servings: 6

Nutrition Value: Calories 523; Carbs 56g; Fat 23g;

Protein 31g

Ingredients

- 2 tsp Butter
- 20 ounces Tagliatelle
- 1 ½ pounds mixed Ground Meat
- 1 ½ pounds Tomato Pasta Sauce
- 1 tsp Oregano
- 1 cup Onions, chopped
- 2 tsp Garlic, minced
- 6 ounces Bacon, diced
- ½ cup White Wine
- 1 cup Heavy Cream
- 1 cup Parmesan cheese grated
- Water, as needed
- Salt and Pepper, to taste

Directions

1. Melt the butter on SAUTÉ mode at High, and cook the onions and garlic for 3 minutes, until soft and fragrant. Add meat and cook until browned, for a few minutes.
2. Stir in the remaining ingredients, except for the heavy cream and Parmesan cheese. Pour in water to cover entirely. Seal the lid and cook for 10 minutes on PRESSURE COOK/MANUAL at High pressure.
3. When ready, do a quick release. Stir in heavy cream and serve with grated parmesan cheese.

288. Elegant Fennel Jasmine Rice

Preparation Time: 15 minutes
Servings: 4

Nutrition Value: Calories 241; Carbs 34g; Fat 14g; Protein 10g

Ingredients

- 1 ½ cups Jasmine Rice
- 1 cup Fennel Bulb, chopped
- 2 Spring Onions, chopped
- 1 cup Parsnips, chopped
- 1 Carrot, chopped
- 2 cups Chicken Stock
- 1 cup Water
- 1 tsp Sage
- 1 tbsp Oil
- Salt and Pepper, to taste

Directions

1. Heat oil on SAUTÉ mode at High, and cook the onions until soft, for 2-3 minutes. Add parsnip, carrots, and fennel and cook for 2 more minutes, until soft. Stir in the remaining ingredients.
2. Seal the lid and cook for 10 minutes on RICE, at High. When ready, do a quick release.

289. Simple Mushroom Risotto

Preparation Time: 15 minutes
Servings: 4

Nutrition Value: Calories 254; Carbs 26g; Fat 16g; Protein 15g

Ingredients

- 1 ½ cups Arborio Rice
- ½ cup dried Chanterelle Mushrooms, soaked, drained, and chopped
- ½ cup Parmesan Cheese, grated
- ¼ cup Onion, chopped
- 1 tsp Garlic, minced
- 4 cups Chicken Stock
- 1 ½ cups Water
- 1 tbsp Butter
- ¼ tsp Salt
- ¼ tsp White Pepper

Directions

1. Melt butter and cook onion and garlic for 2 minutes, until soft and fragrant, on SAUTÉ. Add in the remaining ingredients. Seal the lid and cook for 10 minutes on RICE at High. Do a quick pressure release.

290. Creamy Coconut Rice Pudding

Preparation Time: 20 minutes
Servings: 6

Nutrition Value: Calories 362; Carbs 57g; Fat 8g; Protein 11g

Ingredients

- 2 cups White Rice
- ½ cup Raisins
- 2 Eggs plus 1 Egg yolk, at room temperature
- 8 ounces Milk
- ¼ cup Sugar
- 3 tsp Coconut Oil
- ¼ tsp ground Cinnamon
- ½ tbsp Vanilla Extract
- ¼ tsp Kosher Salt
- ¼ tsp ground Cardamom
- 8 ounces Water

Directions

1. In the pressure cooker, add the oil, water, milk, rice, sugar, cinnamon, vanilla, salt, and cardamom. Press RICE and cook for 8 minutes at High pressure.
2. Once the cooking is complete, perform a quick pressure release. Add the whisked eggs and raisins. Select SAUTÉ at High and cook with the lid off until the mixture boils. Serve warm.

291. Satisfying Saucy Jasmine Rice

Preparation Time: 15 minutes
Servings: 4

Nutrition Value: Calories 299; Carbs 62g; Fat 3g; Protein 7g

Ingredients

- 1 ½ cups Jasmine Rice
- 1 cup Celery, chopped
- 2 spring Onions, sliced
- 1 Carrot, trimmed and chopped
- 3 tsp Olive Oil
- 1 tsp dried Sage
- ¼ tsp ground Black Pepper
- 1 tsp Salt
- 2 cups stock
- 1 cup Water

Directions

1. Select SAUTÉ at High and heat the oil. Add in the onions and cook until translucent. Stir in the carrots and celery and keep stirring for another 2-3 minutes. Add in the remaining ingredients.
2. Select RICE and cook for 10 minutes at High. When ready, do a quick pressure release.

292. Ziti Pork Meatballs

Preparation Time: 25 minutes
Servings: 4

Nutrition Value: Calories 421; Carbs 25g; Fat 23g; Protein 28g

Ingredients

- ¾ pound Ground Pork
- 1 box Ziti Pasta
- 2 Tomatoes, chopped
- 1 cup Veggie Stock
- 3 tsp Oil
- 2 cups Cauliflower Florets
- 2 Bell Peppers, chopped
- ½ cup Cider
- 1 cup Water
- 1 Red Onion, chopped
- ½ tbsp Basil

Directions

1. Combine pork and basil and shape the mixture into 4-5 meatballs. Heat the oil on SAUTÉ at High. Cook meatballs until browned. Set aside. Cook onions, cauliflowers, and peppers for a few minutes, until soft.
2. Stir in the remaining ingredients, including the meatballs. Seal the lid and cook for 20 minutes on PRESSURE COOK/MANUAL at High. When done, quick release the pressure.

293. Adorable Pizza Pasta

Preparation Time: 30 minutes
Servings: 6

Nutrition Value: Calories 491; Carbs 38g; Fat 23g; Protein 35g

Ingredients

- 1 pound Pasta
- 16 ounces Pasta Sauce
- 8 ounces Pizza Sauce
- 1 pound Italian Sausage
- 4 ounces Pepperoni
- 8 ounces Mozzarella Cheese, shredded
- 3 ½ cups Water
- 1 tbsp Butter
- 1 tsp Garlic, minced

Directions

Heat oil on SAUTÉ mode at High. Cook the sausage and garlic for a few minutes, until lightly browned. Stir in the remaining ingredients, except the cheese and half of the pepperoni. Seal the lid and cook for 8 minutes on RICE mode at High pressure. When it goes off, do a quick pressure release. Stir in the cheese and pepperoni. Serve immediately.

294. Delicious Quinoa Pilaf with Almonds

Preparation Time: 20 minutes
Servings: 6

Nutrition Value: Calories 305; Carbs 47g; Fat 8g; Protein 9g

Ingredients

- 1 ½ cups Quinoa
- 2 tsp Butter
- 5 cups Chicken Stock
- 2 White Onions, finely chopped
- 2 Carrots, trimmed and chopped
- Sea Salt and Black Pepper, to taste
- 4 tbsp flaked Almonds, toasted

Directions

1. Select SAUTÉ mode at High and melt the butter. Cook the onions for about 3 minutes, until tender. Add in the carrots and keep cooking for 4 minutes more. Stir in the remaining ingredients, except for the almonds.
2. Select RICE mode and cook for 8 minutes at High Pressure. Do a quick pressure release. Arrange the pilaf on a serving platter and fluff the quinoa with a fork. Serve scattered with toasted almonds.

295. Cheese Tortellini with Broccoli and Turkey

Preparation Time: 30 minutes
Servings: 6

Nutrition Value: Calories 395; Carbs 9g; Fat 23g; Protein 35g

Ingredients

- 3 Bacon Slices, chopped
- 1 ½ pounds Turkey Breasts, diced
- 3 cups Broccoli Florets
- 8 ounces Cheese Tortellini
- ¼ cup Heavy Cream
- ¼ cup Half and Half
- 2 cups Chicken Stock
- 1 Onion, chopped
- 1 Carrot, chopped
- 1 tbsp chopped Parsley
- Salt and Pepper, to taste

Directions

1. Cook the bacon on SAUTÉ mode at High until crispy. Add onions and garlic and cook for 2 minutes, until sweaty Add turkey and cook until no longer pink, for a few minutes.
2. Stir in the remaining ingredients, except heavy cream. Seal the lid, and cook for 8 minutes on RICE mode at High pressure. When ready, release the pressure quickly. Stir in the heavy cream and serve.

296. Chili and Cheesy Beef Pasta

Preparation Time: 15 minutes
Servings: 6

Nutrition Value: Calories 346; Carbs 29g; Fat 14g; Protein 26g

Ingredients

- 1 pound Ground Beef

- 2 Scallions, chopped
- 3 cups Fusilli Pasta, cooked
- 1 tbsp Butter
- ½ cup Cheddar Cheese, grated
- 1 tsp Garlic, minced
- 2 cups Mild Salsa
- ½ cup Tomato Puree
- 1 tbsp Chili Powder
- Water, as needed

Directions

1. Melt the butter on SAUTÉ mode at High, and cook scallions for 3 minutes, until soft. Stir in the garlic and cook for one minute, until fragrant. Add beef and cook until browned, for a few minutes.
2. Stir in salsa, tomato paste, and spices. Seal the lid and cook for 8 minutes on RICE at High. Do a quick pressure release, and stir in cheese and pasta. Cook uncovered for 2 minutes, until well incorporated.

297. Rice Custard with Hazelnuts

Preparation Time: 30 minutes
Servings: 3

Nutrition Value: Calories 444; Carbs 78g; Fat 10g; Protein 11g

Ingredients

- 1 cup Rice
- 4 tbsp Hazelnuts, chopped
- 1 tsp Vanilla Paste
- 1 Egg plus 1 Yolk
- ½ cup Sultanas
- ½ tsp Anise Seed
- 1 cup Milk
- ¼ cup Sugar
- ½ tsp Hazelnut Extract
- 1 ½ cups Water

Directions

1. Pour 1 ½ cups water in the pressure cooker, and lower the trivet.
2. Mix together all ingredients in a baking dish. Place the dish inside the pressure cooker and cover with foil.
3. Seal the lid and cook on BEANS/CHILI for 25 minutes at High. Release the pressure quickly.

298. Darling Spaghetti with Meatballs

Preparation Time: 30 minutes
Servings: 6

Nutrition Value: Calories 306; Carbs 16g; Fat 13g; Protein 27g

Ingredients

- 10 ounces Noodles
- 2 Eggs
- 1 pound Ground Beef
- ¼ cup Breadcrumbs
- ½ small Red Onion, grated
- 1 Egg
- 1 jar Spaghetti Sauce
- ½ tsp Garlic, minced
- Water as needed

Directions

1. Combine the beef, crumbs, garlic, onion, and egg, in a bowl. Mix with hands. Shape the mixture into about 6 meatballs. Add the sauce and spaghetti in your pressure cooker.
2. Pour enough water to cover. Add the meatballs and seal the lid. Cook PRESSURE COOK/MANUAL at High pressure for 15 minutes. When ready, release the pressure naturally, for 10 minutes.

299. Mellow Bulgur and Potato Soup

Preparation Time: 30 minutes
Servings: 4

Nutrition Value: Calories 355; Carbs 65g; Fat 10g; Protein 11g

Ingredients

- ¾ cup Bulgur
- 4 Potatoes, peeled and diced

- 1 Carrot, diced
- 1 tsp Garlic paste
- 1 Celery stalk, chopped
- ½ cup White Onions, chopped
- 3 tsp coconut oil
- 4 ½ cups Chicken Stock
- ½ tsp dried Thyme
- ¼ tsp ground Black Pepper
- 1 tsp Red Pepper, flakes
- ½ tsp Sea Salt

Directions

1. Add all ingredients to the pressure cooker. Select SOUP/BROTH and seal the lid. Cook for 30 minutes at High. Once ready, use a natural pressure release, for 10 minutes.

300. Lemony Rice with Veggies

Preparation Time: 15 minutes
Servings: 4

Nutrition Value: Calories 213; Carbs 34g; Fat 7g; Protein 13g

Ingredients

- 1 cup Rice
- ½ cup Onions, chopped
- 1 cup Broccoli Florets, frozen
- 1 cup Carrots, sliced
- 1 cup Peas
- 1 tbsp Oil
- 2 tsp Lemon Zest
- ¼ cup Lemon Juice
- 2 cups Veggie Stock

Directions

1. Heat oil on SAUTÉ at High, and cook the onions for 2 minutes, until soft. Stir the remaining ingredients.
2. Seal the lid and cook for 10 minutes on RICE at High pressure.
3. Do a quick pressure release. Serve and enjoy!

301. Lush Sausage Penne

Preparation Time: 20 minutes
Servings: 6

Nutrition Value: Calories 413; Carbs 48g; Fat 18g; Protein 21g

Ingredients

- 18 ounces Penne Pasta
- 16 ounces Sausage
- 2 cups Tomato Paste
- 1 tbsp Olive Oil
- 2 tsp Garlic, minced
- 1 tsp Oregano
- ¼ cup Parmesan Cheese, grated
- Water, as needed

Directions

1. Heat oil on SAUTÉ mode at High. Add sausage, cook until browned while crumbling. Add garlic and cook for 1 minute. Stir in the remaining ingredients, except Parmesan and oregano.
2. Cover with water, seal the lid, and cook for 10 minutes on PRESSURE COOK/MANUAL at High. Release the pressure quickly. To serve, top with freshly grated Parmesan cheese and sprinkle with dry oregano.

302. Pineapple and Honey Risotto

Preparation Time: 15 minutes
Servings: 6

Nutrition Value: Calories 374; Carbs 78g; Fat 4g; Protein 5g

Ingredients

- 2 cups White Rice
- ½ cup Honey
- 1 cup Pineapple, crushed
- 3 cups Water
- 2 tbsp Butter
- ½ tsp Vanilla

Directions

1. Place the rice, juice, water, butter, and vanilla in your pressure cooker.
2. Seal the lid and cook for 8 minutes on RICE at High.

3. Release the pressure quickly. Stir in the pineapple and drizzle with honey.

303. Buckwheat Breakfast Porridge with Figs

Preparation Time: 20 minutes
Servings: 6

Nutrition Value: Calories 415; Carbs 58g; Fat 19g; Protein 11g

Ingredients

- 1 cup Buckwheat Groats
- ¼ cup dried Figs, chopped
- 2 Bananas, sliced
- 1 cup Almond Milk
- 2 tbsp Coconut Oil
- ½ tsp Vanilla Extract
- ½ tsp Cinnamon
- ¼ tsp ground Nutmeg
- ½ tsp Kosher Salt
- 2 cups Water

Directions

1. Rinse buckwheat groats under cold water and drain them through a colander. Add buckwheat groats, figs, vanilla, coconut oil, cinnamon, nutmeg, salt to your pressure cooker. Pour in the milk and water.
2. Seal the lid, select PRESSURE COOK/MANUAL and cook for 15 minutes at High pressure. When ready, do a quick pressure release. Carefully open the lid. Top with sliced bananas and serve in a bowl.
3. Charming Bacon and Cheese Pasta
4. Preparation Time: 10 minutes
5. Servings: 6

Nutrition Value: Calories 437; Carbs 72g; Fat 12g; Protein 13g

- **Ingredients**
- 16 ounces Dry Rigatoni Pasta
- 1 cup chopped Onions
- 1 cup diced Bacon
- 2 ½ cups Tomato Puree
- 1 tsp Sage
- 1 tsp Thyme
- ½ cup Cheddar Cheese, grated
- Water, as needed
- Salt to taste
- Freshly chopped basil, to garnish

Directions

1. Fry the bacon on SAUTÉ at High, until brown and crispy, for about 3 minutes. Add the onions and cook for a few minutes, until soft. Stir in rigatoni pasta, tomato puree, sage, thyme, and salt. Add enough water to cover them.
2. Seal the lid and cook for 6 minutes PRESSURE COOK/MANUAL at High pressure. Release the pressure quickly. Stir in the freshly grated Cheddar cheese and serve topped with fresh basil.

304. Heavenly Chicken Enchilada Pasta

Preparation Time: 20 minutes
Servings: 6

Nutrition Value: Calories 567; Carbs 49g; Fat 25g; Protein 31g

Ingredients

- 2 Chicken Breasts, diced
- 3 cups dry Pasta
- 10 ounces canned Tomatoes
- 20 ounces canned Enchilada Sauce
- 1 ¼ cups Water
- 1 cup diced Onion
- 1 tsp Garlic, minced
- 1 tsp Taco Seasoning
- 1 tbsp Olive Oil
- 2 cups Cheddar Cheese, shredded

Directions

1. Heat oil on SAUTÉ at High, and cook the onions until soft, for about 3 minutes. Stir in the remaining ingredients, except the cheese. Seal the lid and cook for 8 minutes PRESSURE COOK/MANUAL at High pressure.
2. Quick-release the pressure. Stir in cheese

and cook for 2 minutes, lid off, on SAUTÉ, until melted.

305. Toothsome Noodles with Tuna

Preparation Time: 20 minutes
Servings: 2

Nutrition Value: Calories 461; Carbs 17g; Fat 29g; Protein 37g

Ingredients

- 8 ounces Egg Noodles, uncooked
- 1 can diced Tomatoes
- 1 can Tuna Flakes, drained
- ½ cup Red Onion, chopped
- 1 ¼ cups Water
- 1 jar Artichoke, marinated and chopped
- 1 tbsp Olive Oil
- 1 tsp Parsley
- ½ cup Feta Cheese, crumbled

Directions

1. Heat oil on SAUTÉ at High, and cook the onions for a few minutes, until translucent. Stir in the remaining ingredients, except cheese. Seal the lid and cook for 5 minutes PRESSURE COOK/MANUAL at High pressure.

When ready, release the pressure quickly. Stir in the feta cheese and serve and enjoy

BEANS & GRAINS

306. Shrimp Rice Paella

Preparation Time: 15 minutes
Servings: 8

Nutrition Values:

Calories: 437
Carbohydrate: 49.1g
Protein: 30.6g
Fat: 13.7g
Sugar: 0.8g
Sodium: 1.08g

Ingredients

- 16 oz. jasmine rice
- 32 oz. frozen wild-caught shrimp
- 4 oz. butter
- 4 oz. chopped fresh parsley
- 2 tsp. sea salt
- 1/2 tsp. black pepper
- 24 oz. chicken broth
- 8 garlic cloves; minced
- 2 pinches crushed red pepper
- 2 medium lemons; juiced
- 2 pinches saffron

Directions:

1. Add all the Ingredients to Instant Pot.
2. Place the shrimp on top.
3. Cover and secure the lid. Turn its pressure release handle to the sealing position.
4. Cook on the *Manual* function with high pressure for 5 minutes,
5. When it beeps; do a Natural release for 7 minutes,
6. If needed; remove the shells of the shrimp and then add the shrimp back to the rice, Stir and serve warm.

307. Pea & Corn Rice

Preparation Time: 13 minutes
Servings: 3

Nutrition Values:

Calories: 356
Carbohydrate: 61.3g
Protein: 7.1g
Fat: 9.2g
Sugar: 3.6g
Sodium: 0.36g

Ingredients

- 1/2 cup frozen garden peas
- 1 cup basmati rice; rinsed
- 1 ½ tbsp. olive oil
- 1/2 large onion; diced small

Salt; to taste

- 1 ½ tbsp. chopped cilantro stalks
- 1 large garlic clove; finely diced
- 1/2 tsp. turmeric powder
- 1/2 cup frozen sweet corn kernels
- 3/4 cup chicken stock
- 1 dollop of butter

Directions:

1. Add oil and onions to Instant Pot and *Sauté* for 5 minutes,
2. Stir in all the remaining Ingredients except the butter.
3. Cover and secure the lid. Turn its pressure release handle to the sealing position.
4. Cook on the *Manual* function with high pressure for 3 minutes,
5. When it beeps; do a Natural release for 7 minutes,
6. Stir in butter and let it melt into the rice, Serve warm.

308. Chorizo Red Beans

Preparation Time: 52 minutes
Servings: 3

Nutrition Values:

Calories: 321
Carbohydrate: 49.1g

Protein: 21.4g
Fat: 5.4g
Sugar: 5.3g
Sodium: 0.64g

Ingredients

- 1 cup red beans; soaked and rinsed
- Freshly cracked pepper
- 1/2 tbsp. cooking oil
- 2 oz. dry (Spanish) chorizo
- 1/2 yellow onion
- 1 ½ garlic cloves
- 1 bay leaf
- 1 ½ cups reduced sodium chicken broth
- 7 1/2 oz. can diced tomatoes

Directions:

1. Add oil, chorizo, garlic and onion to Instant Pot. *Sauté* for 5 minutes,
2. Stir in beans, pepper and bay leaf. Cook for 1 minute; then add the broth.
3. Cover and secure the lid. Turn its pressure release handle to the sealing position.
4. Cook on the *Manual* function with high pressure for 35 minutes,
5. When it beeps; do a Natural release for 20 minutes,
6. Stir in diced tomatoes and cook for 7 minutes on the *Sauté* setting. Serve hot with boiled white rice or tortilla chips,

309. Mix Fried Beans

Preparation Time: 60 minutes
Servings: 6

Nutrition Values:

Calories: 314
Carbohydrate: 49.6g
Protein: 18.1g
Fat: 4.7g
Sugar: 2.5g
Sodium: 0.42g

Ingredients

- 1 lb. pinto beans; soaked and rinsed
- 3/4 cup chopped onion
- 2 garlic cloves; roughly chopped.
- 1/4 tsp. ground black pepper
- 1 ½ tbsp. lard
- 2 cups vegetable broth
- 1/2 jalapeno; seeded and chopped.
- 1 tsp. dried oregano
- 3/4 tsp. ground cumin
- 2 cups water
- 1/2 tsp. sea salt

Directions:

1. Add all the Ingredients to Instant Pot.
2. Cover and secure the lid. Turn its pressure release handle to the sealing position.
3. Cook on the *Bean/Chili* function for 45 minutes,
4. When it beeps; do a Natural release for 20 minutes,
5. Let it cool; then use an immersion blender to puree the mixture, Stir well and serve.

310. Easy Cilantro Rice

Preparation Time: 21 minutes
Servings: 6

Nutrition Values:

Calories: 167
Carbohydrate: 34.8g
Protein: 3.1g
Fat: 1.3g
Sugar: 0.9g
Sodium: 83mg

Ingredients

- 1 1/3 cup white rice
- 1/2 tbsp. butter
- 1/2 yellow onion; diced
- 1 garlic clove; minced
- 2 cups water
- 1/2 tbsp. chicken bouillon
- 1/2 cup peas
- 1/2 tsp. cumin
- 2 oz. can green chilies
- 1/4 bunch cilantro; chopped.

- 3/4 tsp. fresh lime juice
- Salt; to taste

Directions:
1. Add oil, onion and garlic to Instant Pot and *Sauté* for 4 minutes,
2. Add all the remaining Ingredients to the cooker.
3. Cover and secure the lid. Turn its pressure release handle to the sealing position.
4. Cook on the *Manual* function with high pressure for 7 minutes,
5. When it beeps; do a Natural release and remove the lid. Garnish with fresh cilantro and serve.

311. Special Chorizo Pinto Beans

Preparation Time: 52 minutes
Servings: 3

Nutrition Values:
Calories: 337
Carbohydrate: 50.5g
Protein: 21.3g
Fat: 5.7g
Sugar: 5.4g
Sodium: 0.67g

Ingredients
- 1 cup dry pinto beans
- 1/2 tbsp. cooking oil
- 2 oz. dry (Spanish) chorizo
- 1/2 yellow onion
- 1 ½ garlic cloves
- 1 bay leaf
- 1/2 tsp. freshly cracked pepper
- 1 ½ cups chicken broth
- 7 1/2 oz. can diced tomatoes

Directions:
1. Add oil, chorizo, garlic and onion to Instant Pot. *Sauté* for 5 minutes,
2. Stir in beans, pepper and bay leaf. Cook for 1 minute then add the broth.
3. Cover and secure the lid. Turn its pressure release handle to the sealing position.
4. Cook on the *Manual* function with high pressure for 35 minutes,
5. When it beeps; do a Natural release for 20 minutes,
6. Stir in diced tomatoes and cook for 7 minutes on the *Sauté* setting. Serve hot with boiled white rice or tortilla chips,

312. White Beans Curry

Preparation Time: 35 minutes
Servings: 6

Nutrition Values:
Calories: 286
Carbohydrate: 54.1g
Protein: 19.1g
Fat: 1.2g
Sugar: 5.2g
Sodium: 0.61g

Ingredients
- 1 lb. white beans; soaked and rinsed
- 1/2 tsp. red pepper
- 1/2 tsp. ground turmeric
- 1-2 tsp. salt
- 1 bay leaf
- 6 cups unsalted vegetable broth
- 1 tbsp. onion powder
- 2 tsp. garlic powder

Directions:
1. Add all the Ingredients to Instant Pot.
2. Cover and secure the lid. Turn its pressure release handle to the sealing position.
3. Cook on the *Bean/Chili* function on the default settings,
4. When it beeps; do a Natural release for 20 minutes, Stir and serve hot with boiled white rice,

313. Easy Black Bean Gravy

Preparation Time: 35 minutes
Servings: 6

Nutrition Values:
Calories: 289

Carbohydrate: 53.7g
Protein: 18 .7g
Fat: 1.1g
Sugar: 5.8g
Sodium: 0.63g

Ingredients

- 1 lb. black beans; sorted and rinsed
- 1/2 tsp. red pepper
- 1/2 tsp. ground turmeric
- 6 cups unsalted vegetable broth
- 1 tbsp. onion powder
- 2 tsp. garlic powder
- 1 tsp. salt
- 1 bay leaf

Directions:

1. Add all the Ingredients to Instant Pot.
2. Cover and secure the lid. Turn its pressure release handle to the sealing position.
3. Cook on the *Beans/Chili* function on the default settings,
4. When it beeps; do a Natural release for 20 minutes, Stir and serve hot with boiled white rice,

314. Yummy Coconut Rice

Preparation Time: 13 minutes
Servings: 6

Nutrition Values:

Calories: 255
Carbohydrate: 38.9g
Protein: 3.9g
Fat: 9.5g
Sugar: 2g
Sodium: 0.10g

Ingredients

- 1 can coconut milk
- 1 ½ cups jasmine rice
- 1/2 cup water
- 1 tsp. sugar
- 1/4 tsp. salt

Directions:

1. Add all the Ingredients to Instant Pot.
2. Cover and secure the lid. Turn its pressure release handle to the sealing position.
3. Cook on the *Manual* function with high pressure for 3 minutes,
4. When it beeps; do a Natural release for 7 minutes, Serve warm.

315. Easy Bean Mustard Curry

Preparation Time: 24 minutes
Servings: 4

Nutrition Values:

Calories: 373
Carbohydrate: 64.5g
Protein: 21.2g
Fat: 4.7g
Sugar: 16.1g
Sodium: 0.50g

Ingredients

- 2 tsp. mustard powder
- 1/2 cup ketchup
- 1/2 medium onion; chopped
- 1/2 small green bell pepper; chopped
- 1 ½ cans navy beans; rinsed and drained
- 2 tbsp. molasses
- 1/4 tsp. ground black pepper
- 1 ½ slices bacon; chopped.
- 1 tsp. apple cider vinegar

Directions:

1. Select the *Sauté* function on your Instant Pot and add the oil with onion, bacon and bell pepper. Cook for 6 minutes,
2. Add all the remaining Ingredients and secure the lid.
3. Cook on the *Manual* function for 8 minutes on high pressure,
4. When it beeps; do a Natural release for 10 minutes; then release the remaining steam with a Quick release,
5. Garnish with chopped cilantro on top. Serve.

316. Mexican Rice

Preparation Time: 21 minutes

Servings: 3

Nutrition Values:

Calories: 252
Carbohydrate: 53.1g
Protein: 5.6g
Fat: 1.5g
Sugar: 1.9g
Sodium: 0.92g

Ingredients

- 1 cup long-grain white rice
- 1 tbsp. avocado oil
- 1/4 cup onion; chopped
- 2 garlic cloves; finely chopped.
- 1/2 tsp. salt
- 2 tbsp. crushed tomatoes
- 2 tbsp. cilantro; chopped.
- 2 tbsp. sun-dried tomatoes
- 2 cups chicken stock
- 1/4 tsp. cumin
- 1/4 tsp. garlic powder
- 1/4 tsp. smoked paprika

Directions:

1. Add oil, onion and garlic to Instant Pot. *Sauté* for 3 minutes,
2. Stir in rice and mix well with the onion.
3. Add all the remaining Ingredients to the cooker.
4. Cover and secure the lid. Turn its pressure release handle to the sealing position.
5. Cook on the *Manual* function with high pressure for 8 minutes,
6. When it beeps; do a Natural release, Stir and serve warm.

317. Lentil Risotto

Preparation Time: 30 minutes
Servings: 2

Nutrition Values:

Calories: 260
Carbohydrate: 47.2g
Protein: 10.7g
Fat: 3.5g
Sugar: 2.2g
Sodium: 0.24g

Ingredients

- 1/2 cup dry lentils; soaked overnight
- 1 garlic clove; lightly mashed
- 2 cups vegetable stock
- 1/2 tbsp. olive oil
- 1/2 medium onion; chopped
- 1/2 celery stalk; chopped.
- 1 sprig parsley; chopped
- 1/2 cup Arborio (short-grain Italian) rice

Directions:

1. Add oil and onions to Instant Pot and *Sauté* for 5 minutes,
2. Add all the remaining ingredient to Instant Pot.
3. Cover and secure the lid. Turn its pressure release handle to the sealing position.
4. Cook on the *Manual* function with high pressure for 15 minutes,
5. When it beeps; do a Natural release for 20 minutes, Stir and serve hot with boiled white rice,

318. Instant Fennel Risotto

Preparation Time: 29 minutes
Servings: 3

Nutrition Values:

Calories: 238
Carbohydrates: 24.1g
Protein: 6.9g
Fat: 17.5g
Sugar: 1.8g
Sodium: 0.52g

Ingredients

- 1/4 medium fennel; diced
- 1/2 medium brown onion; finely diced
- 1 tbsp. olive oil
- 1/4 bunch of asparagus; diced
- 1/4 tsp. salt
- 1 garlic clove; chopped
- 1 cup Arborio risotto rice

Beans & Grains

- 1 cup vegetable stock
- 1 cup chicken stock
- 1 tbsp. butter
- 3 tbsp. white wine
- Zest of 1/4 lemon
- 1/4 cup grated Parmesan cheese

Directions:
1. Add oil, onion, fennel and asparagus to Instant Pot and *Sauté* for 4 minutes,
2. Add all the remaining Ingredients (except the cheese) to the cooker.
3. Cover and secure the lid. Turn its pressure release handle to the sealing position.
4. Cook on the *Manual* function with high pressure for 10 minutes,
5. When it beeps; do a Natural release and remove the lid. Stir in cheese and serve.

319. Healthy Almond Risotto

Preparation Time: 15 minutes
Servings: 3

Nutrition Values:
Calories: 116
Carbohydrate: 22.5g
Protein: 2g
Fat: 2.1g
Sugar: 0.2g
Sodium: 83mg

Ingredients
- 1/2 cup Arborio (short-grain Italian) rice
- 2 cups vanilla almond milk
- 2 tbsp. agave syrup
- 1 tsp. vanilla extract
- 1/4 cup toasted almond flakes

Directions:
1. Add all the Ingredients to Instant Pot.
2. Cover and secure the lid. Turn its pressure release handle to the sealing position.
3. Cook on the *Manual* function with high pressure for 5 minutes,
4. When it beeps; do a Natural release for 20 minutes, Garnish with almond flakes and serve.

320. Mushrooms Risotto

Preparation Time: 30 minutes
Servings: 2

Nutrition Values:
Calories: 226
Carbohydrate: 42.7g
Protein: 4.4g
Fat: 3.9g
Sugar: 2.3g
Sodium: 60mg

Ingredients
- 1/2 cup cremini mushrooms; sliced
- 1/2 cup Arborio (short-grain Italian) rice
- 1/2 tbsp. olive oil
- 1/2 medium onion; chopped.
- 1 garlic clove; lightly mashed
- 2 cups vegetable stock
- 1/2 celery stalk; chopped.
- 1 sprig parsley; chopped

Directions:
1. Add oil and onions to Instant Pot and *Sauté* for 5 minutes,
2. Add all the remaining Ingredients to Instant Pot.
3. Cover and secure the lid. Turn its pressure release handle to the sealing position.
4. Cook on the *Manual* function with high pressure for 15 minutes,
5. When it beeps; do a Natural release for 20 minutes, Stir and serve hot with boiled white rice.

321. Black Bean Burrito

Preparation Time: 22 minutes
Servings: 4

Nutrition Values:
Calories: 320
Carbohydrate: 23.5g
Protein: 33.1g
Fat: 33.1g
Sugar: 2.1g

Sodium: 0.63g

Ingredients

- 1/2 tbsp. olive oil
- 1/2 small onion; diced
- 1/2 can black beans; rinsed
- 1/2 cup long-grain white rice; uncooked
- 1/2 cup salsa
- 1 cup chicken broth
- 1/2 garlic clove; minced
- 1/2 tsp. chili powder
- 1/4 tsp. Kosher salt
- 3/4 lb. boneless; skinless chicken thighs, cut into 1-inch pieces
- 2 tbsp. chopped cilantro
- 2 tbsp. Cheddar cheese

Directions:

1. Add oil with onion and garlic to Instant Pot and select *Sauté* to cook for 2 minutes,
2. Add all the remaining Ingredients and secure the lid.
3. Cook on the *Manual* function for 10 minutes on high pressure,
4. When it beeps; do a Natural release for 10 minutes; then release the remaining steam with a Quick release,
5. Garnish with chopped cilantro and shredded Cheddar. Serve.

322. Lentils Spinach Stew

Preparation Time: 34 minutes
Servings: 4

Nutrition Values:

Calories: 169
Carbohydrate: 23.2g
Protein: 7.9g
Fat: 5.7g
Sugar: 4.4g
Sodium: 74mg

Ingredients

- 1 cup chopped baby spinach
- 1/2 cup raw lentils
- 1 ½ tbsp. cooking oil
- 1/2 cup chopped onions
- 1 bay leaf
- 1/2 tbsp. grated garlic
- 1/4 tbsp. grated ginger
- 3/4 cup water
- 1 cup fresh tomato puree
- 1/2 green chili; finely chopped.
- 1/4 tsp. turmeric
- 1/2 tsp. coriander powder
- 1 tsp. chili powder
- Salt; to taste
- 1/2 cup fresh cilantro

Directions:

1. Add oil and onions to Instant Pot. *Sauté* for 5 minutes,
2. Stir ginger, garlic paste and bay leaf. Cook for 1 minute then add all the spices,
3. Add lentils, tomato puree and water to the pot.
4. Cover and secure the lid. Turn its pressure release handle to the sealing position.
5. Cook on the *Manual* function with high pressure for 15 minutes,
6. When it beeps; do a Natural release for 20 minutes,
7. Stir in spinach and cook for 3 minutes on the *Sauté* setting. Serve hot with boiled white rice,

323. Mexican Black Beans

Preparation Time: 32 minutes
Servings: 3

Nutrition Values:

Calories: 103
Carbohydrates: 20g
Protein: 4.5g
Fat: 0.6g
Sugar: 1.4g
Sodium: 0.15g

Ingredients

- 1/2 (15 oz.) can black beans; rinsed and drained

- 1/4 cup brown rice
- 3/4 cup water
- 1/4 cup picante sauce
- 1/2 tsp. garlic salt
- Lime juice
- 1 bay leaf
- 1/2 tsp. cumin

Directions:
1. Add all the Ingredients to Instant Pot.
2. Cover and secure the lid. Turn its pressure release handle to the sealing position.
3. Cook on the *Manual* function with high pressure for 22 minutes,
4. When it beeps; do a Natural release for 20 minutes, Stir and serve hot with boiled white rice,

324. Chickpea Spinach Curry

Preparation Time: 34 minutes
Servings: 4

Nutrition Values:

Calories: 180
Carbohydrate: 25.3g
Protein: 6.7g
Fat: 7g
Sugar: 6.9g
Sodium: 78mg

Ingredients

- 1/2 cup raw chickpeas
- 1 cup chopped baby spinach
- 1 ½ tbsp. cooking oil
- 1/2 cup chopped onions
- 1 bay leaf
- 1/2 tbsp. grated garlic
- 1/4 tbsp. grated ginger
- 3/4 cup water
- 1 cup fresh tomato puree
- 1/2 green chili; finely chopped.
- 1/4 tsp. turmeric
- 1/2 tsp. coriander powder
- 1 tsp. chili powder
- Salt; to taste
- Fistful of chopped fresh cilantro

Directions:
1. Add oil and onions to Instant Pot. *Sauté* for 5 minutes,
2. Stir ginger, garlic paste, green chili and bay leaf. Cook for 1 minute then add all the spices,
3. Add chickpeas, tomato puree and water to the pot.
4. Cover and secure the lid. Turn its pressure release handle to the sealing position.
5. Cook on the *Manual* function with high pressure for 15 minutes,
6. When it beeps; do a Natural release for 20 minutes,
7. Stir in spinach and cook for 3 minutes on the *Sauté* setting. Serve hot with boiled white rice,

325. Lentil Chipotle Curry

Preparation Time: 20 minutes
Servings: 3

Nutrition Values:

Calories: 204
Carbohydrate: 29.8g
Protein: 13.4g
Fat: 5.2g
Sugar: 10.8g
Sodium: 0.68g

Ingredients

- 1 cup brown lentils; rinsed and picked over
- 1/2 medium onion; chopped
- 1/2 medium green bell pepper; chopped.
- 1/2 tbsp. canola oil
- 1 chipotle in adobo sauce; seeded and chopped.
- 1/4 cup sun-dried tomatoes; chopped
- 1/2 tsp. ground cumin
- 1 garlic clove; chopped
- 1 ½ tbsp. chili powder
- 1 can (1/4 oz.) diced tomatoes
- 2 cups vegetable broth

- Salt; to taste

Directions:
1. Add oil with onion and bell pepper to Instant Pot and select *Sauté* to cook for 2 minutes,
2. Stir in garlic and chili powder; then sauté for 1 minute,
3. Add all the remaining Ingredients and secure the lid.
4. Cook on the *Manual* function for 12 minutes on high pressure,
5. When it beeps; do a Natural release for 10 minutes; then release the remaining steam with a Quick release,
6. Garnish with chopped cilantro and shredded Cheddar cheese, Serve.

326. Tasty Chickpea Tacos

Preparation Time: 41 minutes
Servings: 6

Nutrition Values:
Calories: 165
Carbohydrate: 25.7g
Protein: 5.3g
Fat: 5.3g
Sugar: 4.3g
Sodium: 60mg

Ingredients
- 1/2 cup raw chickpeas
- 1 ½ tbsp. cooking oil
- 1/2 cup chopped onions
- 1/2 green chili; finely chopped
- 1/4 tsp. turmeric
- 1/2 tsp. coriander powder
- 1 tsp. chili powder
- 1/2 carrot; shredded
- 1/2 tbsp. grated garlic
- 1/4 tbsp. grated ginger
- 3/4 cup water
- 1/2 cup fresh tomato puree
- 1/2 cup green bell pepper; sliced
- Salt; to taste
- 1 tbsp. fresh cilantro
- 6 tortillas

Directions:
1. Add oil and onions to Instant Pot. *Sauté* for 5 minutes,
2. Stir ginger, garlic paste and green chili. Cook for 1 minute then add all the spices,
3. Add chickpeas, tomato puree and water to the pot.
4. Cover and secure the lid. Turn its pressure release handle to the sealing position.
5. Cook on the *Manual* function with high pressure for 15 minutes,
6. When it beeps; do a Natural release in 20 minutes,
7. Stir in shredded carrots and bell pepper. Cook for 10 minutes on the *Sauté* setting. Fill the tortillas with prepared filling and serve.

VEGETABLES

327. Walnut Beets Bowl

Preparation Time: 7 minutes
Servings: 3

Ingredients:

- 1 ½-pounds beets; scrubbed, rinsed
- 2 teaspoons lemon juice
- 1 teaspoon Dijon mustard
- 2 teaspoons apple cider vinegar
- 1 ½ tablespoons olive oil; extra virgin
- 2 tablespoons walnuts; chopped
- 1 ½ teaspoons sugar
- 2 cups water
- Pepper and salt as needed

Directions:

1. Place your Instant Pot on a flat kitchen surface', plug it and turn it on.
2. Open the lid and one by one add the water and beets in the pot. Carefully close its lid and firmly lock it. Then after, seal the valve too.
3. To start making the recipe, press *Manual* button. Now you have to set cooking time', set the timer for 10 minutes. Allow the pot to cook the mixture until the timer goes off.
4. Turn off the pot and press *Cancel.* Allow the built up pressure to vent out naturally', it will take 8-10 minutes to completely release inside pressure.
5. Open its lid and transfer the cooked mixture into a bowl.
6. Drain the beets and chop into bite-sized pieces. In a mixing bowl; add all the ingredients for the dressing except oil and walnuts.
7. Whisk to combine thoroughly and add the olive oil slowly into the dressing; combine well. Add the dressing over the beets, toss and serve!

Nutrition Value:
Calories 151; Fat: 10g; Carbohydrates: 15.2g; Fiber: 3g; Protein 2.7g

328. Zuppa Toscana Recipe

Preparation Time: 35 minutes
Servings: 4

Ingredients:

- 1/2 pounds Ground Italian Sausage (Mild)
- 3 - 4 cups chicken broth
- 2 - 3 slices bacon; chopped
- 1 teaspoon basil; dried
- 3 - 4 medium potatoes; cut into cubes
- 1 tablespoon oil
- 2 garlic cloves; minced
- 1 cup fresh kale; chopped
- 1 tablespoon red pepper; crushed
- 1/2 cup heavy cream or full fat coconut milk
- 1 small onion; chopped
- Salt and Pepper to taste

Directions:

1. Add oil to Instant Pot and press "Sauté" button (*Normal* preset), wait till you see Hot on the display. Add chopped bacon and cook for 2 to 3 minutes. Set aside.
2. Add sausage and cook until browned. Add onion and basil, cook until onion is translucent. Add garlic and cook for 1 to 2 more minutes.
3. Add potatoes, bacon, red pepper and broth, press *Cancel*. Close the lid and turn the vent to *Sealed*.
4. Press *Pressure Cook* (Manual) button, use *+* or *-* button to set the timer for 5 minutes. Use *Pressure level* button to set Pressure to *HIGH*.
5. Once the timer is up; press *Cancel* button and turn the steam release handle to *Venting* position for quick release, until the float valve drops down.
6. Open the lid.

7. Add kale to the Instant pot; close the lid for 5 minutes. Add heavy cream, stir until evenly mixed and then sprinkle with pepper, salt and crushed red pepper.

Nutrition Value:

Calories: 410 g; Total Fat: 30 g; Total Carbohydrate: 6 g; Protein: 12

329. Classic Lentil Gumbo

Preparation Time: 17 minutes
Servings: 6

Ingredients:

- 1 cup chopped celery ribs
- 1 cup chopped okra
- 3 cup vegetable broth
- 1 can diced tomatoes
- 1 teaspoon minced garlic cloves
- 2 tablespoon apple cider vinegar
- 1/2 cup tomato sauce
- 1/2 teaspoon cayenne powder
- 1/2 tablespoon oregano
- 1 cup lentils
- Fresh cilantro
- 1 chopped cauliflower
- 1 tablespoon olive oil
- 1 ½ chopped onions
- 1 tablespoon dried thyme
- 1 chopped red bell pepper
- 1 teaspoon Cajun mix
- Sea salt and Pepper to taste

Directions:

1. Start the Sauté function in Mini Instant Pot and sauté the oil, garlic, celery; and bell peppers for about 5 minutes until they are softened.
2. Add the spices and keep on mixing them for about a minute, Mix all the other ingredients apart from salt and pepper. Mix everything well.
3. Place the lid on the pressure cooker and switch on the High–Pressure function and cook for about 12 minutes.
4. After you are done with cooking, you can add ½-1 teaspoon of salt or kosher salt along with black pepper. Adjust the seasonings as per your taste.
5. Stir the entire thing and keep them warm, It is best not to add extra salt in the lentil gumbo while cooking as the extra salt may ruin the texture of the lentils.
6. Prepare the serving bowls, pour the gumbo; and garnish them with your favorite toppings like red pepper flakes, fresh cilantro, or jalapeño. Enjoy your meal.

Nutrition Value:

Calories: 173, Fat: 3.3g, Carbs: 25g, Protein: 8g

330. Green Beans Stew

Preparation Time: 40 minutes
Servings: 4

Ingredients:

- 1/2 cup dry green beans
- 1 teaspoon ground coriander
- 1/2 teaspoon garam masala
- 1/2 teaspoon cumin seeds
- 1/2 cup red onion; chopped
- 2 large tomatoes; chopped
- 4 garlic cloves
- 1/2 teaspoon cayenne pepper
- 1/4 teaspoon black pepper
- 5 cups water
- 1 teaspoon lemon juice
- 1 teaspoon oil
- 1-inch ginger root; grated
- 1 teaspoon turmeric
- 1 teaspoon salt

Directions:

1. Soak beans for about 15 minutes. Blend onions, garlic, tomato, ginger and spices with 3 teaspoons of water to make a smooth puree and set aside.
2. Add oil to Instant Pot and press "Sauté" button (*Normal* preset), wait till you see Hot on the display. Add cumin seeds. Roast the seeds until fragrant, for 30 seconds.
3. Add the puree, stir and cook until it

thickens, for up to 10 minutes. Press *Cancel* button.
4. Drain beans and add to the Instant Pot. Add water, lemon juice and salt, mix well.
5. Close the lid and turn the vent to *Sealed*. Press *Pressure Cook* (Manual) button, use *+* or *-* button to set the timer for 15 minutes. Use *Pressure level* button to set Pressure to *HIGH*.
6. Once the timer is up; press *Cancel* button and allow the pressure to be released naturally; until the float valve drops down. Open the lid and serve.

Nutrition Value:
Calories: 45 g; Total Fat: 1.5 g; Total Carbohydrate: 7.6 g; Protein: 1.6

331. Cheesy Asparagus Garlic

Preparation Time: 7 minutes
Servings: 4

Ingredients:

- 1 handful asparagus
- 3 teaspoons minced' garlic
- 3 tablespoons grated cheddar cheese
- 1/4 cup butter

Directions:

1. Trim the ends of the asparagus then place in a disposable aluminum pan
2. Sprinkle minced' garlic over the asparagus then drop butter at several places on top. Pour water into the Instant Pot and place a trivet in it
3. Place the aluminum pan with asparagus on the trivet then cover and seal the Instant Pot properly.
4. Select *Steam* setting on the Instant Pot and cook the asparagus for 4 minutes.
5. Once it is done; naturally release the Instant Pot and open the lid
6. Take the aluminum pan out of the Instant Pot and transfer the cooked asparagus to a serving dish.

Nutrition Value:
Calories: 265; Net Carbs: 2.6g; Total Fat: 26.6g; Protein: 4.6g; Carbs: 4g;

332. Green Beans Stir Fry

Preparation Time: 9 minutes
Servings: 4

Ingredients:

- 1/2 lb. chopped' green beans
- 3/4 tablespoon olive oil
- 2 teaspoons minced' garlic
- 1 teaspoon fish sauce
- 1/4 teaspoon salt

Directions:

1. Pour water into the Instant Pot then place a trivet in it.
2. Put the chopped' green beans on the trivet then cover and seal the Instant Pot properly
3. Select *Manual* setting on the Instant Pot and cook the green beans on low for 2 minutes.
4. Once it is done; quick release the Instant Pot and open the lid
5. Remove the cooked green beans from the Instant Pot and transfer to a plate. Wipe and clean the Instant Pot.
6. Pour olive oil into the Instant Pot and select *Sauté* setting. Stir in minced' garlic then sauté until lightly golden brown and aromatic
7. Add green beans to the Instant Pot and season with salt and fish sauce
8. Stir well and press the *Cancel* button. Transfer the cooked green beans to a serving dish then serve.

Nutrition Value:
Calories: 85; Net Carbs: 5.2g; Total Fat: 5.4g; Protein: 2.4g; Carbs: 9.1g;

333. Quinoa Burrito Bowls Recipe

Preparation Time: 25 minutes
Servings: 4

Ingredients:

- 1/2 diced red onion
- 1 ½ cup cooked black beans
- 1 diced bell pepper

- 1 teaspoon extra-virgin olive oil
- 1 teaspoon ground cumin
- 1 cup water
- 1 cup quinoa
- 1 cup salsa
- 1/2 teaspoon Salt

Directions:

1. Heat the olive oil in the Mini Instant Pot. Turn on the Sauté function. Start to sauté the peppers and onions until they soften properly.
2. It will take about 5-8 minutes for the entire process. Add the salt and cumin and sauté for about a minute until you smell beautiful flavors.
3. You should turn off the Mini Instant Pot for a moment, then; start adding the salsa, water; and quinoa along with the beans and seal the lid in a secured manner. Switch on the Sealing function.
4. Cook everything at low pressure for about 12 minutes. The pressure should release naturally once the cooking is done.
5. By the end of cooking time, the quinoa should absorb every bit of the liquid. It will take about 10-15 minutes.
6. Remove the lid now and be careful about the hot steam. Fluff the quinoa with a fork.
7. Serve the dish warm with your favorite toppings. You can also add some shredded lettuce in case you love some additional veggies.

Nutrition Value:
Calories: 163, Fat: 7g, Carbs: 50g, Protein: 13g

334. Quick Peas Risotto

Preparation Time: 20 minutes
Servings: 2

Ingredients:

- 1 cup baby green peas
- 2 celery sticks; make small cubes
- 2 cups vegetable stock
- 1 cup Arborio rice
- 2 cloves garlic; diced
- 3 tablespoons olive oil
- 1 brown onion; diced
- 2 tablespoons lemon juice
- 1/2 teaspoon salt
- 1/2 teaspoon pepper

Directions:

1. Take your Instant Pot and place it on a clean kitchen platform. Turn it on after plugging it into a power socket.
2. Put the pot on *Sauté* mode. In the pot; add the oil, celery, onions, pepper and salt; cook for 4-5 minutes until the ingredients become soft.
3. Mix in the zest, stock, garlic, peas and rice. Stir the ingredients. Close the lid and lock. Ensure that you have sealed the valve to avoid leakage.
4. Press *Manual* mode and set timer for 5 minutes. It will take a few minutes for the pot to build inside pressure and start cooking.
5. After the timer reads zero, press *Cancel* and quick release pressure. Carefully remove the lid, add the lemon juice and serve warm!

Nutrition Value:
Calories: 362; Fat: 13g; Carbohydrates: 52.5g; Fiber: 3g; Protein 8g

335. Mushroom Soup Recipe

Preparation Time: 25 minutes
Servings: 4

Ingredients:

- 1 cup fresh Baby Bella mushrooms; chopped
- 2 teaspoons olive oil
- 1 tablespoon garlic; minced
- 1 teaspoon dried thyme; crushed
- 2 cups cauliflower; chopped
- 4 cups homemade vegetable broth
- 1 yellow onion; chopped
- Salt and Pepper to taste

Directions:

1. Add oil to Instant Pot and press "Sauté" button (*Normal* preset), wait till you see Hot on the display. Add onion and garlic and cook for about 2 to 3 minutes.
2. Add mushrooms and cook for 4 to 5 more minutes. Press *Cancel* and mix in cauliflower and broth. Season with salt, pepper and thyme.
3. Close the lid and turn the vent to *Sealed*.
4. Press *Pressure Cook* (Manual) button, use *+* or *-* button to set the timer for 5 minutes. Use *Pressure level* button to set Pressure to *HIGH*.
5. Once the timer is up; press *Cancel* button and allow the pressure to be released naturally; until the float valve drops down.
6. Open the lid.
7. Puree the soup with an immerse blender.

Nutrition Value:

Calories: 86 g; Total Fat: 12.2 g; Total Carbohydrate: 7.5 g; Protein: 4.1

336. butternut Squash and Mushroom Meal

Preparation Time: 23 minutes
Servings: 2

Ingredients:

- 1-pound butternut squash; cubed
- 1 cup mushroom
- 1/2 cup almond slivers; toasted
- 1/4 cup minced white onion
- 1-pound beans; sliced into 2-inch long slivers
- 1/8 cup minced chives
- 1 tablespoon olive oil
- 1 cup vegetable broth; unsalted
- A pinch of white pepper
- 1/4 teaspoon kosher salt

Directions:

1. Place your Instant Pot on a flat kitchen surface', plug it and turn it on.
2. To start making the recipe, press *Sauté* button. Add the oil and onions; cook for 4 minutes to soften the ingredients.
3. One by one add the mentioned ingredients in the pot (do not add the almonds, chives and beans). Carefully close its lid and firmly lock it. Then after, seal the valve too.
4. To start making the recipe, press *Manual* button. Now you have to set cooking time', set the timer for 10 minutes. Allow the pot to cook the mixture until the timer goes off.
5. Turn off the pot and press *Cancel.* Allow the built up pressure to vent out naturally', it will take 8-10 minutes to completely release inside pressure.
6. Open its lid and add in the beans. Close lid and warm for 2 minutes to warm the beans. Adjust seasoning if needed. Top with almond slivers and chives; serve warm!

Nutrition Value:

Calories 406; Fat: 17g; Carbohydrates: 43g; Fiber: 18.3g; Protein 28g

337. Garbanzo Beans and Potato

Preparation Time: 15 minutes
Servings: 3

Ingredients:

- 1 cup garbanzo beans; cooked
- 2 potatoes; peeled & cubed
- 1 cup diced tomatoes
- 1/2 tablespoon whole cumin seeds
- 1 teaspoon turmeric
- 1 large onion; chopped
- 1/4 teaspoon ginger
- 1 teaspoon coriander
- 1/2 teaspoon salt

Directions:

1. Place your Instant Pot on a flat kitchen surface', plug it and turn it on.
2. To start making the recipe, press *Sauté* button. Add the 1/2 cup of water, cumin seeds and onions; cook for 2-3 minutes to soften the ingredients.

3. Add the potatoes, turmeric, tomatoes, ginger, coriander, bean, salt and 1/4 cup water. Carefully close its lid and firmly lock it. Then after, seal the valve too.
4. To start making the recipe, press *Manual* button. Now you have to set cooking time', set the timer for 5 minutes. Allow the pot to cook the mixture until the timer goes off.
5. Turn off the pot and press *Cancel.* Allow the built up pressure to vent out naturally', it will take 8-10 minutes to completely release inside pressure.
6. Open its lid and transfer the cooked mixture into serving container/containers. Serve the potatoes with your favorite bread or rice.

Nutrition Value:

Calories: 236; Fat: 2g; Carbohydrates: 42g; Fiber: 7.2g; Protein 7g

338. Glazed Cinnamon Honey Carrots

Preparation Time: 4 minutes
Servings: 4

Ingredients:

- 1/4 lb. carrots
- 1/2 tablespoon butter
- 1 tablespoon honey
- 1/4 cup vegetable broth
- 1/2 teaspoon cinnamon
- 1/4 teaspoon salt

Directions:

1. Pell the carrots then set aside. Pour vegetable broth into the Instant Pot then place a trivet in it. Rub the carrots with salt then put on the trivet
2. Cover the Instant Pot with the lid and seal it properly. Select *Manual* setting on the Instant Pot and cook the carrots for 2 minutes.
3. Once it is done; naturally release the Instant Pot then open the lid
4. Take the cooked carrots out of the Instant Pot then place on a plate. Clean and wipe the Instant Pot then put butter in it
5. Return the carrots back to the Instant Pot then drizzle honey and sprinkle cinnamon on top
6. Select *Sauté* setting and cook the carrots for 1 minute. Stir well. Transfer the carrots to a serving dish then serve

Nutrition Value:

Calories: 50; Net Carbs: 6.2g; Total Fat: 0.4g; Protein: 3.9g; Carbs: 10.5g;

339. Spinach and Fusilli Pasta

Preparation Time: 20 minutes
Servings: 3

Ingredients:

- 1-pound spinach
- 1-pound fusilli pasta
- 2 garlic cloves; crushed
- 1/4 cup pine nuts; chopped
- A drizzle of olive oil
- Black pepper and salt to taste

Directions:

1. Take your Instant Pot and place it on a clean kitchen platform. Turn it on after plugging it into a power socket.
2. Put the pot on *Sauté* mode. In the pot; add the oil, garlic and spinach; cook for 6-7 minutes until the ingredients become soft.
3. Add the pasta, salt and pepper; add water to cover the pasta. Close the lid and lock. Ensure that you have sealed the valve to avoid leakage.
4. Press *Manual* mode and set timer for 6 minutes. It will take a few minutes for the pot to build inside pressure and start cooking.
5. After the timer reads zero, press *Cancel* and quick release pressure. Carefully remove the lid; mix the chopped garlic and pine nuts. Serve warm!

Nutrition Value:

Calories: 198; Fat: 1g; Carbohydrates: 6.5g; Fiber: 1g; Protein 7g

340. Mushroom Risotto

Preparation Time: 20 minutes
Servings: 4

Ingredients:

- 1 tablespoon olive oil
- 2 cups vegetable broth
- 1/2 onion; diced
- 2 garlic cloves; minced
- 3 ½-ounce button mushrooms; sliced
- 1 cup risotto rice
- 1/2 tablespoon white wine
- parmesan cheese; grated, for serving
- Salt and Pepper to taste

Directions:

1. Add oil to Instant Pot and press "Sauté" button (*Normal* preset), wait till you see Hot on the display.
2. Add garlic and onion. Sauté for 1 to 2 minutes. Add mushrooms and cook for 3-4 more minutes. Press *Cancel* button.
3. Add rice, broth and white wine, salt and pepper. Close the lid and turn the vent to "Sealed".
4. Press *Pressure Cook* (Manual) button, use *+* or *-* button to set the timer for 6 minutes. Use *Pressure level* button to set Pressure to *HIGH*.
5. Once the timer is up; press *Cancel* button and turn the steam release handle to "Venting" position for quick release, until the float valve drops down.
6. Open the lid; serve topped with parmesan.

Nutrition Value:
Calories: 428 g; Total Fat: 8.6 g; Total Carbohydrate: 20.2 g; Protein: 12.9

341. Buttery Green Beans Recipe

Preparation Time: 15 minutes
Servings: 4

Ingredients:

- 1-pound. fresh green beans
- 2 tablespoons butter
- 1 garlic clove; minced
- 2 cups water
- Salt to taste

Directions:

1. Add water, beans, garlic and salt to the Instant pot. Close the lid and turn the vent to *Sealed*.
2. Press *Pressure Cook* (Manualbutton, use *+* or *-* button to set the timer for 5 minutes. Use *Pressure level* button to set pressure to low.
3. Once the timer is up; press *Cancel* button and turn the steam release handle to *Venting* position for quick release, until the float valve drops down.
4. Open the lid; Add butter and stir a bit, drain excess liquid and serve.

Nutrition Value:
Calories: 86 g; Total Fat: 14.7 g; Total Carbohydrate: 6.7 g; Protein: 11.7

342. Carrots with Dill

Preparation Time: 7 minutes
Servings: 4

Ingredients:

- 1/4 lb. baby carrots
- 1 teaspoon thyme
- 1 teaspoon dill
- 1/4 cup vegetable broth
- 1 tablespoon olive oil

Directions:

1. Peel the carrots then place in a bowl. Drizzle olive oil over the carrots then sprinkle thyme and dill on top.
2. Toss to combine. Pour vegetable broth into the Instant Pot then place a trivet in it
3. Arrange the carrots on the trivet then cover and seal the Instant Pot properly. Select *Manual* setting and cook the carrots on high for 3 minutes
4. Once it is done; naturally release the Instant Pot and open the lid. Transfer the carrots to a serving dish then enjoy

Nutrition Value:

Calories: 30; Net Carbs: 5g; Total Fat: 0.2g; Protein: 0.7g; Carbs: 1.8g;

343. Cauliflower Florets

Preparation Time: 6 minutes
Servings: 4

Ingredients:

- 1½ cups cauliflower florets
- 1 teaspoon cornstarch
- 2 teaspoons sesame seeds
- 1/2 teaspoon ginger
- 1 teaspoon sesame oil
- 1 teaspoon minced' garlic
- 1/4 cup water
- 2 tablespoons soy sauce

Directions:

1. Combine water with soy sauce, sesame oil, minced' garlic, ginger and cornstarch then stir until incorporated.
2. Place the cauliflower florets in the inner pot of an Instant Pot then drizzle the liquid over the cauliflower florets
3. Cover the Instant Pot with the lid and seal it properly. Select *Manual* setting and cook the cauliflower florets on high for 4 minutes
4. Once it is done; naturally release the Instant Pot and open the lid. Transfer the cauliflower florets to a serving dish then sprinkle sesame seeds on top

Nutrition Value:

Calories: 65; Net Carbs: 5.2g; Total Fat: 3.2g; Protein: 2.9g; Carbs: 7.5g;

344. Brussels sprouts Tender

Preparation Time: 3 minutes
Servings: 4

Ingredients:

- 1/2 lb. Brussels sprouts
- 1/4 teaspoon pepper
- 1/2 cup water
- 1/4 teaspoon salt

Directions:

1. Cut each Brussels sprouts into half then place in the inner pot of an Instant Pot. Pour water over the Brussels sprouts then cover and seal the Instant Pot properly
2. Select *Manual* setting on the Instant Pot and cook the Brussels sprouts on high for 1 minute.
3. Once it is done; quick release the Instant Pot and open the lid
4. Strain the cooked Brussels sprouts and place on a serving dish. Sprinkle salt and pepper over the Brussels sprouts then toss to combine

Nutrition Value:

Calories: 50; Net Carbs: 6.2g; Total Fat: 0.4g; Protein: 3.9g; Carbs: 10.5g;

345. Mushroom and Navy Bean

Preparation Time: 40 minutes
Servings: 3

Ingredients:

- 3 cups mushrooms; chopped
- 1 cup navy beans; dried
- 2 tablespoons onion powder
- 1 tablespoon shallot powder
- 2 tablespoons barley
- 1 tablespoon red curry paste
- 1/2 cup farro
- 9 garlic cloves; minced
- 2 tomatoes; diced
- 1 seeded jalapeno pepper; chopped
- Pepper and salt as needed

Directions:

1. Take your Instant Pot and place it on a clean kitchen platform. Turn it on after plugging it into a power socket.
2. Open the lid from the top and put it aside; start adding the beans, faro, barley, mushrooms, garlic, jalapeno, curry paste, shallot and onion powder, pepper and salt.
3. Add water to cover all the ingredients', gently stir them.

4. Close the lid and lock. Ensure that you have sealed the valve to avoid leakage.
5. Press *Manual* mode and set timer for 30 minutes. It will take a few minutes for the pot to build inside pressure and start cooking.
6. After the timer reads zero, press *Cancel* and naturally release pressure. It takes about 8-10 minutes to naturally release pressure.
7. Carefully remove the lid and add the tomatoes. Sprinkle cilantro and scallions; serve warm!

Nutrition Value:
Calories: 238; Fat: 6.5g; Carbohydrates: 38g; Fiber: 1.5g; Protein 11g

346. Tuscan Pasta Recipe

Preparation Time: 20 minutes
Servings: 3

Ingredients:

- 8-ounce penne pasta (any other pasta will also work well)
- 1 bell pepper; chopped
- 1 cup fresh spinach; chopped
- 1/2 onion; chopped
- 1 cup broccoli florets
- 2 cups water
- 1/2 cup mozzarella; grated
- 1/2 cup tomato sauce
- 1 tablespoon olive oil
- 3 ½-ounce cremini mushrooms
- 1 tablespoon parmesan cheese; grated
- Salt and Pepper to taste

Directions:

1. Add oil to Instant Pot and press "Sauté" button (*Normal* preset), wait till you see Hot on the display.
2. Add onion, mushrooms and bell pepper, cook for 3-4 minutes until soft.
3. Add pasta, broccoli, spinach, tomato sauce, water, salt and pepper, press *Cancel* button. Close the lid and turn the vent to "Sealed".
4. Press *Pressure Cook* (Manual) button, use *+* or *-* button to set the timer for 5 minutes. Use *Pressure level* button to set pressure to low.
5. Once the timer is up; press *Cancel* button and turn the steam release handle to *Venting* position for quick release, until the float valve drops down.
6. Open the lid.
7. Add mozzarella, stir well until melted. Serve topped with parmesan cheese.

Nutrition Value:
Calories: 322 g; Total Fat: 7.6 g; Total Carbohydrate: 52.29 g; Protein: 13

347. Spicy Cabbage Wedges

Preparation Time: 10 minutes
Servings: 4

Ingredients:

- 3/4 lb. cabbage
- 1/2 cup water
- 1/2 teaspoon sugar
- 1/4 cup grated carrots
- 1 teaspoon sesame oil
- 1/2 teaspoon cayenne pepper

Directions:

1. Cut the cabbage into wedges then set aside. Pour sesame oil into the inner pot of an Instant Pot then select *Sauté* setting
2. Put the cabbage wedges in the Instant Pot then cook for about 3 minutes until brown on one side. Press the *Cancel* button
3. Sprinkle grated carrots, sugar and cayenne pepper over the cabbage then pour water into the Instant Pot.
4. Cover the Instant Pot with the lid and seal it properly
5. Select * Pressure cook* setting and cook the cabbage on high for 5 minutes
6. Once it is done; naturally release the Instant Pot and open the lid. Transfer the cooked cabbage to a serving dish then serve

Nutrition Value:

Calories: 70; Net Carbs: 7g; Total Fat: 2.5g; Protein: 2.3g; Carbs: 11.6g;

348. Tomato Eggplant and Cheese Lasagna

Preparation Time: 8 minutes
Servings: 4

Ingredients:

- 1½ cup chopped' eggplant
- 3/4 cup diced' tomatoes
- 1/2 cup grated Mozzarella cheese
- 1/2 teaspoon salt
- 1/4 cup tomato sauce
- 1/4 cup diced' onion
- 1/4 cup white wine
- 1/2 teaspoon garlic powder
- 3/4 teaspoon oregano
- 2 tablespoons chopped' parsley
- 1/4 teaspoon pepper

Directions:

1. Place diced' tomatoes in a bowl then add tomato sauce and onion. Season with garlic powder, oregano, salt and pepper then pour white wine over the tomatoes. Stir until combined.
2. Place half of the eggplant on the bottom of a disposable aluminum pan then put half of the tomato mixture over the eggplant. Spread evenly
3. Layer with the remaining eggplant and tomatoes then sprinkle grated Mozzarella cheese on top.
4. Pour water into an Instant Pot and place a trivet in it. Place the aluminum pan with eggplant on the trivet then cover and seal the Instant Pot properly
5. Select *Steam* setting on the Instant Pot and cook the eggplant lasagna for 3 minutes.
6. Once it is done; naturally release the Instant Pot and open the lid
7. Remove the eggplant lasagna from the Instant Pot and serve warm

Nutrition Value:

Calories: 134; Net Carbs: 6.9g; Total Fat: 6.6g;

Protein: 7.9g; Carbs: 11.1g;

349. Savoy Cabbage and Cream

Preparation time: 10 minutes
Cooking time: 9 minutes
Servings: 4

Ingredients:

- 1 cup bacon, chopped
- 1 medium Savoy cabbage head, chopped
- 1 yellow onion, peeled and chopped
- 2 cups vegetable stock
- ¼ teaspoon nutmeg
- Salt and ground black pepper, to taste
- 1 bay leaf
- 1 cup coconut milk
- 2 tablespoons dried parsley

Directions:

1. Set the Instant Pot on Sauté mode, add the bacon and onion, stir, and cook until bacon is crispy. Add the stock, cabbage, bay leaf, salt, pepper, and nutmeg, stir, cover, and cook on Steam mode for 5 minutes. Release the pressure, uncover the Instant Pot, and set it on Sauté mode again. Add the milk, more salt and pepper, if needed, and parsley, stir, and cook for 4 minutes. Divide among plates and serve.

Nutrition Value:

Calories: 160
Fat: 10
Fiber: 2.2
Carbs: 13
Protein: 5

350. Sweet and Spicy Cabbage

Preparation time: 10 minutes
Cooking time: 8 minutes
Servings: 4

Ingredients:

- 1 cabbage, cut into 8 wedges
- 1 tablespoon sesame seed oil
- 1 carrots, peeled and grated

- ¼ cup apple cider vinegar
- 1½ cups water
- 1 teaspoon sugar
- ½ teaspoon cayenne pepper
- ½ teaspoon red pepper flakes
- 2 teaspoons cornstarch

Directions:

1. Set the Instant Pot on Sauté mode, add the oil and heat it up. Add the cabbage, stir, and cook for 3 minutes. Add the carrots, 1¼ cups water, sugar, vinegar, cayenne pepper, and pepper flakes, stir, cover, and cook on the Steam setting for 5 minutes. Release the pressure, uncover the Instant Pot, and divide cabbage and carrots among plates. Add the cornstarch mixed with the remaining water to the Instant Pot, set it on Manual mode, stir well, and bring to a boil. Drizzle over the cabbage and carrots, and serve.

Nutrition Value:

Calories: 90
Fat: 4.5
Fiber: 2.1
Carbs: 11
Protein: 1

351. **Sweet Carrots**

Preparation time: 10 minutes
Cooking time: 15 minutes
Servings: 4

Ingredients:

- 2 cups baby carrots
- A pinch of salt
- 1 tablespoon brown sugar
- ½ tablespoon butter
- ½ cup water

Directions:

1. In the Instant Pot, mix the butter with the water, salt, and sugar and stir well. Set the Instant Pot on Sauté mode and cook for 30 seconds. Add the carrots, stir, cover, and cook on the Steam setting for 15 minutes. Release the pressure, uncover the Instant Pot, set it on Sauté mode, and cook for 1 minute. Serve hot.

Nutrition Value:

Calories: 60
Fat: 0.1
Fiber: 1
Carbs: 4
Protein: 1

352. **Cabbage with Bacon**

Preparation time: 10 minutes
Cooking time: 8 minutes
Servings: 8

Ingredients:

- 1 green cabbage head, chopped
- ¼ cup butter
- 2 cups chicken stock
- 3 bacon slices, chopped
- Salt and ground black pepper, to taste

Directions:

1. Set the Instant Pot on Sauté mode, add the bacon, stir, and cook for 4 minutes. Add the butter and stir until it melts. Add the cabbage, stock, salt, and pepper, stir, cover, and cook on the Steam setting for 3 minutes. Release the pressure, uncover the Instant Pot, transfer the cabbage to plates, and serve.

Nutrition Value:

Calories: 100
Fat: 4
Fiber: 3
Carbs: 7
Protein: 2

353. **Cabbage and Sausages**

Preparation time: 10 minutes
Cooking time: 5 minutes
Servings: 4

Ingredients:

- 3 tablespoons butter
- 1 green cabbage head, chopped
- Salt and ground black pepper, to taste

- 1 pound sausage links, sliced
- 15 ounces canned diced tomatoes
- ½ cup yellow onion, chopped
- 2 teaspoons turmeric

Directions:

1. Set the Instant Pot on Sauté mode, add the sausage, stir, and cook until they are brown. Drain the excess grease, add the butter, cabbage, tomatoes salt, pepper, onion, and turmeric, stir, cover, and cook on the Manual setting for 2 minutes. Release the pressure, uncover, divide cabbage, and sausages among plates, and serve.

Nutrition Value:

Calories: 140
Fat: 6
Fiber: 4
Carbs: 11
Protein: 10

354. Maple-glazed Carrots

Preparation time: 10 minutes
Cooking time: 4 minutes
Servings: 4

Ingredients:

- 2 pounds carrots, peeled and sliced diagonally
- 1 tablespoon maple syrup
- Ground black pepper, to taste
- 1 tablespoon butter
- 1 cup water
- ¼ cup raisins

Directions:

1. Put the carrots into the Instant Pot. Add the water and raisins, cover, and cook on the Steam setting for 4 minutes. Release the pressure, uncover, add the butter and maple syrup, stir, divide the carrots among plates, and sprinkle with black pepper before serving them.

Nutrition Value:

Calories: 60
Fat: 1.1
Fiber: 2.6
Carbs: 12
Protein: 1

355. Carrots with Molasses

Preparation time: 10 minutes
Cooking time: 2 minutes
Servings: 4

Ingredients:

- 16 ounces baby carrots
- Salt and ground black pepper, to taste
- 2 tablespoons butter
- 4 ounces molasses
- 2 ounces water
- 2 tablespoon dill, chopped

Directions:

1. Put the carrots, water, salt, pepper, and molasses into the Instant Pot, stir, cover, and cook on the Manual setting for 3 minutes. Release the pressure, uncover the Instant Pot, add the butter and dill, stir, divide among plates, and serve.

Nutrition Value:

Calories: 60
Fat: 1
Fiber: 2
Carbs: 4
Protein: 3

356. Savory Collard Greens

Preparation time: 10 minutes
Cooking time: 20 minutes
Servings: 4

Ingredients:

- 1 bunch collard greens, trimmed
- 2 tablespoons extra virgin olive oil
- ½ cup chicken stock
- 2 tablespoons tomato puree
- 1 yellow onion, peeled and chopped
- 3 garlic cloves, peeled and minced
- Salt and ground black pepper, to taste
- 1 tablespoon balsamic vinegar
- 1 teaspoon sugar

Directions:

1. In the Instant Pot, mix the stock with the oil, garlic, vinegar, onion, and tomato puree and stir well. Roll the collard greens into cigar-shaped bundles to the Instant Pot. Add the salt, pepper, and sugar, cover, and cook on the Steam setting for 20 minutes. Release the pressure, uncover the Instant Pot, divide the collard greens among plates, and serve.

Nutrition Value:

Calories: 130
Fat: 7
Fiber: 4.5
Carbs: 12
Protein: 4
Sugar: 4

357. Classic Collard Greens

Preparation time: 10 minutes
Cooking time: 25 minutes
Servings: 8

Ingredients:

- 1 onion, peeled and chopped
- 2 tablespoons extra virgin olive oil
- 3 garlic cloves, peeled and crushed
- 2½ pounds collard greens, chopped
- Salt and ground black pepper, to taste
- 2 cups chicken stock
- 2 tablespoons apple cider vinegar
- 1 tablespoon brown sugar
- ½ teaspoon crushed red pepper
- 2 smoked turkey wings

Directions:

1. Set the Instant Pot on Sauté mode, add the oil and heat it up. Add the onions, stir, and cook for 2 minutes. Add the garlic, stir, and cook for 1 minute. Add the stock, greens, vinegar, salt, pepper, crushed red pepper, and sugar and stir. Add the turkey, cover, and cook on the Steam setting for 20 minutes. Release the pressure fast, uncover the Instant Pot, divide greens and turkey among plates, and serve.

Nutrition Value:

Calories: 100
Fat: 1.4
Fiber: 1.7
Carbs: 4
Protein: 6

358. Cauliflower with Pasta

Preparation time: 10 minutes
Cooking time: 10 minutes
Servings: 4

Ingredients:

- 2 tablespoons butter
- 8 cups cauliflower florets
- 2 garlic cloves, peeled and minced
- 1 cup chicken stock
- Salt, to taste
- 2 cups spinach, chopped
- 1 pound fettuccine noodles
- 2 green onions, chopped
- 1 tablespoon gorgonzola cheese, grated
- 3 sundried tomatoes, chopped
- Balsamic vinegar

Directions:

1. Set the Instant Pot on Sauté mode, add the butter, and melt it. Add the garlic, stir, and cook for 2 minutes. Add the stock, salt, and cauliflower, stir, cover, and cook on the Manual setting for 6 minutes. Release the pressure for 10 minutes, transfer the cauliflower to a blender, and pulse well. Add the spinach and green onions and stir. Heat up a pot with some water and a pinch of salt over medium-high heat, bring to a boil, add the pasta, cook according to instructions, drain, and divide among plates. Add the cauliflower sauce, cheese, tomatoes, and a splash of vinegar on top, toss to coat, and serve.

Nutrition Value:

Calories: 160
Fat: 5

Fiber: 3
Carbs: 23
Protein: 13

359. Collard Greens and Bacon

Preparation time: 10 minutes
Cooking time: 26 minutes
Servings: 6

Ingredients:

- 1 pound collard greens, trimmed
- ¼ pound bacon, chopped
- Salt and ground black pepper, to taste
- ½ cup water

Directions:

1. Set the Instant Pot on Sauté mode, add the bacon, stir, and cook for 5 minutes. Add the collard greens, salt, pepper, and water, stir, cover and cook on the Steam setting for 20 minutes. Release the pressure, uncover, divide the mixture among plates, and serve.

Nutrition Value:
Calories: 130
Fat: 8
Fiber: 2
Carbs: 4
Protein: 6

360. Braised Endive

Preparation time: 10 minutes
Cooking time: 7 minutes
Servings: 4

Ingredients:

- 4 endives, trimmed and cut into halves
- Salt and ground black pepper, to taste
- 1 tablespoon lemon juice
- 1 tablespoon butter

Directions:

1. Set the Instant Pot on Sauté mode. Add the butter and melt it. Arrange the endives in the Instant Pot, add the salt, pepper, and lemon juice, cover, and cook on the Steam setting for 7 minutes. Release the pressure naturally, arrange the endives on a platter, add the cooking liquid all over them, and serve.

Nutrition Value:
Calories: 80
Fat: 3.1
Fiber: 0.5
Carbs: 12
Protein: 1.2

361. Endive with Ham

Preparation time: 10 minutes
Cooking time: 20 minutes
Servings: 4

Ingredients:

- 4 endives, trimmed
- Salt and ground black pepper, to taste
- 1 tablespoon white flour
- 4 slices ham
- 2 tablespoons butter
- ½ teaspoon nutmeg
- 14 ounces milk

Directions:

1. Put the endives in the steamer basket of the Instant Pot, add some water to the Instant Pot, cover and cook on the Steam setting for 10 minutes. Heat up a pan with the butter over medium heat, stir, and melt it. Add the flour, stir well, and cook for 3 minutes. Add the milk, salt, pepper, and nutmeg, stir well, reduce the heat to low, and cook for 10 minutes. Release the pressure from the Instant Pot, uncover it, transfer them to a cutting board, and roll each in a slice of ham. Arrange the endives in a pan, add the milk mixture over them, place under a preheated broiler and broil for 10 minutes. Slice, arrange on plates, and serve.

Nutrition Value:
Calories: 120
Fat: 1
Fiber: 2
Carbs: 6
Protein: 23

362. Eggplant Ratatouille

Preparation time: 15 minutes
Cooking time: 8 minutes
Servings: 6

Ingredients:

- 1 eggplant, peeled and thinly sliced
- 2 garlic cloves, peeled and minced
- 3 tablespoons extra virgin olive oil
- Salt and ground black pepper, to taste
- 1 cup onion, peeled and chopped
- 1 green bell pepper, seeded and chopped
- 1 red bell pepper, seeded and chopped
- ½ cup water
- 1 teaspoon dried thyme
- 14 ounces canned diced tomatoes
- Sugar
- 1 cup fresh basil, chopped

Directions:

1. Set the Instant Pot on Sauté mode, add the oil, and heat it up. Add the bell peppers, onion, and garlic, stir, and cook for 3 minutes. Add the eggplant, water, salt, pepper, thyme, sugar, and tomatoes, cover the Instant Pot and cook on the Steam setting for 4 minutes. Release the pressure fast, uncover the Instant Pot, add the basil, stir gently, divide among plates, and serve.

Nutrition Value:

Calories: 109
Fat: 5
Fiber: 3
Carbs: 14
Protein: 2

363. Eggplant Marinara

Preparation time: 10 minutes
Cooking time: 8 minutes
Servings: 2

Ingredients:

- 4 cups eggplant, cubed
- 1 tablespoon extra virgin olive oil
- 3 garlic cloves, peeled and minced
- 1 tablespoon onion powder
- Salt and ground black pepper, to taste
- 1 cup marinara sauce
- ½ cup water
- Spaghetti noodles, already cooked

Directions:

1. Set the Instant Pot on Sauté mode, add the oil, and heat it up. Add the garlic, stir, and cook for 2 minutes. Add the eggplant, salt, pepper, onion powder, marinara sauce, and water, stir gently, cover and cook on the Steam setting for 8 minutes. Release the pressure, uncover the Instant Pot, and serve with spaghetti.

Nutrition Value:

Calories: 130
Fat: 3
Fiber: 2
Carbs: 3
Protein: 3

364. Sautéed Endive

Preparation time: 10 minutes
Cooking time: 15 minutes
Servings: 4

Ingredients:

- 8 endives, trimmed
- Salt and ground black pepper, to taste
- 4 tablespoon butter
- Juice of ½ lemon
- ½ cup water
- 1 teaspoon sugar
- 2 tablespoons fresh parsley, chopped

Directions:

1. Put the endives into the Instant Pot, add 1 tablespoon butter, lemon juice, ½ cup water, sugar, salt, and pepper, stir, cover, and cook on the Steam setting for 10 minutes. Release the pressure, uncover the Instant Pot, and transfer the endives to a plate. Heat up a pan with the remaining tablespoons butter over medium-high heat, add the endives, more salt and pepper, if needed, and parsley.

Stir and cook for 5 minutes. Transfer the endives to plates, and serve.

Nutrition Value:

Calories: 90
Fat: 1
Fiber: 4
Carbs: 4
Protein: 2

365. Endive Risotto

Preparation time: 10 minutes
Cooking time: 20 minutes
Servings: 2

Ingredients:

- ¾ cup rice
- 2 Belgian endives, trimmed, cut into halves lengthwise, and roughly chopped
- ½ yellow onion, peeled and chopped
- 2 tablespoons extra virgin olive oil
- ½ cup white wine
- 2 cups vegetable stock
- 2 ounces Parmesan cheese, grated
- 3 tablespoons heavy cream
- Salt and ground black pepper, to taste

Directions:

1. Set the Instant Pot on Sauté mode, add the oil, and heat it up. Add the onion, stir, and sauté for 4 minutes. Add the endives, stir, and cook for 4 minutes. Add the rice, wine, salt, pepper, stock, stir, cover, and cook on the Steam setting for 10 minutes. Release the pressure fast, uncover the Instant Pot, and set it on Sauté mode. Add the cheese and heavy cream, stir, cook for 1 minute, transfer to plates, and serve.

Nutrition Value:

Calories: 260
Fat: 5
Fiber: 5
Carbs: 13
Protein: 16

366. Babaganoush

Preparation time: 10 minutes
Cooking time: 4 minutes
Servings: 6

Ingredients:

- 2 pounds eggplant, peeled and cut into medium chunks
- Salt and ground black pepper, to taste
- ⅓ cup extra virgin olive oil
- ½ cup water
- 4 garlic cloves, peeled
- ¼ cup lemon juice
- 1 bunch thyme, chopped
- 1 tablespoon tahini
- 3 olives, pitted and sliced

Directions:

1. Put the eggplant pieces into the Instant Pot, add ¼ cup oil, set the Instant Pot on Sauté mode, and heat up. Add the garlic, water, salt, and pepper, stir, cover, and cook on the Steam setting for 3 minutes. Release the pressure, uncover the Instant Pot, transfer the eggplant pieces and garlic to a blender, add the lemon juice and tahini and pulse well. Add the thyme and blend again. Transfer eggplant spread to a bowl, top with olive slices and a drizzle of oil, and serve.

Nutrition Value:

Calories: 70
Fat: 2
Fiber: 2
Carbs: 7
Protein: 1

367. Eggplant Surprise

Preparation time: 10 minutes
Cooking time: 7 minutes
Servings: 4

Ingredients:

- 1 eggplant, roughly chopped
- 3 zucchini, roughly chopped
- 3 tomatoes, cored and sliced
- 2 tablespoons lemon juice

- Salt and ground black pepper, to taste
- 1 teaspoon dried thyme
- 1 teaspoon dried oregano
- 3 tablespoons extra virgin olive oil

Directions:

1. Put the eggplant pieces into the Instant Pot. Add the zucchini and tomatoes. In a bowl, mix the lemon juice with salt, pepper, thyme, oregano, and oil and stir well. Pour this over the vegetables, toss to coat, cover the Instant Pot and cook on the Steam setting for 7 minutes. Release the pressure, uncover the Instant Pot, divide among plates, and serve.

Nutrition Value:

Calories: 140
Fat: 3.4
Fiber: 7
Carbs: 20
Protein: 5

368. Kale with Garlic and Lemon

Preparation time: 10 minutes
Cooking time: 5 minutes
Servings: 4

Ingredients:

- 3 garlic cloves, peeled and chopped
- 1 tablespoon extra virgin olive oil
- 1 pound kale, trimmed
- Salt and ground black pepper, to taste
- ½ cup water
- Juice of ½ lemon

Directions:

1. Set the Instant Pot on Sauté mode, add the oil, and heat it up. Add the garlic, stir, and cook for 2 minutes. Add the kale and water, cover, and cook on the Steam setting for 5 minutes. Release the pressure, uncover the Instant Pot, add the salt, pepper, and lemon juice, stir, divide among plates, and serve.

Nutrition Value:

Calories: 60
Fat: 3
Fiber: 1
Carbs: 2.4
Protein: 0.7

369. Braised Kale

Preparation time: 10 minutes
Cooking time: 10 minutes
Servings: 2

Ingredients:

- 10 ounces kale, chopped
- 1 yellow onion, peeled and sliced thin
- 1 tablespoon kale
- 3 carrots, peeled and sliced
- ½ cup chicken stock
- 1 tablespoon butter
- 5 garlic cloves, peeled and chopped
- Salt and ground black pepper, to taste
- Balsamic vinegar
- ¼ teaspoon red pepper flakes

Directions:

1. Set the Instant Pot on Sauté mode, add the butter, and melt it. Add the carrots and onion, stir, and sauté for 2 minutes. Add the garlic, stir, and cook for 1 minute. Add the kale, stock, salt, and pepper, stir, cover, and cook on the Manual setting for 7 minutes. Release the pressure, uncover the Instant Pot, add the vinegar and pepper flakes, toss to coat, divide among plates, and serve.

Nutrition Value:

Calories: 60
Fat: 2
Fiber: 2
Carbs: 4
Protein: 1

370. Braised Fennel

Preparation time: 10 minutes
Cooking time: 12 minutes
Servings: 4

Ingredients:

1. 2 fennel bulbs, trimmed and cut into quarters
2. 3 tablespoons extra virgin olive oil
3. Salt and ground black pepper, to taste
4. 1 garlic clove, peeled and chopped
5. 1 dried red pepper
6. ¾ cup vegetable stock
7. Juice of ½ lemon
8. ¼ cup white wine
9. ¼ cup Parmesan cheese, grated

Directions:

1. Set the Instant Pot on Sauté mode, add the oil, and heat it up. Add the garlic and red pepper, stir, cook for 2 minutes, and discard the garlic. Add the fennel, stir, and brown it for 8 minutes. Add the salt, pepper, stock, wine, cover, and cook on the Steam setting for 4 minutes. Release the pressure, uncover the Instant Pot, add the lemon juice, more salt and pepper, if needed, and cheese. Toss to coat, divide among plates, and serve.

Nutrition Value:

Calories: 70
Fat: 1
Fiber: 2
Carbs: 2
Protein: 1

371. Easy Cheesy Artichokes

Preparation Time: 10 minutes
Servings 3

Nutrition Value: 173 Calories; 12.5g Fat; 9g Carbs; 8.1g Protein; 0.9g Sugars

Ingredients

- 3 medium-sized artichokes, cleaned and trimmed
- 3 cloves garlic, smashed
- 3 tablespoons butter, melted
- Sea salt, to taste
- 1/2 teaspoon cayenne pepper
- 1/4 teaspoon ground black pepper, or more to taste
- 1 lemon, freshly squeezed
- 1 cup Monterey-Jack cheese, shredded
- 1 tablespoon fresh parsley, roughly chopped

Directions

1. Start by adding 1 cup of water and a steamer basket to the Instant Pot. Place the artichokes in the steamer basket; add garlic and butter.
2. Secure the lid. Choose "Manual" mode and High pressure; cook for 8 minutes. Once cooking is complete, use a quick pressure release; carefully remove the lid.
3. Season your artichokes with salt, cayenne pepper, and black pepper. Now, drizzle them with lemon juice.
4. Top with cheese and parsley and serve immediately. Bon appétit!

372. Chinese Bok Choy

Preparation Time: 10 minutes
Servings 4

Nutrition Value: 83 Calories; 6.1g Fat; 5.7g Carbs; 3.2g Protein; 2.4g Sugars

Ingredients

- 2 tablespoons butter, melted
- 2 cloves garlic, minced
- 1 (1/2-inch) slice fresh ginger root, grated
- 1 ½ pounds Bok choy, trimmed
- 1 cup vegetable stock
- Celery salt and ground black pepper to taste
- 1 teaspoon Five-spice powder
- 2 tablespoons soy sauce

Directions

1. Press the "Sauté" button to heat up the Instant Pot. Now, warm the butter and sauté the garlic until tender and fragrant.
2. Now, add grated ginger and cook for a further 40 seconds.
3. Add Bok choy, stock, salt, black pepper, and Five-spice powder.
4. Secure the lid. Choose "Manual" mode and High pressure; cook for 6 minutes. Once cooking is complete, use a quick pressure release; carefully remove the lid.

5. Drizzle soy sauce over your Bok choy and serve immediately. Bon appétit!

373. Green Cabbage with Bacon

Preparation Time: 10 minutes
Servings 4

Nutrition Value: 166 Calories; 13g Fat; 7.1g Carbs; 6.8g Protein; 2.7g Sugars

Ingredients

- 2 teaspoons olive oil
- 4 slices bacon, chopped
- 1 head green cabbage, cored and cut into wedges
- 1 cups vegetable stock
- Sea salt, to taste
- 1/2 teaspoon whole black peppercorns
- 1 teaspoon cayenne pepper
- 1 bay leaf

Directions

1. Press the "Sauté" button to heat up the Instant Pot. Then, heat olive oil and cook the bacon until it is nice and delicately browned.
2. Then, add the remaining ingredients; gently stir to combine.
3. Secure the lid. Choose "Manual" mode and High pressure; cook for 3 minutes. Once cooking is complete, use a quick pressure release; carefully remove the lid.
4. Serve warm and enjoy!

374. Warm Broccoli Salad Bowl

Preparation Time: 10 minutes
Servings 4

Nutrition Value: 95 Calories; 3.1g Fat; 8.1g Carbs; 9.9g Protein; 3.8g Sugars

Ingredients

- 1 pound broccoli, broken into florets
- 2 tablespoons balsamic vinegar
- 2 garlic cloves, minced
- 1 teaspoon mustard seeds
- 1 teaspoon cumin seeds
- Salt and pepper, to taste
- 1 cup Cottage cheese, crumbled

Directions

1. Place 1 cup of water and a steamer basket in your Instant Pot.
2. Place the broccoli in the steamer basket.
3. Secure the lid. Choose "Manual" mode and High pressure; cook for 5 minutes. Once cooking is complete, use a quick pressure release; carefully remove the lid.
4. Then, toss your broccoli with the other ingredients. Serve and enjoy!

375. Creamed Spinach with Cheese

Preparation Time: 10 minutes
Servings 4

Nutrition Value: 283 Calories; 23.9g Fat; 9g Carbs; 10.7g Protein; 3.2g Sugars

Ingredients

- 2 tablespoons butter, melted
- 1/2 cup scallions, chopped
- 2 cloves garlic, smashed
- 1 ½ pounds fresh spinach
- 1 cup vegetable broth, preferably homemade
- 1 cup cream cheese, cubed
- Seasoned salt and ground black pepper, to taste
- 1/2 teaspoon dried dill weed

Directions

1. Press the "Sauté" button to heat up the Instant Pot. Then, melt the butter; cook the scallions and garlic until tender and aromatic.
2. Add the remaining ingredients and stir to combine well.
3. Secure the lid. Choose "Manual" mode and High pressure; cook for 2 minutes. Once cooking is complete, use a quick pressure release; carefully remove the lid.
4. Ladle into individual bowls and serve warm. Bon appétit!

376. Turnip Greens with Sausage

Preparation Time: 10 minutes
Servings 4

Nutrition Value: 149 Calories; 7.2g Fat; 9g Carbs; 14.2g Protein; 2.2g Sugars

Ingredients

- 2 teaspoons sesame oil
- 2 pork sausages, casing removed sliced
- 2 garlic cloves, minced
- 1 medium-sized leek, chopped
- 1 pound turnip greens
- 1 cup turkey bone stock
- Sea salt, to taste
- 1/4 teaspoon ground black pepper, or more to taste
- 1 bay leaf
- 1 tablespoon black sesame seeds

Directions

1. Press the "Sauté" button to heat up the Instant Pot. Then, heat the sesame oil; cook the sausage until nice and delicately browned; set aside.
2. Add the garlic and leeks; continue to cook in pan drippings for a minute or two.
3. Add the greens, stock, salt, black pepper, and bay leaf.
4. Secure the lid. Choose "Manual" mode and Low pressure; cook for 3 minutes. Once cooking is complete, use a quick pressure release; carefully remove the lid.
5. Serve garnished with black sesame seeds and enjoy!

377. Asparagus with Colby Cheese

Preparation Time: 10 minutes
Servings 4
Nutrition Value: 164 Calories; 12.2g Fat; 8.1g Carbs; 7.8g Protein; 3.3g Sugars

Ingredients

- 1 ½ pounds fresh asparagus
- 2 tablespoons olive oil
- 4 garlic cloves, minced
- Sea salt, to taste
- 1/4 teaspoon ground black pepper
- 1/2 cup Colby cheese, shredded

Directions

1. Add 1 cup of water and a steamer basket to your Instant Pot.
2. Now, place the asparagus on the steamer basket; drizzle your asparagus with olive oil. Scatter garlic over the top of the asparagus.
3. Season with salt and black pepper.
4. Secure the lid. Choose "Manual" mode and High pressure; cook for 1 minute. Once cooking is complete, use a quick pressure release; carefully remove the lid.
5. Transfer the prepared asparagus to a nice serving platter and scatter shredded cheese over the top. Enjoy!

378. Mediterranean Aromatic Zucchini

Preparation Time: 10 minutes
Servings 4
Nutrition Value: 85 Calories; 7.1g Fat; 4.7g Carbs; 1.6g Protein; 3.3g Sugars

Ingredients

- 2 tablespoons olive oil
- 2 garlic cloves, chopped
- 1 pound zucchini, sliced
- 1/2 cup tomato purée
- 1/2 cup water
- 1 teaspoon dried thyme
- 1/2 teaspoon dried oregano
- 1/2 teaspoon dried rosemary

Directions

1. Press the "Sauté" button to heat up the Instant Pot. Then, heat the olive oil; sauté the garlic until aromatic.
2. Add the remaining ingredients.
3. Secure the lid. Choose "Manual" mode and Low pressure; cook for 3 minutes. Once cooking is complete, use a quick

pressure release; carefully remove the lid. Bon appétit!

379. Chanterelles with Cheddar Cheese

Preparation Time: 10 minutes
Servings 4

Nutrition Value: 218 Calories; 15.1g Fat; 9.5g Carbs; 9.9g Protein; 2.3g Sugars

Ingredients

- 1 tablespoon olive oil
- 2 cloves garlic, minced
- 1 (1-inch) ginger root, grated
- 1/2 teaspoon dried dill weed
- 1 teaspoon dried basil
- 1/2 teaspoon dried thyme
- 16 ounces Chanterelle mushrooms, brushed clean and sliced
- 1/2 cup water
- 1/2 cup tomato purée
- 2 tablespoons dry white wine
- 1/3 teaspoon freshly ground black pepper
- Kosher salt, to taste
- 1 cup Cheddar cheese

Directions

1. Press the "Sauté" button to heat up the Instant Pot. Then, heat the olive oil; sauté the garlic and grated ginger for 1 minute or until aromatic.
2. Add dried dill, basil, thyme, Chanterelles, water, tomato purée, dry white wine, black pepper, and salt.
3. Secure the lid. Choose "Manual" mode and Low pressure; cook for 5 minutes. Once cooking is complete, use a quick pressure release; carefully remove the lid.
4. Top with shredded cheese and serve immediately. Bon appétit!

380. Family Cauliflower Soup

Preparation Time: 10 minutes
Servings 4

Nutrition Value: 167 Calories; 13.7g Fat; 8.7g Carbs; 3.8g Protein; 5.1g Sugars

Ingredients

- 4 tablespoons butter, softened
- 1/2 cup leeks, thinly sliced
- 2 cloves garlic, minced
- 3/4 pound cauliflower, broken into florets
- 1 cup water
- 2 cups chicken stock
- 1 cup full-fat milk
- Kosher salt, to taste
- 1/3 teaspoon ground black pepper

Directions

1. Press the "Sauté" button to heat up your Instant Pot. Then, melt the butter; sauté the leeks until softened.
2. Then, sauté the garlic until fragrant, about 30 seconds. Add the remaining ingredients and gently stir to combine.
3. Secure the lid. Choose "Manual" mode and Low pressure; cook for 5 minutes. Once cooking is complete, use a quick pressure release; carefully remove the lid.
4. Ladle into individual bowls and serve warm. Bon appétit!

381. Cauliflower and Kohlrabi Mash

Preparation Time: 15 minutes
Servings 4

Nutrition Value: 89 Calories; 4.7g Fat; 9.6g Carbs; 3.6g Protein; 2.6g Sugars

Ingredients

- 1/2 pound cauliflower, cut into florets
- 1/2 pound kohlrabi, peeled and diced
- 1 cup water
- 3/4 cup sour cream
- 1 garlic clove, minced
- Sea salt, to taste
- 1/3 teaspoon ground black pepper
- 1/2 teaspoon cayenne pepper

Directions

1. Add 1 cup of water and a steamer basket

to the bottom of your Instant Pot.
2. Then, arrange cauliflower and kohlrabi in the steamer basket.
3. Secure the lid. Choose "Manual" mode and Low pressure; cook for 3 minutes. Once cooking is complete, use a quick pressure release; carefully remove the lid.
4. Now, puree the cauliflower and kohlrabi with a potato masher. Add the remaining ingredients and stir well. Bon appétit!

382. Old-Fashioned Stuffed Peppers

Preparation Time: 20 minutes
Servings 3

Nutrition Value: 488 Calories; 38.2g Fat; 7.1g Carbs; 29.1g Protein; 4.1g Sugars

Ingredients

- 2 tablespoons olive oil
- 1 yellow onion, chopped
- 2 garlic cloves, smashed
- 2 tablespoons coriander, chopped
- 1/3 pound ground beef
- 1/2 pound ground pork
- Sea salt, to taste
- 1/4 teaspoon black peppercorns, freshly crushed
- 3 bell peppers, deveined, tops removed
- 2 ripe tomatoes, puréed
- 1 teaspoon dried basil
- 1/2 teaspoon dried oregano
- 1/2 teaspoon dried rosemary
- 1/2 cup Romano cheese, freshly grated

Directions

1. Press the "Sauté" button to heat up the Instant Pot; heat the oil.
2. Once hot, sweat the onions for 2 minutes. Add garlic and coriander cook an additional 30 seconds. Then, stir in ground meat and cook until no longer pink. Season with salt and black peppercorns.
3. Stuff the peppers with this meat mixture; do not pack the peppers too tightly.
4. In a mixing bowl, thoroughly combine pureed tomatoes, basil, oregano, and rosemary. Pour this mixture over the peppers.
5. Wipe down the Instant Pot with a damp cloth; add 1 ½ cups of water and a metal trivet to the Instant Pot.
6. Place the peppers on the trivet and secure the lid. Choose "Poultry" mode and High pressure; cook for 15 minutes. Once cooking is complete, use a quick pressure release; carefully remove the lid.
7. Top with grated Romano cheese, cover, and let it sit in the residual heat. Serve warm and enjoy!

383. Aromatic Tomato Soup

Preparation Time: 10 minutes
Servings 2

Nutrition Value: 339 Calories; 29.5g Fat; 9.1g Carbs; 10.8g Protein; 5.6g Sugars

Ingredients

- 1 tablespoon avocado oil
- 2 cloves garlic, minced
- 2 ripe tomatoes, puréed
- 1/2 cup double cream
- 1/3 cup water
- 1/2 teaspoon basil
- 1 teaspoon dried sage
- Salt, to taste
- 1/4 teaspoon ground black pepper
- 1/2 teaspoon cayenne pepper
- 1/2 cup Colby cheese, shredded

Directions

1. Press the "Sauté" button to heat up the Instant Pot; heat the oil. Once hot, cook the garlic until aromatic.
2. Add the remaining ingredients and stir to combine.
3. Secure the lid. Choose "Manual" mode and Low pressure; cook for 3 minutes. Once cooking is complete, use a quick pressure release; carefully remove the lid.
4. Ladle into individual bowls and serve immediately. Bon appétit!

384. Bok Choy with Tofu

Preparation Time: 8 minutes
Servings 4

Nutrition Value: 133 Calories; 8.6g Fat; 5.1g Carbs; 11.1g Protein; 2g Sugars

Ingredients

- 1 tablespoon olive oil
- 12 ounces extra-firm tofu, pressed and cubed
- 1 ½ teaspoons ginger-garlic paste
- 1 ½ pounds Bok choy
- 1 cup water
- 2 tablespoons coconut aminos
- 1/4 cup rice wine vinegar
- 1 teaspoon smoked paprika
- Himalayan pink salt, to taste
- 1/4 teaspoon ground black pepper

Directions

1. Press the "Sauté" button to heat up the Instant Pot; heat the oil. Once hot, cook the tofu until delicately browned.
2. Add the ginger-garlic paste and Bok choy; sauté 1 minute more. Add the remaining ingredients.
3. Secure the lid. Choose "Manual" mode and Low pressure; cook for 4 minutes. Once cooking is complete, use a quick pressure release; carefully remove the lid.
4. Serve immediately. Bon appétit!

385. Braised Garlicky Endive

Preparation Time: 6 minutes
Servings 3

Nutrition Value: 91 Calories; 5.3g Fat; 9.1g Carbs; 3.6g Protein; 1.8g Sugars

Ingredients

- 1 tablespoon extra-virgin olive oil
- 2 garlic cloves, minced
- 2 large-sized Belgian endive, halved lengthwise
- 1/2 cup apple cider vinegar
- 1/2 cup broth, preferably homemade
- Sea salt and freshly ground black pepper, to taste
- 1 teaspoon cayenne pepper

Directions

1. Press the "Sauté" button to heat up the Instant Pot; heat the oil. Once hot, cook the garlic for 30 seconds or until aromatic and browned.
2. Add Belgian endive, vinegar, broth, salt, black pepper, and cayenne pepper.
3. Secure the lid. Choose "Manual" mode and Low pressure; cook for 2 minutes or until tender when pierced with the tip of a knife.
4. Once cooking is complete, use a quick pressure release; carefully remove the lid. Bon appétit!

386. Italian Pancetta and Cabbage Soup

Preparation Time: 10 minutes
Servings 4

Nutrition Value: 196 Calories; 17.8g Fat; 8.4g Carbs; 2.2g Protein; 2.5g Sugars

Ingredients

- 1 tablespoon olive oil
- 2 ounces pancetta, finely diced
- 1/2 cup shallots, chopped
- 1 red bell pepper, deveined and sliced
- 1 green bell pepper, deveined and sliced
- 1 carrot, sliced
- 2 celery stalks with leaves, diced
- 2 cloves garlic
- 2 ripe Roma tomatoes, puréed
- 3/4 pound green cabbage, cut into wedges
- 4 cups water
- 2 bouillon cubes
- 1 tablespoon Italian seasoning blend
- 1 cup baby spinach

Directions

1. Press the "Sauté" button to heat up your Instant Pot; heat the olive oil. Once hot, cook pancetta until crisp, about 3 minutes; reserve.

2. Now, cook the shallots, peppers, carrot, celery, and garlic until tender.
3. Add tomatoes, cabbage, water, bouillon cubes, Italian seasoning blend; stir to combine.
4. Secure the lid. Choose "Manual" mode and Low pressure; cook for 3 minutes. Once cooking is complete, use a quick pressure release; carefully remove the lid.
5. Lastly, add baby spinach, cover, and let it sit in the residual heat until it wilts. Ladle into four soup bowls and top with the reserved pancetta. Enjoy!

387. Buttery and Garlicky Fennel

Preparation Time: 6 minutes
Servings 6

Nutrition Value: 111 Calories; 7.8g Fat; 8.7g Carbs; 2.1g Protein; 4.7g Sugars

Ingredients

- 1/2 stick butter
- 2 garlic cloves, sliced
- 1/2 teaspoon sea salt
- 1 ½ pounds fennel bulbs, cut into wedges
- 1/4 teaspoon ground black pepper, or more to taste
- 1/2 teaspoon cayenne pepper
- 1/4 teaspoon dried dill weed
- 1/3 cup dry white wine
- 2/3 cup chicken stock

Directions

1. Press the "Sauté" button to heat up your Instant Pot; now, melt the butter. Cook garlic for 30 seconds, stirring periodically.
2. Add the remaining ingredients.
3. Secure the lid. Choose "Manual" mode and Low pressure; cook for 3 minutes. Once cooking is complete, use a quick pressure release; carefully remove the lid. Bon appétit!

388. Vegetables à la Grecque

Preparation Time: 10 minutes
Servings 4

Nutrition Value: 326 Calories; 25.1g Fat; 8.4g Carbs; 15.7g Protein; 4.3g Sugars

Ingredients

- 2 tablespoons olive oil
- 2 garlic cloves, minced
- 1 red onion, chopped
- 10 ounces button mushrooms, thinly sliced
- 1 (1-pound) eggplant, sliced
- 1/2 teaspoon dried basil
- 1 teaspoon dried oregano
- 1 thyme sprig, leaves picked
- 2 rosemary sprigs, leaves picked
- 1/2 cup tomato sauce
- 1/4 cup dry Greek wine
- 1/4 cup water
- 8 ounces Halloumi cheese, cubed
- 4 tablespoons Kalamata olives, pitted and halved

Directions

1. Press the "Sauté" button to heat up your Instant Pot; now, heat the olive oil. Cook the garlic and red onions for 1 to 2 minutes, stirring periodically.
2. Stir in the mushrooms and continue to sauté an additional 2 to 3 minutes.
3. Add the eggplant, basil, oregano, thyme, rosemary, tomato sauce, Greek wine, and water.
4. Secure the lid. Choose "Manual" mode and Low pressure; cook for 3 minutes. Once cooking is complete, use a quick pressure release; carefully remove the lid.
5. Top with cheese and olives. Bon appétit!

389. Caramelized Endive with Goat Cheese

Preparation Time: 10 minutes
Servings 4

Nutrition Value: 221 Calories; 18.5g Fat; 6.6g Carbs; 8.7g Protein; 0.8g Sugars

Ingredients

- 1/2 stick butter
- 1 ½ pounds endive, cut into bite-sized

chunks
- Sea salt, to taste
- 1/3 teaspoon cayenne pepper
- 1/3 teaspoon ground black pepper
- 1/4 cup dry white wine
- 1/2 cup chicken broth
- 1/4 cup water
- 2 tablespoons fresh parsley, roughly chopped
- 2 ounces goat cheese, crumbled

Directions
1. Press the "Sauté" button to heat up your Instant Pot; now, melt the butter. Cook endive for 1 to 2 minutes or until it is caramelized.
2. Season with salt, cayenne pepper, and black pepper. Next, pour in wine, broth, and water.
3. Secure the lid. Choose "Manual" mode and Low pressure; cook for 2 minutes. Once cooking is complete, use a quick pressure release; carefully remove the lid.
4. Serve topped with goat cheese. Bon appétit!

390. Loaded Tuscan Rapini Soup

Preparation Time: 8 minutes
Servings 4

Nutrition Value: 95 Calories; 6.7g Fat; 5.2g Carbs; 4.2g Protein; 1.4g Sugars

Ingredients
- 2 tablespoons butter, melted
- 1/2 cup leeks, sliced
- 2 garlic cloves, minced
- 4 cups broccoli rabe, broken into pieces
- 2 cups water
- 2 cups broth, preferably homemade
- 1 zucchini, shredded
- 1 carrot, trimmed and grated
- Sea salt, to taste
- 1/4 teaspoon ground black pepper
3.

Directions
1. Press the "Sauté" button to heat up your Instant Pot; now, melt the butter. Cook the leeks for about 2 minutes or until softened.
2. Add minced garlic and cook an additional 40 seconds.
3. Add the remaining ingredients. Secure the lid.
4. Choose "Manual" mode and Low pressure; cook for 3 minutes. Once cooking is complete, use a quick pressure release; carefully remove the lid. Bon appétit!

391. Nopales with Sour Cream

Preparation Time: 8 minutes
Servings 4

Nutrition Value: 109 Calories; 7.3g Fat; 8.8g Carbs; 3.5g Protein; 3.7g Sugars

Ingredients
- 1 pound nopales, cleaned and diced
- 1 white onion, chopped
- 2 garlic cloves, smashed
- 2 tablespoons fresh parsley, chopped
- 2 dried chiles negros
- 1 cup ripe tomatoes, chopped
- 1/2 teaspoon mustard seeds
- 1/2 teaspoon Mexican oregano
- 2 tablespoons olive oil
- Sea salt and ground black pepper, to taste
- 1 cup chicken broth
- 1/2 cup sour cream

Directions
Place all ingredients, except for sour cream, in your Instant Pot.
1. Secure the lid. Choose "Manual" mode and High pressure; cook for 5 minutes. Once cooking is complete, use a quick pressure release; carefully remove the lid.
2. Spoon into serving bowls and serve dolloped with sour cream. Bon appétit!

SOUPS AND STEWS

392. Chicken Soup

Preparation time: 10 minutes
Cooking time: 17 minutes
Servings: 4

Ingredients:

- 4 chicken breasts, skinless and boneless
- 2 tablespoons extra virgin olive oil
- 1 onion, peeled and chopped
- 3 garlic cloves, peeled and minced
- 16 ounces chunky salsa
- 29 ounces canned diced tomatoes
- 29 ounces chicken stock
- Salt and ground black pepper, to taste
- 2 tablespoons dried parsley
- 1 teaspoon garlic powder
- 1 tablespoon onion powder
- 1 tablespoon chili powder
- 15 ounces frozen corn
- 32 ounces canned black beans, drained

Directions:

1. Set the Instant Pot on Sauté mode, add the oil, and heat it up. Add the onion, stir, and cook 5 minutes. Add the garlic, stir, and cook for 1 minute. Add the chicken breasts, salsa, tomatoes, stock, salt, pepper, parsley, garlic powder, onion powder, and chili powder, stir, cover, and cook on the Soup setting for 8 minutes. Release the pressure for 10 minutes, uncover the Instant Pot, transfer the chicken breasts to a cutting board, shred with 2 forks, and return to pot. Add the beans and corn, set the Instant Pot on Manual mode and cook for 2-3 minutes. Divide into soup bowls, and serve.

Nutrition Value:

Calories: 210
Fat: 4.4
Fiber: 4.3
Carbs: 18
Protein: 26

393. Potato and Cheese Soup

Preparation time: 10 minutes
Cooking time: 10 minutes
Servings: 6

Ingredients:

- 6 cups potatoes, cubed
- 2 tablespoons butter
- ½ cup yellow onion, chopped
- 28 ounces chicken stock
- Salt and ground black pepper, to taste
- 2 tablespoons dried parsley
- 1/8 teaspoon red pepper flakes
- 2 tablespoons cornstarch
- 2 tablespoons water
- 3 ounces cream cheese, cubed
- 2 cups half and half
- 1 cup cheddar cheese, shredded
- 1 cup corn
- 6 bacon slices, cooked and crumbled

Directions:

1. Set the Instant Pot on Sauté mode, add the butter and melt it. Add the onion, stir, and cook 5 minutes. Add half of the stock, salt, pepper, pepper flakes, and parsley and stir. Put the potatoes in the steamer basket, cover the Instant Pot and cook on the Steam setting for 4 minutes. Release the pressure fast, uncover the Instant Pot, and transfer the potatoes to a bowl. In another bowl, mix the cornstarch with water and stir well. Set the Instant Pot to Manual mode, add the cornstarch slurry, cream cheese, and shredded cheese and stir well. Add the rest of the stock, corn, bacon, potatoes, half and half. Stir, bring to a simmer, ladle into bowls, and serve.

Nutrition Value:

Calories: 188

Fat: 7.14
Fiber: 1.5
Carbs: 22
Protein: 9

394. Split Pea Soup

Preparation time: 10 minutes
Cooking time: 20 minutes
Servings: 6

Ingredients:

- 2 tablespoons butter
- 1 pound chicken sausage, ground
- 1 yellow onion, peeled and chopped
- ½ cup carrots, peeled and chopped
- ½ cup celery, chopped
- 2 garlic cloves, peeled and minced
- 29 ounces chicken stock
- Salt and ground black pepper, to taste
- 2 cups water
- 16 ounces split peas, rinsed
- ½ cup half and half
- ¼ teaspoon red pepper flakes

Directions:

1. Set the Instant Pot on Sauté mode, add the sausage, brown it on all sides and transfer to a plate. Add the butter to the Instant Pot and melt it. Add the celery, onions, and carrots, stir, and cook 4 minutes. Add the garlic, stir and cook for 1 minute. Add the water, stock, peas and pepper flakes, stir, cover and cook on the Soup setting for 10 minutes. Release the pressure, puree the mix using an immersion blender and set the Instant Pot on Manual mode. Add the sausage, salt, pepper, and half and half, stir, bring to a simmer, and ladle into soup bowls.

Nutrition Value:

Calories: 30
Fat: 11
Fiber: 12
Carbs: 14
Protein: 20

395. Corn Soup

Preparation time: 10 minutes
Cooking time: 15 minutes
Servings: 4

Ingredients:

- 2 leeks, chopped
- 2 tablespoons butter
- 2 garlic cloves, peeled and minced
- 6 ears of corn, kernels cut off, cobs reserved
- 2 bay leaves
- 4 tarragon sprigs, chopped
- 1-quart chicken stock
- Salt and ground black pepper, to taste
- Extra virgin olive oil
- 1 tablespoon fresh chives, chopped

Directions:

1. Set the Instant Pot on Sauté mode, add the butter and melt it. Add the garlic and leeks, stir, and cook for 4 minutes. Add the corn, corn cobs, bay leaves, tarragon, and stock to cover everything, cover the Instant Pot and cook on the Soup setting for 15 minutes. Release the pressure, uncover the Instant Pot, discard the bay leaves and corn cobs, and transfer everything to a blender. Pulse well to obtain a smooth soup, add the rest of the stock and blend again. Add the salt and pepper, stir well, divide into soup bowls, and serve cold with chives and olive oil on top.

Nutrition Value:

Calories: 300
Fat: 8.3
Fiber: 8
Carbs: 50
Protein: 13

396. Butternut Squash Soup

Preparation time: 10 minutes
Cooking time: 16 minutes
Servings: 6

Ingredients:

- 1½ pounds butternut squash, baked, peeled and cubed
- ½ cup green onions, chopped
- 3 tablespoons butter
- ½ cup carrots, peeled and chopped
- ½ cup celery, chopped
- 29 ounces chicken stock
- 1 garlic clove, peeled and minced
- ½ teaspoon Italian seasoning
- 15 ounces canned diced tomatoes
- Salt and ground black pepper, to taste
- 1/8 teaspoon red pepper flakes
- 1 cup orzo, already cooked
- 1/8 teaspoon nutmeg, grated
- 1½ cup half and half
- 1 cup chicken meat, already cooked and shredded
- Green onions, chopped, for serving

Directions:

1. Set the Instant Pot on Sauté mode, add the butter and melt it. Add the celery, carrots, and onions, stir, and cook for 3 minutes. Add the garlic, stir, and cook for 1 minute. Add the squash, tomatoes, stock, Italian seasoning, salt, pepper, pepper flakes, and nutmeg. Stir, cover the Instant Pot, and cook on the Soup setting for 10 minutes. Release the pressure, uncover, and puree everything with an immersion blender. Set the Instant Pot on Manual mode, add the half and half, orzo, and chicken, stir, and cook for 3 minutes. Divide the soup into bowls, sprinkle green onions on top, and serve.

Nutrition Value:
Calories: 130
Fat: 2.3
Fiber: 0.4
Carbs: 18
Protein: 6

397. Beef and Rice Soup

Preparation time: 10 minutes
Cooking time: 15 minutes
Servings: 6

Ingredients:

- 1 pound ground beef
- 3 garlic cloves, peeled and minced
- 1 yellow onion, peeled and chopped
- 1 tablespoon vegetable oil
- 1 celery stalk, chopped
- 28 ounces beef stock
- 14 ounces canned crushed tomatoes
- ½ cup white rice
- 12 ounces spicy tomato juice
- 15 ounces canned garbanzo beans, rinsed
- 1 potato, cubed
- Salt and ground black pepper, to taste
- ½ cup frozen peas
- 2 carrots, peeled and sliced thin

Directions:

1. Set the Instant Pot on Sauté mode, add the beef, stir, cook until it browns, and transfer to a plate. Add the oil to the Instant Pot and heat it up. Add the celery and onion, stir, and cook for 5 minutes. Add the garlic, stir and cook for 1 minute. Add the tomato juice, stock, tomatoes, rice, beans, carrots, potatoes, beef, salt, and pepper, stir, cover and cook on the Manual setting for 5 minutes. Release the pressure, uncover the Instant Pot, and set it on Manual mode. Add more salt and pepper, if needed, and the peas, stir, bring to a simmer, transfer to bowls, and serve hot.

Nutrition Value:
Calories: 230
Fat: 7
Fiber: 4
Carbs: 10
Protein: 3

398. Chicken Noodle Soup

Preparation time: 10 minutes
Cooking time: 12 minutes
Servings: 6

Ingredients:

- 1 yellow onion, peeled and chopped

- 1 tablespoon butter
- 1 celery stalk, chopped
- 4 carrots, peeled and sliced
- Salt and ground black pepper, to taste
- 6 cups chicken stock
- 2 cups chicken, already cooked and shredded
- Egg noodles, already cooked

Directions:

- Set the Instant Pot on Sauté mode, add the butter and heat it up. Add the onion, stir, and cook 2 minutes. Add the celery and carrots, stir, and cook 5 minutes. Add the chicken and stock, stir, cover the Instant Pot and cook on the Soup setting for 5 minutes. Release the pressure, uncover the Instant Pot, add salt and pepper to taste, and stir. Divide the noodles into soup bowls, add the soup over them, and serve.

Nutrition Value:
Calories: 100
Fat: 1
Fiber: 1
Carbs: 4
Protein: 7

399. Zuppa Toscana

Preparation time: 10 minutes
Cooking time: 17 minutes
Servings: 8

Ingredients:

- 1 pound chicken sausage, ground
- 6 bacon slices, chopped
- 3 garlic cloves, peeled and minced
- 1 cup yellow onion, peeled and chopped
- 1 tablespoon butter
- 40 ounces chicken stock
- Salt and ground black pepper, to taste
- Red pepper flakes
- 3 potatoes, cubed
- 3 tablespoons cornstarch
- 12 ounces evaporated milk
- 1 cup Parmesan, shredded
- 2 cup spinach, chopped

Directions:

1. Set the Instant Pot on Sauté mode, add the bacon, stir, cook until it's crispy, and transfer to a plate. Add the sausage to the Instant Pot, stir, cook until it browns on all sides, and also transfer to a plate. Add the butter to the Instant Pot and melt it. Add the onion, stir, and cook for 5 minutes. Add the garlic, stir, and cook for 1 minute. Add ⅓ of the stock, salt, pepper, and pepper flakes and stir. Place the potatoes in the steamer basket of the Instant Pot, cover and cook on the Steam setting for 4 minutes. Release the pressure, uncover the Instant Pot, and transfer the potatoes to a bowl. Add the rest of the stock to the Instant Pot with the cornstarch mixed with the evaporated milk, stir, and set the Instant Pot on Manual mode. Add the cheese, sausage, bacon, potatoes, spinach, more salt and pepper, if needed, stir, divide into bowls, and serve.

Nutrition Value:
Calories: 170
Fat: 4
Fiber: 2
Carbs: 24
Protein: 10

400. Minestrone Soup

Preparation time: 10 minutes
Cooking time: 15 minutes
Servings: 8

Ingredients:

- 1 tablespoon extra virgin olive oil
- 1 celery stalk, chopped
- 2 carrots, peeled and chopped
- 1 onion, peeled and chopped
- 1 cup corn kernels
- 1 zucchini, chopped
- 3 pounds tomatoes, cored, peeled, and chopped

- 4 garlic cloves, peeled and minced
- 29 ounces chicken stock
- 1 cup uncooked pasta
- Salt and ground black pepper, to taste
- 1 teaspoon Italian seasoning
- 2 cups baby spinach
- 15 ounces canned kidney beans
- 1 cup Asiago cheese, grated
- 2 tablespoons fresh basil, chopped

Directions:
1. Set the Instant Pot on Sauté mode, add the oil and heat it up. Add the onion, stir, and cook for 5 minutes. Add the carrots, garlic, celery, corn, and zucchini, stir, and cook 5 minutes. Add the tomatoes, stock, Italian seasoning, pasta, salt, and pepper, stir, cover, and cook on the Soup setting for 4 minutes. Release the pressure fast, uncover, add the beans, basil, and spinach. Add more salt and pepper, if needed, divide into bowls, add the cheese on top, and serve.

Nutrition Value:
Calories: 110
Fat: 2
Fiber: 4
Carbs: 18
Protein: 5

401. Chicken and Wild Rice Soup

Preparation time: 10 minutes
Cooking time: 15 minutes
Servings: 6
Ingredients:

- 1 cup yellow onion, peeled and chopped
- 2 tablespoons butter
- 1 cup celery, chopped
- 1 cup carrots, chopped
- 28 ounces chicken stock
- 2 chicken breasts, skinless, boneless and chopped
- 6 ounces wild rice
- Red pepper flakes
- Salt and ground black pepper, to taste
- 1 tablespoon dried parsley
- 2 tablespoons cornstarch mixed with 2 tablespoons water
- 1 cup milk
- 1 cup half and half
- 4 ounces cream cheese, cubed

Directions:
1. Set the Instant Pot on Sauté mode, add the butter and melt it. Add the carrot, onion, and celery, stir and cook for 5 minutes. Add the rice, chicken, stock, parsley, salt, and pepper, stir, cover, and cook on the Soup setting for 5 minutes. Release the pressure, uncover, add the cornstarch mixed with water, stir, and set the Instant Pot on Manual mode. Add the cheese, milk, and half and half, stir, heat up, transfer to bowls, and serve.

Nutrition Value:
Calories: 200
Fat: 7
Fiber: 1
Carbs: 19
Protein: 5

402. Creamy Tomato Soup

Preparation time: 10 minutes
Cooking time: 6 minutes
Servings: 8
Ingredients:

- 1 yellow onion, peeled and chopped
- 3 tablespoons butter
- 1 carrot, peeled and chopped
- 2 celery stalks, chopped
- 2 garlic cloves, peeled and minced
- 29 ounces chicken stock
- Salt and ground black pepper, to taste
- ¼ cup fresh basil, chopped
- 3 pounds tomatoes, peeled, cored, and cut into quarters
- 1 tablespoon tomato paste
- 1 cup half and half
- ½ cup Parmesan cheese, shredded

Directions:

1. Set the Instant Pot on Sauté mode, add the butter and melt it. Add the onion, carrots, and celery, stir, and cook for 3 minutes. Add the garlic, stir, and cook for 1 minute. Add the tomatoes, tomato paste, stock, basil, salt, and pepper, stir, cover, and cook on the Soup setting for 5 minutes. Release the pressure, uncover the Instant Pot and puree the soup using and immersion blender. Add the half and half and cheese, stir, set the Instant Pot on Manual mode and heat everything up. Divide the soup into soup bowls, and serve.

Nutrition Value:

Calories: 280
Fat: 8
Fiber: 4
Carbs: 32
Protein: 24

403. Tomato Soup

Preparation time: 10 minutes
Cooking time: 45 minutes
Servings: 6

Ingredients:

For the roasted tomatoes:

- 14 garlic cloves, peeled and crushed
- 3 pounds cherry tomatoes, cut into halves
- Salt and ground black pepper, to taste
- 2 tablespoons extra virgin olive oil
- ½ teaspoon red pepper flakes

For the soup:

- 1 yellow onion, peeled and chopped
- 2 tablespoons olive oil
- 1 red bell pepper, seeded and chopped
- 3 tablespoons tomato paste
- 2 celery ribs, chopped
- 2 cups chicken stock
- 1 teaspoon garlic powder
- 1 teaspoon onion powder
- ½ tablespoon dried basil
- ½ teaspoon red pepper flakes
- Salt and ground black pepper, to taste
- 1 cup heavy cream

For serving:

- Fresh basil leaves, chopped
- ½ cup Parmesan cheese, grated

Directions:

1. Place the tomatoes and garlic in a baking tray, drizzle 2 tablespoons oil, season with salt, pepper and a ½ teaspoon of red pepper flakes, toss to coat, introduce in the oven at 425°F, and roast for 25 minutes. Take the tomatoes out of the oven and set aside. Set the Instant Pot on Sauté mode, add the oil, and heat it up. Add the onion, bell pepper, celery, salt, pepper, garlic powder, onion powder, basil, the remaining red pepper flakes, stir, and cook for 3 minutes. Add the tomato paste, roasted tomatoes, and garlic and stir. Add the stock, cover the Instant Pot, and cook on the Manual setting for 10 minutes. Release the pressure, uncover the Instant Pot and set it on Sauté mode. Add the heavy cream and blend everything using an immersion blender. Divide in bowls, add basil and cheese on top, and serve.

Nutrition Value:

Calories: 150
Fat: 1
Fiber: 3
Carbs: 3
Protein: 4

404. Carrot Soup

Preparation time: 10 minutes
Cooking time: 16 minutes
Servings: 4

Ingredients:

- 1 tablespoon vegetable oil
- 1 onion, peeled and chopped
- 1 tablespoon butter
- 1 garlic clove, peeled and minced
- 1 pound carrots, peeled and chopped
- 1 small ginger piece, peeled and grated

- Salt and ground black pepper, to taste
- ¼ teaspoon brown sugar
- 2 cups chicken stock
- 1 tablespoon Sriracha
- 14 ounces canned coconut milk
- Cilantro leaves, chopped, for serving

Directions:
1. Set the Instant Pot on Sauté mode, add the butter and oil, and heat them up. Add the onion, stir and cook for 3 minutes. Add the ginger and garlic, stir, and cook for 1 minute. Add the sugar, carrots, salt, and pepper, stir, and cook 2 minutes. Add the sriracha, coconut milk, stock, stir, cover, and cook on the Soup setting for 6 minutes. Release the pressure for 10 minutes, uncover the Instant Pot, blend the soup with an immersion blender, add more salt and pepper, if needed, and divide into soup bowls. Add the cilantro on top, and serve.

Nutrition Value:
Calories: 60
Fat: 1
Fiber: 3.1
Carbs: 12
Protein: 2

405. Cabbage Soup

Preparation time: 10 minutes
Cooking time: 10 minutes
Servings: 4

Ingredients:
- 1 cabbage head, chopped
- 12 ounces baby carrots
- 3 celery stalks, chopped
- ½ onion, peeled and chopped
- 1 packet vegetable soup mix
- 2 tablespoons olive oil
- 12 ounces soy burger
- 3 teaspoons garlic, peeled and minced
- ¼ cup cilantro, chopped
- 4 cups chicken stock
- Salt and ground black pepper, to taste

Directions:
1. In the Instant Pot, mix the cabbage with the celery, carrots, onion, soup mix, soy burger, stock, olive oil, and garlic, stir, cover, and cook on Soup mode for 5 minutes. Release the pressure, uncover the Instant Pot, add the salt, pepper, and cilantro, stir again well, divide into soup bowls, and serve.

Nutrition Value:
Calories: 100
Fat: 1
Fiber: 2
Carbs: 10
Protein: 10

406. Cream of Asparagus

Preparation time: 10 minutes
Cooking time: 25 minutes
Servings: 4

Ingredients:
- 2 pounds green asparagus, trimmed, tips cut off and cut into medium pieces
- 3 tablespoons butter
- 1 yellow onion, peeled and chopped
- 6 cups chicken stock
- ¼ teaspoon lemon juice
- ½ cup crème fraiche
- Salt and ground white pepper, to taste

Directions:
1. Set the Instant Pot on Sauté mode, add the butter and melt it. Add the asparagus, salt, and pepper, stir, and cook for 5 minutes. Add 5 cups of the stock, cover the Instant Pot, and cook on Soup mode for 15 minutes. Release the pressure, uncover the Instant Pot and transfer soup to a blender. Pulse several times and return to the Instant Pot. Set the Instant Pot on Manual mode, add the crème fraiche, the rest of the stock, salt, pepper, and lemon juice, bring to a boil, divide into soup bowls, and serve.

Nutrition Value:
Calories: 80

Fat: 8
Fiber: 1
Carbs: 16
Protein: 6.3

407. Ham and White Bean Soup

Preparation time: 10 minutes
Cooking time: 15 minutes
Servings: 8

Ingredients:

- 1 pound white beans, soaked for 1 hour and drained
- 1 carrot, peeled and chopped
- 1 tablespoon extra virgin olive oil
- 1 yellow onion, peeled and chopped
- 3 garlic cloves, peeled and minced
- 1 tomato, cored, peeled and chopped
- 1 pound ham, chopped
- Salt and ground black pepper, to taste
- 4 cups water
- 4 cups vegetable stock
- 1 teaspoon dried mint
- 1 teaspoon paprika
- 1 teaspoon dried thyme

Directions:

1. Set the Instant Pot on Sauté mode, add the oil, and heat it up. Add the carrot, onion, garlic, tomato, stir, and cook for 5 minutes. Add the beans, ham, salt, pepper, water, stock, mint, paprika, and thyme, stir, cover, and cook on the Bean/Chili setting for 15 minutes. Release the pressure for 10 minutes, uncover the Instant Pot, divide into soup bowls, and serve.

Nutrition Value:
Calories: 177
Fat: 2
Fiber: 1
Carbs: 26
Protein: 14

408. Lentil Soup

Preparation time: 10 minutes
Cooking time: 30 minutes
Servings: 4

Ingredients:

- 2 celery stalks, chopped
- 1 tablespoon olive oil
- 1 small onion, peeled and chopped
- 2 carrots, peeled and chopped
- ½ pound chicken sausage, ground
- 3½ cups beef stock
- 2 teaspoons garlic, peeled and minced
- 1 cup lentils
- 15 ounces canned diced tomatoes
- Salt and ground black pepper, to taste
- 2 cups spinach

Directions:

1. Set the Instant Pot on Sauté mode, add the oil, and heat it up. Add the celery, onion, carrots, stir, and cook for 4 minutes. Add the chicken sausage, stir, and cook 5 minutes. Add the stock, garlic, lentils, tomatoes, salt, pepper, and spinach, stir, cover and cook on the Soup setting for 25 minutes. Release the pressure, uncover the Instant Pot, divide into soup bowls, and serve.

Nutrition Value:
Calories: 175
Fat: 1
Fiber: 1
Carbs: 2
Protein: 2

409. Artichoke Soup

Preparation time: 10 minutes
Cooking time: 20 minutes
Servings: 4

Ingredients:

- 5 artichoke hearts, washed and trimmed
- 1 leek, sliced
- 5 tablespoons butter
- 6 garlic cloves, peeled and minced
- ½ cup shallots, chopped

- 8 ounces Yukon gold potatoes, chopped
- 12 cups chicken stock
- 1 bay leaf
- Fresh parsley, chopped
- 2 thyme sprigs
- ¼ teaspoon black peppercorns, crushed
- Salt, to taste
- ¼ cup cream

Directions:
1. Set the Instant Pot on Sauté mode, add the butter and melt it. Add the artichoke hearts, shallots, leek, and garlic, stir, and brown for 3-4 minutes. Add the potatoes, stock, bay leaf, thyme, parsley, peppercorns, and salt, stir, cover, and cook on the Soup setting for 15 minutes. Release the pressure, uncover the Instant Pot, discard the herbs, blend well using an immersion blender, add salt to taste and the cream, stir well, divide into bowls, and serve.

Nutrition Value:
Calories: 95
Fat: 2
Fiber: 4
Carbs: 15
Protein: 4

410. Carrot Peanut Butter Soup

Servings: 4
Cooking Time: 15 minutes

Ingredients:
- 8 carrots, peeled and chopped
- 1 onion, chopped
- 3 garlic cloves, peeled
- 14 oz coconut milk
- 1 ½ cup chicken stock
- ¼ cup peanut butter
- 1 tbsp curry paste
- Pepper
- Salt

Directions:
1. Add all ingredients into the instant pot and stir well.
2. Seal pot with lid and cook on high for 15 minutes.
3. Release pressure using quick release method than open the lid.
4. Puree the soup using an immersion blender until smooth.
5. Season soup with pepper and salt.
6. Serve and enjoy.

Nutrition Value:
Calories: 416; Carbohydrates: 25.3g; Protein: 8.2g; Fat: 34.2g; Sugar: 12.3g; Sodium: 500mg

411. Healthy Chicken Vegetable Soup

Servings: 6
Cooking Time: 14 minutes

Ingredients:
- 2 chicken breasts, cut into cube
- ½ tsp red pepper flakes
- ¼ cup fresh parsley, chopped
- 1 tsp garlic powder
- 3 cups chicken broth
- 14 oz can tomatoes, diced
- ¼ cup cabbage, shredded
- 1 cup frozen green beans
- ¼ cup frozen peas
- ½ cup frozen corn
- 2 celery stalk, chopped
- 1 carrot, peeled and cubed
- ½ sweet potato, peeled and cubed
- 3 garlic cloves, minced
- ½ onion, chopped
- ½ tsp pepper
- 1 tsp salt

Directions:
1. Add all ingredients into the instant pot and stir well.
2. Seal pot with lid and cook on high for 4 minutes.
3. Allow to release pressure naturally for 10 minutes then release using quick release method.

4. Stir well and serve.

Nutrition Value:
Calories: 171; Carbohydrates: 13.9g; Protein: 18.9g; Fat: 4.6g; Sugar: 5.4g; Sodium: 977mg

412. Chicken Rice Noodle Soup

Servings: 6
Cooking Time: 10 minutes

Ingredients:

- 6 cups chicken, cooked and cubed
- 3 tbsp rice vinegar
- 2 ½ cups cabbage, shredded
- 2 tbsp fresh ginger, grated
- 2 tbsp soy sauce
- 3 garlic cloves, minced
- 8 oz rice noodles
- 1 bell pepper, chopped
- 1 large carrot, peeled and sliced
- 6 cups chicken stock
- 2 celery stalks, sliced
- 1 onion, chopped
- ½ tsp black pepper

Directions:

1. Add all ingredients into the instant pot and stir well.
2. Seal pot with lid and cook on high for 10 minutes.
3. Release pressure using quick release method than open the lid.
4. Stir well and serve.

Nutrition Value:
Calories: 306; Carbohydrates: 18.7g; Protein: 43.1g; Fat: 5.1g; Sugar: 4.3g; Sodium: 1180mg

413. Creamy Squash Soup

Servings: 4
Cooking Time: 15 minutes

Ingredients:

- 4 lbs butternut squash, peeled, seeded, and cubed
- 4 cups beef stock
- ½ tsp sage
- 1 tsp thyme
- 2 garlic cloves, minced
- 1 onion, chopped
- 2 tbsp olive oil
- Pepper
- Salt

Directions:

1. Add oil into the instant pot and set the pot on sauté mode.
2. Add garlic and onion to the pot and sauté for 5 minutes.
3. Add sage, thyme, pepper, and salt and stir for a minute.
4. Add squash and stock. Stir well.
5. Seal pot with lid and cook on high for 10 minutes.
6. Release pressure using quick release method than open the lid.
7. Puree the soup using an immersion blender until smooth and creamy.
8. Serve and enjoy.

Nutrition Value:
Calories: 295; Carbohydrates: 56.4g; Protein: 7.7g; Fat: 8.1g; Sugar: 11.2g; Sodium: 841mg

414. Spicy Mushroom Soup

Servings: 2
Cooking Time: 11 minutes

Ingredients:

- 1 cup mushrooms, chopped
- ½ tsp chili powder
- 2 tsp garam masala
- 3 tbsp olive oil
- 1 tsp fresh lemon juice
- 5 cups chicken stock
- ¼ cup fresh celery, chopped
- 2 garlic cloves, crushed
- 1 onion, chopped
- ½ tsp black pepper
- 1 tsp sea salt

Directions:

1. Add oil into the instant pot and set the pot on sauté mode.

2. Add garlic and onion to the pot and sauté for 5 minutes.
3. Add chili powder and garam masala and cook for a minute.
4. Add remaining ingredients and stir well.
5. Seal pot with lid and cook on high for 5 minutes.
6. Release pressure using quick release method than open the lid.
7. Puree the soup using a blender and serve.

Nutrition Value:

Calories: 244; Carbohydrates: 10.2g; Protein: 3.9g; Fat: 22.8g; Sugar: 5g; Sodium: 287mg

415. Kale Beef Soup

Servings: 4
Cooking Time: 43 minutes

Ingredients:

- 1 lb beef stew meat
- 1 tsp cayenne pepper
- 3 garlic cloves, crushed
- 4 cups chicken broth
- 2 tbsp olive oil
- 1 cup kale, chopped
- 1 onion, sliced
- ¼ tsp black pepper
- ½ tsp salt

Directions:

1. Add oil into the instant pot and set the pot on sauté mode.
2. Add garlic and onion and sauté for 3 minutes.
3. Add meat and sauté for 5 minutes more.
4. Add broth and season with cayenne pepper, pepper, and salt. Stir well.
5. Seal pot with lid and cook on high for 25 minutes.
6. Release pressure using quick release method than open the lid.
7. Add kale and stir well and let sit for 10 minutes.
8. Stir well and serve.

Nutrition Value:

Calories: 333; Carbohydrates: 6.3g; Protein: 40.3g; Fat: 15.6g; Sugar: 1.9g; Sodium: 1137mg

416. Creamy Cauliflower Soup

Servings: 4
Cooking Time: 32 minutes

Ingredients:

- 2 cups cauliflower florets
- 1 tsp pumpkin pie spice
- 5 cups chicken broth
- 3 tbsp olive oil
- 1 onion, chopped
- ¼ tsp salt

Directions:

1. Add oil into the instant pot and set the pot on sauté mode.
2. Add onion to the pot and sauté for 5 minutes.
3. Add cauliflower and cook for a minute. Add broth and season with sea salt.
4. Seal pot with lid and cook on high for 24 minutes.
5. Release pressure using quick release method than open the lid.
6. Puree the soup using an immersion blender until smooth.
7. Add pumpkin pie spice and stir well. Cook on sauté mode for 2 minutes.
8. Serve and enjoy.

Nutrition Value:

Calories: 163; Carbohydrates: 6.7g; Protein: 7.4g; Fat: 12.3g; Sugar: 3.3g; Sodium: 1118mg

417. Kale Cottage Cheese Soup

Servings: 4
Cooking Time: 5 minutes

Ingredients:

- 5 cups fresh kale, chopped
- 1 tbsp olive oil
- 1 cup cottage cheese, cut into small chunks
- 3 cups chicken broth
- ½ tsp black pepper
- ½ tsp sea salt

Directions:
1. Add all ingredients except cottage cheese into the instant pot and stir well.
2. Seal pot with lid and cook on high pressure for 5 minutes.
3. Release pressure using quick release method than open the lid.
4. Add cottage cheese and stir well.
5. Serve hot and enjoy.

Nutrition Value:
Calories: 152; Carbohydrates: 11.7g; Protein: 13.9g; Fat: 5.6g; Sugar: 0.7g; Sodium: 1072mg

418. Simple Kale Chicken Soup

Servings: 4
Cooking Time: 15 minutes

Ingredients:
- 2 cups chicken breast, cooked and chopped
- 2 tsp garlic, minced
- ½ tsp cinnamon
- 4 cups vegetable broth
- 1 onion, diced
- 12 oz kale
- 1 tsp salt

Directions:
1. Add all ingredients into the instant pot and stir well.
2. Seal pot with lid and cook on high for 5 minutes.
3. Allow to release pressure naturally for 10 minutes then release using quick release method.
4. Stir well and serve warm.

Nutrition Value:
Calories: 158; Carbohydrates: 13.1g; Protein: 19.7g; Fat: 2.8g; Sugar: 1.9g; Sodium: 1411mg

419. Mushroom Chicken Soup

Servings: 4
Cooking Time: 25 minutes

Ingredients:
- 1 lb chicken breast, cut into chunks
- 1 tsp Italian seasoning
- 2 ½ cups chicken stock
- 1 small yellow squash, chopped
- 2 cups mushrooms, sliced
- 2 garlic cloves, minced
- 1 onion, sliced
- 1 tsp black pepper
- 1 tsp salt

Directions:
1. Add all ingredients into the instant pot and stir well.
2. Seal pot with lid and cook on high for 15 minutes.
3. Allow to release pressure naturally for 10 minutes then release using quick release method.
4. Remove chicken from pot and puree the vegetable mixture using a blender.
5. Shred the chicken using a fork. Return shredded chicken to the pot and stir well.
6. Serve and enjoy.

Nutrition Value:
Calories: 166; Carbohydrates: 6.1g; Protein: 26.4g; Fat: 3.8g; Sugar: 2.8g; Sodium: 1123mg

420. Coconut Chicken Soup

Servings: 4
Cooking Time: 15 minutes

Ingredients:
- 1 lb chicken thighs, boneless and cut into chunks
- 2 cups Swiss chard, chopped
- 1 ½ cups celery stalks, chopped
- 1 tsp turmeric
- 1 tbsp chicken broth base
- 10 oz can tomato
- 1 cup coconut milk
- 1 tbsp ginger, grated
- 4 garlic cloves, minced
- 1 onion, chopped

Directions:
1. Add ½ cup of coconut milk, broth base, turmeric, tomatoes, ginger, garlic, and

onion to the blender and blender and blend until smooth.
2. Transfer blended the mixture to the instant pot along with Swiss chard, celery, and chicken. Stir well.
3. Seal pot with lid and cook on high for 5 minutes.
4. Allow to release pressure naturally for 10 minutes then release using quick release method.
5. Add remaining coconut oil and stir well.
6. Serve and enjoy.

Nutrition Value:

Calories: 473; Carbohydrates: 29.7g; Protein: 39.5g; Fat: 23.9g; Sugar: 4.7g; Sodium: 560mg

421. Taco Cheese Soup

Servings: 8
Cooking Time: 25 minutes

Ingredients:

- 1 lb ground beef
- 1 lb ground pork
- ½ cup Monterey Jack cheese, grated
- 2 tbsp parsley, chopped
- 4 cups beef broth
- 20 oz can tomatoes
- 16 oz cream cheese
- 2 tbsp taco seasonings

Directions:

1. Add both the ground meats in the instant pot and sauté for 10 minutes.
2. Add taco seasonings, can tomatoes, and cream cheese and stir to combine.
3. Seal pot with lid and cook on high for 15 minutes.
4. Release pressure using quick release method than open the lid.
5. Add parsley and stir well. Top with grated cheese and serve.

Nutrition Value:

Calories: 445; Carbohydrates: 5.7g; Protein: 41.1g; Fat: 28.1g; Sugar: 2.9g; Sodium: 808mg

422. Asparagus Garlic Ham Soup

Servings: 4
Cooking Time: 50 minutes

Ingredients:

- 1 ½ lbs asparagus, chopped
- 4 cups chicken stock
- 2 tsp garlic, minced
- 3 tbsp olive oil
- 1 onion, diced
- ¾ cup ham, diced
- ½ tsp thyme

Directions:

1. Add oil into the instant pot and set the pot on sauté mode.
2. Add onion and sauté for 4 minutes.
3. Add garlic and ham and cook for a minute.
4. Add stock and thyme. Stir well.
5. Seal pot with lid and cook on soup mode for 45 minutes.
6. Release pressure using quick release method than open the lid,
7. Stir well and serve.

Nutrition Value:

Calories: 188; Carbohydrates: 11.4g; Protein: 9g; Fat: 13.5g; Sugar: 5.1g; Sodium: 1099mg

423. Asian Pork Soup

Servings: 5
Cooking Time: 30 minutes

Ingredients:

- 1 lb ground pork
- 1 tsp ground ginger
- ¼ cup soy sauce
- 4 cups beef broth
- ½ cabbage head, chopped
- 2 carrots, peeled and shredded
- 1 onion, chopped
- 1 tbsp olive oil
- Pepper
- Salt

Directions:

1. Add oil into the instant pot and set the pot on sauté mode.
2. Add meat to the pot and sauté for 5 minutes.
3. Add remaining ingredients and stir well.
4. Seal pot with lid and cook on high for 25 minutes.
5. Release pressure using quick release method than open the lid.
6. Stir well and serve hot.

Nutrition Value:

Calories: 229; Carbohydrates: 10.6g; Protein: 29.8g; Fat: 7.2g; Sugar: 5.2g; Sodium: 1443mg

424. Creamy Potato Soup

Servings: 6
Cooking Time: 9 minutes

Ingredients:

- 3 lbs russet potatoes, peeled and diced
- 15 oz can coconut milk
- 3 cups chicken broth
- ½ tsp dried thyme
- 2 carrots, peeled and sliced
- 3 garlic cloves, minced
- 1 onion, chopped
- 2 tbsp olive oil
- Pepper
- Salt

Directions:

1. Add oil into the instant pot and set the pot on sauté mode.
2. Add onion and garlic and sauté for 3-4 minutes.
3. Add remaining ingredients except for coconut milk and stir well.
4. Seal pot with lid and cook on high for 9 minutes.
5. Release pressure using quick release method than open the lid.
6. Puree the soup using an immersion blender until smooth.
7. Add coconut milk and stir well.
8. Season soup with pepper and salt.
9. Serve and enjoy.

Nutrition Value:

Calories: 373; Carbohydrates: 42.3g; Protein: 20.7g; Fat: 20.7g; Sugar: 4.8g; Sodium: 447mg

425. Mexican Chicken Fajita Soup

Servings: 4
Cooking Time: 24 minutes

Ingredients:

- 1 lb chicken breast, boneless
- 1 tsp coriander powder
- 1 tsp ground cumin
- 1 scallion, chopped
- 1 tbsp fresh lemon juice
- 2 cups chicken stock
- 14 oz can tomatoes, diced
- 2 cups bell pepper, chopped
- 1 tbsp garlic, minced
- 1 jalapeno pepper, diced
- 1 cup onion, diced
- 1 tbsp olive oil
- ¼ tsp red pepper flakes
- 1 tsp salt

Directions:

1. Add oil into the instant pot and set the pot on sauté mode.
2. Add garlic, onion, bell pepper, and jalapeno and sauté for 2 minutes.
3. Add chicken, spices, stock, and tomatoes. Stir well.
4. Seal pot with lid and cook on high for 12 minutes.
5. Allow to release pressure naturally for 10 minutes then release using quick release method.
6. Remove chicken from pot and shred using a fork. Return shredded chicken to the pot and stir well.
7. Add lemon juice and stir well.
8. Garnish with scallions and serve.

Nutrition Value:

Calories: 224; Carbohydrates: 14.2g; Protein: 26.6g; Fat: 7g; Sugar: 8.3g; Sodium: 1238mg

426. Butternut Squash Garlic Soup

Servings: 6
Cooking Time: 12 minutes

Ingredients:

- 1 lb butternut squash, cubed
- 2 cups chicken stock
- 1 tsp paprika
- 1/2 tsp dried thyme
- 1/4 tsp red pepper flakes
- 1 onion, diced
- 2 tsp olive oil
- 3 garlic cloves, minced
- 1 lb cauliflower, chopped
- 1/2 cup heavy cream
- 1/2 tsp salt

Directions:

1. Add oil into the instant pot and set the pot on sauté mode.
2. Add onion and garlic to the pot and sauté for 5 minutes.
3. Add paprika, thyme, and red pepper flakes and sauté for a minute.
4. Add squash and cook for 2 minutes. Add cauliflower and stock. Stir well.
5. Seal pot with lid and cook on high for 5 minutes.
6. Release pressure using quick release method than open the lid.
7. Puree the soup using an immersion blender until smooth.
8. Serve and enjoy.

Nutrition Value:

Calories: 115; Carbohydrates: 15.9g; Protein: 3.1g; Fat: 5.7g; Sugar: 4.6g; Sodium: 479mg

427. Tomato Almond Milk Soup

Servings: 6
Cooking Time: 8 minutes

Ingredients:

- 4 cups tomatoes, peeled, seeded and chopped
- 1/2 tsp baking soda
- 1 cup chicken stock
- 1/2 cup heavy cream
- 1 1/2 cups almond milk
- Pepper
- Salt

Directions:

1. Add tomatoes and stock into the pot and stir well. Season with pepper and salt.
2. Seal pot with lid and cook on high for 3 minutes.
3. Release pressure using quick release method than open the lid.
4. Add baking soda to the pot and stir well.
5. Add heavy cream, almond milk, pepper, and salt. Stir well.
6. Puree the soup using an immersion blender until smooth. Cook soup on sauté mode for 5 minutes more.
7. Stir and serve.

Nutrition Value:

Calories: 196; Carbohydrates: 8.4g; Protein: 2.8g; Fat: 18.3g; Sugar: 5.3g; Sodium: 277mg

428. Squash Nutmeg Soup

Servings: 6
Cooking Time: 18 minutes

Ingredients:

- 6 cups butternut squash, peeled and cubed
- 1/8 tsp nutmeg
- 3 cups chicken stock
- 1 onion, chopped
- 2 tbsp olive oil
- 1/8 tsp cayenne pepper
- 2 tsp thyme
- 1/4 cup heavy cream
- Pepper
- Salt

Directions:

1. Add oil into the instant pot and set the pot on sauté mode.
2. Add onion to the pot and sauté for 3 minutes.

3. Add squash, nutmeg, cayenne, thyme, stock, and salt. Stir well.
4. Seal pot with lid and cook on high for 5 minutes.
5. Allow to release pressure naturally for 10 minutes then release using quick release method.
6. Add heavy cream and stir well. Puree the soup using an immersion blender until smooth.
7. Season soup with pepper and salt
8. Serve and enjoy.

Nutrition Value:

Calories: 134; Carbohydrates: 18.9g; Protein: 2.1g; Fat: 7g; Sugar: 4.2g; Sodium: 417mg

429. Tomato Basil Soup

Servings: 6
Cooking Time: 36 minutes

Ingredients:

- 28 oz can tomatoes
- 1 3/4 cup coconut milk
- 1/2 cup fresh basil, chopped
- 1 fresh thyme sprig
- 1 cup carrots, diced
- 1 cup celery, diced
- 3 1/2 cups chicken stock
- 1 cup onion, diced
- 1/3 cup cheddar cheese, grated
- 2 bay leaves
- 1 tbsp butter
- 2 tbsp olive oil
- Pepper
- Salt

Directions:

1. Add olive oil and butter into the pot and set the pot on sauté mode.
2. Add celery, onion, and carrots and sauté for 5 minutes.
3. Add remaining ingredients and stir well.
4. Seal pot with lid and cook on high for 30 minutes.
5. Release pressure using quick release method than open the lid.
6. Puree the soup using an immersion blender until smooth.
7. Stir well and serve.

Nutrition Value:

Calories: 296; Carbohydrates: 15.3g; Protein: 5.3g; Fat: 25.8g; Sugar: 9.2g; Sodium: 844mg

SALADS

430. Lentil Salmon Salad

Servings 4
Preparation Time: 25 minutes

Ingredients:

- Vegetable stock - 2 cups
- Green lentils - 1, rinsed
- Red onion - 1, chopped
- Parsley - 1 2 cup, chopped
- Smoked salmon - 4 oz., shredded
- Cilantro - 2 tbsp., chopped
- Red pepper - 1, chopped
- Lemon - 1, juiced
- Salt and pepper - to taste

Directions:

1. Cook vegetable stock and lentils in a sauce pan for 15 to 20 minutes, on low heat. Ensure all liquid has been absorbed and then remove from heat.
2. Pour into a salad bowl and top with red pepper, parsley, cilantro and salt and pepper (to suit your taste) and mix.
3. Mix in lemon juice and shredded salmon.
4. This salad should be served fresh.

431. Peppy Pepper Tomato Salad

Servings 4
Preparation Time 20 minutes

Ingredients:

- Yellow bell pepper - 1, cored and diced
- Cucumbers - 4, diced
- Red onion - 1, chopped
- Balsamic vinegar – 1 tbsp.
- Extra virgin olive oil – 2 tbsp.
- Tomatoes - 4, diced
- Red bell peppers - 2, cored and diced
- Chili flakes - 1 pinch
- Salt and pepper - to taste

Directions:

1. Mix all above Ingredients: in a salad bowl, except salt and pepper.
2. Season with salt and pepper to suit your taste and mix well.
3. Eat while fresh.

432. Bulgur Salad

Servings 4
Preparation Time: 30 minutes

Ingredients:

- Vegetable stock - 2 cups
- Bulgur - 2 3 cup
- Garlic clove - 1, minced
- Cherry tomatoes - 1 cup, halved
- Almonds - 2 tbsp., sliced
- Dates - 1 4 cup, pitted and chopped
- Lemon juice - 1 tbsp.
- Baby spinach - 8 oz.
- Cucumber - 1, diced
- Balsamic vinegar - 1 tbsp.
- Salt and pepper - to taste
- Mixed seeds - 2 tbsp.

Directions:

1. Pour stock into sauce pan and heat until hot, then stir in bulgur and cook until bulgur has absorbed all stock.
2. Put in salad bowl and add remaining Ingredients:, stir well.
3. Add salt and pepper to suit your taste.
4. Serve and eat immediately.

433. Tasty Tuna Salad

Servings 4
Preparation Time 15 minutes

Ingredients:

- Green olives - 1 4 cup, sliced
- Tuna in water - 1 can, drained
- Pine nuts - 2 tbsp.
- Artichoke hearts – 1 jar, drained and chopped
- Extra virgin olive oil - 2 tbsp.

- Lemon – 1, juiced
- Arugula - 2 leaves
- Dijon mustard - 1 tbsp.
- Salt and pepper - to taste

Directions:

1. Mix mustard, oil and lemon juice in a bowl to make a dressing. Combine the artichoke hearts, tuna, green olives, arugula and pine nuts in a salad bowl.
2. In a separate salad bowl, mix tuna, arugula, pine nuts, artichoke hearts and tuna.
3. Pour dressing mix onto salad and serve fresh.

434. Sweet and Sour Spinach Salad

Servings 4
Preparation Time 15 minutes

Ingredients:

- Red onions - 2, sliced
- Baby spinach leaves - 4
- Sesame oil - 1 2 tsp.
- Apple cider vinegar - 2 tbsp.
- Honey - 1 tsp.
- Sesame seeds - 2 tbsp.
- Salt and pepper - to taste

Directions:

1. Mix together honey, sesame oil, vinegar and sesame seeds in a small bowl to make a dressing. Add in salt and pepper to suit your taste.
2. Add red onions and spinach together in a salad bowl.
3. Pour dressing over the salad and serve while cool and fresh.

435. Easy Eggplant Salad

Servings 4
Preparation Time 30 minutes

Ingredients:

- Salt and pepper - to taste
- Eggplant - 2, sliced
- Smoked paprika - 1 tsp.
- Extra virgin olive oil - 2 tbsp.
- Garlic cloves - 2, minced
- Mixed greens - 2 cups
- Sherry vinegar - 2 tbsp.

Directions:

1. Mix together garlic, paprika and oil in a small bowl.
2. Place eggplant on a plate and sprinkle with salt and pepper to suit your taste. Next, brush oil mixture onto the eggplant.
3. Cook eggplant on a medium heated grill pan until brown on both sides. Once cooked, put eggplant into a salad bowl.
4. Top with greens and vinegar and greens, serve and eat.

436. Sweetest Sweet Potato Salad

Servings 4
Preparation Time: 30 minutes

Ingredients:

- Honey - 2 tbsp.
- Sumac spice - 1 tsp.
- Sweet potato - 2, finely sliced
- Extra virgin olive oil - 3 tbsp.
- Dried mint - 1 tsp.
- Balsamic vinegar – 1 tbsp.
- Salt and pepper - to taste
- Pomegranate - 1, seeded
- Mixed greens - 3 cups

Directions:

1. Place sweet potato slices on a plate and add sumac, mint, salt and pepper on both sides. Next, drizzle oil and honey over both sides.
2. Add oil to a grill pan and heat. Grill sweet potatoes on medium heat until brown on both sides.
3. Put sweet potatoes in a salad bowl and top with pomegranate and mixed greens.
4. Stir and eat right away.

437. Delicious Chickpea Salad

Servings 4

Preparation Time 15 minutes

Ingredients:

- Chickpeas - 1 can, drained
- Cherry tomatoes - 1 cup, quartered
- Parsley - 1 2 cup, chopped
- Red seedless grapes - 1 2 cup, halved
- Feta cheese - 4 oz., cubed
- Salt and pepper - to taste
- Lemon juice - 1 tbsp.
- Greek yogurt - 1 4 cup
- Extra virgin olive oil - 2 tbsp.

Directions:

1. In a salad bowl, mix together parsley, chickpeas, grapes, feta cheese and tomatoes.
2. Add in remaining Ingredients:, seasoning with salt and pepper to suit your taste.
3. This fresh salad is best when served right away.

438. Couscous Arugula Salad

Servings 4

Preparation Time: 20 minutes

Ingredients:

- Couscous - 1 2 cup
- Vegetable stock - 1 cup
- Asparagus - 1 bunch, peeled
- Lemon - 1, juiced
- Dried tarragon - 1 tsp.
- Arugula - 2 cups
- Salt and pepper - to taste

Directions:

1. Heat vegetable stock in a pot until hot. Remove from heat and add in couscous. Cover until couscous has absorbed all the stock.
2. Pour in a bowl and fluff with a fork and then set aside to cool.
3. Peel asparagus with a vegetable peeler, making them into ribbons and put into a bowl with couscous.
4. Add remaining Ingredients: and add salt and pepper to suit your taste.
5. Serve the salad immediately.

439. Spinach and Grilled Feta Salad

Servings 6

Preparation Time: 20 minutes

Ingredients:

- Feta cheese - 8 oz., sliced
- Black olives - 1 4 cup, sliced
- Green olives - 1 4 cup, sliced
- Baby spinach - 4 cups
- Garlic cloves - 2, minced
- Capers - 1 tsp., chopped
- Extra virgin olive oil - 2 tbsp.
- Red wine vinegar - 1 tbsp.

Directions:

1. Grill feta cheese slices over medium to high flame until brown on both sides.
2. In a salad bowl, mix green olives, black olives and spinach.
3. In a separate bowl, mix vinegar, capers and oil together to make a dressing.
4. Top salad with the dressing and cheese and it's is ready to serve.

440. Creamy Cool Salad

Servings 4

Preparation Time 15 minutes

Ingredients:

- Greek yogurt - 1 2 cup
- Dill - 2 tbsp., chopped
- Lemon juice - 1 tsp.
- Cucumbers - 4, diced
- Garlic cloves - 2, minced
- Salt and pepper - to taste

Directions:

1. Mix all Ingredients: in a salad bowl.
2. Add salt and pepper to suit your taste and eat.

441. Grilled Salmon Summer

Salad

Servings 4
Preparation Time: 30 minutes

Ingredients:

- Salmon fillets - 2
- Salt and pepper - to taste
- Vegetable stock - 2 cups
- Bulgur - 1 2 cup
- Cherry tomatoes - 1 cup, halved
- Sweet corn - 1 2 cup
- Lemon - 1, juiced
- Green olives - 1 2 cup, sliced
- Cucumber - 1, cubed
- Green onion - 1, chopped
- Red pepper - 1, chopped
- Red bell pepper - 1, cored and diced

Directions:

1. Heat a grill pan on medium and then place salmon on, seasoning with salt and pepper. Grill both sides of salmon until brown and set aside.
2. Heat stock in sauce pan until hot and then add in bulgur and cook until liquid is completely soaked into bulgur.
3. Mix salmon, bulgur and all other Ingredients: in a salad bowl and again add salt and pepper, if desired, to suit your taste.
4. Serve salad as soon as completed.

442. Broccoli Salad with Caramelized Onions

Servings 4
Preparation Time: 25 minutes

Ingredients:

- Extra virgin olive oil - 3 tbsp.
- Red onions - 2, sliced
- Dried thyme - 1 tsp.
- Balsamic vinegar - 2 tbsp. vinegar
- Broccoli - 1 lb., cut into florets
- Salt and pepper - to taste

Directions:

1. Heat extra virgin olive oil in a pan over high heat and add in sliced onions. Cook for approximately 10 minutes or until the onions are caramelized. Stir in vinegar and thyme and then remove from stove.
2. Mix together the broccoli and onion mixture in a bowl, adding salt and pepper if desired. Serve and eat salad as soon as possible.

443. Baked Cauliflower Mixed Salad

Servings 4
Preparation Time: 30 minutes

Ingredients:

- Cauliflower - 1 lb., cut into florets
- Extra virgin olive oil - 2 tbsp.
- Dried mint - 1 tsp.
- Dried oregano - 1 tsp.
- Parsley - 2 tbsp., chopped
- Red pepper - 1, chopped
- Lemon - 1, juiced
- Green onion - 1, chopped
- Cilantro - 2 tbsp., chopped
- Salt and pepper to taste

Directions:

1. Heat oven to 350 degrees.
2. In a deep baking pan, combine olive oil, mint, cauliflower and oregano and bake for 15 minutes.
3. Once cooked, pour into a salad bowl and add remaining Ingredients:, stirring together.
4. Plate the salad and eat fresh and warm.

444. Quick Arugula Salad

Servings 4
Preparation Time 15 minutes

Ingredients:

- Roasted red bell peppers - 6, sliced
- Pine nuts - 2 tbsp.
- Dried raisins - 2 tbsp.
- Red onion - 1, sliced
- Arugula - 3 cups

- Balsamic vinegar - 2 tbsp.
- Feta cheese - 4 oz., crumbled
- Extra virgin olive oil – 2 tbsp.
- Feta cheese - 4 oz., crumbled
- Salt and pepper - to taste

Directions:
1. Using a salad bowl, combine vinegar, olive oil, pine nuts, raisins, peppers and onions.
2. Add arugula and feta cheese to the mix and serve.

445. Bell Pepper and Tomato Salad

Servings 4
Preparation Time 15 minutes

Ingredients:
- Roasted red bell pepper - 8, sliced
- Extra virgin olive oil - 2 tbsp.
- Chili flakes - 1 pinch
- Garlic cloves - 4, minced
- Pine nuts - 2 tbsp.
- Shallot - 1, sliced
- Cherry tomatoes - 1 cup, halved
- Parsley - 2 tbsp., chopped
- Balsamic vinegar - 1 tbsp.
- Salt and pepper - to taste

Directions:
1. Mix all Ingredients: except salt and pepper in a salad bowl.
2. Season with salt and pepper if you want, to suit your taste.
3. Eat once freshly made.

446. One Bowl Spinach Salad

Servings 4
Preparation Time 20 minutes

Ingredients:
- Red beets - 2, cooked and diced
- Apple cider vinegar - 1 tbsp.
- Baby spinach - 3 cups
- Greek yogurt - 1 4 cup

- Horseradish - 1 tbsp.
- Salt and pepper - to taste

Directions:
1. Mix beets and spinach in a salad bowl.
2. Add in yogurt, horseradish, and vinegar. You can also add salt and pepper if you wish.
3. Serve salad as soon as mixed.

447. Olive and Red Bean Salad

Servings 4
Preparation Time 20 minutes

Ingredients:
- Red onions - 2, sliced
- Garlic cloves - 2, minced
- Balsamic vinegar - 2 tbsp.
- Green olives - 1 4 cup, sliced
- Salt and pepper - to taste
- Mixed greens - 2 cups
- Red beans - 1 can, drained
- Chili flakes - 1 pinch
- Extra virgin olive oil - 2 tbsp.
- Parsley - 2 tbsp., chopped

Directions:
1. In a salad bowl, mix all Ingredients:.
2. Add salt and pepper, if desired, and serve right away.

448. Fresh and Light Cabbage Salad

3. Servings 4
4. Preparation Time 25 minutes

Ingredients:
- Mint - 1 tbsp., chopped
- Ground coriander - 1 2 tsp.
- Savoy cabbage - 1, shredded
- Greek yogurt - 1 2 cup
- Cumin seeds - 1 4 tsp.
- Extra virgin olive oil - 2 tbsp.
- Carrot - 1, grated
- Red onion – 1, sliced
- Honey - 1 tsp.

- Lemon zest - 1 tsp.
- Lemon juice - 2 tbsp.
- Salt and pepper - to taste

Directions:
1. In a salad bowl, mix all Ingredients:.
2. You can add salt and pepper to suit your taste and then mix again.
3. This salad is best when cool and freshly made.

449. Vegetable Patch Salad

Servings 6
Preparation Time: 30 minutes

Ingredients:
- Cauliflower - 1 bunch, cut into florets
- Zucchini - 1, sliced
- Sweet potato - 1, peeled and cubed
- Baby carrots - 1 2 lb.
- Salt and pepper - to taste
- Dried basil - 1 tsp.
- Red onions - 2, sliced
- Eggplant - 2, cubed
- Endive - 1, sliced
- Extra virgin olive oil - 3 tbsp.
- Lemon – 1, juiced
- Balsamic vinegar - 1 tbsp.

Directions:
1. Preheat oven to 350 degrees. Mix together all vegetables, basil, salt, pepper and oil in a baking dish and cook for 25 – 30 minutes.
2. After cooked, pour into salad bowl and stir in vinegar and lemon juice.
3. Dish up and serve.

450. Cucumber Greek yoghurt Salad

Serves:6/
Preparation time: 5 minutes/ cooking time: 0 minutes

Ingredients:
- 4tbsp Greek yoghurt
- 4 large cucumbers peeled seeded and sliced
- 1 tbsp dried dill
- 1 tbsp apple cider vinegar
- 1/4 tsp garlic powder
- 1/4 tsp ground black pepper
- 1/2 tsp sugar
- 1/2 tsp salt

Directions:
1. Place all the Ingredients: leaving out the cucumber into a bowl and whisk this until all is incorporated. Add your cucumber slices and toss until all is well mixed.
2. Let the salad chill 10 minutes in the refrigerator and then serve.

451. Chickpea Salad Recipe

Serves: 4
Preparation Time: 15 minutes

Ingredients:
- Drained chickpeas: 1 can
- Halved cherry tomatoes: 1 cup
- Sun-dried chopped tomatoes: 1 2 cups
- Arugula: 2 cups
- Cubed pita bread: 1
- Pitted black olives: 1 2 cups
- 1 sliced shallot
- Cumin seeds: 1 2 teaspoon
- Coriander seeds: 1 2 teaspoon
- Chili powder: 1 4 teaspoon
- Chopped mint: 1 teaspoon
- Pepper and salt to taste
- Crumbled goat cheese: 4 oz.

Directions:
1. In a salad bowl, mix the tomatoes, chickpeas, pita bread, arugula, olives, shallot, spices and mint.
2. Stir in pepper and salt as desired to the cheese and stir.
3. You can now serve the fresh Salad.

452. Orange salad

Serves: 4 Cooking Time: 15 minutes

Ingredients:

- 4 sliced endives
- 1 sliced red onion
- 2 oranges already cut into segments
- Extra virgin olive oil: 2 tablespoon
- Pepper and salt to taste

Directions:

1. Mix all the Ingredients: in a salad bowl
2. Sprinkle pepper and salt to taste.
3. You can now serve the salad fresh.

453. Yogurt lettuce salad recipe

Serves: 4 Duration of cooking: 20 minutes

Ingredients:

- Shredded Romaine lettuce: 1 head
- Sliced cucumbers: 2
- 2 minced garlic cloves
- Greek yogurt: 1 2 cup
- Dijon mustard: 1 teaspoon
- Chili powder: 1 pinch
- Extra virgin olive oil: 2 tablespoon
- Lemon juice: 1 tablespoon
- Chopped dill: 2 tablespoon
- 4 chopped mint leaves
- Pepper and salt to taste

Directions:

1. In a salad bowl, combine the lettuce with the cucumbers.
2. Add the yogurt, chili, mustard, lemon juice, dill, mint, garlic and oil in a mortar with pepper and salt as desired. Then, mix well into paste, this is the dressing for the salad.
3. Top the Salad with the dressing then serve fresh.

454. Fruit de salad recipe

Serves: 4 Cooking Time: 20 minutes

Ingredients:

- Cubed seedless watermelon: 8 oz.
- Halved red grapes: 4 oz.
- 2 Sliced cucumbers
- Halved strawberries: 1 cup
- Cubed feta cheese: 6 oz.
- Balsamic vinegar: 2 tablespoon
- Arugula: 2 cups

Directions:

1. In a salad bowl, mix the strawberries, grapes, arugula, cucumbers, feta cheese and watermelon together.
2. Top the salad with vinegar and serve fresh.

455. Chickpea with mint salad recipe

Serves: 6
Preparation Time: 20 minutes

Ingredients:

- 1 diced cucumber
- Sliced black olives:1 4 cup
- Chopped mint: 2 tablespoon
- Cooked and drained short pasta: 4 oz.
- Arugula: 2 cups
- Drained chickpeas: 1 can
- 1 sliced shallot
- Chopped Parsley: 1 2 cup
- Halved cherry tomatoes: 1 2 pound
- Sliced green olives: 1 4 cup
- 1 juiced lemon
- Extra virgin olive oil: 2 tablespoon
- Chopped walnut: 1 2 cup
- Pepper and salt to taste

Directions:

1. Mix the chickpeas with the other Ingredients: in a salad bowl
2. Top with oil and lemon juice, sprinkle pepper and salt then mix well.
3. Refrigerate the Salad (can last in a sealed container for about 2 days) or serve fresh.

456. Grapy Fennel salad

Serves: 2 Time to prepare : 15 minutes

Ingredients:

- Grape seed oil: 1 tablespoon
- Chopped dill: 1 tablespoon
- 1 finely sliced fennel bulb
- Toasted almond slices: 2 tablespoon
- Chopped mint: 1 teaspoon
- 1 grapefruit already cut into segments
- 1 orange already cut into segments
- Pepper and salt as desired

Directions:
1. Using a platter, mix the grapefruit and orange segments with the fennel bulb
2. Add the mint, almond slices and dill, top with the oil and add pepper and salt as desired.
3. You can now serve the Salad fresh.

457. Greenie salad recipe

Serves: 4
Preparation Time: 15 minutes
5.

Ingredients:
- Extra virgin olive oil: 2 tablespoon
- Mixed greens: 12 oz.
- Pitted black olives: 1 2 cup
- Pitted green olives: 1 4 cup
- Sherry vinegar: 2 tablespoon
- Pitted Kalamata olives: 1 2 cup
- Almond slices: 2 tablespoon
- Parmesan shavings: 2 oz.
- Sliced Parma ham: 2 oz.
- Pepper and salt as desired

Directions:
1. Stir the almonds, olives and mixed greens together in a salad bowl
2. Drizzle the oil and vinegar then sprinkle pepper and salt as you want.
3. Top with the Parma ham and Parmesan shavings before serving.
4. You can now serve fresh.

SNACKS

458. Carrot Snack

Preparation time: 10 minutes
Cooking time: 6 minutes
Servings: 14

Ingredients:

- ½ teaspoon cinnamon powder
- 1 cup water
- 1 egg white, whisked
- 1 cup baby carrots, grated
- ¾ cup pecans, chopped
- 1 tablespoon honey
- 2 tablespoons coconut flour
- 2 tablespoons flax meal

Directions:

1. In a bowl, mix baby carrots with egg white, cinnamon, pecans, honey, flax meal and coconut flour, stir well and shape 14 balls out of this mix.
2. Add the water to your instant pot, add the steamer basket, add carrot balls, cover and cook on High for 6 minutes.
3. Arrange carrot balls on a platter and serve.
4. Enjoy!

Nutrition Value: calories 120, fat 2, fiber 1, carbs 2, protein 3

459. Mushroom Appetizer

Preparation time: 10 minutes
Cooking time: 12 minutes
Servings: 4

Ingredients:

- 1 pound chorizo, chopped
- 1 pound big white mushroom caps, stems separated and chopped
- 2 tablespoons olive oil
- 1 cup water
- 1 yellow onion, chopped
- A pinch of black pepper

Directions:

1. Set your instant pot on sauté mode, add oil, heat it up, add mushrooms stems, onion and a pinch of black pepper, stir and sauté for 5 minutes.
2. Add chorizo, stir, transfer to a bowl, cool down and stuff mushrooms with this mix.
3. Clean your instant pot, add the water, add the steamer basket, place stuffed mushrooms inside, cover and cook on High for 7 minutes.
4. Arrange on a platter and serve as an appetizer.
5. Enjoy!

Nutrition Value: calories 135, fat 2, fiber 2, carbs 4, protein 12

460. Zucchini Appetizer

Preparation time: 10 minutes
Cooking time: 5 minutes
Servings: 4

Ingredients:

- 3 zucchinis, thinly sliced lengthwise
- 14 bacon slices
- 1 cup water
- ½ cup sun dried tomatoes, chopped
- 4 tablespoons balsamic vinegar
- ½ cup basil, chopped
- Black pepper to the taste

Directions:

1. Put zucchini slices in a bowl, add vinegar, toss a bit and leave aside for 10 minutes.
2. Drain and arrange zucchini slices on a cutting board.
3. Divide bacon slices, basil and sundried tomatoes into each zucchini slices, season with a pinch of black pepper, wrap and secure with toothpicks.
4. Add the water to your instant pot, add the steamer basket, add zucchini rolls, cover and cook on High for 5 minutes.

5. Arrange on a platter and serve.
6. Enjoy!

Nutrition Value: calories 143, fat 2, fiber 3, carbs 5, protein 3

461. Crazy And Unique Appetizer

Preparation time: 10 minutes
Cooking time: 10 minutes
Servings: 2

Ingredients:

- 3 tablespoons curry powder
- 1 cup almond flour
- 1 cup water
- 3 chicken breasts, boneless, skinless and cut into thin strips
- 2 teaspoons turmeric powder
- 1 tablespoon cumin, ground
- 1 tablespoon garlic powder
- Black pepper to the taste

Directions:

1. In a bowl, mix curry powder with flour, turmeric, cumin, garlic powder and black pepper, stir well, add chicken strips and toss to coat.
2. Put the water in your instant pot, add the steamer basket, add chicken strips, cover and cook on High for 10 minutes.
3. Arrange on a platter and serve.
4. Enjoy!

Nutrition Value: calories 100, fat 2, fiber 3, carbs 4, protein 2

462. Almonds Surprise

Preparation time: 10 minutes
Cooking time: 10 minutes
Servings: 10

Ingredients:

- 3 tablespoons cinnamon powder
- 3 tablespoons stevia
- 4 and ½ cups almonds, raw
- 2 cups water
- 2 teaspoons vanilla extract

Directions:

1. In a bowl, mix 1 cup water with vanilla extract and whisk.
2. In another bowl, mix cinnamon with stevia and stir.
3. Dip almonds in water, then in cinnamon mix and place them in a heatproof dish.
4. Add the rest of the water to your instant pot, add the steamer basket, add the dish inside, cover and cook on High for 10 minutes.
5. Transfer almond to a bowl and serve them as a snack.
6. Enjoy!

Nutrition Value: calories 100, fat 3, fiber 4, carbs 3, protein 4

463. Sweet Potato Spread

Preparation time: 10 minutes
Cooking time: 12 minutes
Servings: 6

Ingredients:

- 2 cups sweet potatoes, peeled and chopped
- ¼ cup sesame seeds paste
- 2 tablespoons lemon juice
- 5 garlic cloves, minced
- 1 tablespoon olive oil
- ½ teaspoon cumin, ground
- 2 cups water+ 2 tablespoons water
- A pinch of salt

Directions:

1. Put 2 cups water in your instant pot, add the steamer basket, add potatoes, cover and cook on High for 12 minutes.
2. Transfer potatoes to your food processor, add 2 tablespoons water, sesame seeds paste, lemon juice, garlic, oil, cumin and a pinch of salt and pulse really well.
3. Divide into bowls and serve as an appetizer.
4. Enjoy!

Nutrition Value: calories 130, fat 3, fiber 1, carbs 4, protein 7

464. Mint Dip

Preparation time: 10 minutes
Cooking time: 4 minutes
Servings: 4

Ingredients:

- 1 bunch spinach, chopped
- ½ cup water
- 2 tablespoons mint, chopped
- 1 scallion, sliced
- ¾ cup coconut cream
- Black pepper to the taste

Directions:

1. Put spinach and water in your instant pot, cover and cook on High for 4 minutes.
2. Drain spinach well, transfer it to a bowl, add mint, scallion, cream and black pepper and stir really well.
3. Leave this dip aside for 10 minutes before serving it.
4. Enjoy!

Nutrition Value: calories 140, fat 3, fiber 3, carbs 3, protein 3

465. Popular Shrimp Appetizer

Preparation time: 10 minutes
Cooking time: 2 minutes
Servings: 8

Ingredients:

- 2 pounds big shrimp, deveined
- 4 cup water
- 1 lemon, halved
- 2 bay leaves
- 1 medium lemon, sliced for serving
- ¾ cup tomato paste
- 2 and ½ tablespoons horseradish, prepared
- ¼ teaspoon hot pepper sauce
- 2 tablespoons lemon juice

Directions:

1. Put the water in your instant pot, add halved lemon and bay leaves.
2. Add shrimp, cover and cook on High for 2 minutes.
3. Transfer shrimp to a bowl filled with ice water, cool it down and transfer to smaller bowls filled with ice.
4. In a separate bowl, mix hot sauce with tomato paste, lemon juice and horseradish and whisk.
5. Serve your shrimp with the sauce you made and lemon slices on the side.
6. Enjoy!

Nutrition Value: calories 140, fat 1, fiber 3, carbs 5, protein 2

466. Incredible Scallops

Preparation time: 5 minutes
Cooking time: 6 minutes
Servings: 4

Ingredients:

- 1 jalapeno pepper, seedless and minced
- ¼ cup extra virgin olive oil
- ¼ cup rice vinegar
- ¼ teaspoon mustard
- Black pepper to the taste
- A pinch cayenne pepper
- 1 tablespoon vegetable oil
- 12 big sea scallops
- 2 oranges, sliced

Directions:

1. In your blender, mix jalapeno with olive oil, mustard, black and vinegar and pulse really well.
2. Season scallops with cayenne pepper.
3. Heat up a pan with the vegetable oil over high temperature, add scallops and cook them for 3 minutes on each side.
4. Divide scallops on plates, place orange slices on top and drizzle the jalapeno vinaigrette.
5. Enjoy!

467. Broiled Lobster Tails

Preparation time: 10 minutes
Cooking time: 10 minutes
Servings: 2

Ingredients:

- 2 big whole lobster tails
- ½ teaspoon paprika
- ½ cup coconut butter
- White pepper to the taste
- 1 lemon cut into wedges

Directions

1. Place lobster tails on a baking sheet, cut top side of lobster shells and pull them apart
2. Season with white pepper and paprika.
3. Add butter and toss gently
4. Introduce lobster tails in preheated broiler and broil for 10 minutes.
5. Divide among plates, garnish with lemon wedges and serve right away!
6. Enjoy!

Nutrition Value: calories 140, fat 2, fiber 2, carbs 6, protein 6

468. Delightful Herring Appetizer

Preparation time: 10 minutes
Cooking time: 5 minutes
Servings: 4

Ingredients:

- 10 pieces herring roe, soaked in water for half a day and drained
- 3 cups water
- 2 tablespoons stevia
- 3 tablespoons coconut aminos
- 1 handful mild chili flakes

Directions:

1. In your instant pot, mix water with stevia, aminos, chili flakes and herring roe.
2. Cover, cook on High for 2 minutes, divide into bowls and serve as an appetizer.
3. Enjoy!

Nutrition Value: calories 140, fat 2, fiber 1, carbs 2, protein 3

469. Salmon Patties

Preparation time: 10 minutes
Cooking time: 10 minutes
Servings: 4

Ingredients:

- 1 pound salmon, ground
- 2 tablespoons lemon zest
- Black pepper to the taste
- A pinch of sea salt
- 1 teaspoon olive oil
- ½ cup flax meal

Directions:

1. In your food processor, mix salmon with flax meal, salt, pepper and lemon zest, pulse well, shape 4 patties out of this mix and place them on a plate.
2. Set your instant pot on Sauté mode, add the oil and heat it up.
3. Add patties, cover pot and cook on High for 10 minutes.
4. Arrange patties on a platter and serve.
5. Enjoy!

Nutrition Value: calories 142, fat 3, fiber 2, carbs 3, protein 4

470. Clams And Mussels Appetizer

Preparation time: 10 minutes
Cooking time: 15 minutes
Servings: 4

Ingredients:

- 2 chorizo links, chopped
- 15 clams
- 30 mussels, scrubbed
- 10 ounces veggies stock
- 1 yellow onion, chopped
- 1 teaspoon olive oil
- 2 tablespoons parsley, chopped
- Lemon wedges

Directions:

1. Put the oil in your instant pot, set it on Sauté mode, heat it up, add onions and chorizo, stir and cook for 4 minutes.
2. Add clams, mussels and stock, stir, cover and cook on High for 10 minutes.

3. Release pressure, add parsley, stir, divide into bowls and serve with lemon wedges on the side.
4. Enjoy!

Nutrition Value: calories 142, fat 2, fiber 2, carbs 3, protein 6

471. Special Shrimp Appetizer

Preparation time: 5 minutes
Cooking time: 4 minutes
Servings: 4

Ingredients:

- 2 tablespoons coconut aminos
- 1 pound shrimp, peeled and deveined
- 1 cup chicken stock
- 3 tablespoon stevia
- 3 tablespoons balsamic vinegar
- ¾ cup pineapple juice

Directions:

1. In your instant pot, mix shrimp with aminos, stock, vinegar, pineapple juice and stevia, stir everything well, cover pot and cook on High for 4 minutes.
2. Divide into bowls and serve as an appetizer.
3. Enjoy!

Nutrition Value: calories 132, fat 2, fiber 2, carbs 3, protein 5

472. Stuffed Squid

Preparation time: 10 minutes
Cooking time: 20 minutes
Servings: 4

Ingredients:

- 14 ounces veggie stock
- 3 tablespoons coconut aminos
- 4 squid, tentacles separated and chopped
- 1 cup cauliflower rice
- 2 tablespoon water
- 2 tablespoons stevia

Directions:

1. In a bowl, mix tentacles with cauliflower rice, stir and stuff squid with this mix.
2. Place stuffed squid in your instant pot, add aminos, stock, stevia and water stir, cover and cook on High for 15 minutes.
3. Arrange on a platter and serve as an appetizer.
4. Enjoy!

Nutrition Value: calories 162, fat 3, fiber 2, carbs 3, protein 6

473. Asian-Style Appetizer Ribs

Preparation Time: 25 minutes
Servings 6

Nutrition Value: 331 Calories; 15.8g Fat; 3.1g Carbs; 42.1g Protein; 1.8g Sugars

Ingredients

- 2 tablespoons sesame oil
- 1 ½ pounds spare ribs
- Salt and ground black pepper, to taste
- 1/2 cup green onions, chopped
- 1 teaspoon ginger-garlic paste
- 1/2 teaspoon red pepper flakes, crushed
- 1/2 teaspoon dries parsley
- 2 tomatoes, crushed
- 1/2 cup chicken stock
- 1 tablespoon tamari sauce
- 2 tablespoons sherry
- 2 tablespoons sesame seeds

Directions

1. Season spare ribs with salt and black pepper. Press the "Sauté" button and heat the oil. Once hot, brown your spare ribs approximately 3 minutes per side.
2. Add the remaining ingredients, except for sesame seeds, and secure the lid.
3. Choose "Meat/Stew" mode and High pressure; cook for 18 minutes. Once cooking is complete, use a natural pressure release; carefully remove the lid.
4. Sprinkle sesame seed over the top of your ribs and serve immediately. Bon appétit!

474. Two-Cheese Artichoke Dip

Preparation Time: 15 minutes
Servings 10

Nutrition Value: 204 Calories; 15.4g Fat; 5.6g Carbs; 11.5g Protein; 1.3g Sugars

Ingredients

- 2 medium-sized artichokes, trimmed and cleaned
- 1 cup Ricotta cheese, softened
- 2 cups Monterey-jack cheese, shredded
- 1/2 cup mayonnaise
- 1/2 cup Greek yogurt
- 1 garlic clove, minced
- 2 tablespoons coriander
- 1/4 cup scallions
- 1/4 teaspoon ground black pepper, or more to taste
- 1 teaspoon dried rosemary

Directions

1. Start by adding 1 cup of water and a steamer basket to the Instant Pot. Place the artichokes in the steamer basket.
2. Secure the lid. Choose "Manual" mode and High pressure; cook for 8 minutes. Once cooking is complete, use a quick pressure release; carefully remove the lid.
3. Coarsely chop your artichokes and add the remaining ingredients.
4. Press the "Sauté" button and let it simmer until everything is heated through. Bon appétit!

475. Easy Party Mushrooms

Preparation Time: 10 minutes
Servings 6

Nutrition Value: 73 Calories; 7g Fat; 2g Carbs; 1.7g Protein; 1.1g Sugars

Ingredients

- 3 tablespoons sesame oil
- 3/4 pound small button mushrooms
- 1 teaspoon garlic, minced
- 1/2 teaspoon cayenne pepper
- 1/2 teaspoon smoked paprika
- Salt and ground black pepper, to taste

Directions

1. Press the "Sauté" button and heat the oil. Once hot, cook your mushrooms for 4 to 5 minutes.
2. Add the other ingredients.
3. Secure the lid. Choose "Manual" mode and High pressure; cook for 5 minutes. Once cooking is complete, use a quick pressure release; carefully remove the lid.
4. Serve with toothpicks and enjoy!

476. Herbed Party Shrimp

Preparation Time: 10 minutes
Servings 4

Nutrition Value: 142 Calories; 7.5g Fat; 0.2g Carbs; 18.3g Protein; 0g Sugars

Ingredients

- 2 tablespoons olive oil
- 3/4 pound shrimp, peeled and deveined
- 1 teaspoon paprika
- 1/2 teaspoon dried oregano
- 1/2 teaspoon dried thyme
- 1/2 teaspoon dried rosemary
- 1/2 teaspoon dried basil
- 1/4 teaspoon red pepper flakes
- 1 teaspoon dried parsley flakes
- 1 teaspoon onion powder
- 1 teaspoon garlic powder
- Coarse sea salt and ground black pepper, to taste
- 1 cup chicken broth, preferably homemade

Directions

1. Press the "Sauté" button and heat the olive oil. Once hot, cook your shrimp for 2 to 3 minutes.
2. Sprinkle all seasoning over your shrimp, pour the chicken broth into your Instant Pot, and secure the lid.
3. Choose "Manual" mode and Low pressure; cook for 2 minutes. Once cooking is complete, use a quick pressure release; carefully remove the lid.
4. Arrange shrimp on a serving platter and serve with toothpicks. Bon appétit!

477. Crispy and Yummy Beef Bites

Preparation Time: 25 minutes
Servings 6
Nutrition Value: 169 Calories; 9.9g Fat; 1.1g Carbs; 17.9g Protein; 0.5g Sugars

Ingredients

- 2 tablespoons olive oil
- 1 pound beef steak, cut into cubes
- Sea salt and ground black pepper, to taste
- 1 teaspoon cayenne pepper
- 1/2 teaspoon dried marjoram
- 1 cup beef bone broth
- 1/4 cup dry white wine

Directions

1. Press the "Sauté" button and heat the olive oil. Once hot, cook the beef for 2 to 3 minutes, stirring periodically.
2. Add the remaining ingredients to the Instant Pot.
3. Secure the lid. Choose "Manual" mode and High pressure; cook for 20 minutes. Once cooking is complete, use a natural pressure release; carefully remove the lid.
4. Arrange beef cubes on a nice serving platter and serve with sticks. Bon appétit!

478. Asparagus with Greek Aioli

Preparation Time: 10 minutes
Servings 6

Nutrition Value: 194 Calories; 19.2g Fat; 4.5g Carbs; 2.6g Protein; 2.4g Sugars

Ingredients

- 1 pound asparagus spears
- Sea salt and ground black pepper, to taste
- Homemade Aioli Sauce:
- 1 teaspoon garlic, minced
- 1 egg yolk
- 1/2 cup olive oil
- Sea salt and ground black pepper, to your liking
- 1/4 cup Greek yogurt
- 2 teaspoons freshly squeezed lemon juice

Directions

1. Start by adding 1 cup of water and a steamer basket to the Instant Pot. Place the asparagus in the steamer basket.
2. Secure the lid. Choose "Manual" mode and High pressure; cook for 1 minute. Once cooking is complete, use a quick pressure release; carefully remove the lid.
3. Season your asparagus with salt and pepper; reserve.
4. In a blender or a food processor, mix garlic, egg yolk, and oil until well incorporated.
5. Now, add the salt, ground black pepper, and Greek yogurt. Afterwards, add the lemon juice and mix until your aioli is thickened and emulsified.
6. Serve the reserved asparagus spears with this homemade aioli on the side. Enjoy!

479. Carrot Sticks with Blue-Cheese Sauce

Preparation Time: 10 minutes
Servings 8

Nutrition Value: 202 Calories; 16.8g Fat; 7.1g Carbs; 6.1g Protein; 3.9g Sugars

Ingredients

- 1 pound carrots, cut into sticks
- Himalayan salt and white pepper, to taste
- 1/4 teaspoon red pepper flakes, crushed
- 1 cup water
- Blue-Cheese Sauce:
- 6 ounces blue cheese
- 1/2 cup full-fat yogurt
- 1/2 cup mayonnaise
- 1 teaspoon deli mustard
- 1 tablespoon fresh chives, chopped
- 3 tablespoons water

Directions

1. Simply add carrots, salt, white pepper, red pepper and 1 cup of water to your Instant Pot.
2. Secure the lid. Choose "Manual" mode

and High pressure; cook for 2 minutes. Once cooking is complete, use a quick pressure release; carefully remove the lid.
3. Meanwhile, thoroughly combine the remaining ingredients in a mixing bowl. Serve the prepared carrot sticks with the sauce on the side. Bon appétit!

480. Zingy Zucchini Bites

Preparation Time: 10 minutes
Servings 6

Nutrition Value: 70 Calories; 5.1g Fat; 4.4g Carbs; 3.2g Protein; 0.9g Sugars

Ingredients

- 2 tablespoons olive oil
- 1 red chili pepper, chopped
- 1 pound zucchini, cut into thick slices
- 1 teaspoon garlic powder
- 1 cup chicken broth
- Coarse sea salt and ground black pepper, to taste
- 1/2 teaspoon paprika
- 1/2 teaspoon ground coriander

Directions

1. Press the "Sauté" button and heat the olive oil. Once hot, cook chili pepper for 1 minute.
2. Add the remaining ingredients.
3. Secure the lid. Choose "Manual" mode and Low pressure; cook for 3 minutes. Once cooking is complete, use a quick pressure release; carefully remove the lid. Bon appétit!

481. Kohlrabi Sticks with Hungarian Mayo

Preparation Time: 10 minutes
Servings 6

Nutrition Value: 148 Calories; 13.8g Fat; 5.4g Carbs; 1.5g Protein; 2.6g Sugars

Ingredients

- 1 pound kohlrabi, cut into sticks
- 1 cup water
- Salt and pepper, to taste
- 1/2 cup mayonnaise
- 1 teaspoon whole-grain mustard
- 1/2 teaspoon Hungarian paprika
- 1 teaspoon shallot powder
- 1/4 teaspoon porcini powder
- 1 teaspoon granulated garlic

Directions

1. Add kohlrabi sticks and water to your Instant Pot. Now, season with salt and pepper.
2. Secure the lid. Choose "Manual" mode and Low pressure; cook for 3 minutes. Once cooking is complete, use a quick pressure release; carefully remove the lid.
3. In the meantime, mix the remaining ingredients until everything is well incorporated. Serve with the prepared kohlrabi sticks. Bon appétit!

482. Bok Choy Boats with Shrimp Salad

Preparation Time: 10 minutes
Servings 8

Nutrition Value: 124 Calories; 10.6g Fat; 3.1g Carbs; 4.7g Protein; 1.8g Sugars

Ingredients

- 26 shrimp, cleaned and deveined
- 2 tablespoons fresh lemon juice
- 1 cup of water
- Sea salt and ground black pepper, to taste
- 2 tomatoes, diced
- 4 ounces feta cheese, crumbled
- 1/3 cup olives, pitted and sliced
- 4 tablespoons olive oil
- 2 tablespoons apple cider vinegar
- 8 Bok choy leaves
- 2 tablespoons fresh basil leaves, snipped
- 2 tablespoons fresh mint leaves, chopped

Directions

1. Toss the shrimp and fresh lemon juice in your Instant Pot. Add 1 cup of water.
2. Secure the lid. Choose "Manual" mode and Low pressure; cook for 2 minutes.

Once cooking is complete, use a quick pressure release; carefully remove the lid.
3. Season the shrimp with sea salt and ground black pepper, and allow them to cool completely. Toss the shrimp with tomatoes, feta cheese, olives, olive oil, and vinegar.
4. Mound the salad onto each Bok choy leaf and arrange them on a serving platter. Top with basil and mint leaves. Bon appétit!

483. Game Day Sausage Dip

Preparation Time: 45 minutes
Servings 12
Nutrition Value: 251 Calories; 18.3g Fat; 7.2g Carbs; 14.5g Protein; 5.3g Sugars

Ingredients

- 1 tablespoon ghee
- 3/4 pound spicy breakfast sausage, casings removed and crumbled
- 16 ounces Velveeta cheese
- 8 ounces Cotija cheese shredded
- 2 (10-ounce) cans diced tomatoes with green chilies
- 1 cup chicken broth
- 1 package taco seasoning

Directions

1. Press the "Sauté" button and melt the ghee. Once hot, cook the sausage until it is no longer pink.
2. Add the remaining ingredients.
3. Secure the lid. Choose "Slow Cook" mode and Low pressure; cook for 40 minutes. Once cooking is complete, use a quick pressure release; carefully remove the lid.
4. Serve with your favorite Mediterranean dippers. Bon appétit!

484. Stuffed Baby Bell Peppers

Preparation Time: 10 minutes
Servings 5
Nutrition Value: 224 Calories; 17.5g Fat; 9g Carbs; 8.7g Protein; 5.5g Sugars

Ingredients

- 10 baby bell peppers, seeded and sliced lengthwise
- 1 tablespoon olive oil
- 4 ounces cream cheese
- 4 ounces Monterey-Jack cheese, shredded
- 1 teaspoon garlic, minced
- 2 tablespoons scallions, chopped
- 1/4 teaspoon ground black pepper, or more to taste
- 1/2 teaspoon cayenne pepper

Directions

1. Start by adding 1 cup of water and a steamer basket to the Instant Pot.
2. In a mixing bowl, thoroughly combine all ingredients, except for bell peppers. Then, stuff the peppers with cheese mixture.
3. Place the stuffed peppers in the steamer basket.
4. Secure the lid. Choose "Manual" mode and High pressure; cook for 5 minutes. Once cooking is complete, use a quick pressure release; carefully remove the lid.
5. Serve at room temperature and enjoy!

485. Party Garlic Prawns

Preparation Time: 10 minutes
Servings 6

Nutrition Value: 122 Calories; 5.8g Fat; 2.7g Carbs; 14.2g Protein; 0.5g Sugars

Ingredients

- 2 tablespoons olive oil
- 1 pound prawns, cleaned and deveined
- 2 garlic cloves, minced
- Sea salt and ground black pepper, to taste
- 1 teaspoon cayenne pepper
- 1/2 teaspoon dried dill
- 2 tablespoons fresh lime juice
- 1 cup roasted vegetable broth, preferably homemade

Directions

1. Press the "Sauté" button and heat the

olive oil. Once hot, cook your prawns for 2 to 3 minutes.
2. Add garlic and cook an additional 40 seconds.
3. Stir in the remaining ingredients.
4. Secure the lid. Choose "Manual" mode and Low pressure; cook for 2 minutes. Once cooking is complete, use a quick pressure release; carefully remove the lid.
5. Arrange prawns on a serving platter and serve with toothpicks. Bon appétit!

486. Barbecue Lil Smokies

Preparation Time: 10 minutes
Servings 8
Nutrition Value: 120 Calories; 4.9g Fat; 1.2g Carbs; 17.5g Protein; 0.6g Sugars

Ingredients

- 1 ½ pounds beef cocktail wieners
- 1 cup water
- 1/4 cup apple cider vinegar
- 1/2 tablespoon onion powder
- 1/2 teaspoon ground black pepper
- 1 teaspoon ground mustard
- 2 ounces ale

Directions

1. Simply throw all ingredients into your Instant Pot.
2. Secure the lid. Choose "Manual" mode and High pressure; cook for 2 minutes. Once cooking is complete, use a natural pressure release; carefully remove the lid.
3. Serve with cocktail sticks and enjoy!

487. Two-Cheese and Caramelized Onion Dip

Preparation Time: 15 minutes
Servings 12
Nutrition Value: 148 Calories; 10g Fat; 7.2g Carbs; 7.5g Protein; 4.1g Sugars

Ingredients

- 3 tablespoons butter
- 2 pounds white onions, chopped
- Sea salt and freshly ground black pepper, to taste
- 1/4 teaspoon dill
- 1 tablespoon coconut aminos
- 1 cup broth, preferably homemade
- 10 ounces Ricotta cheese
- 6 ounces Swiss cheese

Directions

1. Press the "Sauté" button and melt the butter. Once hot, cook the onions until they are caramelized.
2. Add the salt, pepper, dill, coconut aminos, and broth.
3. Secure the lid. Choose "Manual" mode and High pressure; cook for 10 minutes. Once cooking is complete, use a natural pressure release; carefully remove the lid.
4. Fold in the cheese and stir until everything is well combined. Serve with your favorite dippers. Bon appétit!

488. Hot Lager Chicken Wings

Preparation Time: 15 minutes
Servings 6

Nutrition Value: 216 Calories; 16.4g Fat; 2.2g Carbs; 12.9g Protein; 0.5g Sugars

Ingredients

- 2 tablespoons butter, melted
- 1 pound chicken thighs
- Coarse sea salt and ground black pepper, to taste
- 1 teaspoon cayenne pepper
- 1 teaspoon shallot powder
- 1 teaspoon garlic powder
- 1 teaspoon hot sauce
- 1/2 cup lager
- 1/2 cup water

Directions

1. Press the "Sauté" button and melt the butter. Once hot, brown the chicken thighs for 2 minutes per side.
2. Add the remaining ingredients to your Instant Pot.
3. Secure the lid. Choose "Poultry" mode and High pressure; cook for 6 minutes.

Once cooking is complete, use a quick pressure release; carefully remove the lid.
4. Serve at room temperature and enjoy!

489. Braised Spring Kale Appetizer

Preparation Time: 10 minutes
Servings 6

Nutrition Value: 103 Calories; 6.1g Fat; 8.1g Carbs; 6.1g Protein; 2.1g Sugars

Ingredients

- 3 teaspoons butter, melted
- 1 cup spring onions, chopped
- 1 pound kale, torn into pieces
- Himalayan salt and ground black pepper, to taste
- 1/2 teaspoon cayenne pepper
- 1 cup water
- 1/2 cup Colby cheese, shredded

Directions

1. Press the "Sauté" button and melt butter. Add spring onions to your Instant Pot and cook for 1 minute or until wilted.
2. Stir in kale leaves, salt, black pepper, cayenne pepper, and water.
3. Secure the lid. Choose "Manual" mode and High pressure; cook for 1 minute. Once cooking is complete, use a quick pressure release; carefully remove the lid.
4. Transfer to a serving bowl and top with grated cheese. Bon appétit!

490. Wax Beans with Pancetta

Preparation Time: 10 minutes
Servings 6

Nutrition Value: 194 Calories; 8.7g Fat; 5.8g Carbs; 24.3g Protein; 2.9g Sugars

Ingredients

- 1 tablespoon peanut oil
- 1/2 cup shallots, chopped
- 4 slices pancetta, diced
- 1 teaspoon roasted garlic paste
- 1 pound yellow wax beans, cut in half
- Kosher salt and ground black pepper, to your liking
- 1 cup water

Directions

1. Press the "Sauté" button to heat up your Instant Pot. Now, heat the peanut oil and sauté the shallot until softened.
2. Now, add pancetta and continue to cook for a further 3 to 4 minutes; reserve.
3. Add the other ingredients; stir to combine
4. Secure the lid. Choose "Manual" mode and Low pressure; cook for 3 minutes. Once cooking is complete, use a quick pressure release; carefully remove the lid.
5. Serve warm, garnished with the reserved shallots and pancetta. Bon appétit!

491. Middle-Eastern Eggplant Dip

Preparation Time: 10 minutes
Servings 10

Nutrition Value: 81 Calories; 6.6g Fat; 5g Carbs; 1.4g Protein; 2.7g Sugars

Ingredients

- 1/4 cup sesame oil
- 2 bell peppers, seeded and sliced
- 1 serrano pepper, seeded and sliced
- 1 eggplant, peeled and sliced
- 3 cloves garlic, minced
- 1 cup broth, preferably homemade
- Kosher salt and ground black pepper, to taste
- 1/2 teaspoon cayenne pepper
- 1/2 teaspoon chili flakes
- A few drops of liquid smoke
- 2 tablespoons coriander, chopped
- 2 teaspoons extra-virgin olive oil

Directions

1. Press the "Sauté" button to heat up your Instant Pot. Now, heat the oil and sauté the peppers and eggplant until softened.
2. Add the garlic, broth, salt, black pepper, cayenne pepper, chili flakes, liquid

smoke, and coriander.
3. Secure the lid. Choose "Manual" mode and Low pressure; cook for 3 minutes. Once cooking is complete, use a quick pressure release; carefully remove the lid.
4. Transfer the mixture to a serving bowl; drizzle olive oil over the top and serve well-chilled. Enjoy!

492. Cheesy Cauliflower Bites

Preparation Time: 10 minutes
Servings 6

Nutrition Value: 130 Calories; 9.6g Fat; 5.1g Carbs; 6.9g Protein; 2g Sugars

Ingredients

- 1 pound cauliflower, broken into florets
- Sea salt and ground black pepper, to taste
- 2 tablespoons lemon juice
- 2 tablespoons extra-virgin olive oil
- 1 cup Cheddar cheese, preferably freshly grated

Directions

1. Add 1 cup of water and a steamer basket to your Instant Pot.
2. Now, arrange cauliflower florets on the steamer basket.
3. Secure the lid. Choose "Manual" mode and Low pressure; cook for 3 minutes. Once cooking is complete, use a quick pressure release; carefully remove the lid.
4. Sprinkle salt and pepper over your cauliflower; drizzle with lemon juice and olive oil. Scatter grated cheese over the cauliflower florets.
5. Press the "Sauté" button to heat up your Instant Pot. Let it cook until the cheese is melted or about 5 minutes. Bon appétit!

493. Goat Cheese and Chives Spread

Preparation time: 10 minutes
Cooking time: 0 minutes
Servings: 4

Ingredients:

- 2 ounces goat cheese, crumbled
- ¾ cup sour cream
- 2 tablespoons chives, chopped
- 1 tablespoon lemon juice
- Salt and black pepper to the taste
- 2 tablespoons extra virgin olive oil

Directions:

1. In a bowl, mix the goat cheese with the cream and the rest of the ingredients and whisk really well.
2. Keep in the fridge for 10 minutes and serve as a party spread.

Nutrition Value: calories 220, fat 11.5, fiber 4.8, carbs 8.9, protein 5.6

494. Chickpeas Salsa

Preparation time: 5 minutes
Cooking time: 0 minutes
Servings: 6

Ingredients:

- 4 spring onions, chopped
- 1 cup baby spinach
- 15 ounces canned chickpeas, drained and rinsed
- Salt and black pepper to the taste
- 2 tablespoons olive oil
- 2 tablespoons lemon juice
- 1 tablespoon cilantro, chopped

Directions:

1. In a bowl, mix the chickpeas with the spinach, spring onions and the rest of the ingredients, toss, divide into small cups and serve as a snack.

Nutrition Value: calories 224, fat 5.1, fiber 1, carbs 9.9, protein 15.1

495. Ginger and Cream Cheese Dip

Preparation time: 5 minutes
Cooking time: 0 minutes
Servings: 6

Ingredients:

- ½ cup ginger, grated
- 2 bunches cilantro, chopped

- 3 tablespoons balsamic vinegar
- ½ cup olive oil
- 1 and ½ cups cream cheese, soft

Directions:

1. In your blender, mix the ginger with the rest of the ingredients and pulse well.
2. Divide into small bowls and serve as a party dip.

Nutrition Value: calories 213, fat 4.9, fiber 4.1, carbs 8.8, protein 17.8

496. Walnuts Yogurt Dip

Preparation time: 5 minutes
Cooking time: 0 minutes
Servings: 8

Ingredients:

- 3 garlic cloves, minced
- 2 cups Greek yogurt
- ¼ cup dill, chopped
- 1 tablespoon chives, chopped
- ¼ cup walnuts, chopped
- Salt and black pepper to the taste

Directions:

1. In a bowl, mix the garlic with the yogurt and the rest of the ingredients, whisk well, divide into small cups and serve as a party dip.

Nutrition Value: calories 200, fat 6.5, fiber 4.6, carbs 15.5, protein 8.4

497. Herbed Goat Cheese Dip

Preparation time: 5 minutes
Cooking time: 0 minutes
Servings: 4

Ingredients:

- ¼ cup mixed parsley, chopped
- ¼ cup chives, chopped
- 8 ounces goat cheese, soft
- Salt and black pepper to the taste
- A drizzle of olive oil

Directions:

1. In your food processor mix the goat cheese with the parsley and the rest of the ingredients and pulse well.
2. Divide into small bowls and serve as a party dip.

Nutrition Value: calories 245, fat 11.3, fiber 4.5, carbs 8.9, protein 11.2

498. Scallions Dip

Preparation time: 5 minutes
Cooking time: 0 minutes
Servings: 8

Ingredients:

- 6 scallions, chopped
- 1 garlic clove, minced
- 3 tablespoons olive oil
- Salt and black pepper to the taste
- 1 tablespoon lemon juice
- 1 and ½ cups cream cheese, soft
- 2 ounces prosciutto, cooked and crumbled

Directions:

1. In a bowl, mix the scallions with the garlic and the rest of the ingredients except the prosciutto and whisk well.
2. Divide into bowls, sprinkle the prosciutto on top and serve as a party dip.

Nutrition Value: calories 144, fat 7.7, fiber 1.4, carbs 6.3, protein 5.5

499. Tomato Cream Cheese Spread

Preparation time: 5 minutes
Cooking time: 0 minutes
Servings: 6

Ingredients:

- 12 ounces cream cheese, soft
- 1 big tomato, cubed
- ¼ cup homemade mayonnaise
- 2 garlic clove, minced
- 2 tablespoons red onion, chopped
- 2 tablespoons lime juice
- Salt and black pepper to the taste

Directions:

1. In your blender, mix the cream cheese with the tomato and the rest of the ingredients, pulse well, divide into small cups and serve cold.

Nutrition Value: calories 204, fat 6.7, fiber 1.4, carbs 7.3, protein 4.5

500. Pesto Dip

Preparation time: 5 minutes
Cooking time: 0 minutes
Servings: 6

Ingredients:

- 1 cup cream cheese, soft
- 3 tablespoons basil pesto
- Salt and black pepper to the taste
- 1 cup heavy cream
- 1 tablespoon chives, chopped

Directions:

1. In a bowl, mix the cream cheese with the pesto and the rest of the ingredients and whisk well.
2. Divide into small cups and serve as a party dip.

Nutrition Value: calories 230, fat 14.5, fiber 4.8, carbs 6.5, protein 5.4

501. Vinegar Beet Bites

Preparation time: 10 minutes
Cooking time: 30 minutes
Servings: 4

Ingredients:

- 2 beets, sliced
- A pinch of sea salt and black pepper
- 1/3 cup balsamic vinegar
- 1 cup olive oil

Directions:

1. Spread the beet slices on a baking sheet lined with parchment paper, add the rest of the ingredients, toss and bake at 350 degrees F for 30 minutes.
2. Serve the beet bites cold as a snack.

Nutrition Value: calories 199, fat 5.4, fiber 3.5, carbs 8.5, protein 3.5

502. Zucchini and Olives Salsa

Preparation time: 5 minutes
Cooking time: 0 minutes
Servings: 4

Ingredients:

- ½ cup black olives, pitted and sliced
- 3 zucchinis, cut with a spiralizer
- 1 cup cherry tomatoes, halved
- Salt and black pepper to the taste
- 1 small red onion, chopped
- ½ cup feta cheese, crumbled
- ½ cup olive oil
- ¼ cup apple cider vinegar

Directions:

1. In a bowl, mix the olives with the zucchinis and the rest of the ingredients, toss, divide into small cups and serve as an appetizer.

Nutrition Value: calories 140, fat 14.2, fiber 1.4, carbs 3.5, protein 1.4

503. Strawberry and Carrots Salad

Preparation time: 5 minutes
Cooking time: 0 minutes
Servings: 4

Ingredients:

- 6 carrots, peeled and grated
- 10 strawberries, halved
- Salt and black pepper to the taste
- 2 tablespoons balsamic vinegar
- 1 tablespoon Dijon mustard
- ¼ cup lemon juice
- 2 tablespoons olive oil

Directions:

1. In a bowl, mix the carrots with the strawberries and the rest of the ingredients, toss, divide between appetizer plates and serve.

Nutrition Value: calories 182, fat 4.3, fiber 2.4, carbs 7.5, protein 3

504. Hot Squash Wedges

Preparation time: 10 minutes
Cooking time: 25 minutes
Servings: 6

Ingredients:

- 6 tablespoons olive oil
- 2 tablespoons chili paste
- 3 butternut squash, peeled and cut into wedges
- 2 tablespoons balsamic vinegar
- 1 tablespoon chives, chopped

Directions:

1. In a bowl, mix the squash wedges with the chili paste and the rest of the ingredients, toss, spread them on a baking sheet lined with parchment paper and bake at 400 degrees F for 25 minutes, flipping them from time to time.
2. Divide the wedges into bowls and serve as a snack.

Nutrition Value: calories 180, fat 4.2, fiber 4.4, carbs 6.5, protein 1.4

505. Shrimp and Cucumber Bites

Preparation time: 5 minutes
Cooking time: 0 minutes
Servings: 8

Ingredients:

- 1 big cucumber, cubed
- 1 pound shrimp, cooked, peeled, deveined and chopped
- 2 tablespoons heavy cream
- Salt and black pepper to the taste
- 12 whole grain crackers

Directions:

1. In a bowl, mix the cucumber with the rest of the ingredients except the crackers and stir well.
2. Arrange the crackers on a platter, spread the shrimp mix on each and serve.

Nutrition Value: calories 155, fat 8.5, fiber 4.8, carbs 11.8, protein 17.7

506. Salmon Rolls

Preparation time: 5 minutes
Cooking time: 0 minutes
Servings: 12

Ingredients:

- 1 big long cucumber, thinly sliced lengthwise
- 2 teaspoons lime juice
- 4 ounces cream cheese, soft
- 1 teaspoon lemon zest, grated
- Salt and black pepper to the taste
- 2 teaspoons dill, chopped
- 4 ounces smoked salmon, cut into strips

Directions:

1. Arrange cucumber slices on a working surface and top each with a salmon strip.
2. In a bowl, mix the rest of the ingredients, stir and spread over the salmon.
3. Roll the salmon and cucumber strips, arrange them on a platter and serve as an appetizer.

Nutrition Value: calories 245, fat 15.5, fiber 4.8, carbs 16.8, protein 17.3

507. Eggplant Bombs

Preparation time: 10 minutes
Cooking time: 45 minutes
Servings: 6

Ingredients:

- 4 cups eggplants, chopped
- 3 tablespoons olive oil
- 3 garlic cloves, minced
- 2 eggs, whisked
- Salt and black pepper to the taste
- 1 cup parsley, chopped
- ½ cup parmesan cheese, finely grated
- ¾ cups bread crumbs

Directions:

1. Heat up a pan with the oil over medium high heat, add the garlic and the eggplants, and cook for 15 minutes stirring often.

2. In a bowl, combine the eggplant mix with the rest of the ingredients, stir well and shape medium balls out of this mix.
3. Arrange the balls on a baking sheet lined with parchment paper and bake at 350 degrees F for 30 minutes.
4. Serve as a snack.

Nutrition Value: calories 224, fat 10.6, fiber 1.8, carbs 5.4, protein 3.5

508. Eggplant Bites

Preparation time: 10 minutes
Cooking time: 15 minutes
Servings: 8

Ingredients:

- 2 eggplants, cut into 20 slices
- 2 tablespoons olive oil
- ½ cup roasted peppers, chopped
- ½ cup kalamata olives, pitted and chopped
- 1 tablespoon lime juice
- 1 teaspoon red pepper flakes, crushed
- Salt and black pepper to the taste
- 2 tablespoons mint, chopped

Directions:

1. In a bowl, mix the roasted peppers with the olives, half of the oil and the rest of the ingredients except the eggplant slices and stir well.
2. Brush eggplant slices with the rest of the olive oil on both sides, place them on the preheated grill over medium high heat, cook for 7 minutes on each side and transfer them to a platter.
3. Top each eggplant slice with roasted peppers mix and serve.

Nutrition Value: calories 214, fat 10.6, fiber 5.8, carbs 15.4, protein 5.4

509. Sage Eggplant Chips

Preparation time: 10 minutes
Cooking time: 45 minutes
Servings: 4

Ingredients:

- 1 tablespoon olive oil
- 2 eggplants, sliced
- ½ tablespoon smoked paprika
- Salt and black pepper to the taste
- ½ teaspoon turmeric powder
- ½ teaspoon onion powder
- 2 teaspoons sage, dried

Directions:

1. In a bowl, mix the eggplant slices with the rest of the ingredients and toss well.
2. Spread the eggplant slices on a baking sheet lined with parchment paper, bake at 360 degrees F for 45 minutes and serve cold as a snack.

Nutrition Value: calories 139, fat 7.1, fiber 4.1, carbs 11.3, protein 2.5

510. Tomato Dip

Preparation time: 10 minutes
Cooking time: 0 minutes
Servings: 4

Ingredients:

- 1 pound tomatoes, peeled and chopped
- Salt and black pepper to the taste
- 1 and ½ teaspoons balsamic vinegar
- ½ teaspoon oregano, chopped
- 3 tablespoons olive oil
- 2 garlic cloves, minced
- 3 tablespoons parsley, chopped

Directions:

1. In a blender, combine the tomatoes with the oregano, salt, pepper and the rest of the ingredients, pulse well, divide into small cups and serve as a party dip.

Nutrition Value: calories 124, fat 4, fiber 2.1, carbs 3.3, protein 3.2

511. Oregano Avocado Salad

Preparation time: 10 minutes
Cooking time: 0 minutes
Servings: 4

Ingredients:

- A drizzle of olive oil
- 4 small avocados, pitted and cubed
- 1 teaspoon mustard
- 1 tablespoon white vinegar
- 1 tablespoon oregano, chopped
- 1 teaspoon honey
- Salt and black pepper to the taste

Directions:
1. In a bowl, combine the avocados with the oil and the rest of the ingredients, toss, divide between appetizer plates and serve.

Nutrition Value: calories 244, fat 14, fiber 12.1, carbs 23.3, protein 8.2

512. Lentils Spread

Preparation time: 2 hours
Cooking time: 0 minutes
Servings: 12

Ingredients:
- 1 garlic clove, minced
- 12 ounces canned lentils, drained and rinsed
- 1 teaspoon oregano, dried
- ¼ teaspoon basil, dried
- 3 tablespoons olive oil
- 1 tablespoon balsamic vinegar
- Salt and black pepper to the taste

Directions:
1. In a blender, combine the lentils with the garlic and the rest of the ingredients, pulse well, divide into bowls and serve as an appetizer.

Nutrition Value: calories 287, fat 9.5, fiber 3.5, carbs 15.3, protein 9.3

513. Chickpeas and Eggplant Bowls

Preparation time: 10 minutes
Cooking time: 10 minutes
Servings: 4

Ingredients:
- 2 eggplants, cut in half lengthwise and cubed
- 1 red onion, chopped
- Juice of 1 lime
- 1 tablespoon olive oil
- 28 ounces canned chickpeas, drained and rinsed
- 1 bunch parsley, chopped
- A pinch of salt and black pepper
- 1 tablespoon balsamic vinegar

Directions:
1. Spread the eggplant cubes on a baking sheet lined with parchment paper, drizzle half of the oil all over, season with salt and pepper and cook at 425 degrees F for 10 minutes.
2. Cool the eggplant down, add the rest of the ingredients, toss, divide between appetizer plates and serve.

Nutrition Value: calories 263, fat 12, fiber 9.3, carbs 15.4, protein 7.5

514. Cheese and Egg Salad

Preparation time: 10 minutes
Cooking time: 0 minutes
Servings: 4

Ingredients:
- 2 tablespoons olive oil
- 12 eggs, hard boiled, peeled and chopped
- Juice of 1 lime
- 14 ounces feta cheese, crumbled
- Salt and black pepper to the taste
- ¼ cup mustard
- ¾ cup sun-dried tomatoes, chopped
- 1 cup walnuts, chopped

Directions:
1. In a bowl, combine the eggs with the oil, and the rest of the ingredients and stir well.
2. Divide into small bowls and serve cold as an appetizer.

Nutrition Value: calories 288, fat 8, fiber 4.5, carbs 15.4, protein 6.7

515. Stuffed Zucchinis

Preparation time: 10 minutes
Cooking time: 40 minutes
Servings: 6

Ingredients:

- 6 zucchinis, halved lengthwise and insides scooped out
- 2 garlic cloves, minced
- 2 tablespoons oregano, chopped
- Juice of 2 lemons
- Salt and black pepper to the taste
- 2 tablespoons olive oil
- 8 ounces feta cheese, crumbed

Directions:

1. Arrange the zucchini halves on a baking sheet lined with parchment paper, divide the cheese and the rest of the ingredients in each zucchini half and bake at 450 degrees F for 40 minutes.
2. Arrange the stuffed zucchinis on a platter and serve as an appetizer.

516. Eggplant And Capers Dip

Preparation time: 10 minutes
Cooking time: 0 minutes
Servings: 4

Ingredients:

- 1 and ½ pounds eggplants, baked, peeled and chopped
- 1 red chili pepper, chopped
- ¾ cup olive oil
- 1 red bell pepper, roasted and chopped
- 1 and ½ teaspoons capers, drained and chopped
- 1 big garlic clove, minced
- 1 bunch parsley, chopped
- Salt and black pepper to the taste

Directions:

1. In a blender, combine the eggplants with the oil, chili pepper and the rest of the ingredients, pulse well, divide into bowls and serve as a party dip.

517. Pomegranate Dip

Preparation time: 10 minutes
Cooking time: 0 minutes
Servings: 6

Ingredients:

- 1 tablespoon olive oil
- 3 garlic cloves, peeled
- 1/8 teaspoon cumin
- 6 tablespoons cold water
- ½ cup tahini paste
- ½ cup pomegranate seeds
- ¼ cup pistachios, chopped

Directions:

1. In a blender, combine the oil with the garlic and the rest of the ingredients, pulse well, divide into cups and serve cold as a party dip.

Nutrition Value: calories 200, fat 1.6, fiber 5.4, carbs 8.5, protein 6.3

518. Lentils and Tomato Dip

Preparation time: 1 hour
Cooking time: 0 minutes
Servings: 6

Ingredients:

- 1 cup red lentils, cooked
- Salt and black pepper to the taste
- 2 tablespoons lemon juice
- 1 garlic clove, minced
- 2 tablespoons tomato paste
- 2 tablespoon cilantro, chopped
- 2 tablespoons olive oil
- 2 teaspoons cumin, ground

Directions:

1. In your blender, combine the lentils with the lemon juice, salt, pepper and the rest of the ingredients, and pulse well.
2. Transfer to a bowl and keep in the fridge for 1 hour before serving.

Nutrition Value: calories 244, fat 8, fiber 12.4, carbs 26, protein 8.5

519. Lentils Stuffed Potato Skins

Preparation time: 10 minutes
Cooking time: 30 minutes
Servings: 8

Ingredients:

- 16 red baby potatoes
- ¾ cup red lentils, cooked and drained
- 2 tablespoons olive oil
- 2 garlic cloves, minced
- 1 tablespoon chives, chopped
- ½ teaspoon hot chili sauce
- Salt and black pepper to the taste

Directions:

1. Put potatoes in a pot, add water to cover them, bring to a boil over medium low heat, cook for 15 minutes, drain, cool them down, cut in halves, remove the pulp, transfer it to a blender and pulse it a bit.
2. Add the rest of the ingredients to the blender, pulse again well and stuff the potato skins with this mix.
3. Arrange the stuffed potatoes on a baking sheet lined with parchment paper, introduce them in the oven at 375 degrees F and bake for 15 minutes.
4. Arrange on a platter and serve as an appetizer.

Nutrition Value: calories 300, fat 9.3, fiber 14.5, carbs 22.5, protein 8.5

DESSERTS

520. Bread Pudding

Preparation time: 5 minutes
Cooking time: 25 minutes
Servings: 4

Ingredients:

- 4 egg yolks
- 3 cups brioche, cubed
- 2 cups half and half
- ½ teaspoon vanilla extract
- 1 cup sugar
- 2 tablespoons butter, softened
- 1 cup cranberries
- 2 cups warm water
- ½ cup raisins
- Zest from 1 lime

Directions:

1. Grease a baking dish with some butter and set the dish aside. In a bowl, mix the egg yolks with the half and half, cubed brioche, vanilla extract, sugar, cranberries, raisins, and lime zest and stir well. Pour this into greased dish, cover with some aluminum foil and set aside for 10 minutes. Put the dish in the steamer basket of the Instant Pot, add the warm water to the Instant Pot, cover, and cook on the Manual setting for 20 minutes. Release the pressure naturally, uncover the Instant Pot, take the bread pudding out, set it aside to cool down, slice, and serve it.

Nutrition Value:

Calories: 300
Fat: 7
Fiber: 2
Carbs: 46
Protein: 11

521. Ruby Pears

Preparation time: 10 minutes
Cooking time: 10 minutes
Servings: 4

Ingredients:

- 4 pears
- Juice and zest of 1 lemon
- 26 ounces grape juice
- 11 ounces currant jelly
- 4 garlic cloves, peeled
- ½ vanilla bean
- 4 peppercorns
- 2 rosemary sprigs

Directions:

1. Pour the jelly and grape juice into the Instant Pot and mix with lemon zest and lemon juice. Dip each pear in this mix, wrap them in aluminum foil and arrange them in the steamer basket of the Instant Pot. Add the garlic cloves, peppercorns, rosemary, and vanilla bean to the juice mixture, cover the Instant Pot and cook on the Manual setting for 10 minutes. Release the pressure, uncover the Instant Pot, take the pears out, unwrap them, arrange them on plates, and serve cold with cooking juice poured on top.

Nutrition Value:

Calories: 145
Fat: 5.6
Fiber: 6
Carbs: 12
Protein: 12

522. Pumpkin Rice Pudding

Preparation time: 30 minutes
Cooking time: 35 minutes
Servings: 6

Ingredients:

- 1 cup brown rice
- ½ cup boiling water
- 3 cups cashew milk
- ½ cup dates, chopped
- Salt

- 1 cinnamon stick
- 1 cup pumpkin puree
- ½ cup maple syrup
- 1 teaspoon pumpkin spice mix
- 1 teaspoon vanilla extract

Directions:

1. Put the rice into the Instant Pot, add boiling water to cover, set aside for 10 minutes and drain. Put the water in milk into the Instant Pot, add the rice, cinnamon stick, dates and salt, stir, cover and cook on the Rice setting for 20 minutes. Release pressure, uncover the Instant Pot, add the maple syrup, pumpkin pie spice, and pumpkin puree, stir, set the Instant Pot on Manual mode and cook for 5 minutes. Discard the cinnamon stick, add the vanilla, stir, transfer the pudding to bowls, set aside for 30 minutes to cool down, and serve.

Nutrition Value:

Calories: 100
Fat: 1
Fiber: 4
Carbs: 21
Protein: 4.1

523. Lemon Marmalade

Preparation time: 10 minutes
Cooking time: 15 minutes
Servings: 8

Ingredients:

- 2 pounds lemons, washed, sliced, and cut into quarters
- 4 pounds sugar
- 2 cups water

Directions:

1. Put the lemon pieces into the Instant Pot, add the water, cover, and cook on the Manual setting for 10 minutes. Release the pressure naturally, uncover the Instant Pot, add the sugar, stir, set the Instant Pot on Manual mode, and cook for 6 minutes, stirring all the time. Divide into jars, and serve when needed.

Nutrition Value:

Calories: 100
Fat: 2
Fiber: 2
Carbs: 4
Protein: 8

524. Rice Pudding

Preparation time: 5 minutes
Cooking time: 15 minutes
Servings: 6

Ingredients:

- 1 tablespoon butter
- 7 ounces long grain rice
- 4 ounces water
- 16 ounces milk
- 3 ounces sugar
- Salt
- 1 egg
- 1 tablespoon cream
- 1 teaspoon vanilla extract
- Ground cinnamon

Directions:

1. Put the butter into the Instant Pot, set it on Sauté mode, melt it, add the rice, and stir. Add the water and milk and stir again. Add the salt and sugar, stir again, cover the Instant Pot and cook on the Rice setting for 8 minutes. In a bowl, mix the cream with the vanilla and eggs and stir well. Release the pressure from the Instant Pot, uncover it, and pour some of the liquid from the Instant Pot over the egg mixture and stir well. Pour this into the Instant Pot and whisk well. Cover the Instant Pot, cook on the Manual setting for 10 minutes, release the pressure, uncover the Instant Pot, pour the pudding into bowls, sprinkle cinnamon on top, and serve.

Nutrition Value:

Calories: 112
Fat: 1.2
Fiber: 0.4
Carbs: 21

Protein: 3.3

525. Ricotta Cake

Preparation time: 30 minutes
Cooking time: 30 minutes
Servings: 6

Ingredients:

- 1 pound ricotta
- 6 ounces dates, soaked for 15 minutes and drained
- 2 ounces honey
- 4 eggs
- 2 ounces sugar
- Vanilla extract
- 17 ounces water
- Orange juice and zest from ½ orange

Directions:

1. In a bowl, whisk the ricotta until it softens. In another bowl, whisk the eggs well. Combine the 2 mixtures and stir very well. Add the honey, vanilla, dates, orange zest, and juice to the ricotta mixture and stir again. Pour the batter into a heatproof dish and cover with aluminum foil. Place dish in the steamer basket of the Instant Pot, add the water to the Instant Pot, cover, and cook on the Manual setting for 20 minutes. Release the pressure, uncover the Instant Pot, allow the cake to cool down, transfer to a platter, slice, and serve.

Nutrition Value:
Calories: 211
Fat: 8.6
Fiber: 0.5
Carbs: 21
Protein: 12

526. Orange Marmalade

Preparation time: 10 minutes
Cooking time: 25 minutes
Servings: 8

Ingredients:

- Juice from 2 lemons
- 3 pounds sugar
- 1 pound oranges, cut into halves
- 1-pint water

Directions:

1. Squeeze the juice from the oranges and cut the peel into pieces. Put the peel in a bowl, cover with water and set aside overnight. In the Instant Pot, mix the lemon juice with the orange juice, water, and peel. Cover the Instant Pot, cook on the Manual setting for 15 minutes, release the pressure, uncover, add the sugar and set the Instant Pot on Manual mode. Cook until sugar dissolves, divide into jars, and serve when needed.

Nutrition Value:
Calories: 50
Fat: 0
Fiber: 0.1
Carbs: 12
Protein: 0.1

527. Berry Jam

Preparation time: 60 minutes
Cooking time: 20 minutes
Servings: 12

Ingredients:

- 1 pound cranberries
- 1 pound strawberries
- ½ pound blueberries
- ounces black currant
- 2 pounds sugar
- Zest from 1 lemon
- Salt
- 2 tablespoon water

Directions:

1. In the Instant Pot, mix the strawberries with the cranberries, blueberries, currants, lemon zest, and sugar. Stir and set aside for 1 hour. Add the salt and water, set the Instant Pot on Manual mode, and bring to a boil. Cover the Instant Pot, cook on Manual for 10 minutes, and release pressure for 10

minutes. Uncover the Instant Pot, set it on Manual mode again, bring to a boil, and simmer for 4 minutes. Divide into jars and keep in the refrigerator until you need it.

Nutrition Value:

Calories: 60
Fat: 0
Fiber: 0
Carbs: 12
Sugar: 12
Protein: 0

528. Peach Jam

Preparation time: 10 minutes
Cooking time: 5 minutes
Servings: 6

Ingredients:

- 4½ cups peaches, peeled and cubed
- 6 cups sugar
- ¼ cup crystallized ginger, chopped
- 1 box fruit pectin

Directions:

1. Set the Instant Pot on Manual mode, add the peaches, ginger, and pectin, stir and bring to a boil. Add the sugar, stir, cover and cook on the Manual setting for 5 minutes. Release the pressure, uncover the Instant Pot, divide the jam into jars, and serve.

Nutrition Value:

Calories: 50
Fat: 0
Fiber: 1
Carbs: 3
Protein: 0
Sugar: 12

529. Raspberry Curd

Preparation time: 10 minutes
Cooking time: 5 minutes
Servings: 4

Ingredients:

- 1 cup sugar
- 12 ounces raspberries
- 2 egg yolks
- 2 tablespoons lemon juice
- 2 tablespoons butter

Directions:

Put the raspberries into the Instant Pot. Add the sugar and lemon juice, stir, cover, and cook on the Manual setting for 2 minutes. Release the pressure for 5 minutes, uncover the Instant Pot, strain the raspberries and discard the seeds. In a bowl, mix the egg yolks with raspberries and stir well. Return this to the Instant Pot, set it on Sauté mode, simmer for 2 minutes, add the butter, stir, and transfer to a container. Serve cold.

Nutrition Value:

Calories: 110
Fat: 4
Fiber: 0
Carbs: 16
Protein: 1

530. Tomato Jam

Preparation time: 10 minutes
Cooking time: 30 minutes
Servings: 12

Ingredients:

- 1½ pounds tomatoes, cored and chopped
- 2 tablespoons lime juice
- 1 cup white sugar
- 1 tablespoon ginger, grated
- 1 teaspoon ground cinnamon
- 1 teaspoon cumin
- ⅛ teaspoon ground cloves
- Salt
- 1 jalapeño pepper, minced

Directions:

1. In the Instant Pot mix the tomatoes with sugar, lime juice, ginger, cumin, cinnamon, cloves, salt, and jalapeño pepper, stir, cover, and cook on the Manual setting for 30 minutes. Release the pressure, uncover the Instant Pot, divide the jam into jars, and serve when

needed.

Nutrition Value:

Calories: 239
Fat: 0
Fiber: 2
Carbs: 59
Sugar: 55
Protein: 0

531. Pear Jam

Preparation time: 10 minutes
Cooking time: 4 minutes
Servings: 12

Ingredients:

- 8 pears, cored and cut into quarters
- 2 apples, peeled, cored, and cut into quarters
- ¼ cup apple juice
- 1 teaspoon cinnamon, ground

Directions:

1. In the Instant Pot, mix the pears with apples, cinnamon, and apple juice, stir, cover, and cook on the Manual setting for 4 minutes. Release the pressure naturally, uncover the Instant Pot, blend using an immersion blender, divide the jam into jars, and keep in a cold place until you serve it.

Nutrition Value:

Calories: 90
Fat: 0
Fiber: 1
Carbs: 20
Sugar: 20
Protein: 0

532. Berry Compote

Preparation time: 10 minutes
Cooking time: 5 minutes
Servings: 8

Ingredients:

- 1 cup blueberries
- 2 cups strawberries, sliced
- 2 tablespoons lemon juice
- ¾ cup sugar
- 1 tablespoon cornstarch
- 1 tablespoon water

Directions:

1. In the Instant Pot, mix the blueberries with lemon juice and sugar, stir, cover, and cook on the Manual setting for 3 minutes. Release the pressure naturally for 10 minutes and uncover the Instant Pot. In a bowl, mix the cornstarch with water, stir well, and add to the Instant Pot. Stir, set the Instant Pot on Sauté mode, and cook compote for 2 minutes. Divide into jars and keep in the refrigerator until you serve it.

Nutrition Value:

Calories: 260
Fat: 13
Fiber: 3
Carbs: 23
Protein: 3

533. Key Lime Pie

Preparation time: 10 minutes
Cooking time: 15 minutes
Servings: 6

Ingredients:

- For the crust:
- 1 tablespoon sugar
- 3 tablespoons butter, melted
- 5 graham crackers, crumbled
- For the filling:
- 4 egg yolks
- 14 ounces canned condensed milk
- ½ cup key lime juice
- ⅓ cup sour cream
- Vegetable oil cooking spray
- 1 cup water
- 2 tablespoons key lime zest, grated

Directions:

1. In a bowl, whisk the egg yolks well. Add the milk gradually and stir again. Add the

lime juice, sour cream, and lime zest and stir again. In another bowl, whisk the butter with the graham crackers and sugar, stir well, and spread on the bottom of a springform greased with some cooking spray. Cover the pan with some aluminum foil and place it in the steamer basket of the Instant Pot. Add the water to the Instant Pot, cover and cook on the Manual setting for 15 minutes. Release the pressure for 10 minutes, uncover the Instant Pot, take the pie out, set aside to cool down and keep in the refrigerator for 4 hours before slicing and serving it.

Nutrition Value:

Calories: 400
Fat: 21
Fiber: 0.5
Carbs: 34
Protein: 7

534. Fruit Cobbler

Preparation time: 10 minutes
Cooking time: 12 minutes
Servings: 4

Ingredients:

- 3 apples, cored and cut into chunks
- 2 pears, cored and cut into chunks
- 1½ cup hot water
- ¼ cup honey
- 1 cup steel-cut oats
- 1 teaspoon ground cinnamon
- ice cream, for serving

Directions:

1. Put the apples and pears into the Instant Pot and mix with hot water, honey, oats, and cinnamon. Stir, cover, and cook on the Manual setting for 12 minutes. Release the pressure naturally, transfer

Nutrition Value:

Calories: 170
Fat: 4
Carbs: 10
Fiber: 2.4
Protein: 3

Sugar: 7

535. Simple Carrot Cake

Servings: 6
Preparation time: 10 minutes
Cooking time: 30 minutes

Ingredients:

- 5 ounces flour
- Salt
- ¾ teaspoon baking powder
- ½ teaspoon baking soda
- ½ teaspoon ground cinnamon
- ¼ teaspoon nutmeg
- ½ teaspoon allspice
- 1 egg
- 3 tablespoons yogurt
- ½ cup sugar
- ¼ cup pineapple juice
- 4 tablespoons coconut oil, melted
- ⅓ cup carrots, peeled and grated
- ⅓ cup pecans, toasted and chopped
- ⅓ cup coconut flakes
- Vegetable oil cooking spray
- 2 cups water

Directions:

1. In a bowl, mix the flour with baking soda, baking powder, salt, allspice, cinnamon, and nutmeg and stir. In another bowl, mix the egg with yogurt, sugar, pineapple juice, oil, carrots, pecans, and coconut flakes and stir well. Combine the two mixtures and stir everything well. Pour this into a springform greased with some cooking spray, add the water to the Instant Pot, and place the pan into the steamer basket. Cover the Instant Pot and cook on the Manual setting for 32 minutes. Release the pressure for 10 minutes, remove the cake from the Instant Pot, let it cool briefly, then cut, and serve it.

Nutrition Value:

Calories: 140
Fat: 3.5

Carbs: 23.4
Fiber: 4.1
Sugar: 5.2
Protein: 4.3

536. Stuffed Peaches

Preparation time: 10 minutes
Cooking time: 4 minutes
Servings: 6

Ingredients:

- 6 peaches, pits and flesh removed
- Salt
- ¼ cup coconut flour
- ¼ cup maple syrup
- 2 tablespoons coconut butter
- ½ teaspoon ground cinnamon
- 1 teaspoon almond extract
- 1 cup water

Directions:

1. In a bowl, mix the flour with the salt, syrup, butter, cinnamon, and half of the almond extract and stir well. Fill the peaches with this mix, place them in the steamer basket of the Instant Pot, add the water and the rest of the almond extract to the Instant Pot, cover and cook on the Steam setting for 4 minutes. Release the pressure naturally, divide the stuffed peaches on serving plates, and serve warm.

Nutrition Value:
Calories: 160
Fat: 6.7
Carbs: 12
Fiber: 3
Sugar: 11
Protein: 4

537. Peach Compote

Preparation time: 10 minutes
Cooking time: 3 minutes
Servings: 6

Ingredients:

8 peaches, pitted and chopped
6 tablespoons sugar
1 teaspoon ground cinnamon
1 teaspoon vanilla extract
1 vanilla bean, scraped
2 tablespoons Grape Nuts cereal

Directions:

1. Put the peaches into the Instant Pot and mix with the sugar, cinnamon, vanilla bean, and vanilla extract. Stir well, cover the Instant Pot and cook on the Manual setting for 3 minutes. Release the pressure for 10 minutes, add the cereal, stir well, transfer the compote to bowls, and serve.

Nutrition Value:
Calories: 100
Fat: 2
Carbs: 11
Fiber: 1
Sugar: 10
Protein: 1

538. Zucchini Nut Bread

Preparation time: 10 minutes
Cooking time: 25 minutes
Servings: 6

Ingredients:

- 1 cup applesauce
- 3 eggs, whisked
- 1 tablespoon vanilla extract
- 2 cups sugar
- 2 cups zucchini, grated
- 1 teaspoon salt
- 2½ cups white flour
- ½ cup baking cocoa
- 1 teaspoon baking soda
- ¼ teaspoon baking powder
- 1 teaspoon cinnamon
- ½ cup walnuts, chopped
- ½ cup chocolate chips
- 1½ cups water

Directions:

1. In a bowl, mix the zucchini with sugar,

vanilla, eggs, and applesauce and stir well. In another bowl, mix the flour with salt, cocoa, baking soda, baking powder, cinnamon, chocolate chips, and walnuts and stir. Combine the 2 mixtures, stir, pour into a Bundt pan, place the pan in the steamer basket of the Instant Pot, add the water to the Instant Pot, cover and cook on the Manual setting for 25 minutes. Release the pressure naturally, uncover the Instant Pot, transfer bread to a plate, cut, and serve it.

Nutrition Value:
Calories: 217
Fat: 8
Fiber: 2
Carbs: 35
Sugar: 22
Protein: 3

539. Samoa Cheesecake

Preparation time: 15 minutes
Cooking time: 1 hour
Servings: 6

Ingredients:

For the crust:
- 2 tablespoons butter, melted
- ½ cup chocolate graham crackers, crumbled
- For the filling:
- ¼ cup heavy cream
- ½ cup sugar
- 12 ounces cream cheese, softened
- 1½ teaspoon vanilla extract
- ¼ cup sour cream
- 1 tablespoon flour
- 1 egg yolk
- 2 eggs
- Vegetable oil cooking spray
- 1 cup water

For the topping:
- 3 tablespoons heavy cream
- 12 caramels
- 1½ cups coconut, sweet and shredded
- ¼ cup semi-sweet chocolate, chopped

Directions:
1. Grease a springform pan with some cooking spray and set it aside. In a bowl, mix the crackers with the butter, stir, spread in the bottom of the pan, and place in the freezer for 10 minutes. In another bowl, mix the cheese with the sugar, heavy cream, vanilla, flour, sour cream, and eggs and stir well using a mixer. Pour this into the pan on top of crust, cover, with aluminum foil and place in the steamer basket of the Instant Pot. Add 1 cup water to the Instant Pot, cover and cook on the Steam setting for 35 minutes. Release the pressure for 10 minutes, uncover, take the pan, remove aluminum foil, and let the cheesecake cool down in the refrigerator for 4 hours. Spread the coconut on a lined baking sheet, place it in the oven at 300° F, and bake for 20 minutes, stirring often. Put caramels in a heatproof bowl, place in the microwave for 2 minutes, stir every 20 seconds, and mix with toasted coconut. Spread this on the cheesecake and set the dish aside. Put the chocolate in another heatproof bowl, place into the microwave for a few seconds until it melts, and drizzle this over the cheesecake, and serve.

Nutrition Value:
Calories: 310
Fat: 8
Fiber: 2
Carbs: 20
Protein: 10

540. Chocolate Pudding

Preparation time: 10 minutes
Cooking time: 20 minutes
Servings: 4

Ingredients:
- 6 ounces bittersweet chocolate, chopped
- ½ cup milk
- 1½ cups heavy cream

- 5 egg yolks
- ⅓ cup brown sugar
- 2 teaspoons vanilla extract
- 1½ cups water
- ¼ teaspoon cardamom
- Salt
- Crème fraîche, for serving
- Chocolate shavings, for serving

Directions:

1. Put the cream and milk in a pot, bring to a simmer over medium heat, take off the heat, add the chocolate and whisk well. In a bowl, mix the egg yolks with the vanilla, sugar, cardamom, and a pinch of salt, stir, strain, and mix with chocolate mixture. Pour this into a soufflé dish, cover with aluminum foil, place in the steamer basket of the Instant Pot, add water to the Instant Pot, cover, cook on Manual for 18 minutes, release the pressure naturally. Take the pudding out of the Instant Pot, set aside to cool down and keep it in the refrigerator for 3 hours before serving with crème fraîche and chocolate shavings on top.

Nutrition Value:

- Calories: 200
- Fat: 3
- Fiber: 1
- Carbs: 20
- Protein: 14

541. Refreshing Curd

Preparation time: 10 minutes
Cooking time: 5 minutes
Servings: 4

Ingredients:

- 3 tablespoons stevia
- 12 ounces raspberries
- 2 egg yolks
- 2 tablespoons lemon juice
- 2 tablespoons ghee

Directions:

1. Put raspberries in your instant pot, add stevia and lemon juice, stir, cover and cook on High for 2 minutes.
2. Strain this into a bowl, add egg yolks, stir well and return to your pot.
3. Set the pot on Simmer mode, cook for 2 minutes, add ghee, stir well, transfer to a container and serve cold.
4. Enjoy!

Nutrition Value: calories 132, fat 1, fiber 0, carbs 2, protein 4

542. The Best Jam Ever

Preparation time: 10 minutes
Cooking time: 5 minutes
Servings: 6

Ingredients:

- 4 and ½ cups peaches, peeled and cubed
- 4 tablespoons stevia
- ¼ cup crystallized ginger, chopped

Directions:

1. Set your instant pot on Simmer mode, add peaches, ginger and stevia, stir, bring to a boil, cover and cook on High for 5 minutes.
2. Divide into bowls and serve cold.
3. Enjoy!

Nutrition Value: calories 53, fat 0, fiber 0, carbs 0, protein 2

543. Divine Pears

Preparation time: 10 minutes
Cooking time: 4 minutes
Servings: 12

Ingredients:

- 8 pears, cored and cut into quarters
- 1 teaspoon cinnamon powder
- 2 apples, peeled, cored and cut into quarters
- ¼ cup natural apple juice

Directions:

1. In your instant pot, mix pears with apples, cinnamon and apple juice, stir, cover and cook on High for 4 minutes.

2. Blend using an immersion blender, divide into small jars and serve cold
3. Enjoy!

Nutrition Value: calories 100, fat 0, fiber 0, carbs 0, protein 2

544. Berry Marmalade

Preparation time: 10 minutes
Cooking time: 20 minutes
Servings: 12

Ingredients:

- 1 pound cranberries
- 1 pound strawberries
- ½ pound blueberries
- ounces black currant
- 4 tablespoons stevia
- Zest from 1 lemon
- A pinch of salt
- 2 tablespoon water

Directions:

1. In your instant pot, mix strawberries with cranberries, blueberries, currants, lemon zest, stevia and water, stir, cover and cook on High for 10 minutes.
2. Divide into jars and serve cold.
3. Enjoy!

Nutrition Value: calories 87, fat 2, fiber 0, carbs 1, protein 2

545. Orange Delight

Preparation time: 10 minutes
Cooking time: 25 minutes
Servings: 8

Ingredients:

- Juice from 2 lemons
- 6 tablespoons stevia
- 1 pound oranges, peeled and halved
- 1-pint water

Directions:

1. In your instant pot, mix lemon juice with orange juice and orange segments, water and stevia, cover and cook on High for 15 minutes.
2. Divide into jars and serve cold.

Nutrition Value: calories 75, fat 0, fiber 0, carbs 2, protein 2

546. Simple Squash Pie

Preparation time: 10 minutes
Cooking time: 14 minutes
Serving: 8

Ingredients:

- 2 pounds butternut squash, peeled and chopped
- 2 eggs
- 2 cups water
- 1 cup coconut milk
- 2 tablespoons honey
- 1 teaspoon cinnamon powder
- ½ teaspoon ginger powder
- ¼ teaspoon cloves, ground
- 1 tablespoon arrowroot powder
- Chopped pecans

Directions:

1. Put 1 cup water in your instant pot, add the steamer basket, add squash pieces, cover, cook on High for 4 minutes, drain, transfer to a bowl and mash.
2. Add honey, milk, eggs, cinnamon, ginger and cloves, stir very well and pour into ramekins.
3. Add the rest of the water to your instant pot, add the steamer basket, add ramekins inside, cover and cook on High for 10 minutes.
4. Garnish with chopped pecans and serve.
5. Enjoy!

Nutrition Value: calories 132, fat 1, fiber 2, carbs 2, protein 3

547. Winter Pudding

Preparation time: 10 minutes
Cooking time: 40 minutes
Servings: 4

Ingredients:

- 4 ounces dried cranberries, soaked for a few hours and drained

- 2 cups water
- 4 ounces apricots, chopped
- 1 cup coconut flour
- 3 teaspoons baking powder
- 3 tablespoons stevia
- 1 teaspoon ginger powder
- A pinch of cinnamon powder
- 15 tablespoons ghee
- 3 tablespoons maple syrup
- 4 eggs
- 1 carrot, grated

Directions:
1. In a blender, mix flour with baking powder, stevia, cinnamon and ginger and pulse a few times.
2. Add ghee, maple syrup, eggs, carrots, cranberries and apricots, stir and spread into a greased pudding pan.
3. Add the water to your instant pot, add the steamer basket, add the pudding, cover and cook on High for 30 minutes.
4. Leave pudding to cool down before serving.
5. Enjoy!

Nutrition Value: calories 213, fat 2, fiber 1, carbs 3, protein 3

548. Banana Dessert

Preparation time: 10 minutes
Cooking time: 30 minutes
Servings: 6

Ingredients:
- 2 tablespoons stevia
- 1/3 cup ghee, soft
- 1 teaspoon vanilla
- 1 egg
- 2 bananas, mashed
- 1 teaspoon baking powder
- 1 and ½ cups coconut flour
- ½ teaspoons baking soda
- 1/3 cup coconut milk
- 2 cups water
- Cooking spray

Directions:
1. In a bowl, mix milk stevia, ghee, egg, vanilla and bananas and stir everything.
2. In another bowl, mix flour with salt, baking powder and soda.
3. Combine the 2 mixtures, stir well and pour into a greased cake pan.
4. Add the water to your pot, add the steamer basket, add the cake pan, cover and cook at High for 30 minutes.
5. Leave cake to cool down, slice and serve.
6. Enjoy!

Nutrition Value: calories 243, fat 1, fiber 1, carbs 2, protein 4

549. Apple Cake

Preparation time: 10 minutes
Cooking time: 1 hour and 10 minutes
Servings: 6

Ingredients:
- 3 cups apples, cored and cubed
- 1 cup water
- 3 tablespoons stevia
- 1 tablespoon vanilla
- 2 eggs
- 1 tablespoon apple pie spice
- 2 cups coconut flour
- 1 tablespoon baking powder
- 1 tablespoon ghee

Directions:
1. In a bowl mix eggs with ghee, apple pie spice, vanilla, apples and stevia and stir using your mixer.
2. In another bowl, mix baking powder with flour, stir, add to apple mix, stir again well and transfer to a cake pan.
3. Add 1 cup water to your instant pot, add the steamer basket, add cake pan, cover and cook at High for 1 hour and 10 minutes.
4. Cool cake down, slice and serve it.
5. Enjoy!

Nutrition Value: calories 100, fat 2, fiber 1, carbs 2, protein 2

550. Special Vanilla Dessert

Preparation time: 10 minutes
Cooking time: 10 minutes
Servings: 4

Ingredients:

- 1 cup almond milk
- 4 tablespoons flax meal
- 2 tablespoons coconut flour
- 2 and ½ cups water
- 2 tablespoons stevia
- 1 teaspoon espresso powder
- 2 teaspoons vanilla extract
- Coconut cream for serving

Directions:

1. In your instant pot, mix flax meal with flour, water, stevia, milk and espresso powder, stir, cover and cook on high for 10 minutes.
2. Add vanilla extract, stir well, leave aside for 5 minutes, divide into bowls and serve with coconut cream on top.
3. Enjoy!

Nutrition Value: calories 182, fat 2, fiber 1, carbs 3, protein 4

551. Tasty And Amazing Pear Dessert

Preparation time: 10 minutes
Cooking time: 6 minutes
Servings: 4

Ingredients:

- 1 cup water
- 2 cups pear, peeled and cubed
- 2 cups coconut milk
- 1 tablespoon ghee
- ¼ cups brown stevia
- ½ teaspoon cinnamon powder
- 4 tablespoons flax meal
- ½ cup walnuts, chopped
- ½ cup raisins

Directions:

1. In a heat proof dish, mix milk with stevia, ghee, flax meal, cinnamon, raisins, pears and walnuts and stir.
2. Put the water in your instant pot, add the steamer basket, place heat proof dish inside, cover and cook on High for 6 minutes.
3. Divide this great dessert into small cups and serve cold.
4. Enjoy!

Nutrition Value: calories 162, fat 3, fiber 1, carbs 2, protein 6

552. Cranberries Jam

Preparation time: 10 minutes
Cooking time: 15 minutes
Servings: 12

Ingredients:

- 16 ounces cranberries
- 4 ounces raisins
- 3 ounces water+ ¼ cup water
- 8 ounces figs
- 16 ounces strawberries, chopped
- Zest from 1 lemon

Directions:

1. Put figs in your blender, add ¼ cup water, pulse well and strain into a bowl.
2. In your instant pot, mix strawberries with cranberries, lemon zest, raisins, 3 ounces water and figs puree, stir, cover the pot, cook at High for 15 minutes, divide into small jars and serve.

Nutrition Value: calories 73, fat 1, fiber 1, carbs 2, protein 3

553. Lemon Jam

Preparation time: 10 minutes
Cooking time: 12 minutes
Servings: 8

Ingredients:

- 2 pounds lemons, sliced
- 2 cups dates
- 1 cup water
- 1 tablespoon vinegar

Directions:

1. Put dates in your blender, add water and pulse really well.
2. Put lemon slices in your instant pot, add dates paste and vinegar, stir, cover and cook on High for 12 minutes.
3. Stir, divide into small jars and serve.
4. Enjoy!

Nutrition Value: calories 72, fat 2, fiber 1, carbs 2, protein 6

554. Special Dessert

Preparation time: 10 minutes
Cooking time: 25 minutes
Servings: 4

Ingredients:

- 3 cups rooibos tea
- 1 tablespoon cinnamon, ground
- 2 cups cauliflower, riced
- 2 apples, diced
- 1 teaspoon cloves, ground
- 1 teaspoon turmeric, ground
- A drizzle of honey

Directions:

1. Put cauliflower rice in your instant pot, add tea, stir, cover and cook at High for 10 minutes.
2. Add cinnamon, apples, turmeric and cloves, stir, cover and cook at High for 10 minutes mode.
3. Divide into bowls, drizzle honey on top and serve.
4. Enjoy!

Nutrition Value: calories 152, fat 2, fiber 1, carbs 5, protein 6

555. Superb Banana Dessert

Preparation time: 10 minutes
Cooking time: 30 minutes
Servings: 4

Ingredients:

- Juice from ½ lemon
- 2 tablespoons stevia
- 3 ounces water
- 1 tablespoon coconut oil
- 4 bananas, peeled and sliced
- ½ teaspoon cardamom seeds

Directions:

1. Put bananas, stevia, water, oil, lemon juice and cardamom in your instant pot, stir a bit, cover and cook on High for 30 minutes, shaking the pot from time to time.
2. Divide into bowls and serve.
3. Enjoy!

Nutrition Value: calories 87, fat 1, fiber 2, carbs 3, protein 3

556. Rhubarb Dessert

Preparation time: 10 minutes
Cooking time: 5 minutes
Servings: 4

Ingredients:

- 5 cups rhubarb, chopped
- 2 tablespoons ghee, melted
- 1/3 cup water
- 1 tablespoon stevia
- 1 teaspoon vanilla extract

Directions:

1. Put rhubarb, ghee, water, stevia and vanilla extract in your instant pot, cover and cook on High for 5 minutes.
2. Divide into small bowls and serve cold.
3. Enjoy!

Nutrition Value: calories 83, fat 2, fiber 1, carbs 2, protein 2

557. Plum Delight

Preparation time: 10 minutes
Cooking time: 5 minutes
Servings: 10

Ingredients:

- 4 pounds plums, stones removed and chopped
- 1 cup water
- 2 tablespoons stevia
- 1 teaspoon cinnamon, powder

- ½ teaspoon cardamom, ground

Directions:
1. Put plums, water, stevia, cinnamon and cardamom in your instant pot, cover and cook on High for 5 minutes.
2. Stir well, pulse a bit using an immersion blender, divide into small jars and serve.
3. Enjoy!

Nutrition Value: calories 83, fat 0, fiber 1, carbs 2, protein 5

558. Refreshing Fruits Dish

Preparation time: 10 minutes
Cooking time: 10 minutes
Servings: 4

Ingredients:
- 1 and ½ pounds plums, stones removed and halved
- 2 tablespoons stevia
- 1 tablespoon cinnamon powder
- 2 apples, cored, peeled and cut into wedges
- 2 tablespoons lemon zest, grated
- 2 teaspoons balsamic vinegar
- 1 cup hot water

Directions:
1. Put plums, water, apples, stevia, cinnamon, lemon zest and vinegar in your instant pot, cover and cook on High for 10 minutes.
2. Stir again well, divide into small cups and serve cold.

Nutrition Value: calories 73, fat 0, fiber 1, carbs 2, protein 4

559. Dessert Stew

Preparation time: 10 minutes
Cooking time: 6 minutes
Servings: 6

Ingredients:
- 14 plums, stones removed and halved
- 2 tablespoons stevia
- 1 teaspoon cinnamon powder
- ¼ cup water
- 2 tablespoons arrowroot powder

Directions:
1. Put plums, stevia, cinnamon, water and arrowroot in your instant pot, cover and cook on High for 6 minutes.
2. Divide into small jars and serve cold.
3. Enjoy!

Nutrition Value: calories 83, fat 0, fiber 1, carbs 2, protein 2

30-DAY MEAL PLAN

DAY	BREAKFAST	LUNCH/DINNER	DESSERT
1	Healthy Banana Oatmeal	Roasted Peppers Soup	Bread Pudding
2	Delicious Blueberry Oatmeal	Chicken and Rice Soup	Ruby Pears
3	Healthy Apple Dates Oatmeal	Chicken and Carrots Soup	Pumpkin Rice Pudding
4	Brussels sprouts with Bacon	Spicy Potato Salad	Lemon Marmalade
5	Flavored Avocado Kale Oats	Salmon Bowls	Rice Pudding
6	Cinnamon Mash Banana Oats	Stuffed Eggplants	Ricotta Cake
7	Delicious Berry Oatmeal	Lentils Soup	Orange Marmalade
8	Banana Nut Oatmeal	Ground Pork and Tomatoes Soup	Berry Jam
9	Cheese Mushroom Frittata	Lamb and Potatoes Stew	Key Lime Pie
10	Fluffy Pancake	Potatoes and Lentils Stew	Peach Jam
11	Spinach Bacon Frittata	Oyster Stew	Raspberry Curd
12	Savory Breakfast Grits	Tomato Soup	Tomato Jam
13	Traditional Pumpkin Pie Oatmeal	Chickpeas Soup	Zucchini Nut Bread
14	Smoked Beef Chili	Fish Soup	Tasty And Amazing Pear Dessert
15	Tomato Pollock Stew	Sausage and Beans Soup	Special Vanilla Dessert
16	Beef Chili with Peppers	Lemony Lamb Soup	Apple Cake
17	Turkey Chili	Chicken and Leeks Soup	Berry Compote
18	Cauliflower Souffle	Lentils Soup	Winter Pudding
19	Lamb Stew with Bacon	Basil Zucchini Soup	Samoa Cheesecake
20	Mediterranean Chili Verde	White Beans and Orange Soup	Stuffed Peaches
21	Spicy Mediterranean Chicken Curry	Tuscan Soup	Peach Compote
22	Mediterranean Vichyssoise	Zucchini Soup	Simple Carrot Cake
23	Creamy Lamb Stew	Cauliflower Cream	Fruit Cobbler
24	Crust-less Breakfast Quiche	Chicken and Orzo Soup	Pear Jam
25	Delicious Egg Bake	Seafood Gumbo	Orange Delight
26	Chocó Cherry Oatmeal	Veggie Soup	Simple Squash Pie
27	Apple Cinnamon Oatmeal	White Bean Soup	Divine Pears
28	Strawberry Oatmeal	Ground Pork and Tomatoes Soup	Berry Marmalade
29	Healthy Green Beans	Lamb and Potatoes Stew	The Best Jam Ever
30	Blueberry French toast Casserole	Potatoes and Lentils Stew	Chocolate Pudding

CONCLUSION

When you commit to a Mediterranean diet, you commit to lots of healthy fats and oils, lots of time with your friends and family, and lots more years of health to come in the future. Don't give up, and don't forget that your body is yours, and yours only – so treat it kindly! Thanks for sticking with us, we wish you the best of luck on your journey towards a healthier, thinner, and more coastal-minded you.

Made in the USA
Monee, IL
08 September 2019